Libralisation and Jo

Libralisation and Journalism

Sanoj Singh

RANDOM PUBLICATIONS
NEW DELHI (INDIA)

Libralisation and Journalism

ISBN 978-93-5111-629-5
© Reserved

Published in 2015 in India by

RANDOM PUBLICATIONS

4376-A/4B, Gali Murari Lal, Ansari Road
New Delhi-110 002
Phone : +9111-43580356, 011-23289044, 011-43142548
e-mail: sales@randompublications.com,
info@randompublications.com, randomexports@gmail.com

Type Setting by : Friends Media, Delhi-110089
Printed at : Mehra Printers, Delhi-110 092

Preface

Environmental journalism is not new to the Indian media. Since early 1970s, the media has been taking interest in the environment, even though in a very staccato manner. But with economic liberalisation since 1991, the role of an environment journalist has drastically changed. Or rather, economic liberalisation has made his role more challenging.

Economic liberalisation has triggered economic boom and has caught the public imagination. Suddenly growth has become the buzzword. India finds it finally refreshing to do away with her 'Hindu growth rate' tag. As the public acceptance of the new economic model deepens, environment as a public good is losing relevance.

This means environment and its related problems like poverty in rural areas is getting less and less favour within the public sphere. This also makes the job of an environment journalist difficult-you have to fight hard against a popular perception to be able to bring back environment into mainstream.

The commercialisation of the electronic media was given a boost as globalisation hit India, bringing about the transformation of Indian television in the early 1990s, accelerated by the combined impact of new communication technologies and the opening up of global markets. Economic liberalisation, deregulation and privatisation contributed to the expansion of Indian media corporations, facilitated by joint ventures with international media conglomerates.

Such developments revolutionised broadcasting in what used to be a heavily protected media market, certainly the most regulated among the world's democracies. Gradual deregulation and privatisation of television has transformed the media landscape, evident in the exponential growth in the number of television channels – from Doordarshan the sole state-controlled channel in 1991 to more than 70 in 2000. Out of these, 19 are in Hindi or English and therefore national in reach, while others cater to regional audiences in their own languages.

The book will be of great interest to the general reader interested in the economic political, reporter, journalism and social problems of the country.

I would like to thank my team for standing beside me throughout my career and writing this book. My special thanks go to "Random Publications" who have published the book.

– *Sanoj Singh*

Contents

1

Newscasts and Political Generations

The young Americans in previous research seemed to resist the idea of writing a life history with newscasts, but the stories they related reveal various conflicts with what they considered a powerful political actor.

They saw themselves as weak compared to television news, which they then attacked with all sorts of criticisms of bias, sensationalism, and triviality. The Spaniards took a greatly different view that led them to feel empowered themselves. That central story emerges from the details reported in this section.

One general observation deserves mention as preface: The forms of news they encountered seem implicated in the ways the young adults in both countries thought and talked about their experiences. Depending on which medium they described, the participants had different ways of writing. About a third of the Spaniards (twelve in all) volunteered to write two life histories, one about newspapers and the other about newscasts.

The two essays by a single writer had a consistency of skill, language, and complexity, and those who wrote at length tended to do so for both topics. However, most of the television vignettes they retold were slightly shorter (and within shorter paragraphs).

The ease of simply referring to images, as well as the abrupt shifts in topics, resulted in essays that did not run quite as long, regardless of which essay came first or whether the writer made small economies by referring in one essay to things already related in the other.

On the whole, the television essays seemed less detailed, tended to mention more images, and told less elaborate stories with thinner descriptions - a pattern similar to that found in the U.S. essays. The contrasts require more formal study because language differences make comparing essays from the two countries difficult.

At least within each national setting the structures of the medium, or perhaps the habits of thought each encourages, were reflected in the ways the young adults wrote about their experiences. In short, the forms of news may delimit how people understand their political worlds.

THE NEWS RITUAL

The participants described a much stronger ritual for watching television news in Spain than in the United States. The differing historical development of television, as well as the cultural heritage in Spain, made watching newscasts a universal practice, reinforcing the importance of family routines for the success of televised news.

Compared to the history of the U.S. medium, television entered Spain later and the industry converted to colour more recently, producing among the participants a greater awareness of the television as a material objects Some of the Spaniards (12.5 per cent) used that sense of the television set to begin and frame their essays (none of the U.S. essays did):

It's easier to remember when you got your first television set or when you changed from black and white to colour (I was nine), just as it's not easy to remember when you saw a car for the first time, although you can always remember the first one you owned. -an urban male, 21

Such material memories extended to the appearance of the newscast. "I remember that they began with a clock that covered the whole screen," said another urban male, 21, "which we used to check our own to see if it was exactly on the time shown." An urban female, 21, recalled that "the broadcast had only one person and was presented about like the radio news used to be, reading from a sheet of paper." Another said the news "seemed made by hand."

In national custom, watching television news became deeply entrenched in Spain.' The midday break from work for many Spaniards traditionally runs from one and four o'clock, and the afternoon news at three consistently has therefore ranked among the highest rated television programmes. "It seemed incredible that my grandparents ate lunch and dinner as fast as possible so they could watch the news," said an urban female regular viewer, 25. "At home it wasn't such an obsession, but we did always eat lunch with the national news in the background." An urban female, 19, said, "At home the television news has always been sacred, at midday as well as in the evening. Whenever the symphonic theme music came on at home, the living room fell silent."

The television ritual dated from the childhood of the young adult generation. (A majority of essays by older adults said they specifically did not watch at a routine time and place. In the Franco era, not everyone owned a television set. "The only television in my village was owned by the parish church," said a rural female occasional viewer, 41, "and we would go there to watch, paying in advance." The older adults also noted the greater appeal of news during the transition. "My interest in TV news," wrote a male regular viewer, 43, "surged as soon as the Franco dictatorship ended. Since that moment I've watched newscasts with real interest as often as possible.")

Although just about everyone adopted the news-viewing habit after Franco's death, attention to broadcast news has even older roots. An earlier generation became attracted through radio in the 1930s. Their grandchildren, the young adults in the study, described the grandparents' current habit of watching el pane and commented on the name, derived from the Spanish Civil War, when people called radio bulletins from the front el pane militar.

The strength of the family news practice produced some conflict, the essays said. Describing the news anchor, an urban female, 21, said, "How could a lady that my parents didn't even know personally get more of their attention than I, their own daughter?" Almost a third (31.3 per cent) mentioned feeling resentful of parents for their news-watching habit, a rate greatly surpassing the very few such expressions in the U.S. television essays. History here intervened with the process of adding more television sets to the home giving Americans the option to choose other programmes. Multiple television sets came later to Spain and hardly get mentioned.

The participants said that in small urban apartments they had few alternatives. "For the smallest ones this began the most painful thirty minutes of the entire day " said an urban female, 21. "It was a torture to not be allowed to talk or squeal for such a long time."

The Americans faced frustrations not only with both parents, who dictated which programme to choose, but also with their fathers, who relaxed with the news while mothers cleaned up. When such differences appeared in their essays, the Spaniards either did not remark on or did not make much of them. The Spanish state monopoly until the 1990s had no commercial competition, making the news on Television Espanola (TVE1 or La Primera) the news.e A further U.S. frustration, with the racism of newscasts, received no mention at all among the Spaniards.

A combination of some gender equality and fewer contested role norms tended to mute the feminist reaction to news watching in Spain. In many cases participants described home routines that included women and men equally. Newscasts themselves also included women. The state channel had female anchors from the participants' earliest memories. Since the addition of a second state channel and three private channels, women continue in anchor positions, although usually in secondary posts (presenting the sports segment, for example, or the weather, both of which appear in national newscasts). The Spanish women also accepted male prerogatives with tolerance. A suburban female regular viewer, 25, said that "it was one of the few things my father always wanted to watch, because the rest of the programmes on television didn't interest him much."

Even when the essays mentioned being told to be silent during the news (21.9 per cent), the demand reiterated the communal quality of the activity. An urban male, 24, said, "I remember that when it didn't interest me and I'd start to talk, my grandparents and parents would all go `Shhh!' and I had to be quiet." No essays mentioned parents getting angry in the authoritative way found in the U.S. cases. The Spanish group also recalled that conversation reinforced the news-watching ritual (9.4 per cent), which hardly received notice in the U.S. group.

During the midday meal, someone in the family would bring up a topic of conversation and refer to what they would see on television. That way I kept getting more interested in the news and in what happened in the world, because if not, I would never understand the conversations at home. -an urban female, 20 Frustrations the Americans felt led them to a feel indifference towards newscasts. Even with the relatively high level of childhood frustration, only some of the Spaniards expressed indifference (9.4 per cent). The ritual in Spain had largely the opposite effect. An urban male, 24, wrote, "A lot of times I could stand watching the newscast because, if all the grown-ups were full of interest and anticipation, they must have been expecting something."

POLITICS

The political experiences in the essays often sprang from the more strongly partisan stance in the Spanish than in the U. S. press. The Spaniards described a three-step recipe for handling the outpouring of partisan news. First, some of them used several news sources:

Luckily my own political opinion doesn't derive from reading just one daily because, as I said, I usually go through several throughout the day, and... I squeeze out what I consider the most... closely adjusted to reality. -an urban male, 28

Second, they employed their knowledge about the political leanings of each paper. "Knowing more or less the ideologies of the newspapers in my country, I try to read critically," wrote an urban female, 20, who concluded that "not all politicians are as good or as bad as they appear." Some essays listed their newspaper preference as a shorthand way of describing their own political position, rather than the other way around. Saying one always reads El Pais, far example, reveals a preference for the left-wing liberal interpretation of events, whereas a dedication to ABC suggests a disposition to conservative and monarchist interpretations.

With a clear sense of the differences, the Spaniards said that, third, they then contrasted what they learned from the news, especially about political matters. "What I do is read and compare so that I can act in the most balanced manner, according to my personal convictions," said a suburban female, 21.

That personal compass helped them retain a discriminating distance. As a rural female, 22, put it, "Reading the newspaper has... helped me get a more critical view.... I've arrived at the conclusion that many times it's best to read without getting too caught up." Especially during elections, wrote a female regular reader, 21, "I think... the facts and opinions are the least trustworthy, due to the number of interests that hide behind that information."

Sometimes participants said the news discouraged them, especially considering what a male regular reader, 25, called "the role certain papers played in our country during recent years by denouncing cases of corruption."

Disappointment with politics came more often from women. "In my political views, reading the daily paper has filled me with irony," wrote an urban female occasional reader, 21. "I think it's better to take it with humor." On the whole, the essays by women seemed slightly less politically oriented than did those by men. The difference also turned up on the questionnaire item for political interest (men 1.2 and women 1.5, on a three-point scale of "very," "somewhat," and "not at all" interested).

In the end, the competing political ideologies in a variety of newspapers, along with some citizens' skills at parsing the messages they read, built a stronger connection to politics. In fact, the young adults seemed to connect with politics more through newspapers than they did through political parties, for which they said they had little sympathy. Only a minority expressed an affinity with any of the three main political parties, socialist PSOE, leftist IU (both 10 per cent), or conservative PP (13.7 per cent), and fully half left the item blank or wrote "none." Yet almost all rated themselves "very" (80 per cent) or "somewhat" (36.7 per cent) interested in politics.

It comes as no surprise that the Spanish participants became newspaper readers while the Americans did not. The Spaniards gave the impression of participating from their earliest years in a family project to bring them into the newspaper-reading habit at home, placing them, of course, within the minority in a country without widespread newspaper reading. The young adults remembered their parents as not pushy or nagging but encouraging, a result that confirms Mannheim's observation of how rarely didactic approaches work in transmitting values between generations. The process comes clear in this extended example:

I remember that my parents used to read me the strange and odd events that happened, from briefs on the last page, and they also explained any important news they'd read. They also urged me to read the paper. They would say, "Oh, did you read this or that happened?" as if for me to have read it were an ordinary thing. That way they encouraged me to take the time, because it was really interesting. They still do that, but now I almost always say yes, I've already read it. What was certain was that I didn't especially like reading the paper. I could read one or two articles but I got tired right away. -an urban male, 24

The essays also said that newspapers enjoyed substantial support from teachers. Unlike the U,S. model of homework, Spanish schools made daily newspaper reading appear painless, through in-class activities and the reinforcement of teachers' behaviour. The media literacy approach, teaching children a critical distance from the press while emphasizing the importance of things reported there, appears to have produced more assiduous reading, rather than the opposite.

The teacher's idea for the class was for us to read a lot of papers of different ideological stripes, to analyse events from different points of view. I refer to this because it was when I changed my attitude towards newspapers. From then on, they interested me much more and I read them differently. I focused on the editorials, as well as on the political stories and their different interpretations. -a female, 27

The material side of the press encourages reading in Spain. Newspapers all have a manageable format, and almost all have reduced the problem of ink rubbing off on the hands. Regular redesigns, whatever their meaning to older readers, appealed to these young adults, who expressed impatience with papers that failed to ride the wave of change. Clear competition at the newsstand also helped build their interest. From a wide selection - national, regional, and local dailies augmented by sports and business papers - some young adults purchased several newspapers just to see how a story was covered (this despite the high cover price, usually equivalent to more than a dollar a copy).

The competition seems not to have degenerated into pandering, although a few of the essays mentioned a recent shift towards more graphic and disturbing coverage. The local paper "has tended to become more aggressive," said an urban female, 19: "All you have to do is compare the same news story in different newspapers." An urban male, 24, wrote that as newspapers try to sell serious news by running it "between curiosities and lighter news... entertainment slowly takes over."

These differences teach some important lessons for newspapers in the United States, despite the contrast in social settings and the Spaniards' exceptional access to news, education, and other advantages. Local newspaper monopolies typical in the United States probably do not encourage readership among the young, but neither do competing papers unless they have ideological differences obvious enough for readers to perceive a difference and sustain the variety.

A clear ideological line, which some U.S. editors might fear would drive readers away, apparently has had the opposite effect in Spain. Support from parents and from teachers seems to have sprung from or responded to the sobriety of the Spanish press as well as its commitment to a political point of view regardless of economic consequences. At school, the U.S. curricula that emphasize doing the hard work of reading at home probably backfire and create resentment.

On the other hand, U.S. resistance to media literacy curricula, because of fears that they will produce troublesome, critical readers, did just that in Spain, with the effect of increasing their interest in newspapers. The empowered readers read more. Finally, although they liked the smaller format and regular design change, the young Spaniards responded with suspicion to efforts to sell the news by packaging it for entertainment value. Their sophistication as readers produces just the sort of tolerance that political theorists expect from a free press in democratic societies a hopeful outcome of ideological competi tion, media literacy, and design innovation.

The similarities between the U.S. and Spanish groups, although far fewer, have more to teach. In both countries, the fate of newspapers paralleled their respective abilities to make news reading a daily ritual at home. Including newspapers as a constant presence in the schools also seems uniformly crucial. The routines of publication and the schedules of production and delivery - the temporal bases of newspapers in modern societies - are just what new electronic versions of newspapers conspicuously lack. Information without a physical form that must get manufactured on regular deadlines may float unattached to temporal processes until readers or electronic publishers invent some other ritual as a replacement.

The same content of the newspaper-another commonality-appealed to the young adults in both countries. News in the paper had to touch close to their lives in each case. Both groups found themselves drawn into the newspaper specifically (as opposed to other news sources) through stories involving people and places they knew. Newspapers have other strengths.

Americans as well as Spaniards mentioned the power of news to recognize events as important and make people seem worthy. At the same time, the content encouraged a placid response: newspapers did not in either country produce the fear incited by U.S. newscasts. In general, when the newspaper's strengths as a setter of daily ritual, as a giver of status, and as a facilitator of calm rationality combined with truly local news content that overlapped the social worlds they inhabited, young adults became readers.

The similarities in the two groups could provide a list of goals for the U.S. press: altering the regulatory environment, the structure of the industry within local and national markets, as well as the content of news and the format for presenting it. Newspapers in the United States would have to make a host of changes at every level to replicate the Spanish experience.

Such a wholesale revision of the U.S. press seems well beyond reasonable expectations for printed newspapers, but perhaps not for electronic forms. The comparison of narratives from Spain and the United States does help account for the failures and successes of newsprint among young citizens, pointing to ways publishers can convey the political information needed to sustain democratic participation.

GENERATIONAL MEMORY

Television news emerged in the previous study as a force that-through an initial major news story - helped young adults identify with their generation.

The U.S. essays focused on the explosion of the space shuttle Challenger as the event to catch attention. Coming from a wider span of ages (eleven years instead of six), the Spanish essays did not agree on a single first event. In those recalling a first story (43.8 per cent), three major events stand out. The story most often cited (12.5 per cent), the death of Generalisimo Franco, lasted more than a month in 1975, prolonged as doctors went to extraordinary measures under pressure from those wishing to extend the Falange regime. The final announcement left a strong impression:

I do remember one image... that had an impact. It was of Carlos Arias Navarro [the head of government] crying before the camera as he announced the death of Franco. I've seen that image many other times, but I believe that the reiteration has served to reinforce in memory that first time it appeared. - an urban male, 24

The young adults also said they (like the U.S. group) shared a universal response with family and friends. A 24-year-old female remarked that after the announcement, "I recall my parents' faces marked with fear for what would happen next."

The event occurred very early in the lives of many participants, some of whom instead referred to one of two subsequent incidents (each 9.4 per cent). Regarding one, the attempted coup d'etat in 1981, a rural female, 22, said, "I remember having seen the news about the golpe de estado of February 23." The essays cited the image of Lieutenant Colonel Antonio Tejero firing shots in the chambers of parliament, with the TVE1 cameras broadcasting live. Others cited, without elaboration, the election of Felipe Gonzalez and the socialist party (PSOE) in 1982.

The important moments in Spain's transition to democracy contain the qualities also found in the U. S. first-story accounts. The essays did not for the most part describe the event, but instead merely pointed to its name or date or principal protagonist. In most cases, the Spaniards said they experienced the event as communal, not in the schools, where the U.S. students watched the shuttle explode, but at home with the family. Both groups remembered the event primarily as visual - in Spain an image of Franco, the king, the colonel, or Felipe Gonzalez, with another telling detail such as tears or senators diving for cover.

Finally, the element of surprise came through in both groups. Even for Franco's death the actual moment, although not unexpected, caught some families with one member away, adding fear to the surprise.

Among the other first news events they recalled, a few mentioned the space shuttle explosion that played so prominently in the U.S. group. Whatever the event, the participants all assigned similar meanings to their first news story. Besides defining the event as universally shared and understood, they centered the retelling on the operation and importance of the news media.

Repetition also played an important role. "I no longer remember if I saw it the year it happened." said a 19-year-old female. "They repeat it almost every year." Finally, the essays follow a pattern of mentioning discussion, which reinforced the event, its significance, its universal interpretation and emotional charge. The shared understanding of a key moment (and in some cases the same moment) in their interaction makes television news central to forming a generation's identity.

BECOMING A VIEWER

A majority of the U.S. television group reported regular or occasional news viewing, and the group's essays generally did not describe any rites of passage leading to a commitment as a viewer. None of the U.S. television essays told a story of trying to join the audience and failing, unlike their counterpart newspaper essays. Although less tortured than the accounts of the U.S. newspaper group, the television essays by Americans reported a variety of tensions and conflicts. Many recalled their parents urging them on, and some complained about the nagging.

Others said they faced social pressure from overachieving relatives or friends. Those who acquired the habit wrote with derogatory language - far from the self-righteous attitude among the U.S. newspaper readers - identifying their high level of news viewing as an addiction, with binges or other extreme swings from time to time. Little wonder they developed an inconsistent and desultory habit of attending to newscasts.

The Spaniards acquired a much higher commitment to watching the news, without much anxiety or complaint. According to the questionnaire, they watched daily for the most part.ll Many identified themselves as habitual viewers (78.1 per cent], and of these, most said they watched every day (84 per cent of habitual viewers).

Regular viewers made up the next largest group (18.8 per cent), only one reported viewing only occasionally, and none reported not watching at all. The only difficulty they cited, newscasters' use of complex language, turns up infrequently. "It was a challenge to connect with what they tried to say, and keeping up to date was a difficult task," said an urban female, 20. "I think only now am I really understanding the news."

The Spaniards said they reached high levels of viewership without much parental urging. Only a minority of the essays said their parents gave any overt encouragement (18.8 per cent), and nearly as many said their parents did not encourage them at all (12.5 per cent). They rated the level of parental encouragement at the midpoint (3 per cent) on the questionnaire, indicating their parents neither encouraged nor discouraged them. The neutral rating makes sense. With the custom of news watching a given, parents had little reason to urge it on the young. A majority called the news a constant, repetitive presence during their middle and late childhood (78.1 per cent).

The content of news programming more often provided the impulse. Several essays mentioned one particular programme: "I remember from a very young age my parents watching `Informe Semanal.' I didn't know what it was, but there were some reports I liked," said an urban female, 21. "At home 'Informe Semanal' is something of an institution." The Saturday evening programme appears to have had the same traditional position among Spanish television news magazines as held in the United States by "60 Minutes" (which no U.S. essay mentioned). The Spanish programme runs more to documentary without a hard news treatment:

One Saturday, during those cold, boring winters of my adolescence, I found myself wide-eyed, watching a story from "Informe Semanal" and without realizing it I got caught up in those reports. I still didn't like the regular newscasts, but on Saturdays I had a regular date to get to know the world. -a female regular viewer, Most participants did not mention the age at which they began watching news for their own interest, rather than as part of the family ritual. Those who did, specified an age ranging from 9 to 16, of course, a strong family tradition made the issue moot in most cases. The essays more often said when the news they watched daily simply began to interest them. Some called their own progression normal. "I've always chosen freely the programmes that were broadcast," wrote a suburban female regular viewer, 25. "At first I liked the children's shows, later I preferred movies, and finally news programmes began to interest me."

In sum, the Spaniards wrote without the disparaging comments of the U.S. newscast viewers and without the self-righteous tones of the U.S. newspaper readers. None of the Spaniards expressed regrets, apologies, or hostility for failing to view (of course, all but two watched news at least regularly). From a young age, the participants considered news viewing an activity for adults (37.5 per cent of the essays mentioned this explicitly), and the general tenor of the writing seems to accept the news as the natural avenue towards adulthood. The routine at home grew uneventfully into an adult habit.

FORM AND CONTENT

The young Americans previously studied did not recall many changes in the look of news. They considered newscasts information, especially appreciated for its visual form, and they had regrets for missing the show. Their preference for news and weather (in that order) reinforced the sense of the centrality of news.

In contrast, the Spaniards considered newscasts with somewhat more reserve. They less often equated television news with information (78.1 per cent) or remarked on missing the broadcasts (perhaps because they simply missed it infrequently). Several essays did highlight the value of the visual content of news, just as the Americans did. An urban female, 21, cited the example of getting a sense of other countries. "With the visuals, it's much easier to remember," she said. The Spaniards, however, had more awareness of its constructed look, commenting more often on the changes in the newscast (40 per cent). The end of the dictatorship brought a general thaw in the style of newscasting. "Back then," said one urban female, 21, "the news was cold and distant from the viewer." (The older Spaniards remembered the old broadcasts vividly.

"The news, back in the time of Franco, was censored and very filtered, and seemed gray and terribly discouraging to me," wrote a 40-year-old male. "They presented a Spain in positive stories that seemed dull and ingenuous, and an exterior world in negative ones, as somewhat dangerous....")

The entry of commercial channels opened the state television stations to competitive pressures, with a resulting increase in sensationalism. A few of the young adults noted specific visual and technological changes in the previous five years, but mostly they commented on the accompanying shift in the tenor of news content, from the values of serious knowledge to the values of entertainment, a transformation that mimics U.S. newscasts.

Everything now seems more like a variety show, like something serious in content but perfectly planned to keep viewers watching the station. The package shines brighter all the time. The coif of the anchor and the smile of the co-anchor contrast with the quantity of negative images and stories. It's quite depressing to watch the news these days. -an urban male, 24

Just over half the Spanish essays expressed a preference for a particular content (56.3 per cent), and weather (the Americans' second favourite segment) figured hardly at all (6.3 per cent). In both countries, news topped the list. For some Spaniards, the interest started early, as it did for a 22-year-old female, who wrote, "I found it enjoyable to know what happened in places with odd names, although at first I didn't understand a thing."

News shared first preference with sports (both 28.1 per cent) among all participants, but by gender the males (like their U.S. counterparts) mentioned sports most often (37.5 per cent, and not one called news a top preference). The women, on the other hand, listed news most often (37.5 per cent) followed by sports (25 per cent), a notable attraction not shared by U.S. women. In some cases, the writers credited interest in sports with leading to their commitment to watch all the newscast, just as in the U.S. examples. "Little by little I began to pick what interested me, at first sports more than anything else," wrote a rural female, 22. "Later I began watching the entire newscast."

The Spaniards acquired the habit of viewing with relative ease, primarily through the news and sports, but they also acquired a critical distance. Besides a sense of how journalists construct news (a result of recent Spanish media history), their response to sports stands in contrast to the Americans' second choice: weather. Sports covers invented games, where weather supposedly reports reality.

INFLUENCES

The Spanish essays were reticent to talk about their moods in detail, and fewer of them said that television news changed their emotional states (53.1 per cent) than did the Americans. Spanish television, at least before the 1990s when commercial stations appeared, did not emphasize danger and violence, and the essays did not refer to many cases of fear during childhood. The Spaniards, even more often than the Americans, listed the various emotions they felt without elaborating. When they did specify, the essays gave examples of human suffering, just as the Americans did. For example, an urban female, 21, wrote, "The images of the charred bodies affected me so much I didn't watch the programme again for several years."

The emotion the Spaniards most often cited, anger (25 per cent), appeared more frequently for women (29.2 per cent) than for men (12.5 per cent), just as in the U.S. group. An urban female, 21, wrote, "The images of terrorist attacks and resulting activities always affect me, but instead of fear, they make me feel anger and helplessness, and that sensation stays with me all day. " The participants sometimes directed their anger towards government policies and politicians. "The story that made me mad, not that long ago and I believe it angered not only me but all of Spain - was the coverage of corruption," said a rural female occasional viewer, 23. (The story she cited enters in the next section.) Anger also focused on the newscasts themselves. An urban male, 21, said the news "provokes my indignation because of the way the stories are treated, usually from the most macabre angle."

Next often the Spaniards cited fear (21.9 per cent), but at less than half the rate of the Americans. In contrast to the U.S. group (in which women, especially from the cities, expressed fear strongly), the Spaniards had no major gap between the numbers of men and women reporting fear or its qualitative expressions. In a typical example, a 26-year-old female regular viewer said, "When the news reports come out about anorexia or depression, the statistics on the incidence of these illnesses are frightening." Such statements cited fear without expressing much emotion.

Sadness, the Americans' most frequent emotion, the Spaniards mentioned least frequently (6.3 per cent), citing happiness twice as often (12.5 per cent). Every instance of these two feelings came from an essay by a woman (in the U.S. group, only women said they ever felt sad, but men expressed happiness more often than did women).

In their emotions, the U.S. group tended to passivity, with men understated in their responses, and women experiencing more volatility. The Spaniards, male as well as female, took a somewhat more active stance, reacting most frequently with anger and newscasts and their content (while understating the passive emotions such as fear and sadness). That pattern extended as well into the actions they took in response to newscasts.

A substantial minority of the Spaniards said television news did have an influence on their actions (34.4 per cent), but none mentioned any changes in dress, hairstyle, or tone of voice - the authoritative airs that some U.S. women said they imitated. Nor did the Spaniards mention news affecting any decisions about their present or future jobs or family. They reported only one action that newscasts influenced: using information in conversations.

If there is something that stands out from watching news on television, it's the comments we make afterwards, whether in the family, with friends or around other people. We have the custom of commenting on a news story and exchanging opinions about it. -an urban male, 23

Another important difference in how the news activated the Spaniards but left the Americans reactive appeared in the precautions they said they took. The tenor of fear did not come through among the Spaniards, who mentioned no precautions and did not appear to share the U.S. fear that one wrong move might spoil their lives. As a result, a majority of the Spaniards (53.2 per cent) maintained that television news did not influence their actions. Like the Americans, they seemed dismissive of the idea that news might affect them. Unlike the Americans, they did not then contradict themselves by listing specific ways the news affected their appearance and actions, including major life decisions.

GESTURAL POLITICS: CIVIL SOCIETY

The study of civil society in Singapore is an academic field attracting significant interest and analysis. It is commonly recognized as an important element in a vibrant and innovative society. Citizen participation in the policy process also plays a crucial role in a modern knowledge-based economy.

Authoritarianism under the PAP People's Action Party has never prevented social organization per se, including the conditional existence of autonomous groups not threatening to the PAP. In fact, at times the PAP has actively but selectively encouraged social organization as a way of embedding the regime.

In early 2005, E. Kay Gillis published a monograph entitled Singapore Civil Society and British Power, tracing the "history" of civil society by investigating "associational activity" in Singapore from 1819 to 1963, or during the era of British power and rule. Gillis found through her research that civil society in Singapore had been strong and effective throughout the period, despite the fact that the British regime was seen as authoritarian, demonstrating that civil society can exist outside a liberal democratic context.

In fact, Gillis argues that civil society, marked by open and autonomous citizen participation in the policy process, played a crucial role in the movement towards the nation's independence. (Others, however, question the existence of contemporary notions of civil society before the formation of the Singapore nation-state). According to Gillis, although civil society started to dismantle during the final period of British rule, it was the then newly elected PAP government's "introduction of domestic restrictive policies on the grounds that the survival of Singapore was at stake" that brought civil society to its lowest ebb.

Although Singapore has since not only survived but prospered economically under the control and rule of the PAP, many of these restrictive—and arguably, repressive—policies continue to affect the cultivation of civil society in contemporary Singapore. Singapore's brand of authori-tarianism, one of the more dubious reasons for its remarkable success over the past four decades, has been characterized by both legal and "extra-legal" limits to independent social and political activities.

While legal limits would include somewhat repressive and political laws such as the Internal Security Act (ISA) and the Societies Act of 1968, the application of what I would call "extra-legal" strategies are far broader. These include, inter alia, "extensive mechanisms of political co-option to channel contention through state-controlled institutions", the creation of quasi-opposition in parliament via the Nominated Member of Parliament (NMP) scheme, as well as the ambiguously framed yet enduring discourse of out-of-bounds markers (or "OB markers"), an important element in our study of civil society in Singapore which will be deliberated in this paper.

The encroachment of the state into many facets of everyday life led to calls, particularly by the newly emerging middle-class Singaporeans, for greater liberalization of the cultural sphere. As a consequence, interests in civil society—both in socio-cultural and political terms—were rekindled from the mid-1980s onwards, though not much happened until the early 1990s. In November 1990, Singapore witnessed its first "changing of the guard" when Goh Chok Tong became the country's second Prime Minister. Upon taking up his new position, Prime Minister Goh declared his intention to embrace a more open, consultative, and consensual leadership style.

To many observers, this meant that Singapore was on course for a less authoritarian mode of rule, which translated to a more participatory form of democracy, and one that would appear to be more sympathetic and welcoming to civil society. The reality, however, was starker than envisaged. While the 1990s saw a revival of interest in the concept of civil society in Singapore, it was also the decade that led to the entrenchment of "OB markers", a golfing terminology that is intended to demarcate the parameters of political debate and thus render civil society meaningless, into Singapore's political lexicon.

Then in January 2004, shortly after then Deputy Prime Minister and Finance Minister Lee Hsien Loong was declared Singapore's next premier, he gave a major speech on the future of politics and society in Singapore at the 35th Anniversary Dinner of the Harvard Club of Singapore. In a speech intended as a preview to his style of rule, Lee laid down his protocol for government-people interaction, as well as the limits of political engagement, by declaring that Singapore "must open up further" by promoting "further civic participation".

Without quite explaining what he meant by "civic" or "opening up", Lee proffered five broad "suggestions"—better read as caveats—on how to promote "civic participation" and therefore build a more "civic society" in Singapore, namely: guidelines for public consultations on new policies or regulations, space for rigorous and robust debate, an emphasis on action or active citizenship, a constructive and "non-crusading" media, and a government that continues to lead the way even as it becomes more open to views. Taking a leaf from his predecessor's book, Lee was in fact pre-empting the "noise" of civil society and political criticism by declaring that he would become an open, inclusive, and consultative leader.

As this paper will go on to contend, the use of populist rhetoric like "openness" and "inclusiveness", as representations of a "civic" and/or "civil" society, must not be taken at face value, since they are often cryptic and ambiguous. Rather, these broad terms and loose concepts exemplify what I would present as "gestural politics", where, "by displaying the "liberal" gestures of the regime, Singaporean voters as well as foreign visitors and investors would be attracted to the new Singapore and its leadership one way or another". In other words, the "gesture" of civil society is more pertinent than its substance. After all, the rise of globalization, along with global (if Western) socio-political influences and rapid advances in media technologies, has meant that it was a matter of time before the government had to deal with the incursion of an increasingly politicized civil society that could threaten PAP rule.

Gestural politics thus helps to "nip the problem in the bud". Recognizing that the concept of civil society comes in various contours, forms, and content, and as such is always arbitrary and ill-defined, it is therefore up to the regime to define, and thus scope, civil society for its own ends and purposes. For better or worse, the equivocal but complex notion of civic and/or civil society makes it particularly amenable to wide (mis)appropriation, hence a "perfect" representation of gestural politics. As Kumar connotes, albeit in another context: "Civil society" sounds good; it has a good feel to it; it has the look of a fine old wine, full of depth and complexity. Who could possibly object to it, who will not wish for its fulfilment?

The discussion that follows provides a broad summary of how the term "civil society" has been employed in Singaporean public (and political) discourse: from its promulgation as "civic" society by George Yeo in the 1990s to its reassertion as a government vision statement calling for "active citizenship" and citizens' "feedback" at the turn of the millennium (especially in Singapore 21: Together, We Make the Difference) from 1999; to its current—and arguably, future—place in a supposedly "new" Singapore of the 21st century, creatively captured by the theme of an "open and inclusive Singapore", first articulated by Lee in January 2004 and followed up in his brief "swearing-in" speech on 12 August 2004. In essence, this paper considers how civil society exemplifies "gestural politics" in Singapore. It argues that while to some extent, engagement with the concept of civil society has become a political necessity, "new" rhetoric about politics and civil society in Singapore remains by and large gestural. Or as Chua puts it in his socio-political assessment of "Singapore in the next decade", the "new" Singapore of the 21st century is likely to be marked by greater liberalization, and not a democratization, of the social, cultural—and indeed public—sphere. The 1990s: Civic Society and Active Citizenship Citizenship is not a reality TV show.

You cannot just watch in the comfort of your home. You need to participate. Every time we participate, we reaffirm our membership and allegiance to our fellow citizens, our community and our country. [Participation] is critical in rooting Singaporeans to the country. (Raymond Lim, Singapore's Minister of State for Foreign Affairs and Trade and Industry)

In June 1991, while government administrators were implementing voter-friendly "consultative" strategies of the "new guard" led by newly installed Prime Minister Goh Chok Tong, the concept of civic society was promulgated in Singapore by a "new guard" minister, George Yeo, who was at the time acting in the portfolio of Information and the Arts] Widely regarded as one of contemporary Singapore's most eloquent politicians, Yeo made his—and indeed Singapore's—seminal speech on "civic society" to suggest a need for Singaporeans to be actively involved not so much in parliamentary, partisan, or lobbyist politics, but in creating a "Singapore soul", marked by a nationalistic and deep emotional attachment to Singapore. His intention was to urge Singaporeans to participate or play a part in enhancing the civic life in and of Singapore so that people will treat the country as home rather than a "soulless hotel" where one can come and go as one pleases.

As Yeo declared: If we are not to be only a hotel, we must have a soul. To develop that soul, we need a lively civic society. The State must pull back some so that the circle of public participation can grow. The use of the term "soul" to refer to one's deep affiliation with the nation is a powerful metaphor. As Nikolas Rose elucidates in his Foucaultian analyses of contemporary governmentality, good government "operates through the delicate and minute infiltration of the ambitions of regulation" into the very interior—or soul—of human existence and experience. Thus, to equate a "lively civic society" with the "soul" of a nation is to effectively forge symmetry between the desires of the individual as citizen and the urge of governments to manage the individual as a participatory subject and cultural citizen.

In this way, the state would be able to, as Yeo puts it quite plainly, "pull back some" to provide "space" for citizens to perform their patriotic citizenship duties. In the case of Singapore during the 1990s, the intention of raising the stakes of civil society-cum-public participation was not so much to enable a thriving public sphere, but to advance and perfect the regulatory apparatuses-cum-technologies of government. Yeo's vision of a civic society is, after all, consistent with then Prime Minister Goh's professed commitment towards a more consultative style of government. The problem though is that the term "civic society" is not quite identical to that of a "civil society". As Singaporean sociologist Chua Beng Huat points out: The difference between the two terms, "civic society" and "civil society" is not some inconsequential play of words, but an indication of one's political stance on the appropriate balance in the relationship between state and society in Singapore.

In other words, when Singaporean politicians use the term "civic society", they are effectively talking about the "civic" responsibilities of citizens as opposed to that of the "rights" of citizenship espoused in the conventional and political understanding of the concept of "civil society". Likewise, Koh Tai Ann suggests that Singapore's model of "civic society" seeks primarily to forestall the potentially destabilizing "politicking" practices of civil society. By placing emphasis on the term "civic"—and the attendant discourses of courtesy, kindness, graciousness, and civility—which spells how citizens ought to behave and conduct themselves publicly, it is hoped that Singaporeans would be discouraged or distracted from real politicking activities.

The choice of the term "civic" by Yeo and other government officials is thus prudent and well-calculated, one that is "consistent with the PAP's language of politics". Even if "civic society" does become interpreted—or confused—as "civil society", the grounds are well covered. At an Institute of Policy Studies conference on civil society in May 1998, George Yeo—who was by then elevated to the full senior status of Minister of Information and the Arts—made a conceptual departure from his original "civic society" speech by declaring that a "civic" society was really Singapore's idea of "civil society". Civil society to Yeo is not just about citizenship in the form of voting rights or the right to carry a Singapore passport, it is more veraciously about enhancing the relationship between state and the non-state for the sake of the nation and its citizens. In trying to depoliticize "civil society", Yeo was in effect attempting to engage—somewhat pre-emptively—the proponents of an autonomous civil society by defining the very terms and tenets of future political engagement. Far from being depoliticized or non-political, this move to carve out a "civic" mode of civil society for Singapore was motivated by political expedience.

Indeed, like most aspects of politics in Singapore, civic or civil society has its own "special meanings", explicable and interpretable only by the PAP. By "pre-defining" civil society, the government could thus go on to talk about various aspects of "civic-ness" and "civility" as captured in less problematic public discourses such as courtesy, kindness, and graciousness.

It could also go on to "proselytize" about the merits of citizen participation in the policy process or "active citizenship", the central theme of "Singapore 21" (the government's 1999 vision of Singapore in the 21st century), knowing full well that free and autonomous participation is mostly absent in a society that is notorious for being politically passive and apathetic. Ho Khai Leong alludes to this problem when he notes that:

The extent to which Singapore citizens can influence policy making depends on the extent to which the PAP allows it to happen. The basic ground rules are set from above and citizenry is merely passively reacting to those regulations.

Although most Singaporeans perceive "Singapore 21" as yet another motherhood statement by the self-proclaimed all-knowing government, the call for "active citizenship" was generally well-received by many people, including those affiliated with local interest groups. The possibility of forging a new "social contract" between the government and its people was sufficiently attractive to groups which had previously existed on the periphery.

Groups such as The Working Committee (TWC), a civil society advocate group, proclaimed in October 1999 that it would be going online to promote civil society. Even the well-known Internet-based association People Like Us (PLU), a group which aims to promote awareness of issues concerning gays and lesbians in society, decided in 2000 to "roll up their sleeves" to publicly discuss about their "active citizenship" roles in conservative Singapore.

That year, an application by the PLU to hold a public forum on "Gays and Lesbians within Singapore 21" was flatly rejected by the Police Public Entertainment Licensing Unit (PELU) on the grounds that mainstream moral values of Singaporeans are conservative, and that Singapore's Penal Code has clear provisions against certain homosexual practices. As Lee summarizes the episode: [A]ctive citizenship and participation in the Singapore context not only has legal, social and cultural limits, but comes with political and ideological boundaries that can and will be strictly enforced at the sole discretion of the authorities.

The PLU's brush with the law enforcers made it clear that while groups with socially "off-centre" or politically sensitive agendas may continue to exist, they should remain "closeted" from the public at all times. Although "Singapore 21" had been depicted as a large-scale consultative project involving some 6,000 ordinary Singaporeans from all walks of life (Singapore 21, "Preface"), it was never intended as a "bottom-up" mass participation exercise, nor was it designed, strictly speaking, to cultivate the growth of civil society.

On the contrary, it became more like a strategic attempt at addressing the long-standing "problem" of political apathy and passivity among Singaporeans, measured predominantly by their seeming disinterest in politics and reluctance to offer feedback via established channels. The concept of feedback, understood quite simply as the expression of one's views on public policy, is deemed one of the most evident and active signs of citizen participation in government. Yet, it has been—and remains—a vexed political issue in Singapore, with a sizeable number of Singaporeans politically apathetic, passively docile, or fearful of reprisal.

As Terence Chong explains with cogency: Past examples of alternative political activism have ingrained in Singaporeans the lessons of challenging the Government. The spectre of incarceration, bankruptcy and exile of political opponents, has, rightly or wrongly, penetrated the middle-class psyche. Apathy thus protects [Singaporeans] from personal distress and embarrassment.

Such apathetic condition is also understandable in view of the fact that the highest consultation channel in Singapore, the centrally controlled Feedback Unit, headed by PAP members of parliament (MPs) and civil servants, was created "out of political necessity" in March 1985:. The formation of the Feedback Unit was a result of the PAP government's frustration at losing two seats to the opposition and winning a smaller share of the popular vote than expected at the 1984 General Election.

As Birch explicates, one of the key words of the post-Lee Kuan Yew's "new guard" has been "feedback", designed not so much to replace a top-down mode of rule, but to manage dissenting voices or public dissonance. At the annual conference of Feedback Groups in Singapore in January 2004, the Minister of State for Foreign Affairs and Trade and Industry, Raymond Lim, reiterated the prime objectives of the Feedback Unit in a speech entitled "Feedback and the Public Purpose" by declaring that:

Feedback makes policy formulation in government a more informed process, ensuring above all that it is relevant. It also makes policy implementation a more effective process, as it enhances public receptiveness based on a better understanding and acceptance of the policy.

Minister Lim's statement makes it quite clear that prime intention of the Feedback Unit is to enhance" public receptiveness" to government policies. It is, in other words, highly functional and predominantly gestural. Any feedback on policies, especially impending and potentially unpopular ones, would thus facilitate the forging of" consensus politics" between the citizenry and the government.

In this way, the concept of feedback or consultation becomes another" gesture" of the government used to gauge political support or otherwise. As a result, those who do not support specific policies would never use established feedback channels to voice their thoughts.

It is interesting to note from a 2003 survey that while 80 per cent of Singaporeans find the Feedback Unit's channels accessible and adequate, and 77 per cent acknowledge the Unit as an effective means for feedback, only about 6,800 feedback inputs--out of a total population numbering more than four million--were received that same year.

By contrast, however, the" Forum" page of the national and most widely read daily, the Straits Times, attracts more than 2,000 letters every month. The Straits Times Forum has become, virtually by default, the most popular site for public feedback and discussion in Singapore, serving to amplify public sentiments on a broad range of social, cultural, economic and, to a lesser extent, political issues. However, it is important to note that while the Forum page has been labelled the" most democratic space in Singapore", the extent to which one can engage in political debate through this forum is almost solely determined by editorial decision and judgement. If the media in Singapore is, as Birch notes in Althusserian terms, an" ideological state apparatus", then genuine or active participation in policy-making via the state-managed newspaper outlet is either futile or not possible, thus reinforcing Ooi Can Seng's (" State-Civil Society Relations and Tourism", in this issue) claim that the Singapore government has been able to re-define civil spaces for its own interests. The corollary is that letters that are deemed politically offensive or destabilizing would not make the cut, thus making the Straits Times Forum a poor example of civil society as it is a socially and politically unproblematic space for the establishment.

The call by" Singapore 21" to embrace" active citizenship" needs to be examined against the backdrop of political hegemony and apathy in Singapore. Calls to participate are typically accompanied by important caveats, including unwritten rules about the limits of participation, exemplified most prominently by OB markers (which the next section of this paper will address). Riding on the context of the Forum, what is not being said tends to speak louder than what is or has been. In this regard," active citizenship" is at best a Machiavellian political gesture aimed at instructing Singaporeans on how to become good and obedient citizens by working with and alongside the state to minimize resistances to government policies. Contrary to the minister's comments in the opening quote to this section, active citizenship in Singapore is precisely a" reality TV show," where citizens who consciously choose to remain apathetic and" inactive" --that is, those who watch the unfolding drama of politics from the comfort of their homes--are the model" participants" in a society that values political compliance and acquiescence.

OB Markers and" New" Politics

Some groups would like [the government] to open faster--not just loosen restrictions but remove them altogether. But while we talk about OB markers and wider fairways, remember that most Singaporeans still do not play golf. Bread and butter issues are still uppermost on their minds. [...] The test of our policies is not how closely we approach an idealized model, but how well we move the majority forward so that we remake Singapore into a dynamic global city and the best home for Singaporeans.

The concept of the OB markers arose following an episode in 1994 dubbed "the Catherine Lim affair". On 20 November 1994, well-known Singaporean novelist and social commentator Catherine Lim's political commentary entitled "One Government, Two Styles" was published in the Sunday edition of Singapore's Straits Times daily. In it, Lim opined that Prime Minister Goh Chok Tong's promise of a more open, consultative, and consensual leadership style had been abandoned in favour of the authoritarian style of his predecessor, referring specifically to the former premier Lee Kuan Yew. This was the gist of Lim's contention:

Over the years, a pattern of governance has emerged that is not exactly what was envisaged. Increasingly, the promised Goh style of people-orientation is being subsumed under the old style of top-down decisions.

POLITICAL ACTIVATION OF THE FAMILY

Our model of family dynamics adopts a "lifespan development" perspective, which recognizes that socialization processes occur throughout a person's life and do not stop once a child reaches adolescence. This approach traces changes in interaction patterns across lifetimes of family members, and focuses on the continual development of the individual.

Families constitute social systems in which role expectations and patterned, predictable behaviour establish homeostatic balance in various domains of interaction, including communication about politics. But relationships and interactions are inherently dynamic, involving adjustments over time and in response to external factors. A family's response to political stimulation provided by an intervention is inherently social - while a father, mother, or adolescent child might initiate political discussion and more frequent use of news media, the family responds collectively to the increased political communication.

We will describe a sequence of activation using the framework of a functional model of political communication in the family. Sociologists have developed functional models to explain counterintuitive patterns of indirect causation in which the consequences of a behaviour or social arrangement appear to be causes of that behaviour. A process might entail uniformity of consequences despite wide variance of activities producing those consequences. The dynamics by which a social system adapts to change involve three elements: homeostatic balance; the structure of behaviours that tends to maintain balance; and disruptions or tensions that upset homeostasis.

Given a family member's increased interest in politics, her developmental goals might require increased communication at home about public affairs. These goals are not necessarily compatible with the relational expectations of others in the family, particularly in low-SES homes, where political issues and controversies are rarely discussed.

For example, the exposure of a spouse to a political controversy at church or at work might result in a disquieting increase in the frequency and intensity of political debates at home, prompting a partner to familiarize herself with the issue. Or, a child's participation in a highly stimulating civics curriculum could represent a source of tension in homes where parents prefer that children avoid bringing up controversial topics.

A parent who observes a child reading the newspaper for the first time and initiating political discussions could perceive higher information needs for herself, and might turn to news media for cognitive orientations that facilitate future discussions.

Campaigns designed to promote citizenship can provide a source of exogenous stimulation or tension that disrupts the structure of social interaction in the family, prompting efforts among family members to restore homeostatic balance. This adjustment process constitutes the behavioural dynamic that might stimulate growth in the political competence of family members.

A family's response to an intervention produces interdependent outcomes that involve reciprocal influence even though only one family member might have been initially exposed to the intervention. Empirical research supports the conceptualization of a process of family activation that follows a five-stage sequence. An individual's response to an intervention includes heightened civic involvement as manifest in increased interest and information seeking (step 1).

The resulting knowledge acquisition and opinion formation motivates interpersonal communication about politics within the family (step 2), prompting increased expectations for political competence among other family members (step 3). As family members achieve compatibility at higher levels of competence, they acquire an increased capacity for reciprocal influence that helps to sustain interest in civic affairs (step 4), which also increases motivation for civic participation outside the home (step 5). A description of this process in terms of distinct stages allows us to explicate the dynamics of intra-family political engagement, but we hasten to add that these processes are interactive in nature and are presented as a heuristic framework rather than as a linear, deterministic model.

STEP 1: INDIVIDUAL RESPONSE

The process we describe as a sequence of political activation hinges on the ability of a mobilization effort to engage at least one family member, who acts as a catalyst for changing the structure of the family's political communication. Exposure to political stimuli is largely driven by psychological involvement, conceptualized as interest or concern about political topics. From the perspective of intervention planners, a key concern is whether involvement varies in response to situational increases in stimulation, or whether involvement represents an enduring predisposition.

Prior research identified two situational factors that influence involvement beyond individual predispositions - the level or prominence of an election and discussion about politics. For example, Sears and Valentino reported that preadults adopt partisan dispositions via intensive exposure to episodic events such as election campaigns. Prominent events as occasions for socialization are important to any model of civic development because political topics are otherwise irrelevant to many adolescents, low-SES adults, and immigrants.

Situational increases in political involvement are associated with information seeking via purposeful use of news media, particularly newspapers. Frank emphasizes that political involvement "is more than a biding interest in politics. When it is stimulated by a situation, involvement may describe a `process of activation' that can lead to communication outcomes such as media use, interpersonal discussion, and political learning." These findings offer an optimistic view of the capacity for interventions to generated widespread interest given a strategy that promotes discussion during election campaigns.

STEP 2: INTERPERSONAL COMMUNICATION

Some family members -perhaps not all - might develop a keener interest in public affairs in response to an increase in the intensity and diffusion of political stimulation. The resulting acquisition of knowledge and opinions provides cognitive resources for use in primary-group interactions, including conversations with family members. The most politically stimulated family member is likely to initiates these discussions, as demonstrated in the "two-step" flow of personal influence.

A basic insight of the two-step model is that information diffusion and social influence are dynamic processes that occur within primary groups.

Following in this research tradition, Beck provided evidence that primary groups appear to be the most important setting for discussion about a presidential campaign. Data collected from a survey of the Ohio electorate immediately following the 1988 election showed that respondents were most likely to discuss the campaign with spouses and co-workers. The family in some respects constitutes an ideal setting for the nurturing of discussions about an ongoing controversy, campaign, or political event. In any group situation, a person's ability to participate in or avoid political conversations is largely determined by the supply of willing discussion partners.

At home, the presence of a spouse and other adult household members should enhance opportunities for political discussion. In comparison to those in formal, public settings, family relationships tend to be intimate, trusting, and long lasting. As such, they provide promising opportunities for interventions to prompt political conversation in light of prior research showing that such conversations involve a certain degree of risk outside of the home. Politics can be a threatening topic, especially in low-SES groups, where it is rarely discussed and where a conversation might challenge a person's sense of personal efficacy. Political discussion occurs more often when relationships are close, contacts are frequent, and participants share similar social characteristics and beliefs. Even in the absence of an intervention, married respondents cite spouses as their most frequent discussion partner for politics. And while several studies show that parent-child discussion about politics occurs infrequently, situational increases in family-based media use are associated with increased frequency of political discussion at home.

STEP 3: EXPECTATIONS FOR CIVIC COMPETENCE

A functional approach to family political communication suggests that individual behaviours prompted by an intervention should not be understood as ultimate and discrete outcomes.

Instead, indications of individual involvement are implicated in an interactive process of stimulated family communication. In the context of an intervention, the heightened salience of public affairs results in increased expectations for competence in political communication within the entire family.

The salience of politics as a discussion topic varies over time in families and in other primary groups; when politics does become prominent, members of a group make adjustments in their political competence, apparently in anticipation of future discussions. Straits observed that individuals who are only slightly interested in politics are significantly more likely to engage in political conversations if a spouse is named as a discussion partner. Family discussion appears to be the key process by which family members achieve similar levels of interest and competence in behaviours such as paying attention to news, acquiring knowledge, expressing opinions, and voting.

But the increased political interest of one family member might create tension in homes where politics is rarely discussed. The social roles inherent in spousal, sibling, and parent-child relationships involve expectations for communicative competence, and in some cases these expectations involve compatibility if not superiority of some family members in certain areas of knowledge, opinion, and behaviour.

Thus, a parent should know more about politics than a child, according to societal convention, and in many homes, spouses might come to expect that they are more or less equal in expertise about public affairs.

An understanding that these expectations should not be violated can be a particularly strong norm in low-SES homes, which are characterized by authoritarian parenting styles and adherence to traditional gender roles. And while the gap in political participation between men and women has narrowed in recent decades, men are on average more likely to know about political topics. In families in which traditional gender roles are valued, a politically activated wife or daughter could violate family norms.

Disruption of prior communication patterns provides impetus for other family members to increase their own competence, stimulating information seeking, knowledge acquisition, and opinion formation. For example, a spouse might disagree with the opinions expressed by a partner who is suddenly inspired by a campaign, but to successfully counter those views she must pay greater attention to politics.

We are assuming here a positive systemic adjustment, as we are articulating a process by which civic interventions can succeed. But a family system will restore balance following disruption of communication norms by one of two routes - the growth we have described, or regression to previous low levels of civic competence. Step 3 is thus the linchpin in this overall process of family activation, as it triggers either an upward or a downward spiral of citizenship. In response to a politically precocious child, a father might exert cognitive effort via media use to maintain a leadership role with respect to knowledge of public affairs. Or he could admonish the child to keep quiet about politics, and thereby maintain role expectations through coercion instead of expertise.

STEP 4: RECIPROCAL INFLUENCE

Compatibility at higher levels of communicative competence provides family members with opportunities to engage each other in ongoing activities that sustain interest in politics. Theorists in developmental psychology characterize the home as a locus of reciprocal influence in which family members affect the behaviour and cognitions of each other. While a reciprocal interaction approach has been applied to spousal and parent-child relationships, this view has not taken firm hold within the literature of family-based political behaviour. Studies in political socialization and related areas tend to assume a topdown flow of influence, from parents to children, or from the most politically competent spouse to the less competent.

Interventions designed to cultivate citizenship generally focus on individuals, but scholars in health communication have demonstrated the effectiveness of targeting families as opposed to individual family members. Rimal and Flora, for example, reported that a campaign directed at the dietary behaviour of households modified not just the eating habits of adults and children, but the impact that the two had on each other.

While the campaign provided a degree of independent influence on the two parties, it also strengthened the capacity of children and parents to influence each other's health behaviours.

Studies on the political involvement of spouses support the contention that family interaction is characterized by mutual adjustment and that changes in the political interest of one member have consequences for the involvement of other family members. Jennings and Niemi documented a strong pattern of homogeneity among eleven indicators of husband-wife politicization. Among the criterion measures and correlations were knowledge (.58), reading newspapers (.50), watching television (.50), election activities (.52), and participation in community affairs (.45). While assortive mating accounts for much of the similarity, the authors controlled for demographic variables in the statistical analysis, and showed how correlations increased over the history of a marriage. The capacity of family members to influence each other's behaviour thus establishes the family as mechanism for political activation, suggesting strategies for interventions to tap into this social energy. An intervention does not have to reach every family member at once to trigger behavioural changes; the stimulation of one member can result in the politicization of the family as a social system. This outcome is reminiscent of "the strength of weak ties" principle, in which an infrequent interpersonal connection might, when activated, lead to a major change in a person's life.

STEP 5: CIVIC PARTICIPA TION

The activation of political interest is thought to occur prior to participation in the formal political system. "The higher the level of psychological involvement, the greater the expected number and variety of political acts in which citizens will engage". But as we will argue in a subsequent section, attempts to explain political involvement using individual-level variables and purely psychological models tend to ignore the micro-social processes that engender civic competence and motivation.

Granted, an increased flow of political information originating from schools, media, and elections induces many individuals to pay attention to public affairs. Social interaction in the family, however, provides a crucial intermediate stage in a sequence of civic activation, translating individual interest into interpersonal communication, heightened expectations for civic competence, and the capacity for reciprocal influence within relationships.

Membership in the family as a kind of domestic sphere, in which individuals provide each other with continuing stimulation about political topics, should also increase motivation for civic participation outside the home. Research on the antecedents of voting demonstrates that interpersonal communication in primary groups is a particularly important stimulus for persons who are only marginally interested in politics. Married people are more likely to vote than similar individuals who are single, separated, or divorced. People with little autonomous motivation may well respond to political stimulation - such as discussion or co-use of news media - from those with whom they have continuing daily relationships. A change in marital status can affect life-space factors such as occupation, residence, and routines of daily life, but Stoker and Jennings argue that even long-lived marriages have evolutionary tendencies with implications for political involvement.

Prior research has demonstrated the importance of the family in the stimulation of voting. In a secondary analysis of turnout for the 1956 presidential election, Glaser compared the actual turnout of couples with what the expected turnout would be if husbands and wives voted independently. Collective turnout behaviour exceeded the expected distribution if the voting of husbands and wives were independent, and marriage was particularly beneficial for low-SES couples in the stimulation of voting.

Glaser noted that similarities in voting in part reflect similar motivations, outside stimuli, and social norms that affect husband and wife simultaneously. But he argued that joint voting and joint non-voting occur so much more often than they would if husband and wife were motivated independently that interaction within the family is probably an additional force that supplements other predispositions. The implications of family influence, however, extend far beyond the recruitment of individuals for participation in the formal political system.

By acquiring discursive habits in the home - such as reciprocity, tolerance for diverse views, turn taking in conversations, and daily discussion about the news - parents and children prepare themselves for participation in civil society. The family's role in boosting civic efficacy deserves more attention from scholars in light of the increasing interest in studying involvement outside the contexts of voting and partisan politics.

2

Challenges of Responsible Journalism

INTRODUCTION

A challenge to the traditional way journalists have practiced their craft has emerged in the past decade. The civic or public journalism movement seeks to redefine the journalist's role and, in the view of some (but not all) observers, alter traditional journalism ethics. The goal of this study is to determine the extent to which rank-and-file newspaper journalists embrace public journalism values and whether these new values displace traditional values, reinforce them, or have no effect.

Traditional journalism emphasizes the values of fairness, balance, and detachment, which in turn establishes newspapers' credibility among the readers and by extension creates a market among advertisers who want their products and services featured in a credible medium. Public journalism pulls back from detachment.

It casts the press in a more active role of presenting information to the readers to motivate community action in order to solve problems and of creating the forum for citizens to become politically active. This role is viewed by critics as a threat to traditional journalism values in general.

To test whether rank and file journalists have accepted public journalism values and whether their acceptance affects support for traditional journalism, this study surveyed news-editorial staff members at daily newspapers throughout the United States. Public journalism coalesced as a movement in the late 1980s and early 1990s.

Jay Rosen, a vocal advocate for public journalism, called for redefinition of the journalist's job—doing public work—which means "living in the present... confronting problems, debating solutions, arriving at decisions that have broad support". Rosen said traditional journalism ethics are secondary to the more fundamental responsibility of journalists to support and promote public work, whereby citizens join the common effort and participate in solutions to civic problems. Many observers have noted that public journalism initiatives have occurred mostly at small- and medium-circulation newspapers. An early experiment in public journalism thrust the *Columbus (GA) Ledger-Enquirer* into a leadership role in community mobilization when in 1988 executive editor Jack Swift led the paper in preparing a series titled "Columbus Beyond 2000: Agenda for Progress". After surveying the community, the paper recommended an agenda for change and helped organize a community task force to promote the changes.

Another project in public journalism came in the decision of the *Charlotte Observer* to move beyond covering the 1992 election in terms of the traditional horse race, in which the candidates set the agenda for coverage. Instead, the newspaper recruited a 1,000-member citizens' panel to establish the agenda for coverage of the politicians. The *Observer* then asked the politicians to respond to issues the panel said were important to them.

In 1994, the *Observer* launched a public journalism project on inner-city violence, about which editor Jennie Buckner said, "We want to rally the entire community to help these most troubled neighbourhoods help themselves". The *Observer* hired a community coordinator (stationed in the newsroom) to recruit participants for community meetings on solutions to crime and joined with television and radio stations in saturation coverage of crime in the targeted communities.

Public journalism had its early critics. In 1994, *Washington Post* executive editor Leonard Downie said, "Too much of what's called public journalism appears to be what our promotion department does, only with a different kind of name and a fancy, evangelistic fervour".

When the *Charlotte Observer* joined with other large North Carolina newspapers in "Your Voice, Your Vote," an effort to pool coverage of the 1996 election campaign and force candidates to respond to voter issues (similar to the 1992 Charlotte Project but on a statewide scale), scathing critiques appeared in the *Washington Post*, the *New York Times*, the *Boston Globe*, and *New Yorker* magazine.

Jonathan Yardley called the effort "a cabal the purpose of which is to take the political agenda out of the hands of the politicians and place it in the hands of journalists... not exactly... good news." Carl Stepp wrote that public journalists create a caricature of the traditional press and worries that collaboration with government to solve problems undermines the press role as a check on government.

Researchers have found it difficult even to define what is meant by public journalism in order to measure it. Davis Merritt described public journalism as experimental, "a philosophy in search of printed expression". One effort to isolate public journalism values, John Bare study of journalist belief systems at three daily newspapers, showed that staff members at the *Wichita Eagle*, which had been involved in public journalism efforts since 1990, scored significantly higher on factors he called Personal Public Journalism and Institutional Public Journalism.

However, for *Raleigh News and Observer* and *Omaha World-Herald* staff members, the traditional investigative and interpretive role of journalists was the dominant belief system.

Given the intense public debate between fervent adherents and detractors, what is the level of support for public journalism values and practices among rank and file journalists? The findings of three nationwide surveys conducted in Fall 1996, including the one reported in this chapter, provide interesting answers to this question about the level of support for public journalism.

An American Society of Newspaper Editors (ASNE) study of "Newspaper Journalists of the '90s" asked 1,191 journalists at 61 newspapers about approval of four public journalism practices, which the study's author acknowledged represented only relatively moderate departures from traditional journalism and avoided some of the more controversial practices that have been implemented in the name of public journalism.

None of the more activist and controversial public journalism strategies were tested. As one would expect, support for these activities that do not depart much from traditional practice was quite high.

Although the ASNE study only tested fairly moderate practices associated with public journalism, a Fall 1996 survey of daily newspaper editors and journalism professors by Don Corrigan and the *St. Louis Journalism Review* asked about more controversial practices that have been employed in public journalism projects. He concluded that no consensus has developed about what defines public journalism and that most journalists remain uncomfortable with many practices identified as public journalism.

Our study sought to determine whether the rank and file newsroom staffers at American daily newspapers support values articulated by public journalism practitioners and activities typical of public journalism projects. Values are ideas or principles that people value, and to obtain them, people are willing to give up other things. Values are what people evaluate as worthwhile.

In our survey, we measured those things journalists value as important in their work, what they see as worthwhile. The research questions the study addressed include the following: Are journalists ready to move beyond the traditional journalism values and practices? Does greater support of public journalism values correlate with less support of traditional journalism values?

Do newsroom supervisors embrace the values of public journalism to a greater extent than do front-line reporters? Do editors and reporters agree with the practices of public journalism projects which have been extensively discussed in professional publications and conferences?

What characteristics among journalists predict greater support for public journalism values and practices? For example, is public journalism, as anecdotal evidence suggests, a small- and medium-circulation phenomenon? And does acceptance of public journalism values correlate with reduced support of traditional journalism values and less sensitivity to traditional ethical dilemmas?

METHOD

We surveyed 1,000 newspaper staff members. In addition to demographic items, the survey included measures of journalists' acceptance of public journalism values and practices. These questions were adapted from variables developed by John Bare in his study of value systems at three newspapers. These questions asked journalists how important public journalism and traditional journalism values are to them personally in their daily work.

In addition to how important values associated with traditional journalism and those associated with public journalism were to them, journalists were asked how they would respond in scenarios that described typical journalistic dilemmas.

In sampling, we had to deal with the paradox that most newspapers are small while most readers receive the larger papers. A simple random sample of the 1,514 daily newspapers would over-represent the readers of small papers and exclude many who read the larger papers. A sample design can represent readers, or it can represent newspapers, but it cannot do justice to both. We chose to represent readers. Our initial sample of 1,000 news editorial staff members at American daily newspapers was therefore drawn with the probability of selection proportionate to the size of the daily circulation.

The sample was therefore self-weighting, representing journalists who serve a random selection of newspaper readers in the United States. When larger newspapers were selected more than once, we chose multiple respondents from those papers in proportion to their size.

For the first and second hits at a newspaper in the sample, we chose at random two names from the 1996 *Editor and Publisher International Yearbook*. For larger newspapers with more than two hits, the third and subsequent staff members were chosen at random from the bylines of local staff writers in a particular issue of the newspaper.

The approach to the selection ensured that supervisors, reporters, and other staff members would be included in the sample. In November 1996, we mailed 1,000 questionnaires containing approximately 100 variables and coded with identification numbers for response tracking. A second and third wave of the survey went to non-respondents.

SOCIAL STRATEGIES

Matters of self-presentation and scope of action are critical to the relations built among researchers, the virtual "places" populating the Internet, and the cultural membership. Correll, for example, was able to convey the location, look, and meanings of the "furniture" of the Lesbian Cafe mostly from her observations of electronic postings, but also from interviews. Compared to Leal's analysis of the relation of TV sets to the domestic material culture in working-class Brazilian homes, the mise-en-scene of the Cafe is not nearly as dense, tactile, and sensuous.

Despite this possibly unfair comparison, "the sense of a common reality [in the Lesbian Cafe] was used by patrons much like physical settings are used by co-present conversationalists—as a source of mutually relevant topics". Like the dialogue one hears in a radio play, conversationalists in the Lesbian Cafe must include many more references in their ordinary talk to objects, the current status of the objects, and the presence or absence of people in and around those objects in order to maintain orientation and sustain a convincing sense of as-if reality. The lean exposition Correll offers would likely be unacceptable in other forms of ethnographic work, but it turns out to be the one that matters to the women who "drink" and socialize there.

Media ethnographers begin their on-line presence in a variety of ways. One mode used by some is that of the unknown, unobtrusive observer. Over a three-year period, Harrington and Bielby collected and printed messages posted on two soap opera BBS's by subscribers to two commercial on-line computer services. They do not report interactions of any kind between themselves and the posters.

Presumably, the computer services were not notified of the initiation of the research activity, nor were the BBS system operators. Interestingly, while the authors appear unconcerned about their own lurker posture, they note the suspicion held by many of the BBS users that their conversations were being overheard by "industry insiders". Scodari also relies on transcripts of fan BBS discourse in interpreting critical reactions to changes in the soap, Another World, although she aligns her own interests much more closely with the fans she quotes than Harrington and Bielby. Open participation characterizes the approach of several other studies and more closely resembles normative field practice. Baym started as an unabashed soap fan and news group contributor and found it easy to continue openly as an analyst of the group:

My position in the [rec.arts.arts.soaps, or r.a.t.s., newsgroup] is that of a participant at least as much as a researcher. As a long-time fan of soap operas, I was thrilled to discover this group. It was only after I had been reading daily and participating regularly for a year that I began to write about it. As the work has evolved, I have shared its progress with the group members and found them exceedingly supportive and helpful. They have acted as research participants as well as subjects and have treated me more as an ambassador than a researcher. The confidence each party had in the other paved the way for Baym to obtain other forms of data besides the news group's messages, especially electronic mail correspondence with several participants and responses to open-ended questions she posted to r.a.t.s. Similarly, Correll's membership in the Lesbian Cafe, and the approval she got from the bar's founder, assisted her in posting queries and interviewing several of the patrons both by e-mail and in person.

Some researchers actually run the facilities that enable computer users to "find" the research project. In an early study, Myers operated a university BBS for two months and set up a number of networked research tools in order to investigate the perceived social context of CMC: on-line surveys, a focus group, and a role-playing game.

More recently, Lindlof et al. launched a Web home page for X-Men fans that offered graphic content (thus participating in the X-Men array of more than 60 Internet locations), links to other X-Men sites, a survey to capture data, and a solicitation for dialogues with on-line X-Men users and page producers. Like the Baym and Correll studies, the research purpose was stated openly in order to invite cooperation; however, its sudden appearance and the research team's initial contacts with users were sometimes met with suspicion, critique (of their knowledge of X-Men), and humorous skepticism.

It became clear that the World Wide Web page of hypertext URLS's (Uniform Resource Locator) that linked to other pages related to the X-Men topic constituted the study's "gatekeeper" in the traditional sense of enabling an initial contact. The study also hints at the possibilities of participatory design in which ethnographers may act as the interpreters of diverse voices, usage interests, and aesthetic tastes in the design of networked systems. A final strategy for consideration moves the researcher physically alongside the user in order to "read" his or her real-time decision making and styles of engagement. The user's dyadic interplay with a computer forms a focal interest, but included in this arena would be the material context of computing (*e.g.*, its location in a room, the CD-ROM's on hand), the institutional culture (*e.g.*, considering open viewing of sex sites as sexual harassment), interpersonal resources or constraints (*e.g.*, informal rules for sharing URL's), and the specific reality of what it means to "do computing" that these signify for users.

Models for this approach exist in the literature on social television viewing and family computer usage. However, since Internet usage is typically a solitary venture, the more promising route would seem to lie in some version of the "shopping with consumers" protocol from the field of consumer behaviour. Accompanying users on their way through the kinetic pathways of virtual space and eliciting talk on a wide range of subjects, either retrospectively or on-the-spot, enables the researcher to understand the more embodied dimensions of CMC.

In effect, the researcher shadows the user's on-site computing. The advantages of the approach are its close proximity to the user and setting, and the ability to comprehend computing performance as an activity that has a rich, localized back stage—that is, as more than lines of type scrolling down a screen.

In ethnographies of embodied social scenes, the researcher must continually negotiate with the culture membership and convince them of the value of the study and the reasonableness of the person doing the research. It is not unusual for ethnographers to have to adjust their persona somewhat differently as they pass through a scene, or disclose different versions of the project, since the members of a group often relate asymmetrically or even conflictively to each other.

CMC ethnographies, as we have shown, also involve some degree of negotiation when anonymous observation is not the method of access. Virtual spaces offer a limited window in which to explain one's purpose, and electronic text is not the most suitable medium for engaging in a sensitive interaction. Trust tends to be a heightened concern where entry and exit and unbridled information disclosure are easily accomplished. Mistakes, once made, can have disastrous results, and be very hard to rectify. Institutional principles for informed consent are now being formulated for research on the World Wide Web, but it will take longer for ethnographers themselves to develop a consensus around protocols for responsible virtual space entry and ways to insure the fair treatment of those they study without compromising very seriously the conduct of enquiry.

TECHNICAL UTILITIES

In this section, we discuss the use of technical utilities for accomplishing research tasks. Some computer systems allow asynchronous communication interactions to be studied either by saving the individual messages, or archiving all postings for later perusal. Most of these have been around for some time. The ones we discuss here are electronic mail, news groups over Usenet, and list servers. Electronic mail is asynchronous (users generally are not communicating in realtime), quick (in terms of transmission and reply), text-based, and configured for dyadic or multiple connections (can be sent one-to-one, one-to-many, or many-to-many). Moreover, e-mail can be stored and manipulated. As Garton and Wellman noted in a recent review:

E-mail can be stored in external memory for future retrieval, searching, editing, and forwarding to others. People can edit their own or other's messages to change their meaning. The historical record of interaction may be used for surveillance of individual and group interactions, to review past decisions (as Oliver North belatedly learned), and to bring new members up to date. What makes this modality particularly suitable for ethnographic research are its personal-contact and archival functions.

For example, in his 9-month participant-observation study of "Zytech," a computer systems firm, Workman utilized e-mail in the following ways:

- Being placed on the company's various distribution lists, which on a daily basis delivered internal documents, minutes of meetings, meeting agendas, and announcements;

- Scheduling interviews;
- Accessing hundreds of BBS's, including Zytech correspondence going back several years;
- Communicating with informants, including follow-ups to FTF interviews.

Though the staggered progress of e-mail interviewing does not promote the same qualities of rapport or spontaneity as personal interviews, it does permit a more elastic time frame for both interviewer and participant to think carefully about the meanings of questions and replies. In another organizational study, special software was used to automatically save the headers (but not the message content) of all departmental e-mail to a designated file whenever a user read or transmitted a message, yielding a non-reactive means of learning who communicates with whom, when, and about what. For ethnographic purposes, the value of this procedure lies in its capacity to augment such methods as interviews or on-site observation.

However, the ability to retrieve and store this information without the users' permission (or below their conscious awareness, even when permission is granted) carries the potential for ethical abuse at worst, and suspicion on the part of participants at best. Usenet is a protocol that describes how groups of messages can be stored on and sent between computers, many of which lay outside of the Internet. In actuality, Usenet forms a "virtual forum" for the electronic community that is divided into a plethora of news groups dedicated to varied areas of interest. News group articles are read and written through programmes called newsreaders that keep track of articles that have been read, allow users to edit what has been read, and enable readers to reply to previously posted messages in the aforementioned study, Baym reported her participant-observation of a news group made up of soap opera aficionados.

Even though some Usenet sites can archive messages off-line, Baym herself saved the messages posted on the r.a.t.s group while she was an active member. Even working with a medium often described as low in social presence or media richness, she was able to develop a "thick" description of the personalities of this community based on features of their postings:

- Signature files (files automatically attached to postings containing identifying information about the sender),
- Humour in the messages,
- Self-disclosure,
- Comments made about personal lives.

By capitalizing on the features of Usenet news groups, variations of focus group interviewing become possible. During a two-month period of operating a public BBS, Myers set up a computer-mediated focus group "to determine what motivated frequent and active BBS use". As an alternative to a simple discussion, a focus group consisting of a theoretically interesting set of users could work on a virtual task. MacGregor and Morrison describe an editing-group protocol in which groups of people were given the opportunity to re-edit existing news reports (including video footage) in order to produce a more "ideal" version, thereby enabling them to understand viewers' journalistic values more concretely.

It is not difficult to see how this task could be adapted to computer news groups and the multimedia capabilities of high-end work stations, although techniques for training and monitoring the users in their editing-group activities would need to be developed. Listserv groups (managed by listserver software) are similar to news groups in that they are discussion groups, but they operate in a completely different way by using the Internet e-mail system to exchange messages. Once a person subscribes to a Listserv group (or Listproc group, as they are called on networks other than the early Bitnet), their name is added to a mailing list that receives postings from everyone else subscribed to the list. Many listservers offer features that allow users to search and retrieve files that are archived, and search the archives using keyword searches. Thus, anyone from a remote site can access archived messages for study from the host computer.

This capability raises interesting ethical issues: How does one receive consent to study the stored communications of users of a particular listserver? Is open access to a person's communications implied in the use of this service? Are the archived files considered the property of the individual subscribers, or are they "owned" in some form of fiduciary relationship by the listserv operator? Because the Internet has developed so rapidly, many such legal and ethical questions have yet to be resolved. The CMC technologies mentioned above have been in place for a while and are generally well known to most researchers. Most of the communication from these sources is asynchronous, *i.e.*, it is archived for later review and becomes an excellent database. However some of the newer systems allow for the actual observation of synchronous, or real-time, communication behaviour. It is to these we now turn.

Some of the more recent real-time technologies are:
- Internet Relay Chat (IRC) systems, or" chat lines";
- The entire gamut of multiple-user technologies, *e.g.*, MUDs (Multiple User Domains, formerly known as Multiple User Dungeons), MOOs (MUD Object-Oriented), and MUSHes (Multi-User Shared Hallucination);
- Groupware,
- Desktop videoconferencing over the Internet. All of these systems operate synchronously and as such more approximate face-to-face communication.

Internet Relay Chat (IRC) is a multi-user synchronous communication capability available worldwide to users with Internet accessibility.

These real time" chat lines" provide for mutithreaded conversations from more than two users in something very similar to an" electronic cocktail party". In these" chat rooms" users are able to don bogus" personas" (false identities) and communicate with interactants from all over the globe. These chat lines are very popular on commercial services like America Online and are now available through various web browsers (*e.g.*, students can" chat" with the president of a university via its Web site).

One step up from IRC is a whole family of computer programmes that allow more than just written conversation in real time. These are multi-user programmes that, in addition to providing text, allow the additional depiction of a physical environment. Multiple User programmes are designed to offer a pseudo-physical dimension via its object orientation. In MOOs, for examples, individuals" virtually" move through" rooms," interact with virtual" objects" such as chairs, doors, and the like, and have virtual conversations with others. As Reid has remarked, in MUDs," text replaces gesture and has even become gesture itself".

A third, more recent technology is found in a generation of software called" groupware." Unlike MUDs, MOOs, MUSHes, MUCKs, and the like that are used more for entertainment and amusement, groupware is being developed mainly for business and professional uses.

Most of the newer groupware programmes use Web-based technology and allow not only for sharing e-mail but for conducting synchronous multiuser conferencing. The promise for ethnographers in this technology lies in the" common thread" that runs through all these programmes--*i.e.,*" the construction of shared memory" and recording of group discussions. In essence, groupware allows for observing the" virtual office," *i.e.,* electronic mail, conferencing, scheduling, shared documents, electronic" whiteboards," and so on, and recording these interactions.

All of this can function in real time or be archived for later study. Appearing now on the horizon is the capability to use the desktop computer for real time videoconferencing.

Using fairly inexpensive video cameras attached to desktop computers, and software such as CU-SeeMe technology, mediated FTF interactions are now available for study. As soon as compression capabilities for full-motion video are perfected, these dispersed FTF interactions, mediated by the computer, can be recorded and used in data analysis.

When considering all these new technologies, the type of research done may have to be dictated by the characteristics of the medium. That is, for asynchronous media, the type of research conducted would be more akin to that for studying other forms of written communication, while synchronous media enable types of research more equivalent to naturalistic observation--*i.e.,* observing the unfolding of communicative events in real time.

It was inevitable that interpretive analysts would turn their attention to the profusion of common culture now moving through the Internet. Forms of ethnographic enquiry are being applied to many of the events that occur in virtual space, although questions remain about how well these approaches engage CMC phenomena. One such question is the appropriateness of" community" as a conceptual device. The conventional idea of community as a stable locus for the practice of ritual, custom, and moral obligation applies to cyberspace groups, albeit in the context of a shifting sense of commitment.

When members can easily come and go, when many" members" do not even post, and when identities cannot be verified beyond the current situation, the power of a community ethos may be weakened considerably. The structural properties of the Internet also raise questions about how far a user community extends. For example, can any array of Web sites found by a search term be considered a" community," and if not, what criteria do we use for including a site in the community set?

Finally, what is the relationship of computer-mediated action to local social networks? It has been suggested, for example, that the growing reliance on computer technology for communicating with distant others may undermine the vitality of public life in so-called real communities or play a role in their economic and social fragmentation. Answers to these and other important issues about virtual community await further and more inventive empirical studies.

If there is one theme that runs through the differences between FTF (embodied) and CIVIC (virtual) ethnography, it is the problem of participation. CIVIC ethnography moves us into questions of what it means to engage in and explain" experience" without being co-present with others. Screen-life is a social sphere of its own with vocabularies, motives, and expectations that increasingly re-interpret the meanings of off-screen-life (*e.g.*, mail becoming known as" snail mail").

Objectifications of life in the screen world are also a part of that world. Computer users do act as textual performers and analysts, and knowingly comment on the skills of other text-makers. The use of symbolic codes like" FOTFL" and the real-time deployment of a character in a MUD are operations that create the affect of participation for users, and it would be unusual for ethnographers; not to consider their situated usage.

However, the sites of semiotic action in CMC are not the texts, but the persons who produce them. The text-threads from a Usenet news group or a stack of e-mail messages exnominate the moments in which they were created and read, and the influences of local institutions on their users' action are seldom seen in the messages themselves. In the years ahead, ethnographers will be struggling with basic questions of what it means to" participate" in simulated worlds as well as with developing tactical ways to participate as researchers. Closely related to the problem of participation are issues of trust and ethical conduct to which we have alluded at various points in this chapter. These issues assume even more importance than usual in research practice due to the greater potential for engaging in covert surveillance of CIVIC social life and the still-unsettled distinctions between" public" and" private" behaviour across the range of cyberspace contexts.

The problem of the stable identifiability of persons who post in Usenet news groups, respond by e-mail, or visit a Web site may also confound the principle of informed consent as a precondition for engaging a human subject's participation. Generally, there is little debate about the need to provide as much disclosure as possible about research procedures to those who are asked to participate, and to shelter them from the possible harmful consequences of participation and subsequent publication.

However, as King notes, extremely wide ranges of" group accessibility" and" perceived privacy" exist on the Internet. The highest accessibility characterizes those public BBS groups that are unmoderated and unregulated, while the least accessible community is" a private, closed e-mail group where the subscription address is not published and there are enforced requirements to join".

Perceived privacy varies in terms of both the sensitivity of the information (in which, for example, a substance abuse support group would seek a very high level of privacy) and the need to disseminate information to the widest possible client group (the National Communication Association's CRTNET would seek a low measure of privacy). Yet a great many Internet conversations can in fact be monitored with relative ease, which complicates the understanding of what is permissible to study and whether observation is truly" covert" if no barriers are erected to keep one from observing.

Of course, it probably does matter to many virtual groups whether it is a naive visitor who is stopping briefly at their fora, or a person whose goal is to cast a long-term, analytic eye on their activities and publish the result. The conventional view holds that any research of on-line participants should" strive to obtain some degree of informed consent whenever possible.... Most importantly, researchers should negotiate their entry into electronic communities, beginning with the `owner' of the discussion, if one exists".

Preserving the dignity and empowerment of the persons being studied, even if their" real" identities and locations are unknown, demands that the researcher take steps to explain all of the elements of the study that may bear on their decision to participate voluntarily. Taking a different view, Jones argues that the highly elusive, evanescent presence and essentially unknowable identity of most of the subjects in cylberspace obviates the need in most cases for pursuing consent formally:" If the research does not involve identifiable subjects, there is no risk to subjects, and therefore the protection of these rights and interests no longer applies".

Jones goes on to argue that the strict application of conventional human subject protections would be especially detrimental to the study of cyberspace, which exists as an arena in which individuals can enjoy the freedom of withholding, revealing, and even fabricating information about themselves.

Somewhere between these positions is King, who states that" the perceived level of privacy with which most members of cyberspace forums post notes is the level that researchers are obligated to protect".

At the stage of publication, she advocates the removal from messages of all headers, signatures, references to the name and type of the group (e-mail, Usenet news group, etc.), and references to any person's name or pseudo-name. It may be that the evolving use of networked systems will alter the customs and arguments for what constitutes" privacy" and" autonomy," in turn informing the ethical practice of ethnography.

RECENT TRENDS IN JOURNALISTIC AUTONOMY

Random surveys, each of more than a thousand U.S. journalists, con ducted every 10 years since the early 1970s suggest that journalism's century-long ascent towards professionalism has stalled and may, in fact, be reversing. The newsroom surveys show a strong trend towards declining journalistic autonomy. Weaver and Wilhoit, who conducted the last two surveys, wrote:

Compared to the early 1970s, journalists in the 1982 sample reported a significant decline in their freedom to decide news story emphasis and editing. The 1992 interviews suggest that newsroom autonomy has diminished further, and at a startling pace. For the first time in three decades, barely half of reporters see themselves [with] the newsroom clout of their predecessors. And the lessening autonomy is occurring at a time when many in the workforce--who entered the profession during a tide of heavy hiring of young staff in the late 1970s and early 1980s--have been in the newsroom long enough to have established their authority.

Four of five journalists laid the loss of autonomy to profit-driven management decisions as well as pressure from government, advertisers, or a hostile public. A comment the researchers deemed typical read: "There is increasing pressure from large corporations, including my own, for bottom-line profit and gains at the expense of long-term quality". By contrast, only 8 per cent said they were hindered by professional standards of ethics, good taste, or objectivity.

Other surveys show a similar trend. A 1993 Associated Press Managing Editors survey of 627 newspaper journalists showed rising discontent from a survey 8 years earlier, particularly among the young, minorities, and best educated. Almost half the journalists with graduate degrees counted themselves dissatisfied enough to want to leave their jobs. "About half of these dissatisfied journalists say they do not have sufficient autonomy on the job," the report said, "they lack resources to do their jobs properly and they are not very impressed with the quality of their newspapers".

A 1995 Associated Press Managing Editors study of newsroom managers also showed less autonomy and greater stress than a similar survey in 1983. "Fully 66 per cent of responding editors said their news hole was reduced in the past year. Half reported losing news staffers who were not replaced. Eighty per cent reported that 'there is more work than I can complete in a normal day'". All of these limitations were imposed from above the newsroom.

Summing up these changes for newspapers in an article titled "The Thrill is Gone," Stepp concluded: "In the age-old battle between the editorial side and the business side, the editorialists have lost the upper hand". In local television--the part of the news industry growing A fundamental principle of ethics is that those with greatest power bear the greatest moral accountability.

Fastest over the past several decades in employment, consumer loyalty, and influence over news practice--the outlook for journalistic autonomy is more dismal still. According to Fink, "In television sheer perversity is at work-a sort of Gresham's Law of Journalism: poor quality, low-cost entertainment shows drive out high quality, high-cost news programming". If these assessments are accurate, journalists are more decision takers than decision makers. While they cannot disavow responsibility for their actions so long as they retain the option to quit their jobs, their authority to produce high-quality ethical news reports is circumscribed, tightly for some, loosely for others. A fundamental principle of ethics is that those with the greatest power bear the greatest moral accountability. Journalism's ethical codes have it backward.

A recent text on media ethics concluded: "[I]t's futile to discuss... efforts by individuals to practice ethical journalism without examining the corporate profit motive and its impact on those efforts". Major American journalism ethics codes, however, not only fail to examine the corporate profit motive, most don't even recognize its existence. Difficult structural ethical questions lie at the heart of journalism conducted by profit-seeking businesses.

Particularly in the modern newsroom where barriers between the business side and the news side have been lowered or eliminated, journalism ethics must speak to potential conflicts of interest with powerful news-shapers outside the newsroom. Drawing on theoretical work by Turow, McQuail, and McManus, at least eight such powerful actors can be identified. In each case there should be both a prescription of an optimal relationship and an enforceable ethical proscription to protect the news department's interest in providing news that maximizes public understanding from the media firm's narrow self-interest in serving the following constituencies:

- Shareholders/Owners. If they seek maximum short-term returns on their investment, they may balk at spending what quality journalism requires.

- Rational advertisers seek the largest audience of potential customers in a context that both lends their claims credibility yet encourages consumption, all at the lowest cost. In contrast, quality journalism seeks the largest audience regardless of customer potential--wealth-and freedom from bias towards advertisers and the ethic of consumption.
- Sources may manipulate the supply of raw material for news in order to gain favorable exposure to their ideas and often themselves. In contrast, ethical journalism gathers information without fear or favour and without regard to the information subsidies of public relations.
- Consumers: More people may be attracted to entertainment information. Further, quality journalism that challenges popular myths and prejudices may drive away some consumers.
- Government: In an environment where parent conglomerates of media firms own companies affected by government regulation or government contracts, or simply by government spending, there may be pressure for biased news in return for favours.
- Parent corporations may exert pressure to report favorably or at least not initiate negative coverage of corporate siblings and their business interests.
- Media firms, represented by the newspaper publisher or TV station general manager or network CEO, may not allocate adequate resources to their news departments given the greater profitability of other choices, such as entertainment programming, or entertainment-oriented sections of a newspaper, or other business interests.
- Pressure groups including social institutions may exert influence on the newsroom for content that does not offend the group's sensibilities or that furthers its agenda. Quality journalism, however, is independent, acting in the best interest of the entire community.

The details of such a structural ethics of journalism are beyond the scope of this chapter. Fresh thinking about how to define, measure, and enforce a new moral code for news is urgently needed. Even the most modest proposal is likely to be highly controversial because structural ethics must negotiate the First Amendment, and more importantly, intrude on the "forbidden," realm of ownership prerogatives of private enterprises. My purpose here has been restricted to demonstrating that the current expressions of national codes of ethics ignore or gloss over the most serious moral issues in contemporary journalism. As long as they do, journalism's codes of ethics are themselves suspect ethically. At best, they are incomplete. At worst, they confuse and discourage needed reforms by permitting those who control the news to deflect criticism from themselves onto their employees.

In Britain, lone motherhood is not a neutral nor an apolitical status; it evokes strong moral evaluations and therefore easily becomes a political symbol.

Although the historical status and treatment of British lone mothers has varied over time, they have almost continually been at the centre of public debates about the state of society in general, but more particularly of 'the family' and the role of women.

Most recently, political and media attention has focused on the doubling of the number of lone parent families in Britain over the past two decades (reaching around 20 per cent of all families with dependent children, over 90 per cent of whom are headed by a lone mother), on the growth of unmarried mothers as a proportion of all lone mothers, and on their increasing reliance on Income Support (the social assistance benefit) rather than on paid work.

Debate has centred around whether lone mothers prefer to live off the state, and may even be created by such policy 'cushioning', or whether they want to be 'self-sufficient' but cannot because welfare policies are unsupportive.

Arguably both views are wide of the mark; research reveals that lone mothers' moral views about 'good' mothering, and how this does or does not combine with paid work, is the crucial issue. Lone mothers received particularly damning attention at the hands of new right politicians and the popular media in 1993, in the context of the then Conservative government's 'back to basics' campaign. Indeed, 1993 has been dubbed 'The year of the lone mother'.

Lone mothers were depicted as a threat to the fabric of society, supposedly rearing delinquent children without the guidance of a proper father, and scrounging benefits and housing off the welfare state. Social policies were called for that would deal with this menace. Lone mothers received further attention in the media as a legitimate cause for social concern during 1996, again functioning as a sort of symbol as part of a national debate about 'moral values', as policies concerning divorce law reform and working mothers were debated.

And towards the end of 1997, lone mothers were once again in the political and media spotlight as a result of the New Labour government's social reforms. Here lone mothers functioned as a symbol in the attempt to restructure social benefits towards welfare-to-work strategies.

Academics have played an important supporting role in media preoccupations with lone mothers. In particular, new right and revisionist/communitarian academics have gained space in the national media, and have propounded what Judith Stacey calls 'virtual social science'.

Here categorical assertion, anecdote and selective readings of 'facts' are posed as unbiased and fault-free authoritative research, in this case purportedly showing that lone mothers are formative members of a British 'underclass'. The US academic Charles Murray gained particular space in the press in the early-mid 1990s, with Cassandra-like statistical and rhetorical predictions that Britain was heading down the same slippery slope as the US, to extensive urban crime, drug use and disorder-where all this was the result of increasing 'illegitimate' births supported by the benefits system. The answer, in this view, is to stop 'supporting' lone motherhood through social policies and instead support the traditional married family.

Such negative portrayals of lone mothers have not gone unchallenged. Attempts have been made by voluntary pressure groups, such as the National Council for One Parent Families, and liberal left professionals and academics, as well as leading figures in the 'liberal' establishment, such as Church authorities, to reinsert a public image of lone mothers as 'normal' women who are doing their best in externally constrained and unfavourable circumstances. In this view, social policies should be enlarged to properly support such women in bringing up their children.

Consequently, mainstream political and media debates about lone mothers in Britain-and corresponding policy proposals-have become polarised between seeing lone mothers as a threat to society or as victims of social problems. Each of these positions, their propagation in the media, the role of academics within this, and the social policies that accompany them, is reviewed in more detail below: particular attention is focused on the ways in which the media have depicted black lone mothers.

But these polarised positions are not the only ways of understanding lone mothers' situation, or of framing the parameters for social policies in response. Indeed, other views may more accurately reflect how lone mothers themselves understand and experience their lives.

These alternative views of lone motherhood are also discussed albeit more briefly, because they have not gained wider legitimacy or currency in national media and political debates, nor influenced policy frameworks to any great extent. The propagation of particular media images of lone mothers and their accompaniment by recommendations for particular social policies, is posed rather simply above. Clearly, the media increasingly inform public understanding and comprehension of the social world, and play a role in placing issues on the political policy agenda-as this volume attests.

Nevertheless, the relationship between mainstream media presentations of lone motherhood and the actual or possible social policies that address their situation is not a relationship of simple stimulus-response.

As in other policy areas, this relationship is more complex, not least because government and political agendas influence and inform media coverage. It is perhaps more useful to see ideological issues lying at the root of both, which relate to shared social understandings about the relationship between individuals, states, markets and families, and to how 'explanations' are constructed in dominant western and academic categorical modes of thought.

REPRESENTATIONS OF LONE MOTHERS
AS A SOCIAL THREAT

One perception of lone mothers expounded in mainstream political and media representations sees them as a social threat: both morally and financially. They are formative members of an underclass that has no interest in providing for itself in legitimate ways. This position links into the underclass theory that has developed in the USA in particular, but has been imported into, and gained influence in, Britain-although it also has its roots in a longstanding British 'social pathology' view of the poor.

This theory posits that, in spatially segregated areas, there is a developing class that has no stake in, and is hostile to, the social order. Lone mothers are seen as active agents in the creation of this underclass. In Britain, young single (that is, never-married) mothers have been focused on as the central culprits.

Lone mothers allegedly choose to have children outside wedlock to gain welfare and housing benefits, and then, supported by the state, they choose not to get a job. Their sons, assumed to be without male authority or roles, are said to drift into delinquency, crime and the drug culture, while their daughters learn and repeat the cycle of promiscuity and dependency. Popular media depictions of lone mothers as a social threat use emotional symbolism more fully than more 'respectable' academic tracts. Media reports, however, both draw on, and are sometimes written by, academics. The American new right/ republican academic Charles Murray has enjoyed particular prominence in the *Sunday Times,* to purvey his virtual social science.

Andrew Neil, when editor of this paper, claimed that he had introduced Murray to the British public and politicians, and sponsored his 'research' in Britain. During the early 1990s and especially in 1993, the *Sunday Times* and other right-wing broadsheets, along with the tabloid press, devoted considerable and regular editorial attention to stories about single mothers and the underclass. They also displayed some raw prejudice in doing so. An editorial in the *Sunday Times* for example argued that:

It is becoming increasingly clear to all but the most blinkered of social scientists that the disintegration of the nuclear family is the principal source of so much unrest and misery. The creation of an urban underclass, on the margins of society, but doing great damage to itself and the rest of us, is directly linked to the rapid rise in illegitimacy... It is not just a question of a few families without fathers; it is a matter of whole communities with barely a single worthwhile role model.

A headline in the same newspaper queried, 'Wedded to welfare-do they want to marry a man or the state?' The *Daily Mail,* with its ideological and political address to 'middle England', offered a similar viewpoint:

The Willenhall estate, on the outskirts of Coventry, houses a large number of single mothers. There are also a lot of young, single men, many living on the proceeds of either crime or benefit fraud and more or less attached to the young women... It is kept afloat by the niggardly (if costly) charity of the state and the local authority, that is to say the taxes paid by traditional two parent families.

The targeting of a particular public housing estate with a supposedly high proportion of young 'underclass' single mothers seems to be a virtual social science technique for delivering messages, and for concretising particular views, as used by Murray and journalists in the popular media. The flagship BBC television current affairs programme, *Panorama,* entitled 'Babies on benefit', broadcast on 20 September 1993, used a similar technique.

In this case it was the St Mellon's council estate in Wales that was portrayed as an underclass breeding ground. This estate had previously received critical attention from the then Conservative Secretary of State for Wales, John Redwood, in a speech arguing for policies that deterred young women from having babies outside marriage and supported by the tax payer. Indeed, the programme makers claimed that they were investigating his contentions. Both Redwood and the *Panorama* programme implied that St Mellon's was typical and could be extrapolated as representative of all lone mothers-despite more considered accounts revealing inaccuracies about the estate and lone mothers generally. Popular media presentations of lone mothers as a social threat link into a conservative new right political view of the state in society, where the welfare provision of housing, benefits and other social provision is castigated as encouraging state dependency, an underclass, and especially single (never-married) motherhood.

Peter Lilley's now infamous 'little list' speech at the 1993 Conservative Party conference, for example, alleged that single mothers were having children to secure welfare benefits and housing, while Stephen Green, Chair of the Conservative Family Campaign, argued that 'Putting girls into council flats and providing taxpayer funded child care is a policy from hell'.

But strands of an underclass discourse are also discernible in the communitarianism underlying the New Labour government's ideas about a 'stakeholder society'. The long-term unemployed, which includes lone mothers, are placed as 'socially excluded'; 'family values' are stressed as the key to a 'decent' and crime-free society, and an element of coercion is required to reintegrate the excluded back into society through paid work. New Labour's view that life in a married two-parent family is better for children and for social cohesion, most notably expounded by Tony Blair and Jack Straw, has been widely reported in the media since 1997.

Media, politicians and academics who promulgate this view of lone motherhood as a threat to society also campaign for social policies that do not reward or encourage such 'self-damaging conduct'.

Consequently, the New Labour government has implemented the previous new right Conservative government's proposal to remove the extra allowances available to (new) lone parents on both the universal child benefit payment and on targeted income-related benefits-with Harriet Harman (then Minister for Social Security and for Women) stating, 'Life is about work, not just about claiming benefit'. Other policy disincentives to lone motherhood advocated by those who hold a social threat view include restrictions on payments to lone mothers who have more children while receiving benefit (as is the practice in some American states). There are also suggestions that young single mothers on benefit should be placed in hostels where their sexual relations and children's upbringing can be supervised. This policy idea has been floated by the New Labour government, in linking hostels with job training-again revisiting proposals of the Conservative government.

Encouragement and reward for traditional male breadwinner/female homemaker couples is also stressed by social threat advocates, with policy proposals to redress the supposed benefit bias towards lone, as opposed to married, parents (another reason given by New Labour for its lone parent benefit cuts). Other policy proposals include a tightening of the divorce law so that fewer lone mother families are created in the first place, as well as advocating 'moral' family and parenting education-the latter being the remit of the government's new National Family and Parenting Institute to be launched in April 1999.

Black Lone Mothers as a Social Threat

Until recently, 'race' and ethnicity were muted features of British social threat representations of lone motherhood. In the wake of the heightened media attention to lone mothers from 1993 onward, however, articles about black lone mothers began increasingly to be reported in the white-dominated media. Under the headline 'The ethnic timebomb', for example, the tabloid *Sunday Express* noted that more than 50 per cent of black families are headed by a lone mother and argued that, 'Almost six in ten black mothers are bringing up children on their own, urged on by the benefit system', implying a direct causal relationship between the incidence of black lone motherhood and the growing social security bill. Such claims ignore the fact that black lone mothers are more likely to be economically active and in full-time employment than their white counterparts; research suggests they also provide healthier lifestyles for their children. The *Sunday Express* article also raises the spectre of 'babyfathers' who-in newspaper accounts-father worryingly large numbers of children with multiple female partners.

Stories about 'babymothers' young black women who are presumed to have children by multiple male partners) also received considerable attention in the broadsheet press. Mainstream radio magazine programmes, such as BBC Radio 4's *The Locker Room* and *Women's Hour,* have also featured discussions about black lone motherhood and its social implications. Much of this coverage has echoed the ongoing debates in black media, especially the tabloid daily, *The Voice*-self-styled 'Britain's best black newspaper'-but there are significant differences between these stories as they are reported in the black press compared with their coverage in the white-dominated media. First, there are no scare stories about social security bills. Second and importantly, there is a sense of debate in the black press, with the black readership responding to 'personal opinion' columns through the letters page. By contrast, coverage of black lone motherhood in the mainstream press tends to be devoid of vigorous questioning or alternatives, with a flat presentation suggesting that 'this is how it is' in the British black population. It is argued elsewhere that the emergence of a focus on black lone mothers in the British mainstream press is linked to the broader social threat concerns discussed above. It is suggested, moreover, that it is through such 'exotic' media explorations of black family life that white people vicariously play out their fears about social breakdown and relationships between men and women.

REPRESENTATIONS OF LONE MOTHERS AS A SOCIAL PROBLEM

In contrast to the view of lone motherhood as a self-created threat to the social order, a second perception of lone mothers widely reported in mainstream media, presents them as victims of externally created problems and in need of help. Stress is laid on the 'facts': in Britain, the majority of lone mothers (just over 50 per cent) are 'mature' divorced, separated or widowed women, rather than young single mothers (with less than 9 per cent being teenagers). Similarly, there is no underclass in the sense of a self-reproducing distinct part of society which stands outside cultural, political and economic norms.

Rather, there is a growing number of people in poverty, including lone mothers, who have essentially the same ambitions as the rest of society, but who are stigmatised and marginalised. The economic and social causes of this marginalisation are beyond the control of those they affect, while the shrinking welfare state only exacerbates difficulties.

According to this perception, lone mothers are seen as social problems. They want paid work to provide for themselves and their children, but are hindered by the structure and nature of the welfare state. From this social problem position, the appropriate policy prescription signals that lone mothers should receive more, not less, state assistance to help them escape poverty and state dependency. By contrast with the social threat perspective discussed above, the social problem framing of lone motherhood is far less common in the tabloid press.

It is mostly limited to broadsheet newspapers with more left wing or 'middle ground' sympathies, such as the *Guardian,* the *Observer* and the *Independent,* which have given a platform to various commentators stressing the poverty and limited options of lone mothers. An article in the *Guardian,* for example, argued that: Reducing the number of single parent families is not an issue about the morality of feckless unmarried women who won't use contraceptives. Two-thirds of single parent families are caused by divorce. What is needed is a genuine political commitment to supporting the family. Better childcare provision for starters...

Despite these broadly sympathetic views, the broadsheets have also published reports by new right/revisionist commentators and, as we noted earlier, they have also been complicit in vicariously playing out social threat views through examinations of black lone motherhood.

Again, academics such as A.H. Halsey and Norman Dennis, taking a revisionist social-problem position, have been given a platform in the mainstream media to advocate a return of the political left to what they call 'ethical socialism', with its 'historic mission to spread the value of the family throughout all the relationships of society'. Indeed, Halsey was one of the commentators featured in the *Panorama* 'Babies-on-benefit' programme. New Labour's commitment to 'the family' as the source of social morality and obligation echoes this ethical socialism. The social problem view of lone motherhood, based on a concern with poverty rather than the fate of 'the family', is dominant among academic social scientists (especially in social policy), however, as well as among welfare practitioners and the British liberal establishment, such as church leaders.

This often reflects a Fabian political inheritance of enlightened state intervention. Jonathan Bradshaw, for example, an academic advisor to the Church of England's commission on the family, supported the Archbishop of Canterbury in arguing that 'lone mothers should be seen primarily as victims and get more help'. Furthermore, the major lobby group for lone mothers in Britain, the National Council for One Parent Families, has also adopted this view of lone mothers. In contrast with the marginalisation of these arguments during the eighteen years of new right Conservative government, there has been renewed lobbying for intervention with the advent of the New Labour government-some of which was disappointed early on with the continuation of some Conservative policies such as the cutting of lone parent benefit.

In Britain, advocates of the social-problem view argue that day-care costs should be taken into account when calculating in work benefits for lone (and other) mothers. In 1994, under the Conservative government, an earnings disregard for formal day-care costs was indeed made available, although at a niggardly level. This suggests that, despite the prevalence of social threat representations of lone mothers in the media at the time, the social problem approach retained influence in British policy-making circles.

This disregard has since been increased by the New Labour government. Other policy suggestions within the social problem mould which have also been taken up by the New Labour government include measures to encourage lone mothers to pursue training and higher education under the New Deal welfare-to-work strategy.

Since autumn 1998, lone parents on income support with a youngest child over school age have been invited to an interview with a personal advisor in their local job centre to discuss 'upgrading' their job skills and/or finding paid work. An expansion of 'after school' care services for children is also part of this New Labour strategy (although this goes no way to matching the levels of public day-care in most other west European countries).

In championing the two-parent family, New Labour politicians are usually careful to say that they do not intend to demonise lone mothers. Jack Straw, for example, in a speech stating that strengthening the institution of marriage as a basis for bringing up children was a cornerstone of 'modern family policy', added, 'We are not in the business of making the job of lone parents more difficult by blaming them as some have done in the past'.

However, while it might be thought that the social-problem view of lone mothers' position had gained political ascendancy since New Labour's election victory in 1997, another suggestion under this perspective has not had such success in reaching the policy agenda.

Rather than increase lone parent 'top up' benefits these have been cut altogether, as we noted above. Indeed, New Labour is effectively combining the social problem view of lone mothers with the social threat view as part of its communitarian approach (a manifestation of its 'third way' between old left and new right). Certainly, lone motherhood continues to be a potent political and media symbol.

There are two alternative views of lone mothers represented in mainstream British media. First, lone motherhood can be seen as part of a general change in family forms and lifestyle patterns, resulting from people's choices about how they live their lives and construct relationships, within a context of over-arching economic, social and cultural change. Policies would thus be predicated upon creating better conditions, and reconciling paid work and family life, for all families rather than focusing on lone mothers alone.

This view is strong at the national level in much of continental Europe, where lone motherhood is less commented on and is much less important as a moral or political symbol than it is in Britain and the USA. While such a lifestyle perspective on lone motherhood may be muted within national media discussions in Britain, appeals to such a view can be seen in the launch of the niche monthly glossy magazine *Singled Out* in 1995. This was aimed at the British 'lone parent' market and covered all aspects of lifestyle, from holidays and cookery, through conducting relationships and child rearing, to financial and legal matters. However, the magazine did not survive its first year-signalling either the lack of a large enough audience who saw themselves as living a 'lone parent' lifestyle, or lone mothers' inability to afford the cover price.

Second, lone mothers can be seen as women who are no longer willing to accept control over their lives by individual men and are thus escaping patriarchy, with access to paid work, contraception, divorce and so on giving them the practical means to be independent. Policies should thus support and encourage this autonomy (including, for some, state support through wages for housework). Such a radical feminist perspective is rarely represented in the national press in its own terms (other than in more marginal publications such as the now defunct *Spare Rib*). Rather, it gets caricatured and castigated as part of the social threat view, where feminists (and socialists) are blamed for supporting lone motherhood and thus social breakdown. Other media can portray lone mothers, particularly black lone mothers, as deriving strength from their embeddedness in supportive female networks.

The low budget black-British film *Babymother,* released in September 1998, thus tells the 'ragga to riches story of single mother Anita, bringing up her children on Harlesden's tough Stonebridge estate, and her struggles to make it as a deejay'.

But journalists who are committed to a social threat view can take an entirely different perspective on the same story: *'[Babymother's]* aim seems to be to encourage immature black women to behave like aggressive, self-pitying trollops, bring up more and more illegitimate children very badly, with no visible means of finance except the taxpayer'. Bigotry of this calibre seems unmoved by facts such as black lone mothers' high rates of employment.

While alternative views may not have had much influence on mainstream media representations of lone mothers or on policy development, they do hold sway amongst lone mothers themselves. Research conducted by two of us draws on interviews with lone mothers in 1994, just after the furore in the media about the moral and financial threat lone mothers posed to British society.

The research revealed that most lone mothers from all social groups held opinions about their position that were congruent with the (nationally muted) escaping patriarchy position, while aspects of the lifestyle perspective were also much in evidence. They often valued freedom to do what they wanted without having to take account of a male partner and were proud of managing on their own. Some also understood themselves to be just a normal part of the diversity of family forms in contemporary British society, especially younger African-Caribbean and white 'alternative' lone mothers who held a more feminist view of families and society more generally.

Given the plethora of bad press that lone mothers have received, voluntary groups representing lone mothers in Britain-most notably the National Council for One Parent Families (NCOPF) and Gingerbread-have made concerted efforts to counter such negative portrayals. Various forms of media coverage, including both newspapers and television programmes, have been influential in shaping the strategies of such organisations. In fact, the NCOPF has emphasised the importance of negotiating the 'right' image of lone mothers. While they maintain that they need to make a case for lone mothers' special needs, they stress that they must be careful to avoid potentially incendiary images that emphasise differences rather than commonalities with other families. Thus both lone mother organisations have been prominent in rebutting dominant social threat political and media images.

In particular, the NCOPF evidenced their concern about harmful media portrayals of lone mothers by challenging the content of the *Panorama* 'Babies-on-benefit' programme. This documentary purported to show the reality of lone motherhood, and alleged that feckless, young, single women were having a string of babies, and living off benefits and in council housing. These never-married mothers supposedly saw no point in gaining employment or in having long-term stable relationships with men as providers and active fathers to their children.

The programme also examined the 'effective' policy option of benefit capping to deal with this phenomenon. The NCOPF complained to the Broadcasting Complaints Commission and went to court over this documentary. As is evident from the press release the organisation put out at the time, they did this because of fears that negative media representations might fuel moves towards punitive social policies: 'At the time when Government is investigating ways to reduce the benefit bill, this *Panorama* has been a disastrous intervention into the debate.'

The NCOPF accused the programme makers and the BBC of presenting an 'unfair, misleading and irresponsible' image of lone mothers. Rather, they asserted, for the majority lone parenthood is an unexpected event in people's lives, and the typical lone parent is a responsible, caring, divorced mother struggling to provide for her children. Interestingly, neither the NCOPF nor Gingerbread responded to the treatment of black 'babymothers' in the mainstream press, for fear of promoting racialised debate about lone mothers that would cut across the 'safe' social problem image of their constituency that they wish to portray.

The dominant social threat and social problem views of lone motherhood in Britain, including discussion about black lone mothers, have been articulated strongly in the national media over the past few years. These perspectives, by defining issues and setting agendas around lone motherhood, are significant components in the policy process. They assign meaning and causes to lone motherhood and construct the parameters within which social policies towards lone mothers should be constituted or changed.

But this is not to imply any direct stimulus-response relationship between media representations and policy formulation; the two interact in complex ways. For their part, the media are highly diverse and, as we have seen, there are alternative ways to frame lone motherhood to those which are predominant in mainstream media: and these do find voice in some niche media (as well as amongst lone mothers themselves).

Relations between media and politicians are reciprocal. It is politicians, along with academics who share their political mission, who have provided copy for the media while, in turn, the media have fuelled public opinion and encouraged particular responses from politicians.

At one level, media and policy representations of lone motherhood as interlinked and mutually reinforcing can be seen simply as the result of a small but influential 'chattering class' of media workers and policy makers (and a few academics) who inhabit a restricted social and geographical world, and who define what is important and what is marginal. What happens in the 'real world' becomes little more than symbolic foils for various political groupings and regroupings. However, even if largely correct, this appealing caricature does little to explain why it is that the social threat and social problem views of lone motherhood are promulgated in the media and by politicians, and not alternative perspectives.

The reasons for this dominance are to be found at deeper social levels; first, at the level of shared social understandings about the relationship between individuals, states, markets and families, and second, at the level of how explanations themselves are normally constructed in dominant and 'educated' modes of thought. On the first level, different welfare state regimes develop different sets of social policy in expressing their particular conceptions of the proper, and gendered, relationship between individuals, families, states and markets, not least with different implications for the position of lone mothers. In Britain, politicians and media workers increasingly seem to share a world view defined in terms of a liberal welfare state regime.

In the liberal welfare state regime (such as the USA) social policy is used to uphold the market and traditional work-ethic norms. Modest and means-tested benefits are aimed at a residualised and stigmatised group of welfare recipients such as lone mothers, and depiction of lone mothers as a social threat more easily attain dominance. Under the conservative welfare regime (with Germany as a type case) states intervene to preserve status difference-including those of traditional gender roles and family forms.

Here lone mothers become peripheralised as mothers without male partners, and the social problem view of lone motherhood more easily gains purchase.

In social democratic welfare state regimes (where Sweden is a type case), social policy reforms de-emphasise the market and emphasise equality rather than the meeting of minimal needs. Both men and women-including lone mothers-are seen as independent worker-citizens who support themselves through participation in the labour market, and social problem and lifestyle views of lone motherhood merge.

Within this, Britain presents a complex, hybrid case, where some elements of the social democratic regime (classically in the NHS) have been inserted into a liberal welfare tradition. Thatcherism, however, marked a rapid return towards the liberal model and, whatever its political differences, 'Blairism' seems to share the same liberal assumptions about the proper relationship between states, markets, families and individuals.

It is the USA that is explicitly taken as a policy role model by both media commentators and politicians rather than the increasingly derided 'European model' (other than by marginalised 'Old Labour' politicians or maverick journalists such as Will Hutton, author of the best-selling book *The State of the Nation*).

On the second level, though, why is it that the dominant view of lone mothers is as a trope for welfare dependency, social marginalisation and even hopelessness? After all, people know from both personal experience and research that most lone mothers do not fit this caricature. Partly, this type of image building depends upon a particular method of explanation commonly used in western thought.

When they use the term 'lone mother' (or 'single parent'), politicians, the media and even voluntary organisations representing lone mothers themselves (such as the NCOPF) are attempting to invoke a particular categorical representation of a type of person-a ready-made classificatory package that serves as a short cut to reading off a particular social situation.

'Lone motherhood' is seen to stand for an a priori, unitary, fixed, coherent, inherent and essentialised set of attributes and characteristics-in other words, the category articulates a particular stereotype-which in Britain easily becomes a negative stereotype to fit in with the preconceptions of the liberal welfare state regime.

This short cut in image building, and in explanation more widely, is often completely misleading because it assumes that the taxonomic group accurately delineates a social group. Taxonomic groups, such as lone mothers distinguished as a particular parental family form, are often different from the real substantive social groups that actually carry through social relationships and actions. It is not just that lone mothers are not a homogeneous or unified population, so that different social groups of lone mothers may behave differently.

Rather, it may not be lone motherhood in itself that is substantively or causally most important for their social behaviour. It may, for example, be membership of a particular ethnic or class group, or location in a particular area, that explains why some lone mothers take up paid work and others do not. Underlying social divisions and differences, however, remain unspoken in taxonomic representations. Nevertheless, lone mothers are not the homogenous group, in terms of social characteristics, that media and politicians invoke when they use the term, and it is therefore extremely unlikely that, as a putative categorical group, they will hold similar views and respond to policy development in similar ways, as maintained by media commentators, politicians, and even many academics. Such categorical thinking, and taxonomic modes of explanation, have their roots in Cartesian thought as a means to produce independent descriptions of social life that are generalisable. This type of conceptualising has received critical attention in a number of ways from philosophers of science such as Wittgenstein to the critical realist, postmodern and feminist theorists of today.

Nonetheless, as a model of understanding and portraying social life (and thus also as a mode of control) it retains enormous purchase and power, underlain as it is by the idea that experts, through their categorisations, have a correct and authoritative access to reality. This is why academics like Murray and Halsey are given media space to confirm stereotypes of lone mothers.

The media and politicians clearly also have greater access to image production and dissemination than most lone mothers. In this way they have the power to impose their categorical version of the reality of lone motherhood-and thus to assert a particular identity of lone mothers, their motivations and behaviour, and the causes of all this-as superordinate and exclusive. A particular image, such as that of lone mothers as a social threat, may be contested by less powerful lobby groups such as the NCOPF. But such attempts to insert an alternative identity for lone mothers into the categorical space still rely on the same unitary and essentialist mode of thought as that dominant in media and political portrayals.

They do not admit, or recognise, diversity within the category, or that the category itself may be cross-cut or even unimportant where other differences (like those of class, ethnicity or location) may be the more influential in explaining motivations, behaviour and causes.

This means, moreover, that the 'categorical identity' that ascribes a particular set of characteristics to the taxonomic group 'lone mothers' is not the same as the various 'ontological identities' of lone mothers themselves-how they think about themselves in relation to others and their situation. These ontological considerations have little authority or power, however, and largely remain invisible unless they are used by the media to support pre-existing categories of lone motherhood as a social threat or a social problem.

ANALYZING CODES OF ETHICS

Although the question of who journalists are is not addressed in national codes, this analysis will count managers who supervise newsroom employees, but not those in other departments. And it includes all news department employees. In newspapers, everyone from the executive editor to contract or freelance reporters and photographers is considered a journalist. In television, everyone working in the news department--from president of the news division at the network and news director at a local station--down to production assistant is included.

Of the four most widely cited codes--enacted by the Society of Professional Journalists, the American Society of Newspaper Editors, the Associated Press Managing Editors, and the Radio/Television News Directors Association--three begin with plausible and lofty language about the role of journalism in a democratic society. The Code of Ethics of the Society of Professional Journalists, for example, begins: "Members of the Society... believe that public enlightenment is the forerunner of justice and the foundation of democracy. The duty of the journalist is to further those ends by seeking truth". Each code then lists more specific do's and don'ts intended to realise these broad goals. The oldest of American journalism's codes, written by the American Society of Newspaper Editors in 1922 and most recently revised in 1975, aims all of its moral injunctions at individual "practitioners," "journalists," and "newspaper men and women." No others are mentioned. Further, the code is cast as a covenant between two parties only, intended to "preserve, protect and strengthen the bond of trust and respect between American journalists and the American people".

The newest code, updated by the Society of Professional Journalists in September 1996, also places responsibility for news solely and directly on journalists. No other actors are assigned moral duties. The code is divided into four sets of moral commands, each of which begins with the phrase, "Journalists should."

The third such injunction says "Journalists should be free of obligation to any interest other than the public's right to know". That heading obliges journalists to "refuse gifts, fees, free travel and special treatment, shun secondary employment, political involvement, public office and service in community organizations" that might conflict with objective reporting. All of these lie within the control of the individual journalist.

He or she must give up some personal benefit to avoid an ethical breach. But parallel with these individual-level injunctions are others in which it is not the journalist's self-interest that must be restrained but that of the corporate or other owner. For example, journalists are obliged to "deny favored treatment to advertisers and special interests and resist their pressure to influence news coverage." Here journalists are asked to decide when the owning corporation must deny itself benefits, such as revenues from advertisers, to avoid an ethical breach. By making no distinction between individual and corporate levels of obligation, the code implies that journalists have this authority.

The Radio/Television News Directors Association code begins: "The responsibility of radio and television journalists is to gather and report information of importance and interest to the public accurately, honestly, and impartially". It contains 10 references to individual broadcast journalists and one to the "broadcasting industry." No other actors are mentioned. The Associated Press Managing Editors' code, revised in 1995, departs from the others in naming an institution, "the newspaper," as the principal subject of moral injunctions. It commands that "the newspaper should report the news without regard for its own interests, mindful of the need to disclose potential conflicts. It should not give favored news treatment to advertisers or special-interest groups". This language reduces the asymmetry of a subordinate class of employees--journalists--making decisions for the corporation that owns the newspaper. But it may not achieve parity.

For newspapers (and television stations) which are part of larger corporations, the subordinate local unit is still being asked to decide an issue that affects the bottom-line of the parent corporation. Given the hierarchical structure of conglomerate corporations, it is more likely that parent corporations will impose policies on their subsidiaries than the reverse. Corporate financial pressures on subordinate firms have occurred despite the protests of the most influential editors. Gene Roberts resigned as executive editor of the Philadelphia Enquirer rather than accept continuing cuts in resources for reporting. Under Roberts the Enquirer won 17 Pulitzer prizes. The corporation applying the pressure was the chain with perhaps the nation's highest reputation for quality, Knight-Ridder.

Common to each of these four national ethics codes is the notion that journalists--individually or in the aggregate--are, or should be, free of business-related constraints imposed by those who pay them and distribute their work. In fact, the obligations are reversed. Corporations employing journalists are expected to conform to the demands of this special class of workers.

Such an arrangement reverses the usual direction of corporate authority. It deprives owners of their traditional right to use their assets as they see fit. Since the First Amendment's guarantee of press freedom has been interpreted as a privilege of the owner and not of the employees or of the community, this reversal might be seen as obstructing the spirit of the First Amendment. Before going any further, we should ask whether this unusual arrangement of employees making decisions for owners actually exists.

Historical evidence indicates that American journalists have been bowing to the demands of owners since the marriage of the steam engine and the printing press gave birth to news as an industry in the 1800s. According to Bates: Will Irwin, Upton Sinclair, George Seldes, Morris Ernst, Oswald Garrison Villard, Leo Rosten, and Robert Lasch all had analysed how profit-seeking interfered with truth-seeking in the press; so had several critics of the 19th century.

The tension between the owner's business interests and journalism was one of the primary reasons Pulitzer proposed professionalizing journalism through higher education at the turn of the 20th century. This struggle was also the centerpiece of the Hutchins Commission's critique of the news at mid century: "The press is... caught between its desire to please and extend its audience and its desire to give a picture of events and people as they really are". Several media historians have noted an accretion of authority for journalists beginning with the waning of the "Yellow Press" at the turn of the 20th century. They note that journalists have become much better educated and compensated than the "ink-stained wretches" of earlier periods of American journalism.

Indeed, two recent court decisions--one each in print and broadcast news--have re-evaluated the U.S. Department of Labor's 50-year-old classification of journalism as a trade protected by wage and hour laws. In December 1994, a federal court judge ruled that former Washington Post reporter Thomas Sherwood was exercising professional prerogatives and receiving a professional level of pay. In April 1996, a federal court of appeals ruled that writers, editors, and producers at NBC News must be classified as "artistic professionals".

The Sherwood case bears directly on journalistic autonomy. In her opinion Judge Norma Johnson noted: Sherwood's job... required him to originate story ideas, piece together seemingly unrelated facts, analyse facts and circumstances, and present news stories in an engaging style. The Court further finds that Sherwood's fact-gathering involved more than passively writing down what others told him. He was required to cultivate sources, utilize his imagination and other skills in seeking information, and continuously develop his finely tuned interviewing skills.

While the evidence that Sherwood was a smart and highly skilled reporter is undeniable, the judge passed over how much the journalist's exercise of authority required permission. The evidence also showed Sherwood's choice of topic and story angle, his choice of sources, his handling of quotes, and the time he had to cultivate sources and write stories all were subject to approval by his superiors. Sherwood worked not within a structure of collegial control but within a hierarchy.

Not even the Post's newsroom meets the standards of autonomy in journalism's national ethics codes. Even at a paper such as the Washington Post, by reputation a paper where reporters have unusual freedom, editors were not elected by their peers, but appointed from above. The most influential manager was selected by business persons outside the newsroom.

Similarly, the resources available to the newsroom were determined not by a committee of journalists but by the parent corporation's board of directors. Were Rupert Murdoch to buy the Post (God forbid!), he could change the operation of the newsroom as quickly as he did when he took over Britain's best-selling newspaper The Sun in 1974 and switched its orientation from labour to conservative.

As owner, Murdoch could dismiss any journalist disagreeing with his notion of news without any hearing or professional due process. And Murdoch could violate journalism's codes of ethics without fear of sanction because none contains enforcement language. The First Amendment would protect Murdoch from any government response. Not even the Post's newsroom meets the standards of autonomy in journalism's national ethics codes. Like many educated and skilled whitecollar employees, these journalists enjoy some authority over their work product. They are not assembly-line workers. But their autonomy is clearly bounded by corporate superiors, not by allegiance to peer standards.

Ironically, during the same half century journalists were gaining those responsibilities Judge Johnson noted, scholars studying the question of who has influence over the news were locating control over the news further and further from reporters and editors. The notion of journalists as arbiters of news was implied in the famous "gatekeeper" study conducted by White. But the 1950s were only half over when Breed contradicted the notion at least of reporter autonomy with his classic survey of 120 journalists at northeastern newspapers. He described a newsroom culture established by management that--usually subtly--enforced management's orientation towards news. The reporters' choice was to go along or get out.

From the 1970s into the early 1980s researchers such as Epstein in network television, Sigal, Sigalman, and Fishman in newspapers, Powers and Bantz, McCorkle, and Baade in local television, Tuchman across several media, and Hirsch reanalyzing White early data, documented that newsroom routines-established more by their employers than by journalists--dictated news content and practice.

In the mid- 1980s Altschull argued that news has always been advertisers. Turow conceptualized journalists as holding only one of 13 power roles that determine media content. Bagdikian located most of the power to shape news well above the newsroom in corporate boardrooms. Soloski argued that professionalism is a widely shared myth in American newsrooms that is manipulated by managers to control news work.

In the 1990s Auletta, Squires, and Underwood described the economic rationalization of network television and newspaper newsrooms in response to profit pressures from owners and the stock market. McQuail proposed an array of social forces outside the newsroom as the determiner of news. Shoemaker and Reese offered a five-level analysis in which owners of media firms exerted the greatest control. McManus theorized that news results from an elaborate compromise among powerful market-driven influences outside the newsroom.

Similarly, scholars who analysed the application of journalism ethics in newsrooms found that journalists are more often the object than the subject of codes. Davenport randomly surveyed 100 newspaper managing editors and an equal number of local television news directors. Eighty per cent of respondents who had written codes said they were imposed on the newsroom by managers with little rank-and-file discussion. In a review of research, Boeyink found that ethics codes were effective only when publishers decided they were important.

Beam surveyed 300 top editors at 60 newspapers of varying sizes. He found that professional autonomy makes more sense considered as an organization level, rather than individual level, variable. Writing about reporters in the American news industry, Fink concluded: "Either you and the hand that feeds you agree on ethics in reporting or writing, or you (not your editor) will be a very unhappy employee--or unemployed".

3

The "Libertarian Press" in Asia

SELF-CENSORSHIP IN THE ASIAN PRESS

The Japanese press is considered the liveliest in East Asia and was ranked the freest in Asia by the Freedom House for 2005. Reporters Without Borders gave Japan the second-highest ranking in Asia in press freedom after South Korea for its 2005 report. Japan's press industry is the largest in the world. It has five national daily newspapers, each claiming a circulation in the millions.

That compares with the top two dailies in the United States -USA Today and The Wall Street Journal - each of which has a circulation of around 2 million. Yomiuri Shimbun, the paper with the largest circulation in the world, has a circulation of 14 million. Asahi Shimbun has a circulation of 12 million. These two Japanese national dailies are the only two newspapers in the world with a circulation surpassing 10 million. The circulations of the other three range from 2.7 million to 5.6 million.

Japanese journalists are well trained and well informed. They have to study for months to pass rigorous exams to even get hired. The exam includes a ninety-minute general intelligence test, a ninety-minute writing test, and a ninety-minute foreign language proficiency test, usually in English, Spanish, French, or Chinese.

Even if a candidate gets good scores, he or she has to pass three to four interviews. Special schools help prepare university students and graduates for the test. But Japanese journalists may find their training and skills wasted under a press club system.

To understand the nature of the Japanese press system, the economic system in Japan has to be examined first. Democracy describes Japan's political system, but freewheeling capitalism is out of the question in Japan although, theoretically speaking, Japan practices free market capitalism. The Japanese economy has thrived and become a dominant force in the global economy under state-guided capitalism.

Instead of regulating the industry, the government helps the industry to grow and compete on the global market. Government and big corporations in

Japan are partners in nation building. Political freedom and rights do not translate into economic liberalism in Japan, which has much to do with the Japanese culture, or the Asian culture.

In Asian societies, especially those under the influence of Confucian thought, the strength of a country is regarded as more important than the profitability of a company, and the well-being of a family is more important than individual rights and freedom. For a country like Japan with limited arable land and scarce resources, the survival and prosperity of the nation take priority in national life. The royal family and often the government are symbols of the nation, and they command respect.

Such a cultural tradition contradicts the Western concept of media as a watchdog and the ultimate goal of libertarian philosophies - man as an end in himself. In Japan, media keep cozy relations with the government and the big industries through the press club system, or "information cartels," which comprise press clubs, industry associations, and media conglomerates, which Freeman (2000) calls "the unholy trinity."

The press clubs channel information from government offices to media organizations. Such a club system discourages independent reporting and thoroughness in journalistic investigations and results in "uniformity of content" and "pro-establishment style of journalism". The information cartels ensure no competition among media outlets and no scoops. In Asian societies, the motto promoted is not Darwin's "survival of the fittest," but the survival of all, which may explain why in many Asian countries, such as Japan, China, and Singapore, comparative advertising is banned.

The club system works well for the Japanese press, which profits from large circulations, high advertising revenue, and exclusive information access from the government. But it is a system designed by the industry to serve media companies' economic interests, a system that has frequently led the press to support state goals.

It is in this sense that the media can be understood as collaborators with the state in the management of society, Freeman said. Such a system discourages investigative reporting and places a premium on relying on official sources rather than alternative information. It interferes with the public's right to receive relevant information in a timely manner.

As a result, all the high-profile political scandals that emerged in the first half of 2002 were not uncovered by the vernacular dailies, but by the non-mainstream weeklies. Because of its less than rigorous reporting, the Japanese press fails to act as a watchdog of the government and is called a lapdog, which was blamed for failing to keep the public informed of the irregularities within the financial industry and the corruption within the government. When the Asian financial crash hit Japan in 1997, the magnitude of the crisis took the public by surprise.

An in-depth analysis of the Japanese press system makes it clear that the ideas available at the "marketplace of ideas" are rather limited. Free competition that is at the very core of the libertarian theory is stifled under the press club system, which also bars reporters from foreign and non-mainstream media outlets from attending exclusive press briefings and getting official press releases. While government control of the press in Japan is not a major issue, control by professional associations and the media organizations themselves is still very effective and produces the same result of a less informed public. The reason why the Freedom House rated the Japanese press as the freest in Asia may be because of the fact that the Japanese government seldom takes direct actions against the press or journalists. In Japan, there is hardly such need, as the press polices itself rather diligently.

Like Japan, South Korea is a newspaper-rich country. South Koreans get their news primarily from daily newspapers. The country has ten national dailies, which are in circulation wars in the millions. In addition, there are 100 free dailies, 314 specialized dailies, 1,999 weeklies, 2,319 monthlies, and 1,245 other periodicals. All newspapers print forty-eight to fifty-six pages for advertising space. In South Korea, each household subscribes to two or three national papers and one local paper, a dream for newspaper owners in any country.

For 2005, the Freedom House rated the press in South Korea "free." And the Reporters Without Borders described the South Korean press as opposite of that of North Korea: "diverse, privately owned and critical of the government". South Korea is a relatively new democracy. After decades of fighting for democracy, South Koreans started to enjoy their political rights in 1987 when a civilian government was sworn in after a general election.

But until Kim Dae Jung, a freedom fighter and folk hero, became president in 1998, the newly found press freedom in South Korea had been contained by its press club system like Japan's, by the common economic interests of the government and big business in South Korea, including the media, and by the influence of Confucian values.

South Korean industries, like those of Japan, used to be guided and supported by the government. The press in South Korea has allied itself with the government and big businesses and is widely seen as "pro-business," "pro-government," and "conservative".

Chong-Hyuk Kim, a reporter for the Joong Ang Ilbo in South Korea, told a Freedom Forum panel that South Korea's ostensibly democratic government barred publishing the size of foreign reserves and foreign debt. He said, "It has become traditional practice between government and media in South Korea not to report critical and important information. The government insisted if that kind of information were revealed, it would be harmful to national security and the national reputation. The media accepted that kind of assertion". The result of such secrecy was the unexpected Asian financial crash in 1997, which hit the South Korean economy hard and caught its people unprepared. A reader of the Chosun Ilbo, one of the largest papers in the country, wrote: "Korean journalism still is a superficial observer of the events and does not carry a torch for the righteous social and ethical standards in a rapidly transforming materialistic society. It still is timid and not impartial and indifferent to power politics".

The press system in South Korea had many similarities with that of Japan until Kim Dae Jung became president in 1998. Since then the South Korean press has started to develop in a new direction, and the press club system is being phased out.

Press freedom in South Korea improved noticeably during the tenure of Kim, when the press became more aggressive in covering the government and more vocal in criticizing government policies. But the unprecedented press freedom in Korean history under Kirn's government was overshadowed by government's crackdown on the major papers with charges of tax evasion in 2001.

Press freedom is still fragile in South Korea, and its press system is in a transitional stage. It remains to be seen if the South Korean press is finally breaking away from self-censorship or if it still wants to maintain good relations with the government and big businesses by avoiding coverage of critical issues.

Self-censorship is not only a major issue in Japan and South Korea but also a major concern in Hong Kong and Thailand. The media in Hong Kong and Thailand are in a category of their own. They are among the freest in Asia when they resort to sensationalism to survive the intense competition.

In Hong Kong, tabloids represent the mainstream press. Practice of yellow journalism, including sensationalized reporting, price wars, and stealing talent from competitors, reached its climax in 1995 and again in 1997. In both Hong Kong and Thailand, the press exercises a high degree of freedom when it is dealing with non-political topics, but starts to be cautious when news stories concern politics, the government, or the royal family.

Before Hong Kong was returned to China, many of the newspapers in the former British colony were pro-British. Since the sovereignty changed hands, more papers are now pro-Beijing. Self-censorship is considered a major concern and the main threat to an independent and free press in Hong Kong despite a great deal of aggressive reporting. Part of the problem of press self-censorship was due to the fact that after Hong Kong was returned to China, the ownership of some of the major newspapers changed hands, including the South China Morning Post. The new press owners have investments on the Chinese mainland and do not want to offend the officials in Beijing. BBC News introduced the media in Hong Kong as editorially dynamic, free, and diverse, but it cited increasing self-censorship and pressures on editorial policies. In Hong Kong, direct government intervention of the press is minimal. However, pressure from the central government in Beijing and new owners of the press makes many editors and reporters wary of how to handle sensitive information or topics.

A public opinion poll found that 48 per cent of the people in Hong Kong believed the local news media practiced self-censorship. The study showed that 62 per cent believed the local news media had qualms when criticizing the central government, while only 34 per cent believed it had concerns in criticizing the local government. "The number of respondents who said the media practices self-censorship has significantly increased, mainly because they think the media has become apprehensive when criticizing the central government," a survey organizer said.

Newspapers in Hong Kong adopted specific strategies in the politics of self-censorship. Francis L. F. Lee and Angel M. Y. Lin argued that in transitional societies such as Hong Kong when political pressure on the press is added to a commercial media system and a professional journalistic culture, the politics of self-censorship often becomes a strategic contest between the media and political actors.

The Ming Pao daily constructed the debate as a factional rivalry in order to position itself as an arbitrator, according to Lee and Lin. In contrast, the popular Apple Daily presented the story as a sovereign people's fight against a powerful entity, which was much more critical towards the central government. "Nevertheless, it also appropriated the dominant discourse, constructed internal contradictions, and decentralized the Chinese central government to smooth out the radicalism of its criticisms".

Jasper Decker, a former staff member at the South China Morning Post, also observed less obvious characteristics of self-censorship, such as the tone and attitude in news stories concerning China. Reporting became less aggressive. Management emphasized the virtues of writing to allow readers to read between the lines. In 1997, the New York Times noted that Ming Pao had "reduced the space given to columnists critical of China and has toned down its previously aggressive reporting of China".

Other newspapers avoided devoting space to politically sensitive topics by assigning their reporters to cover other, non-controversial topics. A content analysis of 1997 editorials of major newspapers in Hong Kong found that 56.2 per cent of the editorials addressed local issues in Hong Kong, while only 8 per cent of the editorials discussed issues in China and 7.6 per cent dealt with topics related to the ties between Hong Kong and China.

Self-censorship was an issue even before 1997. Jim Sciutto, a former Hong Kong journalist, claimed, "Self-censorship is nearly epidemic in Hong Kong, affecting the entire media hierarchy from publishers to beat reporters. A free Hong Kong press is already eroding." In a 1990 survey of Hong Kong journalists, 5 per cent admitted fear of criticizing China in their work, and 54 per cent believed that their fellow journalists felt the same way. The anxiety was not alleviated in the following six years as a similar survey in 1996 found that one in every four journalists expressed concerns over criticizing China.

As much of the self-censorship in Hong Kong was the result of pressure from newspaper editors and owners, some local journalists and researchers argued that it was censorship, not self-censorship on the part of the reporters. Carol Lai, a former chairwoman of the Hong Kong Journalist Association, believed that the influence of editors might have impacted journalists' writing more than any threats from the government. She believed most of the reporters wanted integrity in their reporting, tried to report accurately and objectively and seldom censored themselves. Some editors, however, watered down criticism or killed stories they deemed offensive.

Media owners and editors censored their reporters in the hope of preventing interference from the central government so they could keep their papers in business. Others might wish to expand their investment on the mainland. The Hong Kong Journalist Association noted that the South Chin Morning Post had reduced and diluted its coverage of China since Robert Kuok became an owner in 1993. "In Hong Kong, pro-Beijing forces don't fight the media, they buy it".

In order to be successful, the media in Hong Kong have learned to remain apolitical. Since the late 1960s, major newspapers in Hong Kong have become increasingly less partisan and have avoided taking less popular stand on issues, and instead, have focused more on the market and middle-class liberalism in order to increase profits.

Self-censorship in Hong Kong prompted one Hong Kong journalist to compare Hong Kong tycoons, who toned down their coverage of China, with mainland media outlets, which became more aggressive in their reporting as they sought market share. In the near future, Hong Kong may have to learn a thing or two from the mainland press when it comes to press freedom, according to Mark Simon of the Apple Daily.

In Southeast Asia, the Thai press enjoys a considerable degree of freedom. Its 1997 constitution protects media freedom, freedom of expression, and access to information. Even under the media-unfriendly prime minister Thaksin Shinawatra the media were free to criticize government policies and cover cases of corruption and human rights abuses, but journalists tended to exercise self-censorship regarding the military, the monarchy, the judiciary, and other sensitive issues.

Press freedom is deep-rooted in the Thai culture. However, the tradition of self-censorship in Thailand is as long as its history of a free press. Despite the freedom they enjoyed in the 1980s, Thai editorial writers and reporters censored themselves, mindful that there were unwritten government rules regarding the coverage of the monarchy, government affairs, internal security matters, and Thailand's international image. "Self-censorship is probably a perfect form of political control. Politicians in power don't have to risk creating public ire by openly bullying the media. Media proprietors and journalists know exactly what the 'invisible rules' are". The degree of press freedom and selfcensorship in Thailand is often dependent on the kind of government that is in power. The Thai government under Prime Minister Thaksin provided a telling example.

Since Thaksin came to power, the majority of media outlets were forced into submission. Some journalists lamented that truly independent journalists were now "a rare and endangered species" as too many members of the media were influenced by the lure of political favour, or in fear of political power. The government rewarded media outlets supportive of its policies through the allocation of advertising by telecommunications firms and state enterprises, which resulted in an increasing level of self-censorship. More sophisticated media outlets included mild criticism of the government in their coverage but avoided more serious issues or pursuing issues further.

In such a media environment, anyone in the broadcast media speaking more than "30 per cent of the truth" could get into trouble. The media were thus forced into three categories - government partisans, government mouthpieces, and those that engage in self-censorship. Most mainstream newspapers were won over by the government either through friendly persuasions sweetened with advertising deals or through political pressure, and all television stations were pressured into practicing self-censorship in covering the government.

Using sharper words, The Nation wrote, "...the majority of those who own media outlets sense Thaksin's political invincibility and are prostituting themselves voluntarily. The broadcast media are the most obvious, acting in collusion with the government.... Nowadays, broadcasters are considered strategic partners with the government. Lump-sum financial rewards have made parts of the media into circus dogs that are ready to do summersaults." The print media were no exception, the article said. Publishers were more willing to follow the government line to ensure their business future. Self-censorship was increasingly becoming the normal code of conduct for editors and journalists under Thaksin.

Under a climate of fear and self-censorship within the media community, the Thai media have morphed into the "custodian of the government". In one particular case, the owner of the newsmagazine, Siamrath, exercised self-censorship by canceling the distribution of 30,000 copies of an issue that contained reports critical of the government. In another case, the management of the Bangkok Post removed its editor Veera Prateepchaikul for "irritating" the prime minister by using the word "arrogance". Concerned over the retreat of press freedom, The Nation argued, "The professional integrity of the media should never be conditional on the political power or popularity of a leader, much less his power of patronage to throw financial benefits their way". Two recent court rulings upheld the constitutional rights to freedom of expression in the country, one vindicating former iTV journalists, who were dismissed for refusing to compromise their professional integrity, and the other in favour of media-freedom advocate Supinya Klangnarong and the Thai Post, who were sued for defamation.

Also in 2006, all the free TV channels covered the anti-Thaksin activities, with the exception of only one channel. That was unprecedented under the government of Thaksin. The Freedom House can rate the Thai press as "free," such as in 2002, or "partly free" since 2003. But it is certainly a different kind of free press even though its self-censorship practices are much less systematic than Japan's.

THE "AUTHORITARIAN PRESS" IN ASIA

The press in Singapore and Malaysia is often regarded as the prototype of authoritarian press in Asia. In both countries, the means to control the press are very similar to those used in sixteenth or seventeenth century England, including government censorship, suspension of license, legal actions against the press, and even shutdown of the offending publications. But that is where similarities with Western authoritarianism end.

The authoritarian press theory was based on the historical analysis of sixteenth and seventeenth century England while the authoritarian press in Singapore and Malaysia is shaped more by the Asian cultural tradition and the practical needs of the countries' geo-political realities.

While government authority came more from the absolute power of the monarchy in sixteenth and seventeenth century England, in Asian societies, especially in Singapore, which is under the heavy influence of Confucius's teachings, governments regard themselves both as parents and as rulers, which helps explain why even gum chewing and flushing toilets are regulated.

According to the Confucian hierarchical order of political system, government is the paternalistic figure of the land. "The ruler is the wind. People are the grass. When the wind blows, the grass is sure to bend," Confucius said. But Confucius was also a philosopher. He said, "Authority springs from morality, not force". He believed that people should accept authority, but authority must be just. Confucius asked: "When government leads by the right example, who dares to go astray?" In contrast, authoritarian theory does not address the quality of a government or the morality of the rulers.

Singapore is a society where a no-non-sense government promotes Confucian values of education, hard work and clear moral principles. The Singaporean government is one of the very few in Asia where corruption is rare. The government is as clean as the streets in Singapore, which is often considered the cleanest city in the world. The government in Singapore prides itself on its system of meritocracy and efficiency. Different views are tolerated to a certain extent, but if the press publishes articles the government takes offence to, the government pursues the press relentlessly all the way to the court, which often has a chilling effect on the press.

Confucianism extols cooperative and harmonious relations, which are what the Singaporean government hopes to cultivate both at home and abroad. The government keeps a watchful eye on the press for any stories that address race relations, religion, or problems in neighbouring countries. Such stories are banned in the Singaporean press because of the mixed racial and religious makeup of its population and its often-sensitive relations with its neighbours. Violence and chaos caused by racial and religious differences in neighbouring countries put the Singaporean government on high alert. Former Prime Minister Lee Kuan Yew said that any journalist who did not support Singapore-Malaysia relations would be sent to jail.

Malaysia has many similarities with its neighbour, Singapore, in its treatment of the press, as the two countries were once merged into one for a brief period in their history. Both governments are unequivocal promoters of "Asian values" and loud critics of Western culture.

Asian values in Malaysia include emphasis on the social role of the press, which is for development, and on morality, which in part might have resulted from the Islamic influence in the country. Confucian influences are not as heavy in Malaysia as in Singapore, where Chinese account for about 75 per cent of the population. In Malaysia, Muslims make up about half of the population.

Malaysian leaders, especially former Prime Minister Mahathir, have the government-knows-best attitude. The government has set the goal of making Malaysia a developed country by the year 2020, and it wants the press to help in that endeavor, which means highlighting government development plans, promoting racial and religious harmony by suppressing coverage of racial and religious issues, and controlling Western influences by limiting overseas TV programming to 30 per cent. While the Singaporean government is often criticized for trying to silence dissent and punish the press for negative coverage, the government in Malaysia has promoted positive press coverage on such topics as "Asian values" and national development.

In some aspects, Malaysian media seem to border on the communist system not only in promoting positive news coverage, but also in media ownership. Party press sets the trend in Malaysia, where political parties own major stocks in media agencies.

The ruling political party UMNO owns media giants the New Straits Times and Utusan Malaysia. The Chinese and Indian parties in the country also have acquired major stocks in media agencies that cater to their ethnic groups. The government has a direct stake in the media too by owning the national news agency, Bernama, which has the right to distribute foreign news reports.

Under authoritarian rule, governments do not own the media; they punish the media when they are not happy with the coverage.

One salient feature of the authoritarian press system is government's various ways of punishing and controlling the press when the press is defiant. Even though the Malaysian government punishes occasional rebellious papers, the Malaysian press, especially the mainstream press, mostly saves the government's wrath through compliance with very restrictive press laws.

The Printing Presses and Publications Act of 1984 gives the minister of home affairs the power to revoke publishing licenses without judicial review.

As a result, the Malaysian mainstream press has become so tame that its credibility has been questioned. Zaharom Nain wrote, "... The Malaysian mainstream media - the press and broadcasting - have never aspired to be the guardians of the freedom of speech."

"... The mainstream newspapers' failure to be a credible source of information is a reflection of a journalist's failure in performing her duties professionally," a member of the National Union of Journalists said. The inaction of the press against government suppression of press freedom came under fire too. "The credibility of Malaysian journalists has been damaged as much by dilution of professional standards and ethics as by passivity in tackling legal and administrative restrictions".

ANARCHISM IN THE ASIAN PRESS

Although Asia is rarely known for press freedom, there are some rather free press systems in the region, particularly transitional press systems such as the ones in Taiwan, the Philippines, and Indonesia, where the whole control system was torn down when martial law was ended or strongmen overthrown and where there was tremendous backlash against press control.

But often the enthusiasm for newfound press freedom in these countries leaves the press bordering on a state of anarchy. After decades of government suppression, the press in Taiwan, the Philippines, and Indonesia was enjoying unprecedented freedom and explosive growth when the rules, regulations, and bans were lifted, licenses for starting up newspapers became easier to obtain, and the enthusiasm for starting up newspapers was high. Such outpouring energy overwhelmed the governments in these societies after decades of authoritarian or military rule. These governments had yet to establish trust and credibility among the people and construct new frameworks in regulating the press without the suspicion that democratically elected governments were reintroducing government control over the press. The booming press industry tipped the balance between supply and demand. Intensified competition combined with new press freedom drove many of the papers in these countries to "freakdom" of the press, meaning sensationalism in news coverage.

In Indonesia, now that the press is finally free, the main problem is a lack of professional standards and ethics among journalists. More and more journalists are violating the most sacred principle of the profession: tell the truth. Journalists today are accountable to no one but themselves and their proprietors because of the sweeping deregulation of the media.

The ministry of information was abolished, and gone also was the licensing system. In 1999, a new press law was passed to guarantee freedom. But excesses and abuses of press freedom have ironically prompted calls from the public for the government to restore some control of the press.

Freedom of the press is a double-sided sword, which can expose corruption and injustice but can also hurt the freedom and media if the freedom is abused. Media in Indonesia has changed its role from being a mouthpiece of the government under Suharto to being a critical watchdog today. "Barking headlines, hard-biting editorials, sharp commentaries, satirical cartoons and investigative exposés are now common features of our media".

But the media in general failed to promote the basic principles of journalism, such as accuracy and balanced reporting. Syamsul Muarif, the state minister for information and communication, a new government agency, listed five diseases of the press: pornography, character assassination, false and provocative news, misleading advertisements, and unprofessional journalists.

Media hold up a mirror to the society they cover; in the case of Indonesia, what is reflected is pervasive corruption, which poisons the soul of journalism. Indonesia was rated as the fifth most corrupt country in the world, where corruption spread from the central government to local governments. This culture of corruption gave rise to "envelope journalism" and "bogus journalism". With "envelope journalism," journalists receive cash from news sources to compensate for their low salaries, compromising the integrity of the press. "Many people are willing to provide bribes for journalists to ensure that the press will cover or blow up good stories about them or stop publishing bad news about them." And this is a common practice for almost all private and state organizations. Every day no fewer than 2,000 journalists make their fortune by asking the members of the parliament for money.

The amount offered was so enticing that it attracted fake journalists to news conferences for the enveloped cash, resulting in "bogus journalists," who reached hundreds in Jakarta alone. Some of these bogus journalists were laid-off journalists, while others had no previous connections with the media. "Envelope journalism" brought about public complaints that news stories were inaccurate and failed to cover both sides of a story. Ulin Ni'am Yusron, chairman of the Jakarta Independent Journalists Alliance (AJI), said, "It is too much to ask them to make impartial, quality news if they are underpaid".

In Indonesia, only 30 per cent of about 1,200 publishers in the print media were financially healthy. Therefore, not only journalists can be bought, media organizations can be bought as well. A 2005 survey published by the Alliance for Reform and Democracy in Asia found that 40 per cent of the respondents in

Indonesia did not perceive the media to be free and independent of the government and "other sources". Respondents cited widespread bribery of journalists, the buying of air time on talk shows and other forms of advertisements by public figures, and the efforts of both political parties and big business in establishing their own media or buying into media in order to influence public opinion.

Blame was laid on the lack of professionalism and increasing competition from both the local and foreign media. Nurbaiti contended that the immediate future did not look bright either. The outlook for 2006 was that "the Indonesian media will continue to compromise in the search for balance between profit and quality journalism".

Advocacy journalism sells papers too. During the height of the brutal communal conflict in Maluku province, the Jawa Pos media group was accused of profiting immensely from the conflict, which split up the community along ethnic and religious lines. The group's new paper launched during the middle of the conflict, the Ambon Express, was labeled a "Muslim" daily, and the group's established paper, Suara Maluku, was considered a "Christian" paper. Almost all media outlets in Maluku at that time were accused of taking sides.

The same kind of "provocative reporting" was used during the tension between Indonesia and Malaysia over the disputed Ambalat offshore oil block in the Sulawesi Sea. In their coverage, the Indonesian media failed to promote peace; instead, it contributed to the tension. The national media focused on the possibility of war rather than advocating a peaceful settlement, and the local media preferred to cover the deployment of soldiers or the recruitment of volunteers to attack Malaysia.

In the Philippines, the press claims to be the freest in Asia even though broadcasting is still subject to regulation. Sheila S. Coronel (2000) described the Philippine press as "rowdy," "vibrant," "pluralistic," and "anarchistic." She said Filipino journalists are noisy and powerful. Media exposes have caused the resignation of officials and raised public awareness about important issues. Because of their recent history, Filipino journalists protect their freedom fiercely and are firm believers in the watchdog role of the press. In post-Marcos days, the Philippine media were able to publish information with few restraints. But with few principles of ethics or responsibility to guide them, journalists followed their own set of rules. As a result, accuracy and truth were compromised. Many Philippine journalists believed that journalism was mostly instinctive, and that theories and principles were not much more help than as mere guidesthat there existed no rules specific enough to constitute applicable and reliable standards. "Never has the profession been so cheapened-and cheapened yet by its own practitioners". This belief led to the general deterioration in the quality of the profession. Part of the problem was due to the mushrooming of news media outlets and the growing demand for journalists.

The proliferation of news media outlets depleted the supply of qualified journalists and "opened the profession to invasion by pseudo-journalists, resulting in widespread malpractice".

The news media were criticized for irresponsible and sloppy reporting, for checkbook journalism, and for using its freedom to commercially exploit the public's taste for the sensational. Television bore the brunt of criticism. In the words of a print journalist-turned TV journalist, "Philippine TV has not reached the point of maturity, where we can say that it is really doing things in the service of Filipinos. At this point, it is more of the service of business, making money, fighting the ratings game, and being No. 1". Journalists were eager to present to the public every possible news source without checking his or her credibility. "Anything that would raise the decibel of noise (was deemed to be) good".

A TV reporter who covered the police beat wrote an article in the Philippine Journalism Review, introducing his work. It seemed the most important story to him that day was an action-packed exclusive. The kind of exclusive he was referring to was stories like a fight in a bar between two groups of men. He described that as his "most memorable" story - "The protagonists hurled chairs and exchanged fierce blows (one had his nose bridge badly broken; the other had his face bloodied) until police on patrol intervened. We had everything caught on tape, and my crew and I went home happy with an action-packed exclusive".

Other scoops the reporter and his crew chased included a fire that gutted a car after it crashed into a ten-wheeler, a holdup incident, carjacking in a tunnel, and a fake kidnapping case. Such stories were the focus of his news coverage and the theme of his article. Given the rampant corruption, the high profile problem of murdering journalists and other challenges the country is facing, can the freedom and the power of the media be put to better use?

The news media have also used their freedom to outdo rivals in the race to peddle newspapers and television programmes. When members of the First Philippine Mount Everest Expedition scaled the world's tallest mountain, crews from both ABS-CBN and GMA-7, two TV networks, followed the team to cover the event. Both were exclusive broadcast partners, each network sponsoring its own climbers. Both networks wanted to break the news first and have better videos. And both networks denied that they tried to dictate the pace of the ascent. The competition was viewed as a "ratings war," or "a network war," which the networks denied.

The race in ratings sometimes resulted in tragedy. More than seventy people died in a rush to get inside a sports stadium, where a TV extravaganza sponsored by ABS-CBN was to take place, and the network found itself the subject of news. The motivation for staging the event was again fierce competition between ABS-CBN and GMA-7.

Media ownership pattern, on the other hand, is hardly representative of the interests of different sectors of the society when anybody can buy into the media as long as he or she has money. Media in the Philippines remain an elite enterprise, and newspapers operate in the vested interests of their owners. Media owners sometimes use their newspapers to defend and advance their businesses and political interests. And political patronage in the press is not unusual.

Similar to the situation in Indonesia, money corrupts individual journalists as bribery gets in the way of reporting the truth. "There are many journalists who allow themselves to be used as tools of the government". One reporter wrote about a typical case where a highranking government official was trying to buy her silence with a thick envelope of cash. The reporter was investigating bribery charges against the official and his wife. The reporter was "stunned" and "humiliated" by the matter-of-fact manner in which the bribes were delivered. The case showed the prevalence of corruption in Philippine journalism.

The chase after profits and mounting libel suits against the media prompted growing criticism against the media and calls for improving professionalism. The establishment of Citizen Press Councils and calls for appointing media ombudsmen to keep down libel suits were part of the efforts by the media industry to use the power of a free press more responsibly.

In Taiwan, the press started to enjoy press freedom after martial law was lifted in 1987, and political discussions are much more open in the press since. According to the 2005 Freedom House report, Taiwan is well known for having one of the freest media environments in East Asia because of its firm commitment to judicial independence and economic freedom. Today's media in Taiwan are among the freest and most competitive in Asia.

The media in Taiwan are free and powerful. "For all its shortcomings, the press is free, bold and aggressive". Like their counterpart in the Philippines, the news media in Taiwan play a critical role in exposing government corruption, which would have remained hidden from public view without investigations by the media. Media exposés of corruption cases and scandals involving high-ranking officials resulted in devastating defeats in local elections and resignations of high officials.

However, the media in Taiwan are often criticized for abusing that power and freedom. They are often regarded as a source of social chaos and accused of stirring up disorder by making "unfounded reports" and spreading stories that were not true. Some media organizations tend to be biased or sensationalize their reports. As Taiwan's democracy is sometimes ridiculed as "rambunctious," its media are also considered as lacking accuracy and accountability. To win sympathy and support, the island's embattled president Chen Shui-bian trumped up his family troubles, and the media dutifully sensationalized the story as soap operas. For circulations and ratings, the media spent too much energy on sensationalizing crime stories and the private lives of public figures. One recent example involved a police investigation of a death. For two weeks, the media provided excessive coverage of the case on a daily basis, including the daily activities of the suspect and the police's pursuit.

In another extreme case, the Scoop Weekly, a tabloid magazine, enclosed a VCD of an alleged sexual encounter of a female legislative candidate in one of its issues. The magazine defended itself by saying that the VCDs were enclosed in the magazine as "evidence" supporting the veracity of its investigative reporting.

Some reporters, in the rush to be the first to get the story out, sacrificed accuracy in their reporting rather than tried to find credible sources to check out the facts. And sometimes police complained that newsgathering and reporting got in the way of solving criminal cases. "The freedoms that were so hard to obtain, ironically, now threaten some parts of a society that considers the press the enemy because of its influence and power".

The excesses of press freedom in Taiwan, the Philippines, and Indonesia are typical of press systems in transition from being tightly controlled to almost completely free. The new democracies in Eastern Europe have encountered similar problems, such as the boom of tabloid journalism, the withering of quality press, bribery, and corruption.

The media systems in transition reflect the problems of those societies undergoing major transformations - rough politics in the fight for the power vacuum, partisan press, intense competition because of the new freedom, corruption for lack of a strong and independent judiciary system, weak financial foundation for the media, and lack of training of the journalists.

Democracy is still young in these societies; it will take time for a democratic system to mature. Because of traditions and culture, press freedom in these countries will still have its ups and downs. The newfound press freedom in Asian societies has its own distinctive social and cultural contexts.

ALTERNATIVE PRESS THEORIES AND MODELS

Both Eastern and Western media researchers have tried to redress the deficiencies of the four-theory model by creating their own models. Three more theoretical concepts-development journalism, democratic-participant media, and the revolutionary media-were developed to accommodate the progress and changes in press systems and to supplement the dominant paradigm's four press categories.

Of the new theoretical concepts, development journalism has caused more controversies because the degree of press freedom varies greatly from society to society, and the very concept may imply a role for the government. The controversy also seems to stem from the fact that the deciding factor in creating the four press theories was the presence or absence of press freedom, which was defined mainly in terms of government control. Based on such a criterion, how can one type of press system allow vastly different degrees of press freedom in different societies? When a new concept cannot be fit into the established paradigm, it becomes "controversial."

Progressive, insightful, and creative as these new theories are, they are mostly supplementary to the established four press theories. Ralph Lowenstein developed a "progressive typology," according to which, "press systems evolved from authoritarian to libertarian, to social libertarian or social centralist, and then to a big futuristic question mark". This typology seems to have the same tendency as the established four theories of basing its discussions mainly on the development paths of Western press systems, which makes it less relevant to the evolution of press systems elsewhere in the world.

J. Henry Altschull proposed three basic media models - market, Marxist, and developing. To make the concepts value free, Altschull described them as market, communitarian, and advancing. In trying to reclassify media systems, Altschull brought in the element of culture and belief systems.

He explained that the market system emphasized the "individual" while the communitarian system focused on the "communal life" or the "collective." Altschull also analyzed the role of the media - preserving status quo under both market and communitarian models and advocating change under the advancing model. He explained that there were variations within each model, giving the classification much flexibility.

With the exception of the advancing model describing press systems in the South, Altschull's models were also based mainly on the analysis of Western media systems even though he classified his models also as East, West, and South, where East refers to Marxism and the former Soviet communist bloc in Eastern Europe rather than to Asia.

The only Eastern society mentioned in the analysis was Japan. Altschull explained that despite the variations within the market model, the basic belief systems - hostility to a communitarian belief system - remain intact. "Discord notwithstanding, the broad sweep of the first movement of the symphony is heard throughout the industrialized capitalist world, in Japan as in Denmark and Canada".

Despite Western influence, the Japanese society, steeped in Asian culture and Confucian traditions, has no such hostility. As discussed earlier in this chapter, the press club system in Japan dictates communal behaviour within the industry by discouraging competition and scoops and encouraging collective reporting. A mixture of the East and the West, Japan proves to be a difficult case to be classified.

John C. Merrill's circular model shows that individualistic press systems gravitate towards libertarianism and more collectivistic systems are at the authoritarian end. Merrill said, "... the basic model is a simple spectrum, with authoritarianism at one end and libertarianism at the other. All press systems fall somewhere along this continuum". Merrill's model resembles Altschull's models without the "advancing" or "South" element. Men-ill's model has the merit of built-in flexibility.

The classification of a press system depends on in which direction the system gravitates. But it is still difficult to place Japan on Merrill's model. The Japanese press is mostly free from government control, but it is not individualistic. The press club system emphasizes collective action, but it cannot be described as authoritarian.

The models proposed by Altschull and Merrill represented major improvements over the four-theory model - AltschulPs model moved away from the exclusive emphasis on government control, and Men-ill's model had the merit of built-in flexibility to accommodate different types of press systems and changes within those systems. Despite Men-ill's inclusion of the communitarian factor, the two models still seem to largely rely on Western philosophies, scholarship, and examples of Western media performances.

Jiafei Yin (2003) called for the construction of a new model, which would be based on a broader foundation of both Western and Eastern philosophies and cultural influences, but did not produce an actual model.

Shelton A. Gunaratne brought in both Eastern and Western philosophical, religious, and cultural traditions in building his model-The Dao of the Press. There are two parts to Gunaratne's model: one part is the libertarian-authoritarian (L-A) continuum with varying shades of social responsibility across the continuum, and the other part is a centre-semiperiphery-periphery world system with individuals and groups, nation-states, and the world system at different levels. And all the three levels "autopoietically adjust the degree of free expression" along the L-A continuum.

Gunaratne's model emphasizes both Eastern and Western cultural values in the definitions and interpretations of the term "social responsibility," giving the model much needed flexibility in accommodating different shades of social responsibility found in world cultures. Merrill also addressed the relativity of the concept of responsibility among societies and even within a society.

Similar to many of the previous press theories and models, Gunaratne's L-A continuum also focuses on the libertarian-authoritarian dichotomy, reflecting Western emphasis on freedom and liberty. With the rich heritage of Asian philosophies and cultures, can a new model reflect diverse global cultural values and describe and explain press systems around the world without bias either from the West or the East?

After all, different cultures prioritize values differently. Therefore, press theories that are supposed to address global press systems should have a wider base to reflect a broader, more balanced global view. With adequate attention to factors such as world history, global cultures, and economic pressure, the problems inherent in the four established theories because of the authors' Western bias and their sole focus on governmental influences can be addressed.

For a new paradigm of press theories, the optimal balance between specificity and universality should also be considered. The four theories of the press have the beauty and elegance of a very simple but clear structure - four categories under a dichotomy, which aimed to describe and explain press systems in the whole world. Conveniently general as they are, the four or five theories have difficulties in providing a reliable guide to the global press systems. The universality of the theories is limited. However, if categories are too specific and accurate in describing particular press systems, there may be too many categories for the model to be an effective guide.

One other important factor that needs to be paid attention to in building a more reliable press model is that the model should be dynamic so that it can accommodate the changes in the press systems around the world. Obviously, press systems in the new democracies in Eastern Europe are very different from the press systems in the West even though they all operate under democratic systems now.

The press systems in the new democracies in Asia, such as Indonesia, Cambodia, the Philippines, Taiwan, and South Korea, vary from those in Eastern Europe despite the fact that they are all new democracies and share some similarities.

And the press system in China today cannot be compared with the Chinese press system two decades ago, or the press system in North Korea. It would defeat the purpose of having models if every time any changes occur, new models have to be created.

COMMUNIST PRESS IN ASIA

Today's Asia hosts the majority of the world's remaining communist countries - China, Vietnam, Laos, and North Korea. Trying to understand the press systems in these countries using the Soviet communist press theory as a guide would be misleading.

The communist press theory was based on the model of the Soviet press system, which can't satisfactorily describe the varied press systems in these remaining communist countries today, especially the Chinese press system after more than twenty years of sweeping economic liberalization and opening to the outside world.

The Freedom House rated China 7 for political rights and 7 for civil liberties, not free for 1997-98 (on a scale of one to seven with one being most free and 5.5+ being not free), the same ratings for 1972-73, which meant that for the twenty-five years in between, political rights and civil liberties in the Chinese society remained the same. For its 2005 survey on press freedom, it ranked China the 177th out of a total of 197 countries studied.

The Freedom House rating was in sharp contrast to the 1998 U.S. State Department report, which stated that Chinese citizens benefited from" higher disposable income, looser economic control, greater freedom of movement, increased access to outside sources of information, greater room for individual choice, and more diversity in cultural life". Emmons wrote that," There are those who believe that the media and freedom of speech, in general, never have been as uninhibited as they are today...". Emmons cited in his paper," Surprisingly, the average Chinese citizen enjoys significantly more personal freedom today than ever before".

When China is undergoing economic reforms, what exactly does" media reform" mean? It meant the public's right to know according to late premier Zhao Ziyang; it meant commercializing Chinese media and building a stronger media industry according to late reform architect Deng Xiaoping; and it means the relevance of the media to the people according to current Chinese leader Hu Jintao.

Reforms bring choices, and freedom means having choices. Since the reform started, China's media outlets proliferated. Today China has around 2,000 newspapers, more than 9,000 magazines, 1,000 radio stations, and 200 TV stations broadcasting 2,900 channels. The choices and competition on the media market today stand in sharp contrast to the one voice on the media scene in the past when every city had only one Party paper. Choices, instead of one voice, symbolize the major changes Chinese media consumers have experienced.

Introducing the profit motive, which is absent from the Soviet press model, into the media sector was another reform measure that caused sweeping changes to the industry-it changed the nature of the media in China. Economic reform of the media in China began almost as early as the overall economic reform. And media commercialization becomes an important part of the development of the market economy as the government has adopted a policy of gradually cutting subsidies and encouraging commercialized financing.

Advertising, the capitalist genie, has returned to the world of communist media. To meet the new challenge, the press, including the ones directly under the control of the Party, is becoming increasingly commercialized. Even the official Xinhua news agency and the Party paper, People's Daily, are diversifying their product line to increase profits.

To be competitive on a booming media market, where the number of journalists has doubled in twenty years, media in China have to appeal to the readers, some of them by resorting to sensationalism. To speed up the reform, the government announced in June 2003 that it would end subsidies to all the newspapers in China except three papers and one journal, and all the publications in China had to sever their ties to government departments and stop mandatory subscriptions.

Those titles earning less than 50 per cent of their revenues through voluntarily paid subscriptions had to be shut down. By November that year, a total of 1,452 Party and government newspapers had been affected, 673 of which had been suspended from publication.

The overhaul of the Chinese press system has substantially changed the economic and administrative relationships between the government and the press. From then on, the press has been financially independent of the government, even though the state remains the owner of the press. The biggest challenge facing Chinese editors today is to strike the right balance between being politically correct and economically viable.

In fact, one of the major problems hampering the development of the Chinese press today is the low ethical standards held by some local and commercial papers. Hunan TV, a challenging rival of China Central TV (CCTV), developed a huge following with a series on an orphaned woman looking for her biological parents. In its reporting, the network turned an old rape case into a love story, resulting in being sued. Some media outlets were given warnings and reporters detained for extorting large sums of money from people allegedly involved in wrongdoing.

It is no longer rare in China today that newspapers are exposed for their sensationalism, fabrications, or staged news, which are commonplace in a free press environment but seldom occur under a tightly controlled communist media system. Orthodox communist papers are serious and" clean."

The Soviet press model mostly prescribes a promotional role for the press - the press should be an agitator, an organizer, and propagandist for the socialist cause, but never a watchdog. In the Chinese press today, there is no lack of exposés or negative news, which is a taboo in the rigid communist media model, as bad news is perceived as demoralizing. Given the rampant corruption among government officials in China, some high-level government officials encouraged the press to play the watchdog role by engaging in more investigations. Zhang Baoming, head of the State Administration for Production Safety, called on the media for more active participation in the investigation of major industrial accidents, almost every one of which, he said, was connected with corruption.

Caijing, a financial magazine, made a name for itself for its investigative reporting of the financial sector. Who would have imagined that the communist press would engage in investigative reporting? Former Chinese Premier Zhu Rongji tried to promote the watchdog role of the media.

Commenting on a popular talk show on China Central Television," Focal Point" (Jiaodian Fangtan), which routinely exposes official corruption and mismanagement, Zhu praised the programme as" a mirror and watchdog of the government and a supervisor of the government through public opinion". Wu Guanzheng, secretary of the Central Commission for Disciplinary Inspection, also urged the media to play the watchdog role in the national campaign against corruption. He said media publicity was vital to the campaign, and the authorities should listen to" the voice of the media."

The Zhejiang provincial government encouraged the news media to provide tips directly to its inspection department as the government found it effective to follow and prosecute corruption cases exposed in the media. The government even offered rewards of up to 20,000 yuan ($2,500) if the tips were verified and led to prosecution. In contrast, the municipal government of Nanjing was widely criticized for stipulating that all corruption exposés be signed off by the person exposed in the story.

In Qijiang County, Chongqing municipality, hidden cameras were installed to monitor the performance of government officials. The Southern Metropolis Daily and the Beijing News both carried editorials, arguing that the watchdog role of the media would be much more powerful and effective than the hidden cameras, as it is a bottom-up rather than a top-down approach.

In many cases, the news media are playing such a vigorous watchdog role that a" Witness Protection Law" is being proposed as investigative reporting invites reprisals. Some news sources were detained, jailed, or sent to labour camps. In one case, an editor was beaten to death by Taizhou city police for an embarrassing exposé.

Attacks against journalists have increased in China in recent years as reporters have become more aggressive in reporting sensitive social issues. At least 100 journalists were physically attacked in 2003. In 2002, the central government was investigating provincial government officials in Jiangxi and Zhejiang provinces for punishing journalists who exposed problems in their jurisdictions.

The Soviet communist media did not carry exposés. In China, exposés of high-ranking officials, though allowed, still have to be approved by the government however. One other important feature of the communist press system is the state ownership of the media. The majority of the media outlets in China today are still owned by the state.

However, foreign investment is entering the Chinese media sector, and such investment as mandated by the rules of the World Trade Organization is increasing with the deepening of press reforms. Interest in China among international media groups surged in 2005 after the Chinese government issued rules allowing foreign investment in joint-venture television, radio, and film production companies. News Corporation, Viacom, and Sony Pictures were among the big names involved in joint ventures with Chinese media companies.

The current policy stipulates that investors are denied decision-making power in the media outlets'editorial content. But in practice, the situation is getting murky. The editorial staff of the China International Business, a monthly economic review, gets its salaries from Ringier AG of Switzerland. Such business arrangements are not rare. Many foreign publishers sign deals in media advertising or consulting but actually help produce content. Under the Soviet press system, there was tight control of information and very limited access to government information, resulting in more propaganda than information in the news media. In China today despite government control, access to information has gained substantial progress in recent years.

In 2000, the government of Anhui Province took the unprecedented step of issuing a regulation banning its officials from refusing interviews to the press. Other provinces and cities followed suit. Such regulations were unimaginable before the reforms or under the Soviet media model. The central government now has also installed a spokesman system to meet the needs of the press, both national and international.

In Shanghai, a reporter, based on a city ordinance mandating the disclosure of public information, sued the city planning department for repeatedly declining interviews. This was the first such case in China where a reporter sued a government department for violating his rights to reporting.

The reporter complained that city government departments often denied interviews to him. The city ordinance required city departments to disclose information concerning the economy, city management, and public services. Such ordinance was listed as top priority in the legislative plan of the State Council.

It would make disclosure as the principle and non-disclosure as the exception rather than the other way around as in the past. China is opening up. It has opened up its market to the world, including the media market, even though it is only the entertainment media for now. It is not difficult today to find popular foreign consumer magazines on the newsstands in China.

International Data Group, a Boston publisher, alone has invested $20 million in China, publishing twenty-eight titles and planning another four. These operations are either in the form of joint ventures or through licensing the titles and content for publication in China.

China is also working on an international media centre with a total floor space of 130,000 square meters, which will serve as an office building for more than 100 foreign media organizations in Beijing. And in 2001, Reuters's Qing Niao web site, a site for trade information and e-business, made a low-key entry into China.

The Soviet communist media model was a closed system. But China has opened up, and it wants to reintegrate itself into the world community. The one medium that provides a public forum for the ordinary Chinese and connects the Chinese people directly with the rest of the world is the Internet, which claims about 137 million users in China by the end of 2006, the second largest in the world after the United States.

China has witnessed the fastest growth of Internet use among countries whose annual per-capita is less than $2,000, and the number of net users is expected to increase by at least 15 per cent annually before 2010. The Internet is breaking through the silence of traditional media by posting stories rejected by official newspapers.

With its power of reaching millions of people at the same time, the Internet has directly helped in effecting legislative changes in the country by exposing police brutality, which brought about public outrage on an unprecedented scale and caught the attention of legislators and the government.

The Internet, with its public forums where people can discuss topics shunned by the traditional media, is producing a better informed, more vocal public and a more open society. Inadvertently, it has ushered in a public discourse that has been absent for almost half a century.

It also enabled direct communication between ordinary citizens and government officials. The acceptance of the Internet in China itself is one important indicator of the passing of the rigid communist media system in China, as Internet, a revolutionary medium, defies total control. Some media researchers argue that as long as there is government control, the media in China should be categorized as communist media.

It is true that there is still government control of the media in China - there are news topics on which diversity of opinion is not allowed, there are web sites that are blocked, and there are newspaper editors that have been fired. However, since the start of the reforms, the changes that are occurring in China have substantially reduced government controls.

These changes are happening because of the intention of the government to open up, the new financial independence of the press, the proliferation of media outlets, and the availability of the Internet. Sometimes the sheer size of the country poses a challenge to effective control. For example, when the government could not effectively implement a ban on satellite dishes in 1994, it changed its policy by licensing them instead.

A year later the government also specified permissible programmes and viewing hours. Foreign affairs used to be an area off limits for public discussions in the media. The advent of the Internet with its convenient online forums has made it a hot topic for public debate. Government control of the press is a universal phenomenon. The issue is the degree of control.

In the age of the Internet, total control is out of the question. And in the case of China, that control is being relaxed and challenged from all sides. More recent examples include the suspension and the return of the supplement of a major newspaper in Beijing and the debate over a section of a draft law on managing disasters and accidents.

The weekly" Freezing Point" published by the popular China Youth Daily, which stands out from other newspapers in China for its aggressive reporting and biting commentary, was shut down in late January 2006, and its editors removed to its research department because some government officials were not happy with one article. The case was widely publicized by the media worldwide. The supplement resumed publication one month later following public outcry against such heavy-handedness against the press, including staff letters protesting the actions and an open letter to top Party officials signed by thirteen prominent scholars and former officials who were contributors to the supplement.

The writers of the open letter included Zhu Houze, a former Central Propaganda Department official; Hu Jiwei, a former editor-in-chief of the People's Daily, and He Weifang, a law professor from Peking University, who said," The purpose (of the letter) is to change the current incorrect policies on freedom of speech", The letter said although not all signatories approved of the article, they all supported Freezing Point's right to publish it.

They quoted Chinese leader Hu Jintao as saying no organization in China has special legal privileges. The letter said that the newspaper suspension was neither legal nor sensible and it violated citizens'basic rights to speech and freedom of information, which are their constitutional rights.

Another controversy arose over a draft law on emergency management, which included industrial accidents, natural disasters, and health and public security crises. Part of the draft law addressed the news coverage of emergency situations by the media, stipulating that media outlets could face fines between 50,000 yuan (U.S.$6,250) and 100,000 yuan (U.S.$12,500) if they reported the emergency situations without authorization or released fraudulent reports and if such reports led to serious consequences.

The law was drafted following the aftermath of the outbreak of SARS, when health department officials hid the facts from the public, resulting in rampant rumors in the press and in the streets. Government officials said the purpose of the law was to ensure timely release of accurate information by local officials.

Opposition to the draft law was loud and clear. A legislator, He Keng, said journalism had its own rules and argued that the watchdog role of the media was not strong enough in China. The New Express, a commercial newspaper published by the Yangcheng Evening News, carried an editorial arguing that the law would diminish the watchdog role of the media, that there was no guarantee that the information released by government departments was accurate and that some" natural disasters" were man-made.

In a column in the outspoken Southern Metropolis Daily, Changping pointed out that in the case of coal mine disasters, often local officials and mine owners colluded with each other in covering up the facts of accidents as both profited from the mines. In such situations, how could the media wait for the local government to release accurate information? Changping argued.

One often ignored issue is the self-censorship in the newsrooms in China, which sometimes applies tighter control than the government does for the interests of the media organization or the management. For a lack of laws and regulations, the new media are trying to police themselves. Nineteen web sites jointly issued a set of self-disciplinary rules against bloggers'personal attacks, fabricated stories, plagiarism, and pornographic and violent content. Hosts of the sites said they were ready to delete such materials once they appear on their sites. Min Dahong, a journalism professor said that many big web sites in the world have explicit written rules on deleting or editing users'messages that they regard as abusive, defamatory, offensive, obscene, or in violation of a specific law.

Ultimately how much freedom or control the Chinese media will experience is not only up to the government; it is also up to the editors and reporters of the media, especially those leading media organizations in Beijing, as to how far they will push. So far the most vigorous push comes mainly from local media outside of Beijing.

Following China's example, Vietnam started its own economic reforms in 1986 and" remains wedded to the Chinese model of reform". Its press system is also undergoing similar changes. The liberal economic reforms eroded the pervasive authority of the Party. As a result," Vietnam is no longer as tightly controlled as it used to be although it does remain an authoritarian one-party system". Facing a rise in corruption like China, the government encouraged the press to expose corruption, made new laws to facilitate news gathering, and warned against officials trying to obstruct journalists.

Even though strict censorship still exists in Vietnam today, meaningful independent journalism is possible on certain occasions. There are instances where journalists successfully challenged the police and the court in violating reporters'rights in newsgathering and forced the police and the court to back down. " In terms of freedom, the press here in Vietnam has been getting better and more aggressive". One editor at Lao Dong (Labour), Nguyen Due Tuan, said," There is no question we have more freedom today.... Now, reporters like to see how far they can push and still get their stories published".

Similar to the situation in China, editors in Vietnam now have more discretion in deciding the content of their publications. The press in Vietnam is surprisingly lively in terms of the types of newspapers and magazines. Since the reforms, both the quantity and quality of the press have improved.

The press today is becoming more information oriented than ideology dependent, as the importance of information is generally recognized in a more market-oriented economy. The Internet entered Vietnam in 1997. By the end of 2006, the number of Internet users had reached 14.5 million.

Despite government announcement that access to the Internet would be unrestricted, the Freedom House reported that in 2004 the Vietnamese government suppressed dissent on the Internet with new guidelines of government control and censorship, including a permanent monitoring system aimed at the country's privately run Internet cafes.

Despite the reforms, the majority of the media outlets in Vietnam are still state-owned. But the government has permitted some form of private ownership of periodicals, a bolder step than China's. The condition for ownership is that the publication should be a joint undertaking between the owners and the relevant state agency. An example is the Vietnam Investment Review, the first foreign-owned, Western-style periodical in the country. The government also abolished direct subsidies to the press even though some form of state funding is still continuing.

As a result, the press is forced to become more commercialized, and the survival of the press is subject to market forces, which seems to dictate a success formula of tabloid journalism. Some papers publish uncommon crime stories gathered from police records, all in the name of exposing social problems. In the pursuit of profits, newspapers in Vietnam start to face criticisms about their low ethical standards. Some journalists in Vietnam now claim that they are having more debates on" responsibilities and morals of journalists" than on press freedom.

Early in the reform, the sensationalism and the increasingly aggressive investigative reporting alarmed the Party leaders, who worried that the state was losing control of information flow and wanted to rein in this threatening trend. The government began clamping down on the press in 1989 and tightened control of the media by establishing a new press department aimed at monitoring and controlling press coverage about security matters, issuing new rules regarding passing information to foreign news organizations, amending the 1990 press law, requiring compensation if news coverage leads to losses to the business interests of organizations or individuals.

The government also reminded the press to champion the fight against corruption and other social evils instead of seeking profits alone, but questioning Party rule remains expressly prohibited. The Vietnamese leaders are still ambivalent about the degree of control and the liberal reforms, which help with the country's economic development but threaten the power and control of the Party. North Korea may be the only communist country in Asia left with a press that could still fit the Soviet media model. There has been very little change in the country despite the fact that other remaining communist countries in Asia are undergoing major reforms to open up and revive their economies. Perhaps because of the poor performance of its economy, the widespread and chronic famine, and tremendous external pressure to change, the government is exercising strict control of information flow across its borders.

As a result, information about the country is scarce even with CNN's 2006 documentary, which was shot inside the country with a hidden cell-phone camera. North Korea is the most censored country in the world. Its people experience the world's deepest information void, and the country has no independent journalists.

The main role ascribed to the press is that of spreading the viewpoint of the government. All newspapers and broadcasting stations are under direct government control, and all news is positive. According to the 2003 annual report by Reporters Without Borders, all the news media in the country focused on the personality cult of Kim Jong Il.

The report said three subjects dominated the coverage in the print media: the personality of Kim Jong II, praise of the army, and criticism of the country's foes, especially South Korea, the United States, and Japan. In a story, the official Korean Central News Agency reported that Kim Jong Il was so beloved that after a deadly munitions train explosion in a populated area, people ran into buildings to save the ubiquitous portraits of the" Dear Leader" before they rescued their own family members.

Nothing was mentioned in the news media about the malnutrition among children and urban populations or the failure of the government's" self-reliance" policy. In the leading Party paper, the Rodong Shinmun, commentaries carry greater weight than news stories, and reporters do not compete for scoops among themselves, who are given instructions from the Central Party Committee's propaganda and agitation department on what to cover and in how many pages. Anyone disobeying the instructions is severely punished. Reporters may be jailed for a commentary that deviates from the Party line. Harassment, psychological pressure, intimidation, and round-the-clock surveillance are routine.

The North Korean newspapers do not carry any advertisements except a handful of government notices. For the mass media in North Korea, there is neither private ownership nor market competition. North Korea's revised 1998 constitution guarantees citizens'rights of freedom of speech, of the press, of assembly, demonstration, and association.

But the government prohibits the exercise of these rights in practice. There are strict controls to prevent access to any kind of news coming from abroad. Radios sold in North Korea can receive only domestic programming. Radios obtained from abroad must be altered to work in a similar manner. The national news agency has Internet sites hosted in Japan. Direct access to the web is limited to the privileged few. And to prevent Western influence, very few journalists in North Korea receive training in the West.

It is also hard for the foreign media to do reporting inside the country as they are all portrayed by the regime as liars seeking to destabilize the government. Foreign journalists visiting North Korea have to be on guided tours.

However, in 2006, the Associated Press became the first Western news organization to have a permanent bureau in the country. AP Television News's full-time office in Pyongyang operates in association with the country's state-run broadcaster and is staffed mainly by local reporters. With the increase in international trade, even North Koreans have started to have greater contact with foreigners, which might result in greater access to information from the outside world.

The press in North Korea seems to be the prototype of the communist press, but it does not represent the trend where the press in other communist countries is heading. It is misleading to put the press systems in China, Vietnam, and North Korea in the same category. To do so, media researchers have to disregard the sweeping changes in the Chinese and Vietnamese press.

THE" DEVELOPMENT MEDIA" IN ASIA

Neglected by the authors of the four press theories were media in the poorer countries of the world-development media. The press in South Asia may best be described by the concept of development journalism, a concept developed later to supplement the four theories, as the development of communities and giving voice to the underprivileged are major goals of many of the local media in the region.

The development press is popular in the region perhaps because South Asia is the least economically developed region on the continent. More than half of the world's underweight children lived in India, Bangladesh, and Pakistan, said a recent UNICEF report on the global progress on children's issues.

In India, approximately 47 per cent of the under-five population was underweight. The report found that South Asia was the only region that showed a gender bias with regard to child nourishment, with girls more likely to be underweight than boys. The issue of undernourishment points to the problems of poverty, lack of education, and inequality in the region. In India, communication not only means the transfer of information, but also includes the participation in the society and in the community. The Indian brand of development journalism" focuses on the needs of the poor, the deprived, and the marginalized and emphasizes their effective participation in developmental planning". It motivates the participation of the people and advocates for their interests instead of the views of the policy makers and the planners. And it promotes social justice for all.

Journalists in the country believe that the media should not only carry stories about health campaigns like the one against AIDS but also discuss issues that are important for a civil society because only the mass media can reach the vast rural population and give them a voice in debates affecting their lives.

The mass media can also play a crucial role in social progress, as any transitional society will encounter new attitudes, a new mindset, and a new value system. Development journalism enthusiasts in India conducted workshops for social activists to train them to write stories about development issues and workshops for local editors and journalists to familiarize them with realities and issues in local communities. Commercial newspapers also play a role in development journalism. The Jharkhand-based Prabhat Khabar had been doing development journalism by giving people information on science, information technology, economics, and the comparative financial progress of different states. The paper also conducted" readers'courts," where readers could interact with journalists and discuss ways of improving the quality of the paper, much like the role of the focus groups in civic or public journalism in the United States.

Radio plays a special role in development journalism in South Asia because of its easy and wide reach in the vast rural areas, where literacy rate is still relatively low. The Indian communications NGO (non-government organi-zation) had been highlighting the importance of community radio in India for over half a decade and called for the extension of community broadcasting.

In India, awards are given to mentors of development journalism for encouraging and nurturing journalists to investigate and write on development issues and for supporting journalism initiatives towards" a common social good". Journalists and media researchers in India and Pakistan criticized some of the mainstream media for their elitist approach, focusing on the prominent while ignoring the plight of the underprivileged in rural communities by following Western news values.

The degree of press freedom in South Asia, however, varies considerably from country to country. Once the largest colony in the world, India is the largest democracy in the world today. Only under Prime Minister Indira Gandhi was an attempt made to curtail press freedom by declaring a political emergency to suspend civil rights. The government of Narasimha Rao tried to prevent exposés of government corruption under the pretext of protection of privacy. Despite such government attempts at control, the press in India has largely remained private, free, and vibrant. Cushrow R. Irani, editor-in-chief and managing director of The Statesman, said that India's press today is as free as it chooses to be. N. P. Chekkutty, editor of Media Focus, wrote," The Indian media works in an atmosphere of freedom. We are the purveyors of free thoughts and opinions. We do reflect the freedom of expression the Constitution guarantees to our citizens, and we, therefore, are the epitome of a free, liberal society".

With the freedom it enjoys, the press in India often plays its watchdog role seriously." Newspapers in India are completely free, as free as the newspapers in the United States, as they are privately owned and free of censorship". It is the newspapers that have exposed corruption in India, though some journalists are attacked for their investigative reporting. The Indian press has always been vigilant about protecting its freedom and aggressive in reporting.

Free as it may be as the press in the United States, the Indian press clearly differs from the Western libertarian press system in the perception of its mission. For its social role, the Indian press may be closer to the civic or public journalism in America, which also prescribes an advocacy role for the press. However, in India development journalism represents the aspirations of many journalists, while in America the ethical implications of civic and public journalism are still being debated.

In India, press freedom is guaranteed by the Constitution and the independent court system, which is very similar to the situation in neighbouring Pakistan, formerly a part of India before its independence. Behind India, which has a relatively low literacy rate of 65 per cent, Pakistan's literacy rate is even lower at 38 per cent, which limits the growth of its press industry.

There are about 1,330 newspapers in print in Pakistan, but only 1 per cent of the population buys a newspaper. The press in Pakistan is independent of the government and mostly privately owned.

Major public issues are debated in the press, which has become an instrument for change. In Pakistan no law governs the registration of publications.

In recent years, Pakistan has been moving towards greater press freedom, and its press is among the most outspoken in South Asia. In both India and Pakistan when the government tries to crack down on critical press coverage of the government, the courts often strike down government charges in support of press freedom.

There are exceptions to the constitutional guarantees of the freedom of speech and of the press in Pakistan, the most important of which is the" reasonable restrictions imposed by law in the interest of the glory of Islam". The Constitution prohibits the ridicule of Islam, of the armed forces, or of the judiciary. Development journalism is perhaps less developed in Pakistan than in India. Circulation of newspapers in the rural areas of the country is one of the lowest in the world because of the urban orientation of the papers and the cost of subscription in addition to a low literacy rate. The rural market is largely untapped.

The dramatic increase in the number of publications in recent years is not supported with trained staff. Many journalists, especially rural ones, lack the basic skills to cover the complex issues important to their communities. However, electoral politics has increased the importance of rural centres in the emerging democracy of Pakistan.

Supporting development journalism, the Pakistan Press Foundation (PPF) was established to help raise the standards of journalism, particularly of the vernacular and regional press, and to promote greater awareness of social and development issues through the media. In 1999, PPF restarted the rural journalists'skills development project. By 2002 hundreds of Pakistani rural journalists have attended the workshops. The emphasis of the workshops is on improving basic skills of newsgathering and news writing, as participants are given exercises using actual issues, such as violence against women, environmental issues, child labour, bonded labour, and crime rates. The end of monopoly of the electronic media in Pakistan provides new hopes of reaching a rural audience as radio is acknowledged to be a more suitable and affordable means of providing local communities with a voice of their own. It is more interactive and more suitable for community development. In less than six years, between 2000 and 2006, the broadcast sector completely changed the monolithic landscape that existed for about fifty-three years.

But the proliferation of radio stations has created the co-existence of robust liberty and open lawlessness, and commercial interests dominate the airwaves while development journalism still needs time to take hold. Research on the topic, however, is several steps ahead of the media industry.

Development journalism is regarded as an Asian model of journalism, stemming from the dissatisfaction with the Western news values that do not serve the cause of national development. Western news values of timeliness, prominence, proximity, conflict, and the bizarre exclude the ordinary people in the news unless they are involved in accidents, violence, or catastrophes.

Development journalism, on the other hand, should focus on the educational function of the news, stories about social needs, self-help projects, and obstacles to development. In the exploration of the development journalism model by Asian media researchers, the watchdog role of the media was emphasized, and the media were urged to remain vigilant against government involvement. In Sri Lanka, three newspaper groups dominate the island's newspaper scene - the ANCL, the Upali Newspapers Ltd. and the Wijeya Newspapers Ltd. The ANCL has been under government control since 1973, while the other two are privately owned but have close family connections to political parties.

In the broadcasting sector, Sri Lanka was perhaps the first British colony to introduce radio broadcasting a few years after its inauguration in Europe in 1920s. The country liberalized its radio and TV sectors ahead of the rest of Asia. It permitted the establishment of more commercial radio stations than any other country in the region and put the state-controlled Sri Lanka Broadcasting Corporation under considerable competitive pressure. It also allowed private radio stations to broadcast news and current affairs, unlike some of its neighbouring countries.

Efforts at setting up community radio have never stopped in Sri Lanka. Universities in Sri Lanka and UNESCO played host to regional workshops on community radio for participants from South Asian countries. The goal of such workshops was to make community radio a reality in South Asia and encourage cooperation among community radio advocates in the region. Radio still is a popular medium in South Asia, particularly in rural areas. In Sri Lanka telephone boxes, where a radio station button is installed, allow listeners to contact a station without paying a fee. The system makes it easier for listeners to participate in the programmes and solve problems in the communities.

The mass media in Sri Lanka also play a role in environmental education. Most people in both urban and rural areas use different media outlets as their primary source of environmental education, especially the print media. Television is the next major source of information for the urban population, while radio for the rural population. The media cover environmental issues in the form of news, editorials, investigative stories, entertainment, and educational programmes.

Development journalism in the country can have a bigger potential if the government allows even greater participation by the public in media discussions, which is often limited when there is an increase in guerrilla warfare in the country.

It is evident from the above discussions that the degree of press freedom under the development concept varies from country to country, and that is where the controversy with the concept lies. While one scholar describes it as" the pursuit of cultural and informational autonomy" and" support for democracy" among other goals, another scholar criticizes it as" a rationale for autocratic press control" and" guided press".

Where do all the discussions about the press systems in Asia leave us theoretically? When theories encounter major difficulties in serving as a guide to the understanding of the realities they are supposed to describe, new paradigms are needed. So are the criteria of the Freedom House for assessing global press freedom and civil liberties when their rankings fail to reflect changing realities. Obviously, more factors should be taken into consideration than the current criteria. The Last Rights concluded that the four theories were a" durable" but now" questionable" map and that a" more adequate" map is needed. The book presented inspiring criticism of the four press theories but stopped short of proposing a new paradigm.

4

Function of Journalism in Coverage

INTRODUCTION

Print journalists at first halfheartedly played the celebrated role of "watchdog," in some cases urging readers to be tolerant of Japanese-Americans. But their tolerance, and their time in the "watchdog" role, lasted only until the government put the finishing touches on its policy to deal with alleged fifth column activity, a policy which culminated in the internment. From that point on, print journalists assumed the role of "guard dog," acting as the government's sentry, patrolling for threats to the official version of events that unfolded after Pearl Harbour.

Donohue, Tichenor, and Olien outlined the "guard dog" function as it relates to political reporting, but I argue that it is of particular relevance here. "Guard dog" journalists act as "sentries" for groups who hold power and who have the ability to create their own security systems - in this instance, the federal government, local and state officials, and the military.

Guard dog reporting takes place "when external forces present a threat to local leadership". In writing favorably about dominant groups, journalists tend to "concentrate on individuals while accepting the structure," a tendency seen clearly (and discussed in more detail later) in reporting on the alleged Japanese-American threat to national security. Through their interaction with and dependence on local leaders for information, journalists are trained to suspect potential intruders, and sometimes, as is the case here, "sound the alarm" for reasons that the dominant group may initially be unable to understand.

This inability arises when the authority within the power structure is divided or when part of the power structure is made uncertain by an organized challenge. Along the way, groups who lack power and influence receive little attention from "guard dog" journalists. How a journalist gathers information and writes stories is shaped by the nature of the structure being served and by whom the dominant groups label a threat.

When there is consensus in a community, the guard dog "sleeps," stirring only when an external threat to local leadership materializes. Conflict is reported "in a constrained way and only on certain issues and under certain structural conditions" - in short, when there is conflict between "dominant powers or power blocs". Further, "where different local groups have conflicting interests," Donohue, Tichenor, and Olien argue, "the media are more likely to reflect the views of the more powerful groups".

Such protection highlights "the functions of externally based conflict for reinforcement of local cohesion". Coverage emphasizes the role of dominant groups in addressing issues and correcting problems faced by the community. The guard dog function rejects as "unrealistic" the "watchdog" role of the press taught in so many university journalism classes as a guiding principle for journalistic practice.

The media are not autonomous; they operate as part of the power structure; as such, they "have neither the inclination nor the power to challenge those dominant groups, unless they are already under challenge by other forces". Unable to develop social policy or motivate political action, the media are left to report on actions taken by dominant groups.

If, as in the case of alleged "fifth column" activity explored in this monograph, "these groups and agencies are concerned primarily with an external threat, that will be the agenda of the media.". Questions from reporters that seem to challenge the official view of an event or issue amount to "role playing" driven more by attacks from "contending powers" than by a journalist's desire to expose corruption or challenge action taken by a corporation or agency.

The "guard dog" theory of reporting also runs counter to the view that reporters are little more than "lapdogs," - submissive, dependent, and oblivious to all interests except those of powerful groups. While a "guard dog" journalist does defer to authority, he or she is not completely subservient to dominant interests.

In times of conflict, the work of a "lapdog" journalist would amount to little more than a "defence of the powerful against outside intruders," while the "guard dog" reporter would look for opportunities to report conflict between dominant groups. How deferent a journalist is "depends upon the nature of the community structure as well as on the concentration of power in the larger society".

Finally, the guard dog theory rejects the notion that the media are "equal co-actors" in society's power structure, able to motivate support for policies created by the government, their influence so palpable "that only unusually strong institutions and leaders can counter it". In actuality, reporters are "dependent on the dominant powers" and act to protect "the local power establishment".

Reporters pay a great deal of attention to "nation and society - their persistence, cohesion, and the conflicts and divisions threatening their cohesion". The "tug of war" between the media and dominant powers seen by some is in reality "a result of reporting and reflecting the conflicting views among divided political or economic bodies".

A secondary theoretical strand for this chapter comes from Fiske's work on news as text. Fiske argues for the study of news as a form of discourse - "a set of conventions that strive to control and limit the meanings of the events it conveys". A string of events like those that unfolded after Pearl Harbour are, to use Fiske's term, "unruly." Journalists struggled to make sense of events and to gather information on which to build coverage.

This analysis also explores how journalists applied some of the "strategies of containment" discussed by Fiske to try and routinize coverage of the issues. It is argued, for example, that the government's take on the Japanese American threat became the dominant narrative strand in news coverage of this period; that is, it was "nominated," to use Barthes' term.

Coverage that promoted fairness and tolerance in dealing with Japanese-Americans was "exnominated" once the government took steps to implement its policy for dealing with the Japanese-American issue. For an event to be newsworthy, Fiske argues, it must pertain to "elite" people; it must also be "negative" and "surprising". Of the Japanese-Americans quoted in early coverage, many were prominent business owners and organization officials-the "elite," it could be argued, of the Japanese-American community.

Not only did this reliance on elite sources make it easier for journalists to manage early coverage of the crisis, it also gave them the means to begin marginalizing Japanese-Americans. When journalists began paying more attention to the government's version of events, they all but stopped using Japanese-Americans as sources. Instead, they looked only to prominent government and military officials for the lion's share of their information.

As Fiske notes, "the socially powerful tend to be familiar to us as individuals, the powerless or the voices of opposition are familiar mainly as social roles, which are filled by a variety of forgettable individuals". Donohue, Tichenor, and Olien conclude their discussion of the "guard dog" function with a series of hypotheses formulated to guide further exploration of journalistic practice:

In any structure, the intensity of press reporting and editorializing about a public issue is directly proportional to the degree to which top power positions are uncertain as a result of organized challenge.

Media are more likely to report attacks on individuals in power roles than attacks on power structures. Guard dog media reporting is less intense when the strategies of powerful actors are confined to the traditional roles of political conflict. Media coverage tends to be evaluated as more favorable among groups and occupations occupying more established and dominant power positions, compared with groups and organizations having less established power.

Questioning of the guard dog role is more likely in a highly pluralistic structure than a less pluralistic one. The balance of the monograph will be a test of these hypotheses built on coverage by journalists at three of the nation's most important newspapers of alleged "fifth column" activity by Japanese-Americans.

This case study of the "guard dog" function of the press is built on a textual analysis of the New York Times, San Francisco Chronicle, and Los Angeles Times from December 8, 1941-the day after the attack on Pearl Harbour - to February 19, 1942, the day FDR issued Executive Order 9066.

In all, the main news sections of seventy-two issues of each newspaper were reviewed. The New York Times was selected because of its reputation as the nation's "newspaper of record." The Los Angeles Times and Chronicle were included because they were, and continue to be, two of the most widely read newspapers on the West Coast.

Articles, columns, and letters to the editor that discussed Japanese-Americans, alleged fifth column activity, or calls for or against evacuation of Japanese-Americans were analysed for recurring thematic elements and thematic changes. The goal of the analysis was to chart the emergence of the "guard dog" function, and to show how journalists framed coverage of the alleged Japanese-American threat to national security.

President Franklin D. Roosevelt's decision in 1942 to intern more than 140,000 Japanese-American citizens is one of the darkest chapters in the nation's history. Constitutional rights were trampled; possessions were seized, lives destroyed - all in the name of eliminating a non-existent threat to national security. Justification for Roosevelt's action came from fabricated reports of potential "fifth column" activity by Japanese-Americans from military officials bent on marshaling support for the United States' entry into World War II.

Issued by Roosevelt on February 19, 1942, Executive Order 9066 empowered the Secretary of War to "exclude any and all persons, citizens, and aliens, from designated areas in order to provide security against sabotage, espionage, and fifth column activity". Immigrants born in Japan (Issei) and second generation Japanese-Americans (Nisei) were not allowed to work or travel anywhere on the West Coast.

They were rounded up and sent first to "assembly centres," and then to one of ten relocation centres run by the civilian-staffed War Relocation Authority. On December 7, Roosevelt empowered Attorney General Francis Biddle to have the FBI arrest a set number of enemy aliens. On December 8, the Department of justice closed the borders of the United States both to enemy aliens and to "all persons of Japanese ancestry, whether citizen or alien".

By December 11, nearly 1,400 Japanese-Americans, by then classified as "dangerous enemy aliens," had been taken into custody. The Aliens Division of the Department of Justice, created by Congress in 1940, maintained lists of aliens who would be interned once war began. The Aliens Division was run by John Franklin Carter, a former journalist.

It was Carter who sent FDR a report from West Coast businessman Curtis Munson in which Munson claimed that while most Issei and Nisei were loyal to the United States, "there are still Japanese.who will tie dynamite around their waist and make a human bomb out of themselves".

Despite Munson's report, military officials at first concluded that "widespread sabotage by Japanese is not expected" and that "identification of dangerous Japanese in the west coast is reasonably complete". Nevertheless, 3,000 enemy aliens-half of them Japanese -were interned during the week following Pearl Harbour; the Treasury Department soon froze their bank accounts.

On December 19, 1941, General John DeWitt made the first military proposal for internment. The strongest advocates for internment would include then California Attorney General Earl Warren, later a revered champion of civil rights during his time on the Supreme Court, and DeWitt, who, along with Secretary of War Henry Stimson, encouraged Roosevelt to pursue evacuation as a viable means of ending the Japanese-American "threat" to national security.

Warren told a Congressional committee in February 1942 that Japanese-American sabotage and treachery would inevitably surface: "I believe that we are being lulled into a false sense of security.our day of reckoning is bound to come". In fact, DeWitt lied in his report to Roosevelt about the existence of the threat, a lie left unchallenged for more than four decades, until a federal appeals court ruled that the statute of limitations did not cancel the claims of Japanese-American evacuees whose property was seized before they were interned.

The Supreme Court relied on incomplete evidence when it held that possible subversive activities justified the evacuation of Japanese-Americans, the appeals court ruled. A key purveyor of this "incomplete evidence," according to a number of historians and institutions acting on behalf of Japanese-Americans, was the print media.

Acting far more pliant than the "guard dog" described by Donohue, Tichenor, and Olien, journalists were willing pawns in the government's attempts to paint Japanese-Americans as a threat to national security. Anecdotal evidence cited in accounts written by these historians offers some support for this claim. The Los Angeles Times, for example, announced on December 8 that California was "a zone of danger".

"We have thousands of Japanese here," a Times reporter wrote, "some, perhaps many are good Americans. What the rest may be we do not know, nor can we take a chance in the light of yesterday's demonstration that treachery and double-dealing are major Japanese weapons". After Pearl Harbour, Daniels contends, the Los Angeles Times called on "alert keen-eyed citizens" to finger what were surely "spies, saboteurs, and fifth columnists in their midsts". And it was not the first time that newspapers on the West Coast had attacked Asian-Americans.

In 1905, the San Francisco Chronicle lashed out at Asian immigrants in a series of articles supporting attempts by California's political parties and the American Federation of Labour to end immigration from China and Japan. Stories from the Chronicle carried headlines like "Crime and Poverty Go Hand in Hand with Asiatic Labour" and "Japanese a Menace to American Women".

Four decades later, an immediate call came from a number of journalists to deal decisively with the potential Japanese-American threat; according to Hosokawa, "other voices took up the cry as the days passed, until newspaper and radio commentators were baying like a pack of wolves on a hot trail."

West Coast newspapers "abandoned [their] tradition of supporting the underdog, seeking the truth, unmasking the demagogues, and demanding fair play". Syndicated columnist Henry McLemore brashly called for internment: "herd `em up, pack `em off, and give `em the inside room in the badlands". No journalist was more ardent about evacuation than Scripps-Howard columnist Westbrook Pegler, who advocated putting all Japanese-Americans under surveillance and suspending their habeas corpus rights.

For every hostage killed by the Axis powers, Pegler argued, the United States should kill "100 victims out of [American] concentration camps". At the time, however, the federal government was not actively considering evacuation. In a memo to Roosevelt, Attorney General Nicholas Biddle said that an attack on the West Coast by the Japanese was not imminent.

Hysteria, "and, in some instances, the comments of the press and radio announcers have resulted in a tremendous amount of pressure being brought to bear" on Warren and California Governor Culbert Olson, Hoover said in a memo to Biddle.

But joining Pegler in warning readers about the potential for a Japanese attack on the West Coast was revered columnist Walter Lippmann. At DeWitt's request, Lippmann, in his February 20, 1942 column, told his readers that he agreed with Warren, who argued that because the Japanese and Japanese-Americans were all the more dangerous since they had not yet engaged in any surreptitious activity. Inactivity, Lippmann wrote, was "a sign that the blow is well-organized and that it is held back until it can be struck with maximum effect".

More than twenty years later, Lippmann stood by his work: "There is no doubt that the rights of the [Japanese-American] citizens were abridged by the measure, but I felt then, and still do, that the temper of the times made the measure justified". Lippmann's quick assent to DeWitt's wishes contradicts his standing in the eyes of many scholars as "the most wise and forceful spokesman for objectivity" in journalism.

Indeed it was Lippmann who wrote that "men who have lost their grip upon the relevant facts of their environment are the inevitable victims of agitation and propaganda. The quack, the charlatan, the jingo, and the terrorist can flourish only where the audience is deprived of independent access to information".

The government and the military capably filled the role of charlatan as the period between Pearl Harbour and Executive Order 9066 unfolded, encouraging stories of decisiveness even as they wavered about the correct course of action. But for their part, reporters did not, to use Hosokawa's words, begin "baying like a pack of wolves on a hot trail."

They gradually fell into the role of "guard dog" discussed by Donohue, Tichenor, and Olien, focusing for at least a short time on the patriotism shown by Japanese-Americans. Only as the crisis unfolded - and the government deployed a policy to deal with it - did print reporters shift coverage to the fifth column threat fabricated by officials. We turn now to a detailed textual analysis of how this coverage unfolded.

AN ORGANIZED CHALLENGE

Two seemingly paradoxical strands of news coverage emerge immediately after Pearl Harbour: the first focused on efforts by Japanese-Americans to show their patriotism and loyalty to the United States and their support of the U.S war effort; the second revolved around glowing reports by journalists on efforts by law enforcement officials to detain Japanese nationals and Japanese-Americans.

Fiske might argue that the competing strands of coverage were a by-product of the "unruly" nature of a story that was still taking shape. Like the law enforcement officials working to develop a policy for dealing with Japanese-Americans, print journalists were trying to make enough sense of events to provide adequate coverage for their readers.

By writing at great length about efforts to detain Japanese-Americans, reporters reminded their readers that local, state, and federal officials still had the ability to "create security systems" - in short, to protect American citizens. Donohue, Tichenor, and Olien note that reporters "are on guard against all intruders so long as the authorities are acting in unison and the power relationships among them are stable".

A cynic might argue that law enforcement officials wanted to create the illusion of instability in order to muster support for their containment efforts. While the threat to national security never existed, there probably was a sincere belief on the part of law enforcement officials that the nation was in danger. But instead of trying to stem the "confusion about who is running things,", officials, still trying to craft a policy in the wake of Pearl Harbour, decided to put a bit of manufactured "confusion" to work for them in order to sustain their version of stability. And instead of examining the validity of the government's claims, journalists, who themselves were trying to manage coverage of the story, accepted and disseminated the information. Thus, on December 8, 1941, a page one story in the Los Angeles Times was headlined "Japanese Aliens Roundup Starts." The story, placed next to a story on the reaction of Los Angeles residents to the attack on Pearl Harbour, told of how "a great man hunt was underway," as the FBI sought "300 alien Japanese suspected of subversive activities".

In this story, like many of the others reviewed here, journalists quoted only federal and local law enforcement officials. The reporter described how FBI agents "grabbed" eighteen Japanese-Americans in West Los Angeles and how the "roundup" was the culmination of "months of investigation by FBI agents" led by Special Agent Richard Hood, who had been busy preparing "an index file of suspicious Japanese."

Federal officials, the story said, "planned to hold persons rounded up at various outlying police stations.until a concentration camp is decided upon." Here, the federal government's policy was still forming; nevertheless, journalists showed an early tendency to "sound the alarm" about the as yet unknown threat.

As Donohue, Tichenor, and Olien argue, "[m]aximum uncertainty in the structure occurs when countervailing groups have the capacity to challenge the established power, and thereby raise a realistic possibility that the power relationships may be altered".

But as noted earlier, this threat was manufactured; by reporting what would become an ongoing tally of arrests, reporters allowed federal and state officials to convey the false sense that the nation's position of power was uncertain - that Japanese-Americans living on the West Coast would inevitably alter the nation's power structure.

Thus, even as law enforcement officials were coming to grips with the ramifications of Pearl Harbour, reporters seemed to be creating conditions conducive to an "official version" of events. As we will see, the "intensity" of reporting about the incarceration of Japanese-Americans would increase as days passed.

In addition, the December 8 Times story focused on how the problem of Japanese-Americans living in the area impacted local officials, not JapaneseAmericans themselves or the system of government in place. As Donohue, Tichenor, and Olien note, "guard dog media display a tendency to concentrate on individuals while accepting the structure". But the December 8 issue of the Times included a page two story that exemplifies the second theme seen in the newspapers reviewed here after the attack on Pearl Harbour: the loyalty and patriotism shown by Japanese American citizens. Under the two-column headline "Japanese-Americans Pledge Loyalty to United States," the story told of how the Japanese American Citizens League (JACL) pledged its "fullest cooperation and its facilities to the United States Government".

In a statement, the JACL deplored the attack, and urged FDR to declare war on Japan. The story quoted Shuji Fujii, editor and publisher of Doho, a Japanese newspaper, as saying that Japanese-Americans would be loyal to the United States. Fujii made his feelings known in a telegram to FDR. Also quoted was Yasuchi Sakimoto, an official with the Japanese Fishermen's Association.

Sakimoto said that his members, many of whom would come under fire as the government began manufacturing a fifth column threat, would "turn to agriculture as a means of support during the present conflict". On the same page, the Times ran a story about an apology from the Japanese consul to Los Angeles, Kenji Nakauchi, for Japan's actions. The reporter referred to Nakauchi as "slight" and "bespectacled" in the second paragraph of the story.

In response to the reporter's question, Nakauchi said 20,000 "Japanese nationals" and the same number of Nisei lived in the Los Angeles area. Under a two-column photo of Nakauchi in the centre of the page reading a copy of the Times with an enormous headline reading "War! Japs Bomb U.S. Base" was a caption that told readers Nakauchi was "surprised and shocked" about the attack.

Internment camps were not necessary, he said, especially since German and Italian Americans living in Vancouver were not interned when war with Germany began. Nakauchi was the subject of a shorter story in the December 9 Times which reported that he was "probably the calmest Japanese in Los Angeles."

A third loyalty-related Times story on December 8 told readers that it was "business as usual" in the Little Tokyo section of Los Angeles. "[T]he Japanese populace went about its ordinary Sunday business with an air of resigned calm" despite a steady, daylong flow of curious sightseers, the reporter wrote. News of the attack "failed-on the surface at least-to create much of a stir," according to the reporter. Japanese-Americans "were discussing the news in little knots on street corners." The story concluded with the news that a Committee of Eleven had formed "to maintain loyalty to the United States on the part of the Japanese population here". Local law enforcement officials did not take Japanese American citizens at their word.

The next day, federal, state, and local officials closed all Japanese-owned businesses in the district. The pejorative language used by Times reporters carried over from the previous day's coverage: "little clusters of Japanese gathered to discuss the wholesale display of American authority". Page five of the December 9 Times featured a five-column photo of seven JACL members and Los Angeles Mayor Bowron.

Ken Matsumoto of the JACL is seen holding the American flag; the photo's heading reads "Citizens Offer Loyalty Pledge to Flag." The accompanying story, headlined "Japanese-Americans Ready to Aid Nation," included a statement from the JACL's Anti-Axis Committee which read in part: "the enemy will try to sabotage our usefulness by inciting race hysteria. Let us be vigilant".

A story on the same page told of efforts by Los Angeles school officials to deal with the antiJapanese sentiment shown by many students. Their plan was a response to rumors circulating about everything from school closures to bombing raids. In a particularly ironic statement, Los Angeles School Superintendent Kersey said "the spreading of inflammatory rumors is a powerful weapon of the adversary to undermine morale".

The article talked about everything but easing the strain felt by Japanese-American students, other than a closing quote from Kersey that a "continuing spirit of tolerance should be shown to all who actively support the ideals we are defending".

It is tempting to applaud journalists for creating a tenor of tolerance in their coverage of events in the days after Pearl Harbour. However, their approach serves an important "guard dog" function: it tries to inspire readers to feel the sense of "local cohesion" that Donohue, Tichenor, and Olien discuss.

Thus, stories about loyalty and patriotism shown by Japanese Americans were in fact a tool used by print journalists to help officials keep order until a policy emerged. As they tried to make sense of Pearl Harbour, officials simply did not need the commotion or controversy-at least not yet.

Like the Times, the Chronicle on December 8 gave a prominent position (the bottom of page one) to a bylined story about Japanese-American attempts to prove loyalty to the United States. The Chronicle article went to greater lengths to show how strenuously Japanese-Americans would back the United States - and how far they had to go to do it. The three-deck headline read: "We Are Loyal Americans - We Must Prove It to All of You".

Ironically, the photo accompanying the story showed Hangiro Fujii, a Japanese national and a local business owner, being led away by San Francisco police officers. Chronicle reporter Milton Silverman led the story with a quote (a rarity in news stories) from JACL President Saburo Kido: "The hour is here. We are Americans!" After delivering his message of patriotism to the fifty-six JACL chapters around the county, Kido "walked away from the radio. He smiled - as he and his people have always smiled when they are tense and worried. He thought of the Japan has never seen". Kido thought of "the new Japanese-Americans, now, who were born in this country, who are American citizens, who have a new loyalty to face." Silverman assumes, of course, that Japanese-American citizens had to prove their allegiance to the United States.

But he quoted Kido as saying just that: Japanese-Americans "have been proclaiming their loyalty - the time to prove their true feelings has arrived." Eight paragraphs into the story, Silverman underscored the distinction made by the photo of Fujii; Kido, he said, "speaks for most of the 150,000 Japanese in this country.

Most of them - 70 per cent of them - are American, born in this country." As if reassuring his readers that their Japanese-American neighbours were not a threat, Silverman made clear that "most of them have never seen Japan, can't read or speak Japanese".

Older Japanese, including Toyoji Abe, publisher of the New World-Daily Sun, a Japanese-language newspaper, know "that their children owe no loyalty to Japan: They are Americans." Silverman quoted Abe as saying that he hoped "to remain in this country as a law-abiding resident, co-operating wherever possible with the American authorities," an attitude he claimed was shared by other Japanese-Americans.

Upon hearing of Pearl Harbour, Silverman wrote, "these men swallowed the most bitter pill they could imagine. They discovered their new country was attacked by their old country, and they made their decisions. They went American". Patriotism and loyalty were also the themes of a four-column San Francisco Chronicle photo of a group of Japanese-American soldiers huddled around a car, listening to war reports on the radio.

The banner above the photo read "Japanese Would Fight Japan," even though the soldiers were correctly identified in the caption as Japanese-Americans. "In a few months," the caption read, "they may be fighting on, and against, the soil their parents left." But like Kido and Abe, quoted in Silverman's story, "there was no hesitancy in this group," the caption read. "The attack was treacherous. The counter-attack should be relentless."

For the moment, Japanese-Americans were still a significant part of the news frame constructed by journalists covering the impact of Pearl Harbour. They had been given the chance to show their patriotism, even if journalists had in effect deployed their loyalty in order to help officials maintain order and cohesion. In addition, these early stories served a more destructive purpose: they marginalized - or, as Gitlin might argue, "domesticated"- Japanese-Americans, even though they posed no threat, and were, for the most part, loyal citizens.

In their coverage, journalists created two groups of Japanese-Americans: the officials and the masses; only official, high-ranking Japanese-American officials were quoted, a finding consonant with Donohue, Tichenor, and Olien's claim that conflict is reported only when it involves "dominant powers or power blocs". If there was any anti-American sentiment on the part of Japanese-Americans, it was not covered. Moreover, the average Japanese-American citizen appeared in stories as a cartoon-like, flag waving caricature. With this part of the story established, journalists were now primed to "sound the alarm" about the threat allegedly posed by Japanese nationals.

They soon moved beyond Japanese-American patriotism, beyond what Barthes (1973) calls "inoculation." Reporters allowed Japanese-Americans - for Barthes, "radical voices" - "a controlled moment of speech," one which ensured that "the social body [was] strengthened and not threatened by the contrast between it and the radical".

The guard dog function also offers a possible explanation for journalists' willingness to cover this angle: reporters often act as "fair weather friends for those with marginal positions of power". Journalists shed light on Japanese-American patriotism only until the government developed a policy for dealing with them.

Further, even in stories with a patriotic themes, reporters cited "official" Japanese-American sources in order to better manage the story, a practice that would continue, even when Japanese-Americans were nearly absent from the pages of these newspapers.

Eventually, the lives of Japanese-Americans would be "exnominated," to use Barthes' term. Homages to Japanese-American loyalty would end abruptly as coverage focused on the government's effort to win the war. Journalists continued their extensive coverage of roundup efforts. A page one headline in the December 8 Chronicle announced "Japanese in the U.S.: S.R Joins the Nation in Rounding Up Suspicious Characters and Some Business Men".

The reporter gave the local roundup a sense of national context, leading with "federal agents and troops moved into Japanese communities from San Francisco to Norfolk, Virginia, [and] Alaska to the Panama Canal shortly after noon yesterday and took into custody an undisclosed number of Japanese nationals."

The Chronicle story touched on incarceration efforts in San Diego, Sacramento, and New York. Police blocked off little Tokyo in Los Angeles, referred to in the story as "headquarters for 60,000 Japanese in Southern California. The Times reporter noted that "traffic was halted on First Street" in Little Tokyo in order to "prevent incidents". The Chronicle reported that "a number of people were picked up" by law enforcement officials, a fact missed or not included in the Little Tokyo story by the Times reporter.

The focus here is still on individual law enforcement officials exerting power, as Donohue, Tichenor, and Olien would argue. Nowhere is the structure from which their power emanates examined or challenged. Moreover, reporters were writing less about Japanese-Americans as individuals; Japanese-Americans were reduced to the number of people rounded up during a raid.

This suggests a corollary to the "guard dog" function: while conflict is reported to the extent that it affects individuals, those creating the conflict - even if that conflict is imagined or unrealized - are represented by journalists as a group of faceless, nameless individuals.

As law enforcement officials rounded up Japanese nationals, journalists began to engage in what Fiske calls "claw back"; they attempted to mediate this turn of events "into the dominant value system without losing [its] authenticity". The language used by the Chronicle reporter in the story cited earlier, for example, reinforces a positive image of law enforcement officials. The reporter wrote that a Japanese man "was hustled" into the local immigration station; FBI agents "swooped down" on a predominantly Japanese part of San Francisco.

Agents also arrested a man who was the "head man" of the local Japanese "colony" and who was also the editor of a Japanese newspaper. The article also gives a glowing description of how law enforcement officials "threw a blockade around the big Japanese fishing villages" on Terminal Island in Los Angeles Harbour.

Japanese fishermen coming home from the day's work "were herded into wire enclosures" by soldiers. To be sure, government officials were acting outside their traditional roles by rounding up Japanese-Americans, which in part explains the extensive coverage by journalists, the guard dog theory argues. Reporting would become even more intense when the federal government moved into the uncharted territory of internment.

FACTORS AFFECTING MEDIA COVERAGE

A somewhat different though complementary view of the phenomenon of popular-culture culpability is seen from the perspective of Shoemaker and Reese. Their approach examines how media content is influenced by factors in the context in which it is created.

Though one could view their theoretical perspective as examining media content as shaped by external social processes in a unidirectional (external forces lead to media content) manner, we argue that their theory can be expanded to examine the interrelated, multidirectional, dynamic relations between all elements-content, producers, public.

In Mediating the Message, Shoemaker and Reese identify five major spheres of influence on media content, from the most microscopic to the most macroscopic. We use these labels to identify sources of influence on the producers of news content as well as on the content itself. Though the labels are presented individually, we argue for their overlapping, multidirectional relationship with content as journalists go about the social practice of determining how to cover "the news." We introduce the levels of influence here briefly and will then apply them to each of the three events examined in this chapter.

The most microscopic level of influence on media content is the individual level, that is, the influence exerted by the individual reporter or columnist, the copy editor, and the editor-each person who has a hand in creating the news content. This can include deciding what constitutes news, selecting the angle of the story, writing the story, and editing it. Some of the factors that influence content decisions at the individual level are personal feelings, tastes and preferences, values, opinions, and the professional backgrounds and training of those directly involved in content decisions. The media routines level focuses on the routines, or standard procedures, for gathering and disseminating news. Among the influences found at this level are news values-those characteristics that make an event newsworthy, such as deviance from the norm, sensationalism, prominence, proximity, timeliness, conflict or controversy, human interest, and impact on audience members or society as a whole.

Other media routines include objectivity, the five "Ws" (answering who, what, when, where, and why in every report), pack journalism, competition, reliance on other media for information or for whole stories, localism (getting the local angle on a story that takes place far away), simplicity (offering pat "answers" because complex situations are hard to explain and hard for readers to understand quickly), and over-reliance on a handful of sources.

The next level of influence, moving towards a more macroscopic perspective, is the organizational level. Analysis at the organizational level focuses on the impact of policies, managers, and owners of the organization in which the media content is produced. It is difficult to discuss influences at this level, as we do not know what went on in each newsroom during coverage of these three events. However, the opinions of upper management or concerns of those in the circulation or advertising-sales departments can influence coverage, as can organizational policies such as the degree of autonomy allowed to each reporter.

The extramedia level has to do with elements and factors outside of the media organizations themselves, such as news sources, advertisers, government, interest groups, and the audience. This level includes actual, direct influences as well as the influence that news media personnel's perceptions of what these entities might do or how they might feel that also shape content. While influence of advertisers might weigh against extensive blaming of popular culture in news coverage, for example, pressure from some interest groups and activists, as well as governmental concern, could weigh towards the pursuit of this angle.

In terms of perceptions of audience preferences, some journalists may believe that audiences want to see and read about violence, sensationalism, scandal, and the lives of celebrities. This perception could have a profound impact, because giving the audiences "what they want" will presumably sell newspapers and space to advertisers. Thus, angles that have popular appeal may be advanced while more esoteric or abstract angles, such as the notion that society in general is responsible or that a complex nexus of forces are at fault, may take a back seat.

The notion of audience preference is also a cultural one. de Mooij argues the one such preference that is culturally bound is America's adherence to a cause-and-effect paradigm. She argues that it is a cultural norm in the United States to expect to have a logical explanation for any given event and that any event has concrete and measurable answers to the question of what caused it. Journalists, if following this cultural norm or if presuming audiences follow it, may provide a concrete explanation rather than leave the tragedies unexplained. Subscribing to this cause-and-effect paradigm can be viewed as an individual influence on the part of reporters and editors, an extramedia influence that takes the shape of conceptions about audience preferences, or an ideological influence that entails broad-based cultural and societal beliefs.

The ideological level includes the influences that broad systems of beliefs and values have on the news-gathering process. Among the factors at play here are notions of "elite" and "popular" media, representations that define "mainstream" and "deviant" content, and the concept of hegemony. The latter suggests that entities enjoying political and economic power in existing societal structure will act in the interest of thwarting social change in order to protect their dominant status. We predict that these three case studies will show the use of defensive strategies when other media are, indeed, blamed.

Through the use of labels such as "tabloid," "paparazzi," and "trash TV" to draw theoretically distinct lines, journalists may construct readings of their own stories as the dominant discourse and those of "tabloid" media and "trash TV" as deviant.

A subtext exists in this type of criticism that suggests a need to save people from their own tastes in media and popular culture. This is similar to the points raised by Bird and Jensen above, and is the central theoretical element of the study at hand. de Mooij's suggestion that as part of American culture, we-as members of society-need someone or something to blame whenever there is a tragedy, also has implications for hegemony and social order. In order for members of society to feel secure about the world around them, there has to be a rational cause, with a clearly identifiable source of blame, for each event. Thus, it is much more satisfying to place blame on a specific, tangible targetin this case, the non-elite media-rather than advancing the more unsettling notion that something is amiss in society at large.

The first case study involves the death of Princess Diana of Wales and the automobile accident that took her life and the lives of Dodi al Fayed and Henri Paul on August 31,1997. The accident occurred shortly after midnight in Paris when the Mercedes Benz in which the princess and her friend were travelling crashed in a tunnel near the Seine River. Dodi al Fayed and Henri Paul, the driver, were found dead at the scene. The princess died a few hours later of injuries she sustained in the crash.

The event was reported in newspapers around the world. The larger U.S. and U.K. newspapers gave extensive coverage to the event in the days following the crash. For example, on the first day of coverage The London Observer ran 28 articles, The New York Daily News ran 10 articles, and The Atlanta Journal and Constitution ran four articles.

This case study is based on analysis of those articles and others that were published in English-language newspapers from the day of the crash, August 31, 1997, through the day of Diana's funeral, September 6, 1997, when the focus of coverage shifted from the accident to the funeral. The articles were retrieved from the General News archive of LEXIS-NEXIS Academic Universe. In all, 507 stories were reviewed for relevant content, and those with relevant content were studied more closely.

Often, the first news reports of a tragic and unexpected event will present only the basic facts of the story, answering the fundamental journalistic questions of who was involved, what happened, when it happened, and where it happened, without speculation as to the causes of the event. It usually takes another day or more for the "how" and "why" questions to be answered.

However, this was not the case in the early reporting on Princess Diana's death. Answers to the "how" and "why" questions were included in the initial reports of the event because tabloid-press photographers were said to have been chasing the princess's car at the time of the accident.

Approximately 11 photographers, sources said, some on motorcycles and others in a car, set out after Diana and Dodi's Mercedes when it left the Ritz hotel in Paris. The photographers were apparently trying to get pictures that would confirm rumors of a romance between Diana and Dodi.

Several sources in the earliest stories claimed that the photographers caused the accident. Among them were Paris police, unspecified police, French journalists (their sources unnamed), a photographer for a London paper, Agence-France Presse (the French news agency), and British reporters.

No eyewitnesses to the crash were quoted in the early coverage-in other words, no source knew for certain that the photographers had actually caused the accident (and some sources even claimed that the car had lost the photographers). In spite of this, the idea that the photographers caused the accident became a part of every story reporting the facts of the event. The Boston Heraldbegan an article by Joseph Mallia (Aug. 31,1997) with "Princess Diana and her companion Dodi Fayed were killed in a high-speed car crash early today in a tunnel near the Seine River in Paris, as their Mercedes was being pursued by photographers."

The Hindu of India began a story (no byline, Aug. 31) with "Britain's Princess Diana and her millionaire companion, Dodi El-Fayed, were killed in a car crash early on Sunday while being chased by photographers on motorcycles in a road tunnel in the French capital Paris." The third paragraph of an Associated Press story that ran in The Buffalo News on August 31 read "The crash happened shortly after midnight in a tunnel along the Seine River at the Pont de l'Aima bridge. It came as paparazzi-the commercial photographers who constantly tailed Dianafollowed her car, police said." During the week after the fatal crash, when coverage of the event was at its most intense, nearly every article contained at least one source who blamed the producers of popular culture for Diana's death. Among these were family members and family representatives, dignitaries, ordinary citizens, and journalists themselves.

Other sources who blamed "the paparazzi," "the press," "the media," or "the tabloids" (sometimes including tabloid-style television shows) were an Arizona talk-radio host and many of his callers, Britons living in the United States (usually interviewed in pubs), un-named TV commentators, and David Perel, executive editor of the American tabloid The National Enquirer. Perel was quoted in several newspapers as saying that reckless action by the paparazzi probably caused the accident.

Some family members of the crash victims extended the blame to all photographers who pursue celebrities for photos to be printed in tabloid newspapers. Ellen Tumposky and Mike Claffey of The New York Daily News (Aug. 31) reported "The dead Egyptian playboy's father, Mohammed Al-Fayed, blamed the tragedy on the paparazzi, who were being held for questioning by Paris police. There is no doubt in Mr. Al-Fayed's mind that this tragedy would not have occurred but for the press photographers who have dogged and pursued Mr. Fayed and the princess for weeks,' a spokesman for the Egyptian billionaire said."

The Houston Chronicle (byline Houston Chronicle News Services, Aug. 31) reported "(Michael Gibbons), a spokesman for Buckingham Palace, noting that the incident occurred while the couple were being chased by photographers, said it was 'an accident waiting to happen.'... he repeated the palace's anger at the actions of photographers who pursue the royal family around the world." Other family members blamed not only tabloid-press photographers but also the editors and publishers of gossipy tabloid publications. The London Observer was one of the first to report a scathing statement from Diana's brother.

"This is not a time for recriminations," said Earl Spencer, "but I would say that I always believed the press would kill her in the end. But not even I could imagine that they would take such a direct hand in her death as seems to be the case. It would appear that every proprietor and editor of every publication that has paid for intrusive and exploitative photographs of her, encouraging greedy and ruthless individuals to risk everything in pursuit of Diana's image, have blood on their hands today."

None of the first-day stories reporting the reactions of world leaders and diplomats (such as President Clinton, the Singapore government, and the Pope) contained quotes that blamed popular culture. However, on the second day of coverage, several French government officials made statements blaming the paparazzi, as reported in The Hindu (by Vaiju Naravane, Sept. 1).

The president of the French Parliament, the former prime minister, Mr. Laurent Fabius... said that death precipitated by paparazzi proves that "photos, words and attitudes can also, in a certain sense, kill. These people must now face their responsibility."...The government's spokeswoman, Ms. Catherine Trautmann, who is also France's Culture Minister, was more vehement in her denunciation of the paparazzi. Princess Diana was the victim of the stubbornness of the press, she declared.

"The singlemindedness of the press had increased dramatically these past weeks... The circumstances of her death have thrown up questions about the functioning of this profession and above all of our society," Ms. Trautmann added. Among the stories that reported the reactions of ordinary citizens, most contained at least one source who blamed either the paparazzi who pursued the Mercedes or the press in general. Most of these "average-citizen" sources did not distinguish between the popular press and the elite press or their producers, nor did the reporters attempt to make any distinction for the sources. The blame laid by these sources was among the most vitriolic. The New York Daily News (article by Barbara Ross, Aug. 31) reported:

Britons in New York mixed their grief at Princess Diana's death with criticism of the press for its relentless pursuit of her.... Beverly Dorking, 25, of Leeds in northern England, said, "...she's been dogged and hounded by the media. They've been in her face since she was 19, and now they've taken away the world's most popular woman." Nicola Shigley, 24, of northern England, predicted a backlash against the media. She accused the media of spending "the last 10 years trying to put the woman to an end."

The San Diego Union-Tribune (article by Lillian Salazar Leopold, Aug. 31) reported "'The press has a lot to answer for,' said Mary Simpson, also of Liverpool. 'They hounded her to death. Literally, now.'"

The Seattle Times (article by Chris Solomon, Aug. 31) reported "Mitch Lease, 23...reflected bitterly on the circumstances of her death, a chase by photographers. I think the media should have given her a break a long time ago, and now they've killed her.'" The London Observer (article by Roy Greenslade, Aug. 31) reported "In one bitter outburst on BBC TV, a woman demanded that a reporter and his cameraman slop filmmg. 'You've done this Io her,' she screamed. 'You're to blame. The media, the papers, all of you.'" Some articles blamed popular culture by quoting other publications and thereby demonstrating what seemed to be a world-wide consensus as to who was to blame for the tragedy. A London Observer article (byline: "foreign staff," Aug. 31) read:

The French newspaper Liberation gave over its whole front page to a picture of (Diana) with the headline, "One photo too many. "... Italy's La Stampa took up the same theme, stating tersely: "Dead for a photo".... Hong Kong newspapers agonised over their own home-grown paparazzi, with the Oriental Daily News recalling that a local pop singer, Leslie Cheung, had crashed his Porsche while being pursued by photographers. It branded paparazzi as "criminals of a thousand years." The Daily Star, a Bangladesh newspaper, said that "Western press and society will need to embark on a long search of their souls to come to terms with the sense of guilt Diana's death must generate."

Alongside the just-the-facts stories and reaction stories were articles focused primarily on the causes of the accident. Many of these stories found some aspect of popular culture (either the photographers who chased Diana's car that night, tabloid-press photographers in general, tabloid newspapers, the editors and publishers of tabloid newspapers, or any member of the press who had purchased paparazzi photos) to be at fault. The tone of these articles was often angry and disgusted.

Earl Spencer's statement was used in several of these stories as a starting point for further discussion of the role of the paparazzi in Diana's death. Dave Walker, writing for TAe Arizona Republic (Sept. 1), began such a story by asking "Do the media have blood on their hands for the death of Princess Diana? That's what her brother, Earl Spencer, suggested in the aftermath of the car wreck..."

Walker went on to cite several sources who agreed with Spencer, including Dodi's father, Mohamed al Fayed, unnamed network television commentators, and Phoenix-area talk-radio host Charles Goyette, whom Walker quoted: "'The media are clearly to blame,' said Goyette, summing up the majority opinion among his callers. 'The consumers of this trash don't have the culpability, the media do.'"

An article in The Glasgow Herald (by Catherine Macleod, Sept. 1) quoted a source who followed Spencer's lead and blamed all the producers of tabloid newspapers: "...the Prince of Wales's biographer Jonathan Dimbleby said: 'It isn't only the reporters and photographers, it's those who hired them.' He added: 'It's the editors and proprietors who too often, offer glossy excuses about the public interest who need now to examine their consciences.'"

Some of the stories that discussed causes were actually editorials expressing the views of the writer or writers. For example, The London Observer (no by-line, Aug. 31) expressed the following opinion: "Anyone in the British Press who has bought and used the pictures snatched by paparazzi on so many previous utterly private occasions helped ensure that the ravening pack would be on the trail on Saturday night." Some of these articles were written in a narrative stylo, retelling the facts of the story dramatically while characterizing the photographers as degenerates. For example, Michael Daly of The New York Daily News (Aug. 31) wrote:

No matter how fast her car sped through the Paris night, the paparazzi on the motorbikes were sure to stay right behind her, for she was with the man said to be her lover.... The following Sunday, she was swarmed by those only interested in violating her private life.... They were still after the couple when she arrived in France.

The hounds kept baying, right up to early this morning, when motorcycles sped after Diana's car along the Seine. Her pursuers were right out of the 1961 movie "La Dolce Vita," in which a photographer named Paparazzo chases his prey on a motorscooter.... They chased the biggest score ever right to her death. The frenzy that began with "The Kiss" ended in two children being left without their mother.

Similarly, Luke Harding, Owen Bowcott, John Hooper, Paul Webster, Alex Bellos, Stephen Bates, and Chris Mihill of The London Observer (Aug. 31) wrote:

Even before Princess Diana and Dodi Fayed had strolled through the baroque central corridor of the Ritz hotel in Paris...the paparazzi were lurking in wait.... (Diana and Dodi's) presence was common knowledge among the small, ruthless, multilingual band of photographers who pursue her, very lucratively, for a living.... Around 7 p.m. on Saturday Diana left the Ritz in a chauffeur-driven car to do some shopping in the Champs Elysee. The press pack were, reportedly, in close pursuit....

Quite a few stories blamed "the press" in general or "the media" in general, not distinguishing the mainstream press from the tabloid press.

Among these were stories reporting that Diana herself had condemned the practices of the British press in an interview published in a French newspaper the week before the accident. J. Frank Lynch of The Atlanta Journal and Constitution (Aug. 31) reported "In Great Britain, 'the press is ferocious," Diana said in the article in the French daily Le Monde. 'It forgives nothing and is only hunting down mistakes. Each act is twisted; each gesture is criticized.'"

A number of stories about the causes of Diana's death divided the blame among several culprits. One of these culprits was Henri Paul, the driver of the Mercedes. On the first day of coverage, many articles noted that Paul had been driving at a speed well above the limit and that he lost control of the car, thus implying that the accident was at least partly his fault.

When the news of Paul's very high blood-alcohol level (which was more than three times the French legal limit) was released on day two, he became the target of finger-pointing in many more articles. However, none of the stories that blamed Paul let the producers of popular culture off the hook completely. An editorial in The Arizona Republic (no byline, Sept. 3) argued:

The swift and reckless rush to judgement, the desire to fix certain blame for the death of Diana, is also destructive and promises to leave victims. Misplaced blame might mask sorrow's pain, but it does not heal.

Diana Spencer, queen of celebrity, died from the impaired judgement of millions. We'll name a few. The paparazzi, a subset of photojournalists identified first and perhaps forever as the villains who ended the strange, fairy-tale existence of a lovely young woman, continue to receive disproportionate blame. Seven photographers face some type of charges related to the fatal crash.... So what of the judgement of those editors and publishers who buy sleaze and resell it under some loose definition of news? Impaired?

Morally warped? Yes.... And, so whal of the judgement of millions of readers who purchase the product now blamed for the death of a princess? Impaired? Warped? Yes.... However, in this tragedy, the person whose impaired judgement seems most responsible for the death of Princess Diana, is the man behind the wheel of the car carrying her and her boyfriend....

One of the few articles to seriously consider the culpability of Henri Paul was published by The Boston Globe (Sept. 1). (This story also contained several sources who blamed the paparazzi at the scene and the press in general.) Author Peter S. Canellos wrote:

Ralph Whitehead, a journalism professor at the University of Massachusetts, said all the hand-wringing over the misdeeds of media is "a momentary hysteria."

Unless proof emerges that paparazzi on motorcycles actually interfered with the progress of Diana's car, responsibility for the accident should rest with the driver, he said. The Mercedes limousine was traveling faster than 60 miles per hour-perhaps much faster-in a tunnel where the speed limit is 30, police said. The princess and her companion, Dodi Fayed, did not appear to be wearing seatbelts.

"What would Diana and the rest of the people in the car have lost if they'd been overtaken by photographers?" Whitehead said. "If you're a celebrity, you have a right to regard the paparazzi as a pain in the neck. But it's not the right response to put your life in jeopardy by speeding away."

For a few days, there was a bit of a tug of war between those sources representing the photographers (primarily their lawyers) and those representing the driver (the Fayed family and Paul's co-workers). Some of the stories printed on days two through seven offered opinions as to which party deserved more blame, while others blamed Western society as a whole for its fascination with celebrities.

In an article called "Time Has Come to Point Finger in Right Direction," Steve Wilson of The Arizona Republic (Sept. 3) wrote "I would like to interrupt all the finger-pointing in Princess Diana's death-do the paparazzi or the drunken driver deserve the most blame?-for this important message: It's the culture, stupid. Or more precisely, it's the stupid, celebrity-obsessed culture."

When the playwright Arnold Wesker spent several months at the offices of the *Sunday Times,* gathering background material for his drama *The Journalists,* he decided to produce an account of his observations. The resulting slim volume caused such offence to some of those he observed that its publication was held up for five years. This was his conclusion:

The journalist knows his world is among the least perfect of all imperfect worlds. Most are raring to get out and write books-the best of them do, frustrated by small canvases and the butterfly life of their hard earned thoughts and words. Wesker was not, suffice to say, overly impressed by what he found.

Indeed, his book conveys a sense of bemusement that grown men (as national newspaper journalists in the main then were) could want to subject themselves to such demeaning work. More than a quarter of a century later, many people outside the media seem still to share that view. The industry has changed out of all recognition: relatively large numbers of journalists at all levels are women and not a few are black; and technological advance, long delayed while the trade unions remained strong, has transformed the job.

Yet the popular image of journalism appears often to remain that of the unscrupulous, dog-eat-dog press of 1920s Chicago, immortalised on stage and screen in *The Front Page*. There is undoubtedly a fear of the media, but above all there is a lack of understanding. And nowhere is that lack more evident than in the world of social policy.

NO TABLETS OF STONE

Probably the single most common misconception about what I do is that I do it to edict, or that it is at least pre-determined according to policy positions and protocols. One assumption is that my editor decrees which stories are to be covered, how they should be treated and what editorial line is to be taken.

Alternatively, because of the *Guardian's* liberal image, other people assume such matters are thrashed out in policy discussions involving me and other colleagues. Either way, there is a widespread belief that I approach the working week with a shopping list of news and feature issues to be written about, and with detailed briefing on the angle to take on each. The reality is that papers are much more chaotic operations than their readers ever imagine. While it would be wrong to say there is no top-down editorial diktat, the great bulk of day-to-day decisions about coverage are taken by individual writers or desk editors without reference to colleagues, let alone the editor.

There are two circumstances in which the editor will insist on something being reported. One is when the paper is running a campaign on a particular issue, as with the *Independent's* focus in the mid-1990s on the emerging pattern of abuse of children and young people in residential care over the previous thirty years. To sustain the momentum of such a campaign, developments which ordinarily might not meet the criteria for publication will be carried in what is, in effect, reserved editorial space.

The other circumstance is what is known as an 'editor's must', a term laden with significance and with implied adverse consequences should expectations not be fulfilled. As the words suggest, they refer to a story that must be carried, no matter what. This can range from a pet hobbyhorse to something the editor half heard on the radio that morning.

For many years, one national paper would regularly carry reports of the most obscure issues to do with sailing on the River Crouch in Essex. More common is an elliptical reference by the editor, of a deputy, to an 'interesting' issue. This will be taken by their lieutenants as a clear instruction to ensure the said issue is covered fully in the next edition.

By and large, though, journalists take on-the-run decisions about what to cover, and what not, on the basis not of any written or even verbal orders or guidelines but according to an almost intuitive sense of what is important and what fits the bill for the paper in question. For the *Guardian,* with its particular constituency, this means a greater-than-average interest (though not as great as people often think) in social policy issues. For the *Daily Mail,* with its well-known stance on 'traditional' family values, this means a bigger appetite for stories about marriage, divorce and abortion.

This is not to say that the process of putting together a paper-or, for that matter, a TV or radio programme-is without structure. On a national paper, the day begins with an editorial conference at which desk editors representing the various departments of news and features review that morning's product, assess the efforts of the competition and, usually, pat themselves on the back for a job well done.

The conference then turns to the next day's issue, with each department-essentially home news, foreign, features, city and sport-outlining the events and issues they plan to cover.

At this stage, the listing may simply be, 'Home Office press conference on crime figures', or it may be a more detailed, 'Crime up: Home Secretary to announce new measures'. (With the modern trend of pre-briefing, rare indeed is the announcement not already trailed in the press by government spin doctors.) And listing at this point does not necessarily mean that the proposed article will end up in print.

News and features lists change as the day goes on and plans can be torn up and rewritten well into the evening. Indeed, when the first editions of the dailies become available after 10 p.m.-there is a swap system among the main titles-good stories in the rivals are picked out, checked for veracity and written up for later editions. What is read in the first version of the paper in Cornwall and Scotland can, therefore, differ considerably from what is read in later versions in London.

Setting the Leader Line

While the morning meeting is the main planning forum, there are further, though smaller, editorial conferences as the day wear on and the pace of the operation picks up. These include a leader conference at which the senior journalists who write the editorial comments-usually not, contrary to popular belief, the editor-decide which issues to tackle.

They may discuss what line to take, although much again is left to the individual's assumptions about the paper's values. Exceptionally, there may be a general debate among the staff about a leader line-on the merits of the Gulf

War, for example-but the usual pattern is for the leader writer to discuss the issues with the relevant specialist correspondent.

As with so much else to do with the media, those on the outside, looking in, tend to overestimate the sophistication of what is a fairly crude process.

In an analysis of the *Guardian*'s coverage of alleged ritual child abuse in Rochdale in 1990, Meryl Aldridge has remarked upon the fluctuating leader line: here supportive of social services, there critical in a 'very un-*Guardian*-like way. She concludes that the position the paper eventually arrived at, supporting the families involved against social services, may have had a historical basis: Yet over Rochdale, after an initial struggle, the paper leapt to the parents' defence, ditching the concerns of its stereotype readership. One possible explanation of this apparent paradox is the newspaper's roots, as the *Manchester Guardian,* in the northwest. As a result, over Rochdale, it reacted more like a local paper than a liberal national broadsheet.

The prosaic truth is that the varying leader line through the saga reflected the differing views of two leader writers. The apparent supremacy of one position in such situations results less from informal, intellectual debate, more from practical considerations such as one party going on leave.

Where News Comes from

Whereas general reporters are assigned to stories chosen by a news editor, specialists typically propose stories to the news desk. Whether proposals are taken up depends on the individual news editor's view and the number of story ideas already on the newslist.

Most days, I will put forward two or three ideas in the expectation of being asked to write one or two, of which one may get into the paper. I rely heavily, indeed too heavily, for story ideas on institutional sources.

That means Whitehall, leading professional associations and, increasingly under the contract culture, voluntary groups. Pressure not to miss a government announcement is an enormous incentive to do the job from your desk, and a corresponding disincentive to take time out to see social policy in practice. People are often surprised, and by implication disappointed, at how little I see on the ground of what I write about in the abstract. It is a failing I readily admit to, though I like to think I witness more practice than do most of my peers. Other sources of material are the 'trade' press, the specialist weeklies or monthlies, and tip-offs from readers. The Thatcher/Major years, when there was a clampdown on the passing of information by public servants to the media, undoubtedly slowed the flow of tips and certainly that of confidential documents.

It was on charges of breach of confidentiality that one of my best sources, nurse Graham Pink, was eventually disciplined by NHS managers in Stockport-though not, thankfully, before his powerful testimony of hospital elderly care had already had a profound impact on public and political opinion.

The Labour government elected in 1997 promised protection for whistle-blowers, as in fairness had the Major administration. But experience of the first years of Labour rule suggested that public sector workers were, if anything, even less likely to pass information than they had been under the Conservatives. This obviously had some political basis, in that sources have very often been trade union activists who would at least have been giving Labour the benefit of the doubt, but it also suggested that there was to be no return to the days of brown paper envelopes arriving at newspaper offices by the sackful.

Working as a Specialist

As a specialist, my job is to patrol the areas for which I am responsible. I am there to make sure that the paper does not miss stories that appear elsewhere, to produce exclusive stories of our own and to provide interpretation of, and sometimes informed comment on, emerging issues.

I also see my role in part as acting as a bridge between the paper and the interest groups, professional and user, on my patch. In this respect, the trick is to be and remain a perfectly balanced bridge, leaning in particular not too far towards the 'client group', for want of a better term.

The most heinous crime a specialist can commit is to go native, to become too closely identified with their professional sources. This is not generally a question of corruption, certainly not in social policy, but it can over time become easy to adopt professional perspectives on issues such as resource constraints-*i.e.* there is never enough-than to question the use of resources already available.

One information source that never dries up, sadly, is the constant stream of people dissatisfied, and very often angry, with the treatment they have received from public services. Indeed, the growth of a more consumerist attitude towards such services, in contrast to the gratitude of the '1945 generation' at having any services at all, seems to be fuelling dissatisfaction. I receive calls and letters every day, almost without fail, from people who feel at their wits' end with social security, the Child Support Agency, the NHS and, most often, social services. The most distressing approaches are those from parents who believe their children have unjustifiably been taken into care. Rarely can such complaints be explored, not least because of social services' reluctance to discuss them on grounds of client confidentiality. But it is difficult to find the time to look into any grievance.

Contrary to widespread supposition, specialists in the press are very much one-person shows: there is no research backup and rarely any designated understudy on the general reporting staff. It would be quite possible to spend all the time pursuing readers' problems. In order to do the job, you end up pursuing almost none.

The good Story

What makes a good story? It seems to be to the eternal bafflement of social policy professionals that good practice does not win headlines; that journalists are not falling over themselves to report, 'Child saved from abuse' or 'Patient treated successfully'.

Social services journalist Anne Fry has it about right, 'A good story-contrary to popular social work belief-is not about some worthy policy development, practice initiative or social services personality. It is about raw emotion, disagreement between professionals and, best of all, culpability'.

This came to a head, not for the first time and surely not for the last, in coverage of the early joint reviews of social services departments by the Audit Commission and the Social Services Inspectorate. While many of the first thirty review reports were positive, media attention focused on a handful that were critical, notably those on Sefton, Barking and Dagenham, Sheffield and Coventry. Social services leaders were angered by the imbalance and, at the 1998 social services conference, Rita Stringfellow, chair of the Local Government Association's social affairs and health committee, publicly criticised the 'unhelpful' language being used by this writer and, indeed, by the newly-appointed chief inspector of social services, Denise Platt.

Government ministers sought to blame the media for dwelling on the few negative reports, and ignoring the rest, but the fact was that the Whitehall publicity machine had deliberately played up the negative joint review reports in order to portray the Labour administration as tough on poor social work. If there was a media conspiracy, the politicians were very much party to it.

Culpability is very much top of the media agenda: witness the (usually frustrated) demands for at least one head to roll on publication of every enquiry report into a so-called 'care-in-the-community killing'.

But other factors can serve to raise the level of interest in stories. Research for the Department of Health on communication and the risks to public health has identified ten 'media triggers' likely to make a story about a health risk a major one.

They are:
- Questions of blame
- Alleged secrets and attempted cover-ups
- Human interest through identifiable heroes, villains, dupes, etc. (as well as victims)
- Links with existing high-profile issues or personalities
- Conflict (between experts and/or between experts and the public)
- Signal value: the story as a portent of further ills ('What next?')
- Many people exposed to the risk, even if at low levels ('It could be you!')
- Strong visual impact

- Sex and/or crime
- Snowballing of reportage: the fact that something is a major story is often itself a story, and this becomes self-fuelling as media compete for coverage.

Most of these factors can be said to have general application. But in the field of social policy, I would add an eleventh trigger: that the story has development potential, that it can be turned into something more than the sums of its present parts.

One of the most hilarious, but at the same time cautionary, accounts of this has been written by sociologist Robert Burgess, now Vice-Chancellor at Leicester University. He had been awarded a research grant to lead a study of children's knowledge of nutrition, as part of the Economic and Social Research Council's Nation's Diet initiative.

The first media treatment of this, in a regional daily paper, was fairly accurate. But as the story was picked up, sequentially, by news agencies and other papers, it became increasingly distorted into a shape more to the media's liking. In the end, the *Sun* reported: Din-dins prof hunts chip kids. A professor is to share bags of chips with kids for two years-to find out why they prefer junk food to school dinners. Sociologist Robert Burgess, dubbed Doctor Din-Dins, will visit schools around the country and follow children on lunchtime trips. In a similar vein, though mercifully less extreme, much of the media went into overdrive in December 1997 about the threat to the great British doorstep. This was supposedly posed by amendments to the building regulations to make homes wheelchair accessible.

'Hilda Ogden would be tearing out her curlers-they're planning to do away with the great British doorstep, ' lamented the *Daily Mail*.

The fact that the change would apply only to new properties was played down; that it was part of a bigger package to improve general accessibility and was supported by organisations including the Chartered Institute of Housing, the Royal Institute of British Architects and the Consumers' Association, was scarcely mentioned at all. The converse of this compulsion to push stories beyond their natural limits is to be found in media coverage of the voluntary sector. Here is a burgeoning, £13 billion-slice of the economy, employing almost 500,000 paid staff and at least 3 million volunteers, delivering a fast-growing wedge of public services. Yet it is as if the media do not want the sector to have grown up.

Coverage remains very much stuck in a 1950s charity time warp of good-cause fundraising, lifeboats, guide dogs and helping sick children. Even on the broadsheet national papers, there is a clear antipathy to stories that treat the leading charities as the big businesses they now are. But stories exposing the 'fat-cat' salaries of charity bosses, earning in excess of £65,000 a year for running multi-million-pound operations, are lapped up.

As a specialist correspondent, the challenge is to survive within this environment, observing the unwritten rules about what is a good story and demonstrating obeisance to some of the (least objectionable) prejudices, while keeping faith with your constituency. The tension implicit in this can be very great. It has been with increasingly heavy heart over recent years that I have approached the task of covering enquiry reports on care-in-the-community homicides. On one hand, it has been clear that the reports have been revealing fewer and fewer insights into the underlying problems and have been contributing to a grossly distorted picture of mental health care.

On the other hand, when the rest of the media are carrying the reports in full and gruesome detail, it is simply not an option to argue for no coverage. The compromise is to try to present the issues in as restrained and balanced a way as possible.

This is not to say that, by doing so, you are seeking to protect your professional contacts. Of course it is true that specialists rely on their contacts and cannot afford to risk being cut off by betraying confidence or reporting in an overly hostile manner. But it is impossible to avoid reporting critically, when justified, and experience suggests that most social policy professionals take a mature view of this.

Over the past ten years, I could count on the fingers of one hand the number who have reacted so adversely to something I have written that further working relations have been damaged.

Playing the System

One of the lasting impressions of specialising in this field is how poor the social policy world appears to be at shaping the media agenda. If you remain purely reactive, as too many seem to, coverage tends to be framed by the trigger factors: blame, cover-up and so on. 'But you never print the good news!' comes the protest. And it is undeniably true, as discussed above, that you will never find a paper clearing page one for a graphic account of the successful rehabilitation of a young offender.

But that is not to say that the promotion of positive images is a lost cause. For all the media bias against social workers, and there undoubtedly is such bias, the profession has in recent years been pleasantly surprised to find itself praised for its counselling and other work in the aftermath of civil disasters.

Skilful, proactive handling of the media has even been known to turn near-catastrophe (in every sense) into a veritable public relations triumph, as in the case of the abduction and return of baby Abbie Humphries from the Queen's Medical Centre, Nottingham, in 1994.

So what kind of news and feature ideas am I looking for? The essential answer is anything which offers robust evidence, quantitative or qualitative, of the functioning of both society and the controls upon it. Social welfare agencies are sitting on a wealth of this kind of information, but very rarely do they seek to make use of it. Whitehall has recently woken up to this, beginning quite aggressively to market the social data series held by the Office for National Statistics.

One result has been a much higher media profile for the various official surveys and one-off reports based upon them. While it would be absurd to suggest that a voluntary organisation could match the number-crunching of the Government's statistical arm, even the smallest charity is likely to have sound empirical evidence of the social issues it works with.

Put into the public domain in the right way and at the right time, for timing is a great deal in successful use of the media, such evidence could be invaluable. As regards promotion of good practice, the *Guardian* is unique among national papers in having a weekly supplement, *Society,* devoted to social policy in the broadest sense. Yet, with honourable exceptions such as the Joseph Rowntree Foundation, it is remarkable how few organisations seek to have their work highlighted in this way.

This may reflect fear of being 'stitched-up' by the press, of being drawn on to territory you do not wish to discuss and of saying things you do not mean to say, but I believe the professional magazines encounter a similar reticence. In stark contrast to the private sector, where even the smallest advance of process is trumpeted abroad, those in the public service seem diffident to a fault.

Problems of Client Confidentiality

There is, however, understandable caution about publicity when it might involve identifying service clients. This is one of the principal causes of strain between the media and social policy practitioners. Papers, just as much as TV and radio, are these days looking to personalise policy stories.

If you approach the news desk with a proposal to cover a research report, the first question will be, 'Are there any case studies?' Very often, availability of a case study will be the difference between the paper carrying a substantial article on a report or survey, and carrying nothing at all.

The problem of client confidentiality is clearly greater in some spheres than others. It is perfectly reasonable that people with mental health problems, for example, may be reluctant to be profiled in the press or interviewed by electronic media. But too many social welfare organisations assume automatically that none of their clients would want to be identified. Too often, no effort is made to find case studies or negotiate conditions by which their anonymity could be preserved. While news and features editors naturally prefer people to be named, and indeed pictured, when push comes to shove there is always room for pseudonyms and pictures in silhouette.

Some of the more media-wise charities have absorbed this lesson to good effect: it would be unthinkable of the NSPCC, for one, to issue a report without having lined up a selection of families and/or workers prepared to talk about their relevant experiences.

Even MIND, the mental health charity, is now invariably able to find service-users willing to speak to reporters on one basis or another. Statutory service-providers remain way behind on this, however, and very often refuse even to ask clients about the possibility of co-operating with the media. If they did, they might very well be surprised by the response.

Missing the Trick

Unfortunately, it is not just in terms of failure to help personalise issues that many social welfare organisations are missing a media trick. The bulk of my daily postbag goes straight into the wastebin, very often unread beyond the first couple of lines, because it is hopelessly irrelevant to the interests of a national paper. I receive astounding numbers of press releases about openings of day centres and health units, launches of training packs and Web sites, sponsored events and cheque presentations (complete with cheesy photographs), even though there is not a shred of evidence that my paper ever carries such things.

Many, depressingly, come from public relations consultants doubtless charging fat fees for their special expertise in accessing the media. I also receive considerable numbers of press statements written in jargon impenetrable even to me, let alone the general public, or put together in such an unappealing way that you might conclude there was some intent to discourage interest. This is the opening paragraph of a press release on a revolution in training for the 2 million people working in health and social care:

The two National Training Organisations (NTOs) which are being established for the Personal Social Services and Health Care sectors will work together on key projects and initiatives. The two NTOs, whilst covering distinct areas, also have a range of shared issues and concerns which will benefit from joint working.

This, similarly, is the opening of a press statement on a prestigious international conference of experts on mental illness among older people. It shows all the signs of having been written by a committee. Today...experts in the care of the elderly discussed the enormous challenges which face both the developed and developing worlds in coping with the serious mental health problems of aging populations. They paid particular attention to the burden of dementia, the illness most devastating to the individual, distressing to the care-giver and demanding of society, which is estimated to affect some 22 million people worldwide.

It is vitally important to put in the first paragraph the main hook to lure journalists who will scan only a few lines. This is the opening of a press release from a leading insurance company:

XXX have surveyed more than 1,000 customers on the issue of effective eyesight and discovered that nearly nine out of ten of those questioned feel that motorists should have their vision tested more regularly for road safety purposes. Hardly very surprising, you might think. Nine paragraphs later, at the very end, the company spokesman is quoted, 'In our survey, nearly one in five of our over-50 customers felt they knew someone whose eyesight was poor enough to cause a danger to other road users, yet that person continued to drive.'

Many organisations fail to realise that the chances of getting something into the papers are much improved if the material relates to something of current debate. At the same time, there is a general lack of appreciation that, while papers can and do make last-minute changes to cover an emerging issue, most features are planned a week or two in advance. Almost weekly I am asked on a Monday if I can get something into *Guardian (Society)* forty-eight hours later.

The short answer is no. The overriding problem I encounter, however, is a simple failure on people's part to read the paper: to look at what is carried, and what is not, and to tailor submissions accordingly. It may seem blindingly obvious, but it very often appears to be beyond even the most pricey public relations agency.

Worrying Trends

Anybody reading the press closely for the past few years must have been struck by the changes that have taken place. Certainly any direct comparison of a broadsheet paper with an issue of the same title a decade ago is arresting. There are fewer stories, fewer words to the page and the overall content is a lighter, frothier mix. Pages are dominated by packages of words and pictures: a main article, though typically no longer than 600 words, together with a large photograph and usually a box or panel giving bullet points or a list of related facts (as in, 'Six other unhappy lottery winners' or 'Ten more celebrity alcoholics').

There is a new emphasis on the arts and a seemingly insatiable, if somewhat incestuous, appetite for stories about the media. Above all, there is a concentration on 'lifestyle' and consumer issues. This trend, which some have called 'dumbing-down', has extended also to television and radio. It has made it increasingly difficult to win editorial space and airtime for policy matters, especially if they cannot be presented in terms that the media can easily assimilate. Some issues of considerable importance have gone almost wholly unreported in the media because of this. The Labour government's reforms of the NHS in 1999, for example, have simply been ignored by most papers and electronic media because of their complexity.

As most people, and most news desks for that matter, never understood the Conservatives' NHS internal market system, it was argued, it mattered little if Labour's further change-introduction of primary care groups and trusts-therefore went unexplained and unexplored. This carries all kinds of dangers, however.

The lesson of the fiasco of the Child Support Agency in the early 1990s was that when the political process fails, producing unworkable legislation, and the media in turn fail to exercise proper scrutiny, the outcome is disastrous for society. Thus, too, the media excused themselves on grounds of the complexity of the issue. It is all very well devoting double-page feature spreads to searing questions of the day such as, 'Should men wear shorts?', but there are wider responsibilities to bear in mind. The other important trend in recent coverage of social policy has been the rise of the spin doctor. The 1997 Labour government did not invent the black art, contrary to popular belief, but it certainly put it into practice with enthusiasm and ruthlessness.

The significance is twofold. First, the rigorous briefing of favoured journalists ahead of a government policy announcement means that the 'line' is firmly established before any detail officially emerges. Should the details then fail to support that line, or suggest another, it is very difficult to swim against the tide. It is doubly difficult for TV journalists who, very often, have been tipped the wink to prepare background filming to support the line being briefed. With that film in the can, they are pretty much locked on to the line. And with TV following the line, it becomes even more unlikely that individual newspaper journalists will be able to argue for anything different.

The influence of TV cannot be overestimated: it is not unknown for national papers to turn upside down their take on a story to fall in step with the BBC early evening bulletin. The second significance of spin doctors is that they dislike specialist correspondents. We know too much. Much the preferred conduit for briefings is the parliamentary lobby, where what is said is not only unattributable, but supposedly never uttered, and where political journalists will generally take at face value what they are told.

Ministers can in this way launch crackdown after crackdown, fly policy kite after kite, without ever being challenged too closely on detail, cost, or indeed whether they have already said as much, or something wholly contradictory, some time previously. Since the change of government, the number of opportunities for specialists to quiz ministers at press conferences or other events has fallen sharply. Access to departmental officials has also been curtailed. Again, the trend cannot be a healthy one for proper scrutiny of policy making, for the overall working of checks and balances.

INCREASE MEDIA COVERAGE

In a 1999 e-mail survey of 2,500 business reporters and editors for the Marshall School of Business, University of Southern California, more than 65 per cent said that PR people were the least likely to be considered a useful source for new story ideas. In fact, 60 per cent said PR people never or rarely give insightful comments that contributed to story assignments. What is behind the hostility and mistrust of PR people from the media? Quite bluntly, we have an image problem. As an industry, we often do not understand a reporter's needs. We are not very good at representing our services to our clients, and we have few ways to measure (or even quantify) our value. (Despite the fact that agencies average a mere three per cent net margin, clients still thinks PR is expensive!)

At least political spin doctors are held in awe. Mainstream business journalists have sour opinions of publicists caused by the endless assault of extravagant promotions, vapid press releases, and the flood of e-mails, FAXes and voice mails in a constant "follow-up" mode. Individually, we seem to know those aggressive techniques and silly promotions won't get marginal coverage in even a marginal newspaper or magazine. Yet collectively the assault continues, implying ignorance or disregard for the realities of journalism. Each bad experience further diminishes the good intentions of professional practitioners. The current model is broken. How can PR professionals change the framework of media relations to encourage a more enlightened approach? One idea is to stop looking at the media as an adversary but as a partner (or perhaps a customer) in a larger process.

THE MEDIA SUPPLY CHAIN

You can't pick up a business magazine today without hearing about "supply chain management," formal cooperation between customer and vendor to facilitate commercial transactions and eliminate inefficiencies on both sides. Supply chain management is an enlightened view of a formerly adversarial relationship. Rather than bare-knuckled confrontation, supply chain management emphasizes shared goals, responsibilities and cooperation for mutual benefit... but only with the most trusted suppliers.

In a sense, the supply chain analogy can apply to the process of "making news." PR is an important part (but only one part) of the elaborate process of delivering accurate, unbiased and timely information to the general public on a continuous basis. (Most journalists will recoil at this analogy, since news is reported, not manufactured. However, the chain of events and common interests make it true enough, and it is certainly a more noble description than the existing model.)

In the media supply chain, no money changes hands. The publicist provides excellent quality raw materials in the form of appropriate story ideas, press releases, fact sheets, executive interviews, product samples, B-roll, etc. In fact, sometimes just a good idea and a well-timed phone call is value enough! The media's job is to transform these materials, gathered together with dozens of their own ideas and sources, into high-quality finished goods (The News) on a monthly, weekly, or daily basis. These stories attract and retain readers, which allow media owners to make money by selling advertising or subscriptions. The entire news gathering process is designed to filter out "impurities" that detract from the value of the media's product: crass, overt commercialism, cloying, hackneyed, or vapid copy, factual errors, inconsequential observations, and other PR sins. Once quality is assured, the newsroom adds insight, objectivity and crisp writing, then sends it to their printing/broadcasting folks for timely, high-quality mass production and delivery.

So far, there are no bold new PR ideas here. Most PR professionals already know the process could be better. Better publicists instinctively know the rules and act accordingly. But the concept of a media supply chain ennobles the effort for the rest of the industry. It provides an easy-to-understand analogy to prevent shortcuts and transgressions. Identifying PR as part of larger whole forces publicists to consider its responsibilities in a larger chain of events. When we understand the value of pitching good-quality stories, we take large steps to improving our overall media effectiveness.

Between the checks and balances, reporters and publicists have one powerful, shared goal: we both want to make the front page with colourful, interesting stories that are accurate, creative and effective. Most publicists get into trouble when they focus too much on their client obligations, and not enough on their responsibilities to journalists. That's a shame, since our relationships with the media are often the most valuable ones we have.

Finally, the supply chain analogy is more easily comprehended and respected by senior management. Any good executive instinctively grasps the importance of conforming to customers' requirements. (A process-oriented description gives the long-suffering product publicist a novel excuse why the president's portrait is not on the front cover of FORTUNE magazine this month!)

IMPROVING CUSTOMER SERVICE

Our primary function in the media supply chain is to give journalists terrific story ideas their publication or programme can use to attract and retain an audience. However, we have hundreds of competitors, each of whom are equally helpful.. or brutally persistent. In this buyer's market, what can we do to endear ourselves to the media, to become a favored supplier? First, like any customer-focused supplier, we must thoroughly understand our buyer's requirements. Each magazine, newspaper, or television and radio programme has a unique and distinct voice and style. We should become expert on their needs, then suggest ideas that make sense in the context of the publication or show.

If we anticipate new story ideas and materials before our customers ask for them, and we deliver these ideas in a timely manner (ahead of our customers' competitors), we will be a favored, reliable vendor. Second, our customers are busy. We should recognize that and do everything possible to reduce our customers' workload. All story pitches should include conveniently packaged information, credible, easily verifiable facts, authoritative and concise spokespeople, interesting visuals. Is the backgrounder written in a jargon-free language, understandable by the average reader? Did we make or beat the reporter's deadline?

Third, we should be pragmatic. We are selling a limited range of story ingredients at a time, our customers may need something else. If we get no reply or no interest, it is not personal. It probably means the answer was no. An aggressive salesperson may make an occasional sale through forceful persistence, but he or she will forever lose the opportunity to build a long-term relationship.

FINDING STORIES THAT SELL THEMSELVES

The best benefit of looking at the bigger picture of a media supply chain is never having to "sell" another story. One of the most effective PR placement techniques is to understand the media's needs so well that the story sells itself, there is no need to push. A good reporter instinctively sees the essential elements of a good story, no matter how unknown the client.

Behind every tough reporter is a tougher editor. Before reading a single word of copy, any good editor will likely ask: "Is it news? Is it timely? Is it relevant? Is it of interest to our readers? Is the information complete? And most important of all, will it amuse me?" If you can not honestly answer yes to all these questions, then any reporter you work with is unlikely to defend your idea to his or her boss.

So what do you look for? Where do you extract the good raw materials for great stories, the ones that get approved by the editor? This question is especially important for your media relations effectiveness when your company's products aren't particularly familiar or important.

There are no easy answers, but I have found that a deliberate thinking process can often help uncover most of the important elements. Whether you're writing a pitch letter or press release, it is useful to review this list to make sure you give your clients (the media) the very best story you can find.

Benefits: Why would anyone want to buy your product, retain your services, or attend your event? What's in it for ME? This is the most important question to ask at the beginning of any publicity project, yet it is often taken for granted due to ignorance or arrogance.

Avoid being a tiresome cheerleader. Be an informed skeptic. Find the people in your organizations that really understand why customers buy from your company. More importantly, find out what makes your product, service, or client so special compared to everyone else's. Make it a point to know the competitive environment, so you'll emphasize the most important features, and why. Talk to salespeople. Regularly. In fact, go on at least four sales calls a year with your salespeople. Understand the curmudgeonly, prospective customer at the business end of the supply chain. The one that wearily has read every trade magazine article, knows every player, and is numb to technobabble. Then write your release for him. In fact, writing for prospective customers is much more important that writing for existing customers. The reason is simple: customers do not buy your products. Prospective customers buy your products. Therefore, product and service PR is effective when it attracts and persuades people who have never heard of your company, or never considered your products, and are too busy to care.

A product feature is merely a bullet point on a fact sheet. Finding out who shot the bullet and what they were aiming at - often makes the story complete.

Context: A good story pitch starts with a solid connection (a hook) to a current or future event. What is going on in the world today? Where do you fit in? Mainstream editors grow weary of publicists that can't connect product pitches to the real world.

One good exercise is to read this morning's paper and try to find a way to relate a client's product to today's major headlines. Then do some indepth research to confirm your hunches. You may wind up with a much more insightful, exciting media angle than you expected._

Details: Detailed explanations to a buyer's experiences in solving a problem are often the most effective elements in successful pitches, releases and case studies. Specifically, what are the details behind the buyer's motivation?

Most buying decisions are money-based: a calculated decision to invest money to save (or make) even more money. They should never be described with vague and amateurish (non-newsworthy) phrases such as "trust," "quality" and "leadership."

Buyers, however, are occasionally reluctant (or incapable) of revealing the extent of their savings, lest they create advantage for their competitors, inflated value for you, the vendor, or political embarrassment for themselves for missed opportunities. That creates a vacuum: how to document the basic point of the story with compelling facts.

When you hear a vacuous, empty phrase (left column), start digging through the story angles on the right column.

Diligence: Be relentless in your pursuit of newsworthy, underlying facts of your product's benefits and competitive environment. Why did the customer include your company on the short list? What are the intriguing features of your product that deliver the essential benefits?

For example, in making precision machine tools, exactly why is precision and accuracy important? A cliche like "quality" is an insufficient explanation. Any reputable magazine will reject it and the rest of your story. Often, the reasons why those standards were written reveal a much better story. Since the late 1960s, machine tools have become 100 times more accurate and precise.

What's driving this trend? During the same time, the U.S. Government began to institute new pollution standards for automobiles. Coincidence? In fact, numerous conversations with engineers revealed a causal relationship between higher machine tool precision and improved fuel economy, lower emissions standards... and, yes, even better quality - better engine reliability and less frequent tune UPS.

If you want to find out why someone bought a particular brand, don't just ask one person. Dig deeper. As 'It turns out, the basketball stadium at the University of North Carolina demanded a particular brand of insulation facing to enhance the crowd roar. The insulation company did not know this, nor did the builder, but the architect spent six months performing acoustical testing on dozens of insulation samples before choosing one brand.

Persistence pays off with better stories that convince prospects to become customers. Never be satisfied with a superficial explanation of a purchasing decision.

Objectivity and skepticism: Occasionally our heads nod when they should shake. Don't be persuaded simply because your boss or client signs your paycheck. If you can't convince an objective outsider of your story's news value, you will never convince a good reporter. Communicators have an advantage in this area. We are the universal donors of business communications. We have an inalienable right to ask dumb questions. Use this right to your advantage. Seek sound explanations to tough questions. You can always write "up," but it is more time-consuming to have to go back and seek further explanation, or to pitch a story that can't be used.

Jargon-less language: Arno Penzias, the Nobel— laureate from Bell Labs, once remarked about the importance of using plain-English to help sell complicated technology: "If you can not explain why your technology is important to a waitress in an all-night diner, then you have big problems."

Be an advocate for free speech - copy that is free from complicated, technical terms, or cumbersome sentences. No one else in your organization will do it. It is your responsibility to protect your company's reputation, both to the media and its customers. Each useless sentence, jargon-filled paragraph, or frivolous press release diminishes the media's opinion of your entire company, and erodes your professional credibility.

Connect visions to reality: Bridges stay up because scientists and engineers think in precise, definite terms. However, most PR people are abstract, clever thinkers that have trouble remembering where they parked their cars. We love to hunt for creative story ideas in unlikely places. To turn these ideas into real stories, however, we need the cooperation of subject matter experts. And often they have little time (or patience) for us "non-traditional" thinkers. Behind the scientist's steep learning curve hides a kindly mentor who loves to talk and explain. You can reap the benefits of bringing out that side of them by showing them you respects their expertise and asking for their honest help. Together, you share a keen interest in accurately telling others who are not as familiar with it about their work and accomplishments.

To build a bridge, a good publicist should consider an interview plan to open folks up. Here is a suggested list of questions that are designed, at once, to flatter and elicit interesting details that may otherwise be hidden'.

- How did you ever come up with that concept?
- How did you convince management to let you go ahead?
- So, how does this differ from (name competitor's version of similar project)?
- What was the worst problem you ran into?
- Did it turn out how you expected?
- But how does the thing work?
- Did you find applications for it along the way that you didn't expect?
- What other industries could you use that in?
- How long did it take, from start to finish?
- What would you change, if you could go back and start over again? What's next?

It is not possible to answer these questions in less than 50 words. In the process, the answers may reveal new threads and ideas that can be woven into more interesting story ingredients. Be sure to include a "closer" question. If the interviewer has not yet spilled the story, these questions will be the cue to do so. "Who else should I talk to?" or "What have I forgotten to ask?" followed by "What haven't we talked about?" Be prepared for another whole side of the project/product to appear, enough for another release or two. This technique works especially well unlocking engineers who seem programmed to parse their answers to only the question asked.

Finally, cultivate internal credibility. Build a reputation for knowing your markets, technology, and industry almost as well as your internal experts. Good internal reporting depends upon earning the respect and active cooperation of knowledgeable peers. Publicists create the most value for their paying clients by attending to the needs of the unpaid clients: reporters, editors and producers that use our stories. The concept behind the media supply chain reveals, and in fact, legitimizes the publicist's role in journalism. It reveals the futility of trying to push stories on customers that won't (and can't) use them, and moves public relations people towards more sophisticated, valuable roles.

As any good marketer will tell you, it is much easier to "sell" a product to a customer who already wants to buy. The most effective product publicists pursue interesting, topical and accurate story ideas with uncompromising zeal. In the essential link between our stories and our customers, we owe it to both clients and the media to practice this enlightened supply chain mentality to improve our individual effectiveness and the collective reputation of the industry. While the debate over whether the Internet as a whole should be judged as a credible source of news and information has ebbed as more users have flocked to news sites sponsored by traditional media, the question remains of how much faith users should place in certain online components such as Weblogs (also known as blogs). Weblogs, diarystyle Web sites that generally offer observations and news listed chronologically on the site as well as commentary and recommended links,1 surged in popularity after the events of 9/11.

Bloggers (those who create blogs) and traditional journalists argue over how much faith to place in messages posted on the blogosphere (the blogging universe). But while several studies have examined credibility of online media, scholars have paid little attention to how credible users judge Weblogs. Metzger, Flanagin, Eyal, Lemus, and McCann argue that one weakness of online credibility studies is that they examine only the Web and ignore other Internet components.

Alternative sources of news and information, such as Weblogs, have been ignored. However, their credibility deserves attention for several reasons: First, they are a growing phenomenon, increasing from an estimated 30,000 in 1998 to at least three million by the beginning of 2004. Second, while the number of blog users is small (only 17 per cent of Internet users have ever visited a blog), their influence may exceed their readership. Because many blog users are politically interested and active, they are wooed by tech-savvy politicians. For instance, blog users may have given a boost to presidential hopeful Howard Dean.

Also, many journalists consider blogs a trustworthy source of information and rely on them for information and story ideas. Blogs have been credited for bringing to light stories ignored by the traditional media, such as racist remarks by Senate Majority Leader Trent Lott that led to his resignation. This study surveyed Weblog users online to investigate how credible they view blogs as compared to other sources. This study will also explore how reliance on Weblogs, as well as traditional and online media sources, predicts credibility of Weblogs.

TRADITIONAL MEDIA AND CREDIBILITY

Beginning in the 1940s, many researchers studied the impact of the credibility of sources on interpersonal influence, examining what characteristics made a speaker persuasive. Similarly, researchers examined characteristics of persuasive messages. Studies of the credibility of a medium, however, arose from concerns in the newspaper industry first about the rising number of people turning to radio for news and then about the number relying on television. The rise of the Internet has led to a host of recent credibility studies comparing traditional sources with this emerging medium.

NON-TRADITIONAL MEDIA AND CREDIBILITY

Credibility research has focused almost entirely on mainstream media, particularly newspapers. Many of these studies were conducted by news organizations that feared that falling credibility would signal further decline in readership and advertising profits.

CREDIBILITY OF NON-TRADITIONAL MEDIA

Several studies have explored the impact of non-traditional media such as talk radio and late night talk shows in the last three presidential elections on voters and on the campaign itself while others have explored the content of such non-traditional media. While scant attention has been paid to how credible voters find information in non-traditional media, anecdotal evidence suggests that users judge them as more credible than mainstream media.

For instance, scholars have noted that talk radio and talk television emerged as forces in the 1992 presidential campaign because the public was dissatisfied with media coverage. Users could talk directly to candidates or to talk show hosts, rather than have information filtered through the press. While traditional media attempt to balance coverage, talk radio hosts openly attack both opposition candidates as well as what they perceive as liberal media coverage. Political talk show hosts present themselves as true authorities on political issues while claiming traditional media hide or lie about facts, a suspicion apparently held by talk show listeners. Finally, listeners may trust the information they receive from talk radio because they believe the hosts are more open about their biases than traditional journalists who subtly interject their views into their stories.

EARLY INTERNET USERS AND CREDIBILITY

Some of the earliest Internet credibility studies were conducted before traditional media became established in online publishing. During the mid-1990s the Internet was compared to a frontier outpost where discussion was "free, sometimes pointed, often blunt, and frequently rebellious." Critics suggested several reasons why the Web should be judged as a less credible source of information than traditional media: Anyone could post information to the Web, and these sites created by individuals spouting their views often appeared as credible as those hosted by reliable sources. Such sites lacked editorial oversight and did not have the professional and social pressures to provide accurate and unbiased information. Also, the Internet was rife with rumors and misinformation, and several parody sites, which looked like official sites, sprouted up on the Internet.

However, the public, particularly Internet users, did not share these fears. While some studies found that the Internet lagged behind traditional media in terms of credibility, most found Web information just as, or more, credible.

Many of these studies only examined Internet users. However, when studies compared users to non-users, findings indicated that those who relied on the Internet for news and information were more likely to judge it as credible.

WEBLOG CREDIBILITY

Clear lines have been drawn between blog users and traditional journalists on the question of blog credibility. Critics advance the same arguments made against the Internet in its earliest days. Anyone can create a blog, and bloggers are not bound by ethical and professional standards of trained journalists. Indeed, a leading blogger, Sean-Paul Kelley of the Agonist, was accused of stealing information from a subscription intelligence service and posting it to his Weblog. Similarly, bloggers are not bound by standards of objectivity; most have strong views that they express openly. As Instapundit blogger Glenn Reynolds says, "A blog is a disclosure of the blogger's biases." Weblogs do not undergo gatekeeping or editing to cull misinformation, sharpen prose, and ensure what is written is fair. Finally, many bloggers use pseudonyms such as Loco Parentis, Big Arm Woman, or No Watermelons, making it difficult to judge the credibility of the information, on their site. Blogs do rely, however, on peer review of other bloggers to point out mistakes that can be easily and prominently corrected. Users may find Weblogs more credible because they are independent rather than controlled by corporate interests; bloggers may discuss issues traditional media shy away from because they might hurt corporations. Blogs also run stories from around the world that were unavailable or ignored by traditional media. Like political talk radio listeners, then, Weblog users are likely to consider blogs a highly credible source of information.

TRADITIONAL MEDIA USE AND WEBLOG CREDIBILITY

Observers relate the rise in blogs to growing distrust and dislike of the traditional media, particularly after 9/11, which saw the number of blogs increase due to the perception that traditional media coverage was overly sympathetic to Arab nations and their peoples. Most bloggers and their readers are conservative, viewing the media as liberal, and tend to see blogs as a new and better journalism that is opinionated, independent, and personal. While studies of traditional media suggest that opinionated writing lowers credibility, bloggers and blog readers contend that Weblogs contain thoughtful analysis of the news events missing from mainstream media. Bloggers and readers criticize the media, and some sites, such as talkingpointsmemo.com, buzzmachine.com, and asmallvictory.net, are devoted to critiquing media coverage. Bloggers and readers routinely fact check stories in traditional media and gleefully point out errors.

While bloggers and blog readers are critical of traditional media, they do not ignore them. Instapundit's Reynolds notes that to be a critic of the media means that you must pay attention to them. Because most bloggers are not independent newsgatherers, they must rely heavily on the Web for their content, and much of that comes from traditional media. Also, bloggers often try to lend authority to their sites by providing links to traditional media sites.

Conversely, although journalists may perceive bloggers as "wannabe amateurs badly in need of some skills and editors," they increasingly rely on blogs for story tips, information, and access to stories from media throughout the world. Further, while many political blogs are written by armchair observers spouting their views, many journalists and some news organizations like MSNBC host their own blogs.

Studies consistently show that heavy media users judge the Internet as highly credible. Indeed, traditional media use in some studies is the strongest predictor of Internet credibility. Those who go online for political news and information tend to be political junkies, heavy users of traditional political sources of information such as CNN, Sunday morning public affairs shows, and newsmagazines. The Internet supplements rather than replaces traditional sources of political information. Also, traditional media users tend to be highly media literate, knowing what sources to trust and what to discard, and have learned where to go online for credible news.

INTERNET USE AND WEBLOG CREDIBILITY

Studies of mainstream media suggest that the more people rely on the media for news and information, the more they will judge that information as credible. Similarly, people judge their preferred news source as the most credible. Many studies examining Web credibility also find that the more people go online the more credible they rate the information they find. Greer discovered that amount of time online was the strongest predictor of whether an online medium would be judged as credible. On the other hand, Johnson and Kaye discovered that for both political and sports news, amount of Web use failed to predict online credibility, a finding supported by others. Johnson and Kaye found that Internet users were not heavy users of traditional media and speculated that because of their limited experience with traditional media, they were not well trained to judge which Internet sources are credible.

Anecdotal evidence suggests that Internet use would predict Weblog credibility. First, blog users are heavy Internet users. Blog users are likely to be media literate and know what sources they trust and do not trust.

BLOGS AND POLITICAL ATTITUDES

With the exception of trust in the government, political variables have not proven strong predictors of online credibility. For instance, Johnson and Kaye found that political trust was the second strongest predictor of credibility of online newspaper and TV news, and strong partisans tended to judge online media as believable. Political attitudes may have little influence on online credibility because studies suggest that online users, rather than being socially isolated and apathetic, are politically interested and are more likely to seek out information from the media than the general public. However, researchers are split on whether they are more knowledgeable than the average citizen. While trust in government initially was not a strong predictor of credibility, it has emerged as a stronger influence as the audience has become more mainstream and trust in government has increased.

Political variables may have a limited effect on credibility judgements of blog users because many are strong political activists. While some Weblogs and blog readers lean towards the left, the blogosphere is predominately right of centre, either conservative or libertarian. Blog readers are also political junkies. The American Demographic survey found that political sites were the second most visited type of Weblogs behind personal or family blogs.

BLOGS AND DEMOGRAPHICS

Studies of the Web offer conflicting findings about the influence of demographics on Web credibility. Earlier studies found that those who judged the Internet as credible were, paradoxically, those who tended to use the media the least: young females of lower education and income. Demographic influence, however, sometimes declined after controlling for other factors. Some recent studies have also found fewer connections between demographics and credibility, particularly after controlling for other factors. Johnson and Kaye speculated that as the Web has moved from being a bastion of young, white, wealthy, well-educated males to one that is more demographically mainstream, the influence of demographics has declined.

However, Flanagin and Metzger reported that men rated both message and site credibility significantly higher than women. Johnson and Kaye, in a study of how online experience influenced credibility judgements, found that demographics proved to be the strongest predictor of credibility, with young men with lower education rating the Internet as less credible.

The authors speculated that because men had been online longer than women, spend more time online, and engage in more activities, that experience may help them judge which sites are credible and which ones are not. Demographics should predict Weblog credibility because, like the Web in general during the mid1990s, the blogosphere is populated with younger white men of high incomes.

RESEARCH QUESTIONS

This study poses the following research questions:
RQ1: To what degree will Weblog users view Weblogs as a credible source of information?

RQ2: Will Weblog users judge Weblogs as significantly more credible than other online sources?

RQ3: Will Weblog users judge Weblogs as significantly more credible than traditional sources of information?

RQ4: To what degree will reliance on Weblogs predict Weblog credibility after controlling for demographics, political attitudes, interest and knowledge of non-political news, as well as reliance on traditional and other online media?

METHOD

A survey aimed at Web log readers was posted online from 23 April to 22 May 2003. The survey was linked from 131 Weblogs of diverse ideologies and 14 Weblog-oriented bulletin boards/electronic mailing lists. Respondents also learned about the survey from announcements sent to Weblog-oriented chat rooms and to bloggers who agreed to post the survey URL. Additionally, a "snowball" technique was used where respondents could automatically forward the survey to fellow blog readers.

Generating a random sample of Weblog users would be very difficult because there is no central registry of blog readers or any way to identify them from Internet users who do not access Weblogs. Unlike telephone and mail surveys, samples cannot be produced through census lists or random digit-dialing-type techniques such as random e-mail generators. Therefore, this study employs a convenience sample. Although the findings cannot be generalized to Internet or Weblog users as a whole, they do present a picture of the 3,747 survey respondents.

DEPENDENT MEASURES

Media credibility is generally defined as the worthiness of being believed, and it is often measured as a multidimensional construct consisting of believability, accuracy, fairness, and depth of information. Respondents were asked to rate on a 5-point scale the degree of believability, fairness, accuracy, and depth of Weblogs. The 5-point scale ranged from "not at all" to "very" (believable, fair, accurate, or in-depth). Scores were combined into a Weblog credibility index.

INDEPENDENT MEASURES

Credibility of Traditional and Online Sources

Respondents were asked to compare traditional and online media in terms of believability, fairness, accuracy, and depth using the same 5-point scale. Respondents marked their assessments of traditionally delivered broadcast television news, cable television news, newspapers, radio news, talk radio, and news magazines, and of the following online sources: broadcast television news sites, cable television news sites, newspaper sites, radio news sites, and news magazines sites. Scores were combined into a credibility index for each traditional and online medium (alphas for traditional media range from.87 to.92 and for online media from.83 to.89).

Source Reliance

Past studies indicate that the credibility of a medium or source of information is strongly related to reliance on a source. Using a 5-point scale ranging from "heavily rely on" to "don't rely at all," respondents assessed their levels of reliance on the same six traditional media and five online sources.

Political Attitudes

Respondents assessed their knowledge and involvement in politics and in non-political issues in relation to their Weblog use. Using a 5-point scale ranging from "greatly increased" to "greatly decreased," respondents judged whether Weblogs influenced their involvement in politics and their knowledge about political and general news issues. Respondents also indicated their degree of interest in politics, in general news, and in current events on a 0 to 10 scale.

Trust in the government was measured as a summated index of three items from the National Election Studies conducted by the University of Michigan: "Most of our leaders are devoted to service," "Politicians never tell us what they really think," and "I don't think public officials care much about what people like me think." The response options for each attitude item ranged from "strongly disagree" (1) to "strongly agree" (5). The polarity was reversed on the second and third statements to create the index (alpha =.75).

Demographics

Gender, age, income, and education data were also collected.

Data Analysis

First, frequencies were run on the Weblog, online sources, and traditional media credibility indices. second, paired f-tests were calculated to compare the credibility of Weblogs to each online and each traditionally delivered medium. Lastly, hierarchical regression was conducted to examine whether reliance on Weblogs predicts credibility of Weblogs after controlling for demographics, political attitudes, general news interest and knowledge, and reliance on traditional media and online sources.

The predictors were entered into the regression models as blocks, with demographic variables entered first, followed by political and general news variables. Measures of reliance on traditional media were entered third, followed by reliance on online sources.

RESULTS

Respondent Profile

The online survey was completed by 3,747 respondents. Almost 9 out of 10 Weblog readers are white (89.3 per cent), and 76.5 per cent are male. The respondents are highly educated, with 92.6 per cent reporting some college or higher, and 41.8 per cent earning more than $65,001 per year.

Just over half (52.5 per cent) credit Weblogs with increasing their levels of political involvement. Almost 9 out of 10 claim that they have become more knowledgeable about politics (87.3 per cent) and about general news and current events (88.7 per cent) since they started reading Weblogs. Almost three-quarters of the respondents are very interested in politics (64.9 per cent) and general news and current events (67.8 per cent). They are politically interested and knowledgeable, but only moderately trusting of government. Slightly less than one-half (47 per cent) report high to very high levels of trust in the government, 30.9 per cent are moderately trustful, and 22.1 per cent claim low to very low degrees of trust. Respondents have been online for just over 71/2 years, spending about 9.1 hours per week interacting with bloggers, reading comments, and following links to additional information, and have been doing so for 1 year and 9 months on average, which coincides with the post 9/11 popularity surge of Weblogs. Additionally, 64.5 per cent seek information from what they consider conservative or very conservative Weblogs, whereas only 16.3 per cent turn to liberal or very liberal Weblogs, and the remaining 20.2 per cent look for more moderate information. The demographic profile of the respondents and the types of Weblogs they visit closely mirror Weblog reader profiles reported by others.

CREDIBILITY OF ONLINE AND TRADITIONAL SOURCES

Weblogs

RQf asks about the credibility of Weblogs. Almost three quarters (73.6 per cent) of Weblog readers view Weblogs as moderately to very credible and only 3.5 per cent consider them "not at all" or "not very credible". When the credibility index is broken into its four components (believable, fair, accurate, depth), depth of information emerges as a Weblog's strongest attribute; 72.2 per cent of respondents think of Weblogs as "moderately" to "very" in-depth sources of information.

Weblogs are judged moderately to very believable by 59.6 per cent. Blog users seem to acknowledge that accuracy of Weblogs may be questionable; 50.2 per cent consider them "somewhat" or "not very" accurate. Additionally, respondents seem aware of Weblog biases with 61.6 per cent claiming that Weblogs are "somewhat" or "not very" fair.

Online Media Sites

Weblog readers rated online newspapers the most credible of online media, although all online sources were generally thought of as only "somewhat" credible. However, only 42.7 per cent rate online newspapers as "moderately" or "very" credible. Online radio news sites and broadcast television sites were judged as the least credible with 26.7 per cent and 29.0 per cent, respectively, considering them as "not very" or "not at all credible."

Traditional Media

Traditional media do not fare much better. Printed newspapers and news magazines had the highest percentage of respondents rating them as moderately to very credible sources, 46.5 per cent and 43.7 per cent, respectively; however, both had an almost equal percentage rating them as "somewhat" credible. Generally, Weblog users view traditional media as only "somewhat" credible. Weblogs Compared to Online Media Sites. RQ2 asked whether respondents view Weblogs as more credible than other online sources. Paired sample t-tests were used for comparisons. Weblogs were more credible than any other online source: online broadcast television, online cable television news, online newspapers, online news magazines, and online radio news. Online broadcast television and online radio news have the lowest mean credibility scores, whereas online newspapers had the highest.

Weblogs Compared to Traditional Media. RQ3 involved comparing Weblogs to traditionally delivered media. Weblogs were judged significantly more credible than any traditional medium: broadcast television news, cable television news, newspapers, news magazines, radio news, and talk radio. Broadcast television and over-the-air talk radio are the two least credible traditional sources and newspapers and newsmagazines the most credible.

Predictors of Weblog Credibility

RQ4 asks whether Weblog credibility can be predicted by Weblog reliance after controlling for reliance on traditional media and other online sources, and political attitudes, general news interest and knowledge, and demographics.

Even after controlling for other variables, reliance on Weblogs is a strong positive and significant predictor of perceptions of Weblog credibility. The more users rely on Weblogs, the higher their assessments of credibility. Reliance on Weblogs explains between 12.7 per cent and 14.6 per cent of the perceptions of Weblog credibility. Reliance on five of the six traditional media and on the online sources also significantly, but weakly, predicts Weblog credibility; however, all but two of those relationships were negative. Reliance on traditional media accounts for an additional.1 per cent - 1.8 per cent of the variance, and reliance on online sources for an additional 1 per cent. Political involvement, political knowledge, political interest, and general news knowledge are weak, but consistent, predictors of Weblog credibility, but general news interest is not. Trust in government is also a weak, but significant, predictor. The political and general news variables, however, explain a greater percentage of the variability (about 15 per cent) than do the online and traditional reliance measures and about the same amount as the Weblog reliance variables. None of the demographic variables predicts Weblog credibility.

Reliance on Broadcast Television and Online Broadcast Television Web sites

Perceptions of Weblog credibility are significantly, but negatively and weakly, predicted by reliance on broadcast television news and their online counterparts. The less Weblog users rely on broadcast television news and broadcast news Web sites, the more they rely on Weblogs and, thus, the higher they rate Weblog credibility.

Reliance on Cable Television Neius and Online Cable Television Web sites

Reliance on cable television news significantly, but weakly, predicts credibility of Weblogs. The more a Weblog reader relies on cable television news the higher the credibility of Weblogs. Conversely, less reliance on cable television news sites leads to perceptions of Weblog credibility. Those Weblog readers who view Weblogs as credible are more likely to watch cable television news than to connect to cable television news online.

Reliance on Newspapers and Online Newspapers

Reliance on both printed and online newspapers predicts Weblog credibility, respectively. Less reliance on newspapers and their online sites leads to higher Weblog credibility.

Reliance on Radio News, Talk Radio, and Radio News Sites

Over-the air talk radio is a significant and positive predictor. The greater the reliance on talk radio, the higher the Weblog credibility. Online radio news, on the other hand, is a significant but negative predictor. Weblog users who rely on talk radio but not on online radio Web sites for news and information are more likely to judge Weblogs as highly credible. Reliance on broadcast radio news is the only medium, traditional or online, that is not a significant predictor.

Reliance on News Magazines and Online News Magazines, Reliance on both print and online news magazines significantly, but negatively and weakly, predicts Weblog credibility. Weblog readers with low levels of reliance on news magazines are more likely to rate Weblogs as highly credible.

DISCUSSION

This study surveyed Weblog users online to discover how credible they viewed blogs and how judgements of Weblog credibility compare to traditional and online media sources. This study also explored the degree to which reliance on Weblogs, as well as traditional and online media sources, predicts Weblog credibility.

Almost three-quarters of respondents view Weblogs as moderately to very credible and only 3.5 per cent rate them not at all or not very credible. An important reason users say they rely on blogs is because they provide more depth and more thoughtful analysis than is available in other media.

On the other hand, fewer than four in ten thought blogs were fair. However, while fairness may be considered a hallmark of traditional journalism, bias is likely seen as a virtue by blog users. The majority rate themselves as conservative and almost two-thirds said they sought information from conservative or very conservative sites. Blog readers are seeking out information to support their views and are likely to consider conservative information they receive from blogs as highly credible. Users view blogs as a new and better form of journalism than the mainstream media, one that is opinionated, analytical, independent, and personal.

Not surprisingly, then, Weblog users judged blogs as significantly more credible than other media. However, this does not mean that bloggers do not consider some mainstream media credible. The plurality considered both online and traditional newspapers, traditional news magazines, and online cable television news as moderately to very credible and both online news magazines and traditional cable television news also recorded moderate credibility scores. These ratings for print media and cable television were similar to those found in a study of politically interested Internet users.

The moderate scores for print media and cable news may reflect bloggers' and blog readers' paradoxical attitude towards traditional media. They may distrust the media, but bloggers link to media sites and pay attention to media content, even if only to hunt for mistakes and look for what they consider bias. Weblog reliance was the only strong predictor of Weblog credibility. These results parallel studies of traditional media that the more one uses a medium, the more credible one judges it.

Amount of reliance may also be a strong predictor of Weblog credibility because media consumers determine the credibility of a source by using various cues such as reputation of the medium and style of delivery. For newbies, Weblogs may not appear credible. Most are a series of short journal entries with links to other information; they do not look like traditional media. Furthermore, the personal, opinionated writing style that attracts blog users may put off some newcomers used to the more balanced, disinterested writing style of traditional media.

Finally, while traditional media claim to be non-biased, most news Weblogs make no apologies for being conservative, liberal, or libertarian. Visiting blogs of a different political stripe than one's own may be particularly off putting for a new user. But as the user finds a blog with views matching his or her own and adjusts to the style of reporting, subsequent greater use of the blog may mean he or she will judge it credible.

Past studies have found that reliance on traditional media consistently is the strongest predictor of online credibility. This study found that both online and traditional media reliance were weak predictors of Weblog credibility. More important, most relationships were negative, meaning that those who rely little on traditional media are more likely to view blogs as credible. Past studies have found that the Internet has served as a supplement to traditional information for news and information. Internet users are news junkies who judge online and traditional sources as equally credible and rely on both to survey the news environment. However, blog users distrust traditional media and see Weblogs as a viable alternative.

However, the more blog readers use talk radio, the more credible they view Weblogs, even though blog users did not rate talk radio as highly credible. In many ways, Weblogs are online versions of talk radio. Talk show listeners can talk directly to talk show hosts or guests; Weblog users can either e-mail the blog host directly or post comments to the blog. Both blogs and talk radio are dominated by conservative hosts who openly attack political opponents and what they perceive as liberal press coverage.

Blog users may trust information they receive from Weblogs because they believe the hosts do not hide their biases. Similarly, while blog readers praise Weblogs for their depth of coverage, talk radio also is applauded by its users for depth. While early studies suggested that talk radio listeners were socially isolated and politically alienated, later studies presented talk radio listeners as politically interested and active, with high levels of political involvement and political knowledge, but low levels of trust in government. This study's Weblog users also were politically interested, involved, active, and knowledgeable, but with only moderate trust in government. Furthermore, these variables positively, though weakly, predicted credibility of Weblogs.

Weblog credibility was also positively, though weakly, predicted by cable television use. Blog users who tire of the so-called liberal leanings of broadcast news may be taking shelter in cable networks such as Fox who have aligned themselves on the right end of the political spectrum. The study has limitations, of course. Reaching the small population of Internet users who have visited blogs is a challenge because traditional methods of data collection do not readily apply to the Internet. Though posting a survey online is recognized as an effective method of collecting data, limitations arise from the lack of random selection.

This study relied on a self-selected convenience sample, and, therefore, results cannot be generalized to the Internet as a whole or even to blog users. As Babbie noted, however, in situations where random probability sampling is not possible, non-probability sampling is acceptable. The Internet is conducive to purposive sampling, as subsets within the larger population of users can be identified and solicited through announcements posted on message boards, sent out to special mailing lists, and through hyperlinks posted on key online sites, as employed here.

Careful use of this type of purposive sampling generates results that may be representative of a specific subset of Internet users, but not the larger population. Still, the demographic profile of the Weblog readers who responded to this study and the types of Weblogs they visit closely mirror the Weblog reader profiles reported by others. This study suggested that demographically, Weblog users resembled early Internet users: white males with high incomes and high levels of education. Past research indicates that as Internet users became more representative of the demographic mainstream, credibility scores for online and traditional media rose. Future studies could find if Weblog users follow a similar trend, or whether blog readers remain a distinct group of Internet users who maintain their dislike and distrust of the traditional media.

5

Development of Press in India

Journalism came to India in 1785 when the first newspaper was established by an Englishmen called Hickey. Because of the intellectual nature of journalism, the subsequent history of newspapers in India is extremely interesting. The realization of the power of the print media was bound to be grasped by those exploiting and those resisting exploitation. Journalism has its bright periods and its dark days. There were periods of sustained growth and also phases of repression and major crises. The communications revolution and the information explosion of recent decades have spawned new forms of journalism and news-gathering methods, not always of high quality and sometimes of doubtful integrity. The darkest patch of Indian Journalism was the emergency of 1975-77 when the press was fully deprived of its innate freedom. In the following pages the reader will find a comprehensive overview of the origins, development and growth of journalism in India, from the last years of the eighteenth century to the post-independence surge in the power of the fourth Estate.

HISTORY OF PRESS IN INDIA

COLONIAL JOURNALISM

The printing press preceded the advent of printed news in India by about 100 years. It was in 1674 that the first printing apparatus was established in Bombay followed by Madras in 1772. British colonialism brought newspaper publishing to India, beginning with the *Bengal Gazette* in 1780, founded by James Augustus Hicky, a disgruntled employee of the East India Company, who described the journal as 'a weekly political and commercial paper open to all parties, but influenced by none'. And the first Hindi daily, *Samachar Sudha Varshan*, began in 1854.

"Newspaper history in India is inextricably tangled with political history," wrote A. E. Charlton (Wolseley 3). James Augustus Hicky was the founder of India's first newspaper, the Calcutta General Advertiser also known as *Hicky's Bengal Gazette*, in 1780. Soon other newspapers came into existence in Calcutta and Madras: the *Calcutta Gazette*, the *Bengal Journal,* the *Oriental Magazine,* the *Madras Courier* and the *Indian Gazette*. While the *India Gazette* enjoyed governmental patronage including free postal circulation and advertisements, *Hicky's Bengal Gazette* earned the rulers' wrath due to its criticism of the government. In November 1780 its circulation was halted by government decree. Hicky protested against this arbitrary harassment without avail, and was imprisoned. The *Bengal Gazette* and the *India Gazette* were followed by the *Calcutta Gazette* which subsequently became the government's "medium for making its general orders".

The *Bombay Herald*, *The Statesmen* in Calcutta and the *Madras Mail* and *The Hindu*, along with many other rivals in Madras represented the metropolitan voice of India and its people. While *Statesman* voiced the English rulers' voice, *The Hindu* became the beacon of patriotism in the South. *The Hindu* was founded in Madras as a counter to the *Madras Mail*.

Patriotic movements grew in proportion with the colonial ruthlessness, and a vehicle of information dissemination became a tool for freedom struggle. In the struggle for freedom, journalists in the twentieth century performed a dual role as professionals and nationalists. Indeed many national leaders, from Gandhi to Vajpayee, were journalists as well. Calcutta, Madras, Bombay and Delhi were four main centers of urban renaissance which nourished news in India. It was only during and after the seventies, especially after Indira Gandhi's defeat in 1977, that regional language newspapers became prevalent.

There were nationalist echoes from other linguistic regional provinces. Bengal, Gujarat, Tamil, Karalla, Punjab and Uttar Pradesh produced dailies in regional languages. Hindi and Urdu were largely instrumental in voicing the viewpoints and aspirations of both Hindus and Muslims of the Northern provinces. As communalism and religious intolerance increased before and after partition, Urdu remained primarily the language of Muslims, as Pakistan chose this language as its lingua franca. After partition, the cause of Urdu and its newspapers, suffered a setback as Hindu reactionaries began to recognize the association of Urdu with Islam and Pakistan.

William Bolts, an ex-employee of the British East India Company attempted to start the first newspaper in India in 1776. Bolts had to beat a retreat under the disapproving gaze of the Court of Directors of the Company The *Hickey's Bengal Gazette or the Calcutta General Advertiser* was started by James Augustus Hickey in 1780. The *Gazette*, a two-sheet newspaper, specialised in writing on the private lives of the Sahibs of the Company. He dared even to mount scurrillious attacks on the Governor-General, Warren Hastings', wife, which soon landed "the late printer to the Honourable Company" in trouble.

Hickey was sentenced to a 4 months jail term and ₹.500 fine, which did not deter him. After a bitter attack on the Governor-General and the Chief Justice, Hickey was sentenced to one year in prison and fined ₹.5,000, which finally drove him to penury. These were the first tentative steps of journalism in India. B.Messink and Peter Reed were pliant publishers of the *India Gazette*, unlike their infamous predecessor. The colonial establishment started the *Calcutta Gazette*. It was followed by another private initiative the *Bengal Journal*. The *Oriental Magazine of Calcutta Amusement*, a monthly magazine made it four weekly newspapers and one monthly magazine published from Calcutta, now Kolkata.

The *Madras Courier* was started in 1785 in the southern stronghold of Madras, which is now called Chennai. Richard Johnson, its founder, was a government printer. Madras got its second newspaper when, in 1791, Hugh Boyd, who was the editor of the *Courier* quit and founded the *Hurkaru*. Tragically for the paper, it ceased publication when Boyd died within a year of its founding.

It was only in 1795 that competitors to the *Courier* emerged with the founding of the *Madras Gazette* followed by the *India Herald*. The latter was an "unauthorised" publication, which led to the deportation of its founder Humphreys. The *Madras Courier* was designated the purveyor of official information in the Presidency.

In 1878, The Hindu was founded, and played a vital role in promoting the cause of Indian independence from the colonial yoke. It's founder, Kasturi Ranga Iyengar, was a lawyer, and his son, K Srinivasan assumed editorship of this pioneering newspaper during for the first half of the 20th century. Today this paper enjoys the highest circulation in South India, and is among the top five nationally.

Bombay, now Mumbai, surprisingly was a late starter - *The Bombay Herald* came into existence in 1789. Significantly, a year later a paper called the *Courier* started carrying advertisements in Gujarati.

The first media merger of sorts: The *Bombay Gazette*, which was started in 1791, merged with the *Bombay Herald* the following year. Like the *Madras Courier*, this new entity was recognised as the publication to carry "official notifications and advertisements".

'A Chronicle of Media and the State', by Jeebesh Bagchi in the *Sarai Reader 2001* is a handy timeline on the role of the state in the development of media in India for more than a century.

Bagchi divides the timeline into three 'ages'. The Age of Formulation, which starts with the Indian Telegraph Act in 1885 and ends with the Report of the Sub-Committee on Communication, National Planning Committee in 1948 The Age of Consolidation that follows stretches from 1951, with the extension of the Indian Telegraph Act to the whole of India and ends with the promulgation of the "Indecent Representation of Women (Prohibition) Act" in 1985. The current age is the Age of Uncertainty, which began in 1989 with the introduction of the Prasar Bharati (Broadcasting Corporation of India) Bill. As newspapers became widely available they acted as a harbinger of modernity, contributing to the construction of a national identity. Despite very low literacy and strict press laws introduced by successive British colonial administrations, the press played a key role in the nationalist movement, even if its pioneers came from a small westernised, educated elite. Such was Ram Mohan Roy, a versatile Bengali intellectual who established the nationalist press in India in the early 1820s by starting three reformist publications – the *Brahmanical Magazine*, in English, the *Sambad Kaumudi* in Bengali, and the *Mirat-ul-Akhbar* in Persian. At the same time, at the other end of the country, Fardoonji Murzban launched the *Bombay Samachar* in 1822, which is still in existence as a Gujarati daily.

Roy's contemporary, Lord William Bentinck, a relatively liberal Governor General, supported Indian efforts at reforms and, as a result, by 1830 there were 33 English language and 16 Indian language publications in operation. In subsequent decades many more nationalist newspapers and magazines appeared.

Among the more notable publications were *Rast Goftar* edited by Dadabhai Naoroji, the founder of the Indian National Congress and *Shome Prakash* in Bengali founded in 1858 by Iswar Chandra Vidyasagar. The influence of Indian-language newspapers had grown so much by 1870 that they were perceived as a threat by the colonial administrations, which led to the Vernacular Press Act of 1878, aimed at silencing any attempts by the Indian language press to criticise the government. Mass illiteracy, poverty and repressive press laws were serious handicaps to the development of the press. Yet the availability and expansion of printing technology to Indian languages radically changed the face of journalism. Within a century of the publication of the *Bengal Gazette*, more than 140 newspapers in Indian languages were in operation, articulating a nascent nationalism.

As nationalism evolved so did the idea that the freedom of the press was a basic right to be cherished and fought for. Indian industrialists started their own newspapers with a clear anti-colonial stance. Most nationalist leaders were involved in activist, campaigning journalism, none more than Mahatma Gandhi, who realised the importance of the written word and used Gujarati, his mother-tongue, as well as English, to spread the message of freedom.

Writing in *Young India* in 1920, he defended the right of newspapers to protest against press laws. Radio, which began regular broadcasting in 1927 (though All India Radio was founded as a public broadcasting service in 1936), remained in the hands of the colonial powers who used the airwaves to legitimise the Raj. By 1941, about 4,000 newspapers and magazines were in print in 17 languages and the underlying theme was the end of colonial rule.

Towards the end of the British Raj, the press could be broadly divided into three categories: the establishment papers such as *The Statesman* and the *Times of India*, the nationalist press's *Hindustan Times*, The *Indian Express* and *The Hindu,* and the Indian language publications such as *Anand Bazaar Patrika* in

Bengali, *Kesari* in Marathi, *Sandesh* and *Bombay Samachar* in Gujarati, *Matribhumi* in Malayalam and *Aaj* in Hindi.

THE MEDIA AT INDEPENDENCE

Even after independence, the legacy of anti-colonialism continued to influence Indian media. India inherited from the British the combination of a private press and a Government-controlled broadcasting system. Given the diversity of the press, it was critically aware and, by and large, acted as a fourth estate in a fledgling democracy, while the electronic media was used for what came to be known as 'nation-building.' In a vast, geographically and culturally diverse country with 16 official languages and more than 800 dialects, and great disparity in the levels of development, national media had a crucial role to play to develop a sense of Indianness.

All India Radio (AIR), was seen as the key instrument for national development in a largely illiterate country, and the leadership was keen to develop this as a means of mass persuasion. As elsewhere in the developing world, Indian leaders found it difficult to relinquish political control over broadcasting, the most potent instrument of mass persuasion and propaganda. It was also argued that an uncontrolled broadcasting system could destabilise the country, given its traumatic birth, which saw one million people killed and more than 15 million displaced, the result of the partition as the British divided and quit India in 1947. The violent legacy of the partition dictated that the national media had to be very sensitive to ethnic, cultural and religious considerations. The journalists' task was to help in overcoming the immediate crisis of political instability that followed independence and to foster the long-term process of modernisation and nation-building, reflecting the dominant ideology of the newly emergent and activist state.

Just a year after independence, India's first Prime Minister, Jawaharlal Nehru, told the constituent assembly which was drafting India's constitution, 'my own view of the set up for broadcasting is that we should approximate as far as possible to the British model, the BBC; that is to say, it would be better if we had a semi-autonomous corporation. Now I think that is not immediately feasible'. (Chatterjee, 1991: 182) Consequently, the public broadcasting monopoly became little more than a propaganda service for Government. Like other public-sector departments, it was over-bureaucratised and its performance was dull. How far it succeeded in serving any developmental purposes is also open to debate.

The introduction of television in 1959 as a pilot UNESCO-sponsored educational project reflected the initial attitude to the medium as an educational tool and a means for disseminating state policies and public information. The state television channel (Doordarshan) was part of AIR until 1976, when it became a separate department under the Information and Broadcasting Ministry.

The aim of the national broadcasters was to educate, inform and create a feeling of national identity and help maintain national unity. Doordarshan followed the AIR broadcasting code, which prohibited, among other things, criticism of friendly countries, attacks on religions or communities, incitement to violence, or material affecting the integrity of the nation.

Other sections of the electronic media were also employed by the state for propaganda purposes. Newsreels produced by the Indian Film Division, a wing of the Ministry of Information and Broadcasting, were used to promote government policies. As a study by the Press Institute of India observed: '[newsreels] are not only controlled by the Government but their theme and content are also dictated by it. Since films have a tremendous educational and propaganda value, it is mandatory for all cinema houses to show newsreels...' In addition, the Government could indirectly influence the private print media, through control of newsprint and advertising and subsidising pro-government newspapers and news agencies.

Despite such direct and indirect interference by the Government, the relative autonomy of the private print media contributed greatly to the evolution of democracy in India. As democracy took root, various political parties and groupings representing the whole ideological spectrum started up their own newspapers and magazines. Even among the mainstream press, ideological leanings reflecting political and cultural affiliations could be detected in the tone, tenor and treatment of stories.

During Nehru's tenure as Prime Minister (1947-1964), Indian media seemed to follow the democratic agenda. Most newspapers, even those owing allegiance to extreme political parties, believed that the multi-party system of Government had taken a firm root in the country and a free press was integral to its success. Unlike most other developing countries, the Government in India tolerated criticism on the editorial pages of national press. This tolerance gave Indian journalists – most coming from an urban middle-class milieu – high professional standards and a space to engage in critical debates on socio-political and economic issues. More importantly, the proactive and investigative, often adversarial, role of journalists, contributed to the evolution of an early-warning system for serious food shortages and thus a preventive mechanism against famine – an annual scourge during the British Raj.

Nehru had a genuine interest in promoting national consensus through the mass media. However, the political manipulations of Nehru's daughter Indira Gandhi, Prime Minister from 1967 to 1977 and again from 1980 to 1984, strained this consensus. Especially during the emergency of 1975-77 when censorship was rife, journalists were detained and the national broadcasting organisations reduced to becoming the mouthpiece of the ruling party and its leader. Despite blatant misuse of the electronic media, Indira Gandhi lost the 1977 election to the Janata Party – a loose grouping of right-wing and centrist parties. The coming to power for the first time of a non-Congress coalition had a positive impact on the growth of Indian media, partly because it catapulted several regional leaders into the national limelight, thereby promoting the regional press.

The Janata government promised autonomy for the electronic media and appointed a 12-member working group (known as the Verghese Committee) to develop a policy framework for the broadcast media. The result of their deliberations, published in 1978 (the Prasar Bharati Bill), recommended the establishment of an independent National Broadcasting Trust, Akash Bharati, to run both Doordarshan and AIR. However, more than two decades after the introduction of the bill, the official broadcasting media remain under strict Government control. What has changed, however, is its revenue-generating structure, as Doordarshan rapidly commercialised, a process intensified by the increasingly neo-liberal governments of the 1980s. As a result, television became much more entertainment-oriented: its soaps – originally borrowing from the success of telenovelas in Brazil and Mexico (a mix of education, information and entertainment using education entertainers) – were altered to meet the needs of advertisers.

THE PRESS COMMISSIONS

Press Council is a mechanism for the Press to regulate itself. This unique institution is rooted in the concept that in a democratic society the press needs at once to be free and responsible.

If the Press is to function effectively as the watchdog of public interest, it must have a secure freedom of expression, unfettered and unhindered by any authority, organised bodies or individuals. But, this claim to press freedom has legitimacy only if it is exercised with a due sense of responsibility. The Press must, therefore, scrupulously adhere to accepted norms of journalistic ethics and maintian high standards of professional conduct.

Where the norms are breached and the freedom is defiled by unprofessional conduct, a way must exist to check and control it. But, control by Government or official authorities may prove destructive of this freedom. Therefore, the best way is to let the peers of the profession, assisted by a few discerning laymen to regulate it through a properly structured representative impartial machinery. Hence, the Press Council.

A need for such a mechanism has been felt for a long time both by the authorities as well as the Press itself all over the world, and a search for it resulted in the setting up of the first Press Council known as the Court of Honour for the Press in Sweden in 1916. The idea gained quick acceptance in other Scandinavian countries, and later in other parts of Europe, Canada, Asia, Australia and New Zealand. Today, the Press Councils or similar other media bodies are in place in more than four dozen nations. The basic concept of self-regulation in which the Press Councils and similar media bodies world over are founded, was articulated by Mahatma Gandhi, who was an eminent journalist in his own right, thus: " The sole aim of journalist should be service. The newspaper press is a great power, but just as unchained torrent of water submerges the whole country side and devastates crops, even so an uncontrolled pen serves but to destroy. If the control is from without, it proves more poisonous than want of control. It can be profitable only when exercised from within."

Pandit Jawaharlal Nehru while defending Press freedom, warning of the danger its irresponsible exercise entails stressed: " If there is no responsibility and no obligation attached to it, freedom gradually whithers away. This is true of a nation's freedom and it applies as much to the Press as to any other group, organisation or individual."

The First Press Commission (1954) came across in some section of the Press, instances of yellow journalism of one type or another, scurrilous writing-often directed against communities or groups, sensationalism, bias in presentation of news and lack of responsibility in comment, indecency and vulgarity and personal attacks on individuals. The Commission, however, pointed out that the well-established newspapers had, on the whole. Maintained a high standard of journalism. They had avoided "cheap senstationalism and unwarranted intrusion into private lives." But it remarked that " whatever the law relating to the Press may be, there would still be a large quantum of objectionable journalism which, though not falling within the purview of the law, would still require to be checked." It was of the view that the best way of maintaining professional standards of journalism would be to bring into existence a body of of people principally connected with the industry whose responsibility it would be to arbitrate on doubtful points and to censure any one guilty of infraction of the code of journalistic ethics.

The Commission recommended the setting up of a Press Council. Among the objectives visualised for the Council were: " to safeguard the freedom of the press", " to ensure on the part of the Press the maintenance of High standards of public taste and to foster due sense of both the rights and responsibilities of citizenship" and " to encourage the growth of sense of responsibility and public service among all those engaged in the profession of journalism." The Commission, recommended the establishment of the Council on a statutory basis on the ground that the Council should have legal authority to make enquiries as otherwise each member, as well as the Council as a whole, would be subject to the threat of legal action from those whom it sought to punish by exposure.

The Commission said that the Council should consist of men who would command general confidence and respect of the profession and should have 25 members excluding the Chairman. The Chairman was to be a person who was or had been a Judge of the High Court and was to be nominated by the Chief

Justice of India. The Press Council of India was first constituted on 4th July, 1966 as an autonomous, statutory, quasi-judicial body, with Shri Justice J R Mudholkar, then a Judge of the Supreme Court, as Chairman. The Press Council Act, 1965, listed the following functions of the Council in furtherance of its objects:

- To help newspapers to maintain their independence;
- To build up a code of conduct for newspapers and journalists in accordance with high professional standards;
- To ensure on the part of newspapers and journalists the maintenance of high standards of public taste and foster a due sense of both the rights and responsibilities of citizenship;
- To encourage the growth of a sense of responsibility and public service among all those engaged in the profession of journalism;
- To keep under review any development likely to restrict the supply and dissemination of news of public interest and importance;
- To keep under review such cases of assistance received by any newspaper or news agency in India from foreign sources, as are referred to it by the Central Government.
  Provided that nothing in this clause shall preclude the Central Government from dealing with any case of assistance received by a newspaper or news agency in India from foreign sources in any other manner it thinks fit;
- To promote the establishment of such common service for the supply and dissemination of news to newspapers as may, from time to time, appear to it to be desirable;
- To provide facilities for the proper education and training of persons in the profession of journalism;
- To promote a proper functional relationship among all classes of persons engaged in the production or publication of newspapers;
- To study developments which may tend towards monopoly or concentration of ownership of newspapers, including a study of the ownership or financial structure of newspapers, and if necessary, to suggest remedies therefor;
- To promote technical or other research;
- To do such other acts as may be incidental or conducive to the discharge of the above functions.

The Act of 1965 provided that the Council shall consist of a Chairman and 25 other members. Of the 25 members, 3 were to represent the two houses of Parliament, 13 were to be from amongst the working journalists, of which not less than 6 were to be editors who did not own or carry on the business of management of newspapers and the rest were to be the persons having special knowledge or practical experience in respect of education and science, law, literature and culture. By an amendment of the Act in 1970, the membership of the Council was raised by one to provide a seat for persons managing the news agencies.

The Chairman under the Act on 1965, was to be nominated by the Chief Justice of India. Of the three Members of Parliament, two representing Lok Sabha were to be nominated by the Speaker of the Lok Sabha and one representing Rajya Sabha, was to be nominated by the Chairman of the Rajya Sabha. The remaining 22 members were to be selected by a three-man Selection Committee comprising the Chief Justice of India, Chairman of the Press Council and a nominee of the President of India. The Chairman and the members were to hold office for a period of three years provided that no member could hold office for a period exceeding six years in the aggregate.

When in the early years of the Council's existence a grievance was aired about the selection of a category of members, Parliament embarked on a search for a meticulous formula which would ensure uncompromising impartiality and fairness in the selection of Chairman and other members. This led to the amendment of the 1965 Act entrusting this work to a Committee comprising the incumbent of the three highest offices which are considered as an embodiment of these attributes, namely, Chairman of Rajya Sabha, Speaker of Lok Sabha and Chief Justice of India. But, the pursuit for still less subjective scheme continued. Even a statistical formula was evolved for equitable presentation of the various representative organisations of the profession.

As has been referred to earlier, composition of the nominating committee was changed by an amendment of the said Act in 1970, according to which the Chairman and the members from the press were to be nominated by a Nominating Committee consisting of the Chairman of the Rajya Sabha, the Chief Justice of India and the Speaker of the Lok Sabha.

The amending Act of 1970 introduced several other provisions in the Act. The manner of selection of persons of special knowledge or practical experience was specified. It provided that of the three persons to be nominated from among such people, one each shall be nominated by the University Grants Commission, the Bar Council of India and the Sahitya Academy. It also provided for raising the membership of the Council to give one seat to the persons managing the news agencies. Out of the six seats for proprietors and managers of newspapers, two each were earmarked for big, medium and small newspapers. No working journalist who owned or carried on the business of management of newspapers could now be nominated in the category of working journalists. Also, it was specified that not more than one person interested in any newspaper or group of newspapers under the same control, could be nominated from the categories of editors, other working journalists, proprietors and managers.

The Nominating Committee was empowered to review any nomination on a representation made to it by any notified association or by any person aggrieved by it or otherwise. The amended Act also barred renomination of a retiring member for more than one term. Where any association failed to submit a panel of names when invited to do so, the Nominating Committee could ask for panels from other associations or persons of the category concerned or nominate members after consultation with such other such individuals or interests concerned as it thought fit.

Under the original Act, the Chairman was nominated by the Chief Justice of India. But, after this amendment, nomination of the Chairman was also left to the Nominating Committee.

The Council set up under the Act of 1965 functioned till December 1975. During the Internal Emergency, the Act was repealed and the Council abolished w.e.f. 1/1/1976.

Press Counicl of 1979

A fresh legislation providing for the establishment of the Council was enacted in 1978 and the institution came to be reviewed in the year 1979 with the very same object of preserving the freedom of the press and of maintaining and improving the standards of Press in India. The present Council is a body corporate having perpetual succession. It consists of a Chairman and 28 other members. Of the 28 members, 13 represent the working journalists. Of whom 6 are to be editors of newspapers and remaining 7 are to be working journalists other than editors. 6 are to be from among persons who own or carry on the business of management of newspapers. One is to be from among the persons who manage news agencies. Three are to be persons having special knowledge or practical experience in respect of education and science, law and literature and culture. The remaining five are to Members of Parliament: three from Lok Sabha, and two from Rajya Sabha.

The new Act provides for selection of the Chairman by a Committee consisting of the Chairman of the Rajya Sabha, the Speaker of Lok Sabha and a person elected by the members of the Council from among themselves. The twenty representatives of the Press are nominated by the associations of aforesaid categories of the newspapers and news agencies notified for the purpose by the Council in the each category. One member each is nominated by the University Grants Commission, the Bar Council of India and the Sahitya Academy. Of the five Members of Parliament, three are nominated by the Speaker of the Lok Sabha and two by the Chairman of the Rajya Sabha. The term of the Chairman and the members of the Council is three years. A retiring member is eligible for renomination for not more than one term.

An extremely healthy feature of the Indian Press Council is the scheme and procedure of the nomination of its Chairman and other members, following a long search based on the experience of several years of functioning of the Council. Despite being a statutory body, the Government and its authorities have been completely kept out of the nomination process except for publishing the notification in the official gazette of the names of the members nominated. Nor has it been left to any individual to decide, however eminent or highly placed he may be.

A totally non-subjective procedure which leaves no scope for the interference or influence by Government or any other agency was evolved with remarkable ingenuity. The scheme is in force since the enactment of the Press Council Act of 1978 under which the revived Press Council was set up in 1979.

Objects and Functions of the Council

The objects of present Press Council are substantially the same as were laid down under the Act of 1965 and it is not necessary to repeat them here. But the functions have undergone some change in that the three of the functions listed in the earlier Act were not included in the 1978 Act as they were considered to be burdensome for the Council to perform. These related to (a) promoting the establishment of such common services for the supply and dissemination of news to newspapers as may, from time to time, appear to it to be desirable;(b) providing facilities for proper education and training of persons in the profession of journalism; and (c) promoting technical or other research.

In addition, the Act of 1978 lists two new functions of the Council: (I) to undertake studies of foreign newspapers, including those brought out by any embassy or any other representative in India of a foreign State, their circulation and impact; and, (ii) to undertake such studies as may be entrusted to the Council and to express its opinion in regard to any matter referred to it by the Central Government.

The other functions remain the same as enumerated in the Act of 1965.

Power of the Council

The powers of the Press Council are provided in Section 14 and 15 of the Act as under:

Power to Censure Section 14:1) Where, on receipt of a complaint made to it or otherwise, the Council has reason to believe that a newspaper or news agency has offended against the standards of journalistic ethics or public taste or that an editor or a working journalist has committed any professional misconduct, the Council may, after giving the newspaper, or news agency, the editor or journalist concerned an opportunity of being heard, hold an enquiry in such manner as may be provided by the regulations made under this Act and, if it is satisfied that it is necessary to do, it may, for reasons to be recorded in writing, warn, admonish or censure the newspaper, the news agency, the editor or the journalist, as the case may be:

Provided that the Council may not take cognisance of a complaint if in the opinion of the Chairman, there is no sufficient ground for holding an enquiry.

- If the Council is of the opinion that it is necessary or expedient in public interest so to do, it may require any newspaper to publish therein in such manner as the Council thinks fit, any particulars relating to any enquiry under this section against a newspaper or news agency, an editor or a journalist working therein, including the name of such newspaper, news agency, editor or journalist.
- Nothing in sub-section (1) shall be deemed to empower the Council to hold an enquiry into any matter in respect of which any proceeding is pending in a court of law.
- The decision of the Council under sub-section (1), or sub-section (2), as the case may be, shall be final and shall not be questioned in any court of law.

General Powers of The Council

5 of 1908

15.(1) For the purpose of performing its functions or holding any enquiry under this Act, the Council shall have the same powers throughout India as are vested in a civil court while trying a suit under the Code of Civil Procedure, 1908, in respect of the following matters namely:-

- Summoning and enforcing the attendance of persons and examining them on oath;
- Requiring the discovery and inspection of documents;
- Receiving evidence on affidavits;
- Requisitioning any public record or copies thereof from any court or office;
- Issuing commissions for the examination of witnesses or documents; and
- Any other matter, which may be prescribed.

(2) Nothing in sub-section (1) shall be deemed to compel any newspaper, news agency, editor or journalist to disclose the source of any news or information published by that newspaper or received or reported by that news agency, editor or journalist.

45 of 1860

(3) Every enquiry held by the Council shall be deemed to be a judicial proceeding within the meaning of sections 193 and 228 of the Indian Penal Code.

- The Council may, if it considers it considers it necessary for the purpose of carrying out its objects or for the performance of any of its functions under this Act, make such observations, as it may think fit, in any of its decisions or reports, respecting the conduct of any authority, including Government.

Fundings of the Council

The Act provides that the Council may, for the purpose of performing its functions under the Act, levy fee at the prescribed rates from registered newspapers and news agencies. Apart from this, the Central Government has been enjoined to pay the Council by way of grant such sums of money as the Central Government may consider necessary, for the performance of its functions.

Functioning of the Council

The Council discharges its functions primarily through the medium of its Enquiry Committees, adjudicating on complaint cases received by it against the Press for violation of the norms of journalism or by the Press for interference with its freedom by the authorities. There is a set procedure for lodging a complaint with the Council.

A complainant is required essentially to write to the editor of the respondent newspaper, drawing his attention to what the complainant considers to be in breach of journalistic ethics or an offence against public taste. Apart from furnishing to the Council a cutting of the matter complained against, it is incumbent on the complainant to make and subscribe to a declaration that to the best of his knowledge and belief he has placed all the relevant facts before the Council and that no proceedings are pending in any court of law in respect of any matter alleged in the complaint; and that he shall inform the Council forthwith if during the pendency of the enquiry before the Council any matter alleged in the complaint becomes the subject matter of any proceedings in a court of law. The reason for this declaration is that in view of Section 14(3) of the Act, the Council cannot deal with any matter which is sub judice.

If the Chairman finds that there are no suffecient grounds for enquiry, he may dismiss the complaint and report it to the Council; otherwise, the Editor of the newspaper or the journalist concerned is asked to show cause why action should not be taken against him. On receipt of the written statement and other relevant material from the editor or the journalist, the Secretariat of the Council places the matter before the Enquiry Committee.

The Enquiry Committee screens and examines the complaint in necessary details. If necessary, it also calls for further particulars or documents from the parties. The parties are given opportunity to adduce evidence before the Enquiry Committee by appearing personally or through their authorised representative including legal practitioners. On the basis of the facts on record and affidavits or the oral evidence adduced before it, the Committee formulates its findings and recommendations and forwards them to the Council, which may or may not accept them. Where the Council is satisfied that a newspaper or news agency has offended against the standards of journalistic ethics or public taste or that an editor or working journalist has committed professional misconduct, the

Council may warn, admonish or censure the newspaper, the news agency, the editor or journalist, or disapprove the conduct thereof, as the case may be. In the complaints lodged by the Press against the authorities, the Council is empowered to make such observations as it may think fit in respect of the conduct of any authority including government. The decisions of the Council are final and cannot be questioned in any court of law. It will thus be seen that the Council wields a lot of moral authority although it has no legally enforceable punitive powers.

The Enquiry Regulations framed by the Council empower the Chairman to take suo motu action and issue notices to any party in respect of any matter falling within the scope of Press Council Act. The procedure for holding a suo motu enquiry is substantially the same as in the case of a normal enquiry except that for any normal enquiry a complaint is required to be lodged with the Council by a complainant. For the purpose of performing its functions or holding an enquiry under the Act the Council exercises some of the powers vested in a Civil Court trying a suit under the Code of Civil Procedure, 1908, in respect of the following matters, namely:-

- Summoning and enforcing the attendance of persons and examining them on oath;
- Requiring the discovery and inspection of documents;
- Receiving evidence on affidavits;
- Requisitioning any public record or copies thereof from any court or office;
- Issuing commissions for the examination of witnesses or documents; and
- Any other matter, which may be prescribed.

The Council expects the parties to cooperate with it in the conduct of its business. At least in two cases where the Council noticed that the parties were literally uncooperative or adamant, it exercised, its authority under Section 15 of the Act to compel them to appear before it and/or to furnish record etc. In the complaint of some Chandigarh journalists against the Chief Minister and the Government of Haryana, the erstwhile Council had to warn the authorities about the use of Council's coercive powers if they failed to respond to the notices sent by the Council. Similarly, in the famous case of B G Verghese against The Hindustan Times, the Birlas were directed to provide complete correspondence exchanged between Shri Verghese and Shri K K Birla.

The Council, in 1980 had proposed amendment of the Act, for empowering the Council to recommend to the authorities concerned, denial of certain facilities and concessions in the form of accreditation, advertisements, allocation of newsprint or concessional rates of postage for a certain period in the case of a newspaper which was censured thrice by the Council. Acceptance of the Council's recommendations on the part of the authorities was sought to be made obligatory. The Council was further of the view that, as in the case of newspapers, the power vested in it under Section 15(4) of the Press Council Act, 1978, to make such observations as it may think fit, in any of its decisions or reports, respecting the conduct of any authority including government, should expressly include the power to warn, admonish or censure such authorities and that the observations of the Council in this behalf should be placed on the Table of both the Houses of Parliament and/or of the Legislature of the State concerned. In the year 1987, the Council reconsidered the matter and after detailed deliberations, decided to withdraw its proposal for penal powers because it was of the reconsidered opinion that in the prevalent conditions these powers could tend to be misused by the authorities to curb the freedom of the Press.

Since then, time and again, suggestions/references have been made to the Council that it should have penal powers to punish the delinquent newspapers/journalists. In response, the Council has consistently taken the view that the moral sanctions provided to it under the existing scheme of the Act are adequate. The suggestion was repeated by the Union Minister for Information and Broadcasting in his inaugural address to the International Conference of Press Councils held in New Delhi in October, 1992, but the Council unanimously rejected it with the following reasoning:-

" Were the Council to be endowed with the power to impose sanctions/penalties, it would be equitable that the power to impose sanctions applies also when complaints are made by the Press against the Government and its authorities. A power to impose meaningful sanctions raises a number of issues, including, (a) the onus of proof; (b) the standard of proof; (c) the right to and cost of legal representation; and (d) whether review and/or appeal would be available. The effect of any or all of these issues may militate against the basic premise, that the Press Council's provide a democratic and efficient and inexpensive facility for hearing of the complaints, and that the consequent inevitability would, in effect, become courts, excercising judicial power and well known problems of access, cost, formality and delay would equally apply, thus defeating the basic purpose of the Press Council."

In December 1992 the Council received a reference from the Central Government soliciting its views on "whether a procedure can be laid down to ensure that newspapers/magazines censured by the Press Council for breach of guidelines in connection with communal writings, can be deprived of incentives from government, such as advertisements etcetera, and whether the Press Council would be in a position to suggest what action should be taken when it holds a newspaper/magazine guilty of breach of guidelines." The Council considered the matter in the meeting held in June1993 in the light of the stand adopted by it in the past against arming the Council with punitive powers. Having considered the matter in depth, the Council felt that the moral authority presently exercised by the Council is quite effective and the Council does not need any punitive powers in showing the Press the path of self-regulation. The Council, however, decided that if the newspaper is censured twice for any type of unethical writings within a period of three years, copies of such decisions should be forwarded to the Cabinet Secretary to the Government of India and to the Chief Secretary of the concerned State Government for information and such action, as may, in exercise of their discretion, be deemed to be appropriate in the circumstances of the case. The Council decided that that the period of three years will be taken as preceeding three years counted backwards from the date of the second censure.

Some of the Important Adjudications Rendered and Guidelines Issued by the Council

Since its establishment in 1966, the Council has rendered several momentous adjudications and issued guidelines which may have a lasting impact on the press in the country. The following are some of the important cases in which adjudications have been pronounced. The details are given at annexure A1-40

Communal Writings:

- Government of Orissa vs. Desh, Calcutta Weekly (1968 A.R. 25-27) (A-1)
- Government of Mysore vs. Zam Zam, Urdu Weekly of Bangalore (1969 A R 56-57) (A2)
- The Council initiated suo-motu action against the following papers and after due enquiry, while dropping the cases, it observed that restraint by the Press is necessary during the period when the country is passing through a tense phase resulting from conflict over such sensitive issues as communal riots: (1980 A R 131-146) (A-3)
- Dainik Jagran
- Asli Bharat
- Current
- Free Press Journal
- Shri Varsha
- Malayala Manorama
- Northern Indian Patrika

3(a) Dy. Commissioner, Hazaribagh Vs Ranchi Express (A R 86-87)

- Shri Shopat Singh Makkasor Vs. Rajasthan Patrika 18 th A R (231-232)
- Shri Zile Singh Chahal, General Secretary, All India Jat Maha Sabha, Rohtak versus Vishwa Mail Evening Daily, Kota. 18 th AR (234-235)

Defamation

- Government of Goa, Daman and Diu versus Blade (1969 A R 12-14) (A-4)

- P K Bansal Versus Surya India (12 th AR 218-222) (A-5)
- Madhu Limaye Vesus Indian Express (13 th AR 139-158) (A-6)
- Harikishan Singh Surjeet Vs Indian Express (13 th AR 125-139) (A-7)
- Vasant Sathe Vs The Independent (12 th AR 242-252) (A-8)
- Sh H N Kumar, Municipal Councillor as representative of the Municipal Committee, Madikheri Vs Editor 'Shakti', Kannada Daily, Madikheri. AR 1994 (A9)
- Sh Vatal Nagaraj, MLA, Karnataka Legislative Assembly, Bangalore Vs. Lankesh Patrika (111-112) 17th AR
- Complaints of Mrs Phanali Singhal versus Independent and The Hindustan Times (16 th AR Page 123,128,129-132)

Investigative Reporting

- R C Bhargava, Chairman, Maruti Udyog Ltd. Vs The Statesman 15 th AR (130-142) (A-10).

Obscenity and Bad Taste

- Delhi Adminstration Vs Confidential Advisor (1969 AR 50-52) (A-11)
- Sh Dinesh Bhai Trivedi, MP Rajya Sabha Vs. The Sunday Statesman Miscellany (14 th AR 531-536) (A-12)

Right to Privacy

- Sr. Cyrilla-Superior Franciscans of St. Mary of Angles/Fr. Placido Fonseco Vs. The Indian Express, Free Press Journal, Times of India and Samna (13 th AR 92-110) (A-13)
- Dr Vasudha Dhagamwar, Executive Director, MARG Vs India Today AR 1993 (A-14)

VI.. Right to Reply

- Shri T K Mahadevan Vs The Illustrated Weekly of India (1981 AR 130-135) (A-15)
- Dr Walter Fernandes Vs Surya India (11 th AR 233-235) (A-16)
- P K Bansal Vs Surya India (12 th AR 218-222) (A-5)
- Madhu Limaye/Harkishan Singh Surjeet Vs Indian Express (13 th AR 139-158) (A-6)

Pre-Publication Verification

- Government of Assam Vs Dainik Asom (1982 AR 82-85) (A-17)
- D N Saikia, Deputy Secretary, Government of Assam Vs. The Press Trust of India and The Statesman (12 th AR 140-142) (A-18)
- 3 (I) Government of Goa, Daman and Diu Vs Blade (1969 AR Pg 12-14) (A-4)

(ii) P K Bansal Vs Surya India (12 th AR 218-222) (A-5)

(iii) Madhu Limaye Vs Indian Express (13 th AR 139-158) (A-6)

(iv) Harkishan Singh Surjeet Vs Indian Express (13 th AR 125-139) (A-7)

(v) Vasant Sathe Vs The Independent (12 th AR 242-252) (A-8)

4. Deepak Vohra Vs Sunday Mail (PCI Review July 1994 59-71) (A-19) 16th AR 133-144

Right of the Press to use its own column

*   Shri Ashok Mehta, DUJ, IUJ, PUCL Vs Times of India (Aug. 4-5, 1998)

Threats to Press Freedom

*   Malayala Manorama Versus Government of Kerala (PCI Review, January 1983 Page 62) (A-20)
*   Malayala Manorama Versus various State Governments. (PCI Annual Report 1968, Page 38) (A-21).
*   Blitz Versus District Administration of Dehradun (PCI review April 1984, Page 30) (A-22).
*   Mahajati Versus Government of Assam (PCI Review, October 1983, page 55) (A-23).
*   Suo Motu action by Press Council of India against the Government of Karnataka (PCI Review April 1982, page 36) (A-24)
*   Madhya Pradesh Small Newspapers Association Versus Municipal Commissioner. (PCI Annual Report, 1972, page 66) (A-25).
*   Searchlight Versus Deputy Commissioner of Ranchi. (PCI Annual Report 1972, page 65) (A-26).
*   Dainik Janambhumi Versus Government of Assam. (PCI Annual Report 1980, page 56) (A-27)
*   Chandigarh Union of Journalists Versus Government of Haryana. (PCI Annual Report 1974, page 68) (A-28)
*   U.P. Small and Medium Newspapers Editors Council Versus District Magistrate, Hardoi. (PCI Review January 1983, page 58) (A-29)
*   Suo Motu action by Press Council of India (Annual Report 1983, page 37) (A-30)
*   Sarita Mukta Versus Government of Madhya Pradesh (PCI Annual Report 1981, page 60) (A-31)
*   Suo motu action-attacks on Gujarat Samachar (Annual Report 1986, page 44) (A-32)
*   Shri Rama Shanker Prasad, Bihar Vs S.P. Nalanda 15 th AR page 24-25

Advertisement and Press Freedom

*   Tribune Versus Government of Haryana (PCI Annual Report 1979, page 45) (A-33)

- Saptahik Mujahid Versus Government of Assam. (PCI Review July 1983 page 44) (A-34)
- Searchlight and Pradeep Vs Government of Bihar (PCI Annual Report 1974, Page 11) (A-35)
4. Amar Ujala (Bareilly and Meerut Editions) Vs Distt. Admn, UP 15 th AR 66-67

Impropriety and Press Freedom

- Arjun Baan Versus Pargana Officer of Tehsil Briswa, UP (PCI Annual Report, 1983, Page 40)(A-36)
- Press Correspondent, Hind Samachar Versus Government of Punjab(PCI Annual Report 1973, page 27) (A-37)
- Vishwa Manav Versus S.P., Badayun (PCI Review October 1983, page 52) (A-38)
- Ex Member of ParliamentVersus Government of Andhra Pradesh (PCI Annual Report 1972, Page 7) (A-39)
- Complaint of P Rajan Vesrsus Mathrubhumi (AR 1989-90 page 72)(A-40)
- Atul Maheshwari, Editor, Amar Ujala, Hindi Daily, Meerut Vs ECI (17 th AR Page 45)
7. Shri Ritendra Mathur, Panchjanya Versus PRO, MP Legislative Assembly (June 98)

A study of these adjudications would show that the Council has been unquestionably successful in its efforts towards achieving the objects set before it of not only preserving the freedom of the press but also ensuring that the standards of journalism are maintained and improved. While the authorities, after Press Council's intervention, have been seen to be generally refraining from indulging in putting undue pressure on the Press, the press-persons too have tended to restrain themselves from the kind of journalism that could undermine the standards expected of them. The moral impact of the Council has come to be widely recognised. The tremendous increase in the number of complaints from 80 in 1979 to 1075 in 1997 is ample proof of the faith expressed by mediamen and the public alike, in the working, importance and need for a body like the Council at the helm of the fourth estate.

Code of Conduct

Section 13 (2) (b) of the Press Council Act, 1978, enjoins the Council to build up a Code of Conduct for newspapers, news agencies and journalists in accordance with the high professional standards to help and guide the newsmen. Building of such a Code is a dynamic process which has to keep pace with time and events. The expression "build up" indicates that the code may be evolved by the Press Council on case by case basis through its adjudications. A compendium of broad principles evolved by the Press Council through its adjudications/guidelines was first published in the year 1984 by the Council in collaboration with the Indian Law Institute under the title " VIOLATION OF JOURNALISTIC ETHICS AND PUBLIC TASTE" This compilation of principles is sorted out from the decisions or adjudications of the Council or the guidelines issued by it or its Chairman. In 1986, the second part of the compendium entitled "VIOLATION OF FREEDOM OF THE PRESS" relating to adjudications and principles in matters or complaints against the government and its authorities which were of important and far reaching nature and which involved observations respecting the conduct of any authority including government was published.

Since 1986 there has been a continuous increase in the institution of complaints and their disposal by the Press Council with consequent acceleration of the process of building up the code. In 1992, the Council brought out " A Guide to Journalistic Ethics" containing principles of journalistic ethics culled out from the adjudications of the Council and the guidelines issued by it in their wake.

As several more decisions of far reaching importance relating to the rights and responsibilities of the press have been rendered since then by the Council, a 162 page elaborate and comprehensive second edition of the guide has been issued. It also deals with the concept of right to privacy and lays down the guidelines to be followed in this behalf. The law of defamation has also been dealt with in some of its aspects for the guidance of the press, public servants and public figures. The Council has in an important adjudication respecting alleged defamation of public officials of a Municipal Committee held that the remedy of action for damages against the Press or the media is simply not available to public officials with respect to their acts and conduct relevant to the discharge of their official duties, even if the publication is based on facts and statements which are not true, unless the official establishes that the publication was made with reckless disregard for the truth.

In such a case it will be enough for the defendant (member of the press or media) to prove that he acted after a reasonable verification of the facts; it is not necessary for him to prove that what he has written is true. But where the publication is proved to be false and actuated by malice or personal animosity, the defendant would have no defence and would be liable for the damages. However, a public official enjoys the same protection as any other citizen in matters not relevant to the discharge of his duties. Of course, judiciary and Parliament and State Legislatures represent exception to this rule as the former is protected by the power to punish for its contempt and the latter by their privileges under Articles 105 and 194 respectively of the Constitution. The Council has further held that this does not mean that the Official Secrets Act, 1923 or any similar enactment or provision having the force of law does not bind the press or media. It has also been held that there is no law empowering the State or its officials to prohibit or to impose a prior restraint upon the press/media.

In regard to public official's claim to privacy, the Council has laid down that if there is a clash between the public official's privacy and the public's right to know about his personal conduct, habits, personal affairs and traits of character impinging upon or having a bearing on the due discharge of his official duties, the former must yield to the latter.

However, in matters of personal privacy which are not relevant to discharge of his official duties, the public official enjoys the same protection as any other citizen.

This Guide as a whole suggests a way of steering safely and responsibly through the minefield of legal, moral and ethical problems which confront the editors, journalists and owners of newspapers everyday. The Guide is not a compilation of cast-iron principles but contains broad general principles, which, if applied with due discernment and adaptation to varying circumstances of each case, will help the journalists to self-regulate the conduct of their profession along the path of professional rectitude. These are by no means exhaustive nor are they meant to obtain a rigidity which could hinder the unfettered working of the Press.

BROAD PRINCIPLES EVOLVED

Some of the broad principles evolved by the Council in course of its adjudication on various subjects both in respect of standards of journalism and the freedom of the Press are summarised as under:

JOURNALISTIC STANDARDS

Communal Writings

Scurrilous and inflammatory attacks should not be made on communities and individuals. Any news on communal events based on rumours will be violative of the journalistic ethics. Similarly, distorted reporting making important omissions will not be correct. While it is the legitimate function of the Press to draw attention to the genuine grievance of any community with a view to seeking redress in a peaceful and legal manner, there should be no invention or exaggeration of grievances, particularly those which tend to promote communal discord.

It will be highly conducive to the creation of a healthy and peaceful atmosphere if sensational, provocative and alarming headlines are avoided, and acts of violence or vandalism are reported in such a manner as may not undermine people's confidence in law and order machinery of the State and may at the same time have the effect of discouraging and condemning such activities.

Defaming a community is a serious matter and ascribing to it a vile, anti-national activity is reprehensible and amounts to journalistic impropriety.

There is no impropricty in publishing historical facts in order to warn the present generation against repetition of past mistakes even though these mistakes may not be palatable to a particular community.

There is no objection in making statements about religious communities if they are couched in temperate language and are not exaggerated or incorrect.

Journalistic impropriety

Some of the principles evolved by the Council through its adjudications in respect of journalistic impropriety are:

Any matter discussed or disclosed in confidence ought not to be published without obtaining the consent of the source. If the editor finds that the publication is in the public interest, he should clarify it in an appropriate footnote that the statement or discussion in question was being published although it had been made "off the record".

An advertisement containing anything unlawful or illegal, or the one which is contrary to good taste or journalistic ethics or propriety should not be published.

Proper care should be taken by newspapers in maintaining accuracy in respect of quotations.

Where a newspaper is charged with violation of journalistic ethics, a plea that it has ceased publication will afford the editor no defence, since it is his conduct which is subject of the complaint.

Obscenity and Bad Taste

The meaning of taste varies according to the context. For a journalist it implies that "which on grounds of decency or propriety he should not publish". Where a matter has "a tendency to stimulate sex feelings" its publication in a journal meant for the lay public, young or old, undesirable. Exploitation of sex falls short good taste. Public taste is to be judged in relation to the environment, milieu as well notions of taste prevailing in contemporary society.

The basic test of obscenity is whether the matter is so gross or vulgar that it is likely to deprave or corrupt. Another test is whether depiction of the scene and language used can be regarded as filthy, repulsive, dirty or lewd.

Whether a story is obscene or not, will depend on such factors as literary or cultural nature of the magazine, and the social theme of the story. The relevancy of a picture to the subject matter of a magazine or a paper has a bearing on the question whether the matter published falls below the standards of public taste. One of the relevant factors for judging whether the picture falls below the standard of public taste will be the purpose or nature of the magazine - whether it relates to art, painting, medicine, research or reform of sex.

The Press Council expressed concern over the increasing instances of obscene advertisements in the print media. It was opposed to censorship but favoured preventive steps to check any obscene material at pre-publication stage. Since most of such advertisements are routed through advertising agencies, the Council felt that this task should not be difficult if these agencies were to exercise more caution and restrain in preparing and releasing the advertisements that may be considered objectionable to family viewing by an average citizen. It felt that the Association of Advertising Agencies of India as an Umbrella organisation of all these advertising agencies could play a very meaningful and positive role in the matter and sought its cooperation to contain advertisements that are likely to damage the socio-cultural ethos of the country in the longer run. The Council appealed to the newspapers also to carefully scrutinize the advertisements received by them either directly from the advertisers or through the advertising agencies and exercise a self-restraint by rejecting such advertisements as may be considered obscene and objectionable. It has also reiterated the following guidelines framed by it to counter against obscene publication.

"Newspapers shall not display advertisements which are vulgar or which through depiction of a woman in nude or lewd posture, provoke lecherous attention of males as if she herself was commercial commodity for sale".

Whether a picture is obscene or not, is to be judged in relation to three tests; namely

(i) Is it vulgar and indecent?

(ii) Is it a piece of mere pornography?

(iii) Is its publication meant merely to make money by titillating the sex feeling of adolescents and among whom it is intended to circulate? In other words, does it constitute an unwholesome exploitation for commercial gain.

Other relevant considerations are whether the picture is relevant to the subject matter of the magazine. That is to say, whether its publication serves any preponderating social or public purpose, in relation to art, painting, medicine, research or reform of sex.

Right of Reply

The prime principle that emanates from the various adjudications on this subject upholds the editors discretion in publication of letters. He would, however, be expected to voluntarily rectify an incorrect statement or report on a matter of public nature; the general reader can claim a locus standi on the basis of the public right to know. Besides, any person who has been specifically referred to in a publication can claim an automatic right to reply in the columns of the paper. Though the Council does not have the power to force a newspaper to publish, a rejoinder it may direct it to publish the particulars of the enquiry against it.

Pre-verification of News

Verification of news is necessary before publication, especially when the report has slanderous or libellous overtones or could lead to communal tension; nor can the publication of rumours as views of a cross-section of people be justified under any circumstances. The editor shall make necessary amends when any false or distorted publication is brought to his notice.

Defamation - Scurrilous writings

Under the second exception to Section 499 of the Indian Penal Code it is not defamation to express in good faith any opinion whatever respecting the conduct of a public servant in the discharge of his public functions, or respecting his character, so far as his character appears in that conduct, and no further. The Council has accordingly held the opinion that fair comments on the public life cannot be held to be improper. But if any factual statements are made, they must be true and correct. In case a defamatory element is involved, more good faith will not be a defence in any civil action for damages.

Right to privacy Vs. Public figures

The Press Council of India formulated guidelines to achieve a balance between the right to privacy of the public persons and the right of the press to have access to information of public interest and importance. The issue under heated debate at both national and international level and the international conference of the World Association of Press Councils (WAPC) held in April 1998 in Delhi, stressed that there is a need for reconciliation between three competing constitutional values at play on this count, viz: (a) an individual's right to privacy, (b) freedom of the press, and (c) the people's right to know about public figures in public interest.

The Council has prepared a report on the issue and framed the guidelines as follows:-

"Right to privacy is an inviolable human right. However, the degree of privacy differs from person to person and from situation to situation. The public person who functions under public gaze as an emissary/representative of the public cannot expect to be afforded the same degree of privacy as a private person. His acts and conduct are of public interest ('public interest' being distinct and separate from 'of interest to the public') even if conducted in private may be brought to public knowledge through the medium of the press. The press has, however, a corresponding duty to ensure that the informations about such acts and conduct of public interest of the public person is obtained through fair means, is properly verified and then reported accurately. For obtaining the information in respect of acts done or conducted away from public gaze, the press is not expected to use surveill devices. For obtaining information about private talks and discussions, while the press is expected not to badger the public persons, the public persons are also expected to bring more openness in their functioning and co-operate with the press in its duty of informing the public about the acts of their representatives".

FREEDOM OF THE PRESS

Threats to Press Freedom

An attack on a paper or those connected with it editorially or in management with a view to pressurising or intimidating them for the opinion expressed in the paper, constitutes a gross interference with the freedom of the Press.

Tendencies to coerce newspapers to desist from publishing facts or toe a particular line are matters of concern.

The local administration is expected to help the journalist to perform his duties without being under duress or pressure.

Implication of an editor of a newspaper in a fabricated case by the police authorities with a view to harassing him for his treatment of the news or critical writings amounts to interference in the freedom of the Press.

Groups raids on newspaper offices by unruly mobs interferes with the freedom of the Press. Suitable precautionary protective measures ought to be taken by the police. The same applies to blockade of newspapers offices.

Harassment and victimization of journalists by police is a direct attack on the freedom of the Press.

Seizure of camera and removal of film by police from a Press Photographer while covering the news would amount to preventing the journalist from performing his duties and is a matter to be viewed seriously.

Filing of motivated frivolous cases against a journalist would amount to interfering with his functions.

Any attempt by a minister to browbeat a reporter into toeing his line in the matter of reporting would be inconsistent with maintaining the proper standards of ministerial conduct towards the Press.

Disaccreditation and withdrawal of housing facilities from a newspaper correspondent because of articles/news items written by him would amount to an attempt to pressurise the correspondent and, therefore, the Press.

The Press and Registration of Books Act, 1867, does not empower the District Magistrate to obtain "Assurance Letters" from prospective editors before granting or refusing a declaration.

Declaration of newspapers under the Press and Registration of Books Act, 1867, cannot be cancelled on the ground that the newspapers concerned were indulging in yellow journalism. Any complaint in regard to yellow journalism should be filed with the Press Council. Closeness of the date of appearance of a critical article and the date of disaccreditation would be material factors determining whether the disaccreditation was on account of that article.

Advertisement and Press Freedom

The giving or withholding of advertisements, whether by individuals or by the government as a lever to influence the editorial policy constitutes a threat to and jeopardises the liberty of the Press, meaning in this context the freedom of the editor. This is especially so in case of the government since it is the trustee of public funds and, therefore, bound to utilise them without discrimination.

Advertisements, from any party including the government cannot be claimed as a matter of right by a newspaper. Government can frame its policy of placing advertisements based on objective criteria. But this should be based upon publicly stated principles without taking into consideration the editorial policy of the paper.

If an editor is guilty of an action or an impropriety de hors his paper, he can be proceeded against personally but this would not justify denial of advertisements to the paper of which he happens to be the editor. This applies to an employee or even the proprietor of a newspaper.

The outside activities of the editor or other journalists might throw light on what he wrote for the paper, and in the event of such writings being improper, action against the paper is justified. However, this is for improper publication and for the employees' activities de hors the paper. (Ibid)

Impropriety and Press Freedom

It is improper to offer an inducement to a journalist to adopt a particular line of comment, and for the journalist to accept such an inducement. In the event of improper inducement being offered by the government the situation would be worse, since, then the media would become an arm of law enforcement. (Ibid)

It is improper for a journalist to accept an assignment which would be incompatible with the integrity and dignity of his profession or exploitation of his status as journalist. (Ibid) The editor of a newspaper cannot be asked to divulge the source of information of a letter published in his paper.

Asking a journalist to divulge his personal and confidential source of information amounts to violation of his obligation to report on events of public interest and constitutes a threat to Press freedom.

The editor of a newspaper cannot be directed by the police to alert his correspondent against the publication of a news item relating to the acts of the police, as it would be against the fundamental right of the Press.

The motivated stoppage of subscription of teleprinter service of a news agency due to the feeling that reportage of a certain situation was exaggerated and to pressurize the agency would amount a threat to the freedom of the press.

Singling out news despatches to a newspaper and arrest of editors for activities in discharge of their professional duties and issue of warning letter from the government to newspapers to desist from publishing anything relating to certain activities of some groups, could legitimately give rise to an apprehension of threat to the freedom of the Press.

GUIDELINES AND POLICY FORMULATIONS

The Council has issued guidelines and recommended policy framework on various matters concerning the Press and the people. In addition, the Chairmen of the Council have been guiding the Press through statements whenever a serious situation arose in which the Press was expected to work with restraint and circumspection. They also reacted sharply through such statements whenever organised major offensives were made against the Press.

In 1969, the Council issued a 10-point guidelines laying down norms and standards in reporting and commenting on matters which bear on communal relations. Without being exhaustive the guidelines listed and explained what would be offending against journalistic propriety and ethics, and should, therefore, be avoided.

Again, in the wake of the happenings in Ayodhya in 1990, the Council while reiterating the 1969 guidelines, issued another 12-point guidelines in the light of the new experience. The Council said that the principles outlined in it should be inculcated at every level of the media from training stage upwards and made a standard of external accountability. These principles laid down certain 'dos' and don'ts for both the Press and the State.

The Council has over the years formulated policy framework in respect of such subjects as rules of accreditation, newsprint, advertisements, selection of journalists for accompanying the President, the Prime Minister etc., on their foreign tours. As stated earlier, the Council has, following a decision taken in its meeting in October 1982, published two compendiums of its adjudication; one each on violation of journalistic ethics and violation of freedom of the Press, giving at the end of a similar set of cases the principles underlying the adjudications.

Special Enquiries

Apart from enquiring into the regular complaints, the Council has held a number of special enquiries, mostly suo motu, but sometimes on complaints into incidents and matters concerning the Press.

Report on Deshar Katha, Tripura 1990

Following a complaint by Shri Gautam Das, Editor, Daily Deshar Katha, a Bengali newspaper of Agartala, Tripura, regarding frequent violent attacks on the employees and hawkers of his newspapers by Congress (I) workers, the Press Council set up a Special Committee to make a thorough on-the-spot enquiry. The Committee visited Agartala and heard the representatives of the

Government of Tripura and the complainant. As a result the Government of Tripura assured that they would take all necessary steps to prevent recurrence of such incidents and provide full security to Deshar Katha.

Ayodhya Report 1990

A special enquiry was set up on the Ayodhya happenings in 1990 and another in 1992. Their reports were made public in 1991 and 1993 respectively. In the first enquiry, the Council found four Uttar Pradesh dailies Jagran, Aj, Swatantra Bharat and Swatantra Chetna, guilty of publishing reports which constituted a grave violation of norms of journalistic ethics. The Council censured* these newspapers for violation of the norms. The Council also criticised the Uttar Pradesh Government for its many lapses in dealing with the situation and its behaviour towards the Press. It expressed serious concern over the authorities taking recourse

*Jagran has challenged this decision of the Council before the Allahabad High Court, which is pending. to punitive and preventive action in excess of the demand of the situation and deplored invoking provisions of non-existent Press (Objectionable Matters) Act, 1951, and misapplying the provisions of the Press and Registration of Books Act, 1867.

Ayodhya Report 1993

In the wake of the demolition of the disputed shrine at Ayodhya on 6.12.1992 came the reports of numerous attack on journalists/press media photographers/cameramen who were covering the happenings at Ayodhya on 6.12.1992 and thereabout. As the matter was of great urgency and concern, a Special Enquiry Committee headed by the Chairman of the Council was set up to enquire into the matter. Prior to this the Chairman had already issued an appeal urging restraint and moderation on the part of the press while reporting events and presenting comments bearing on communal relations. Simultaneously, he expressed concern on the incidents of assaults on journalists when, they in discharge of their professional duties, were trying to cover the events. He also appealed to the authorities to ensure that the press is allowed to function freely and fearlessly to disseminate information on matters of public importance.

The Special Committee set up vide order dated 14.12.1992 collected oral and written evidence at its sittings at Ayodhya, Faizabad, Lucknow and Delhi and submitted its report to the full Council on 7.1.1993. The report as adopted by Council was released on 8.1.1993.

Punjab Report 1991

An enquiry was held into the pressures and problems confronting the Press and its personnel during acts of terrorism in Punjab. Adopting the report of the

Special Committee, captioned 'Overcoming Fear' the Council extended its full support to the Punjab Press in its efforts to inform the people truthfully and impartially of the events and circumstances in the State and in resisting any code or norm sought to be imposed on it through force or intimidation by any extraneous authority or organisation.

J&K Report 1991

Similarly, a special enquiry was held on the problems faced by the Press in Jammu and Kashmir. Adopting the report of this committee in July 1991, the Council said the critical importance of information and communication in the complex and difficult situation in Kashmir had not been adequately realised either by the government or by the media itself. It suggested a series of measures to respond effectively to the various aspects of the situation. The full report was later published under the caption 'Crisis and Credibility'.

Bihar Report 1993

The report on increasing incidents of assaults on journalists and the pressures/impediments in the way of free functioning of the Press in the State of Bihar adopted by the Council on March 31, 1993 advised the Press and the authorities to put their relations on more healthy footings.

Report on AIDS and the Media 1993

The report on 'AIDS AND THE MEDIA' laid down certain do's and don'ts for the media advising them that from sporadic news AIDS must become campaign target. At the same time, the Press should bear in mind that the 'public interest' which may justify publication of a matter within the preserve of personal privacy, must be a 'legitimate interest' and not prurient or morbid curiosity.

Defence Report 1993

Yet another report of June 1993 captioned 'Pen and Sword' advocated an attitude of greater openness in Defence related information.

J & K Report 1994

The Council's latest report of 1994 on "Threats to the media from militant organisation in J & K" has recommended prompt dissemination of information at government level to counter militant propaganda. The report has also advised the Government to provide institutional and area security to the media personnel who face threats from the militants for taking independent stand.

The Model Advertisement Policy 1994

In the year 1994 the Council formulated uniform Advertisement Policy for application throughout India. It provides a succinct criteria for approval of newspapers for empanelment by the authorities for advertisements.

Guidelines on 'Pre-poll' and 'Exit-polls' Survey

The Press Council of India having considered the question of desirability or otherwise of publication of findings of pre-poll surveys and the purpose served by them, is of the view that the newspapers should not allow their forum to be used for distortions and manipulations of the elections and should not allow themselves to be exploited by the interested parties.

The Press Council, therefore, advises that in view of the crucial position occupied by the electoral process in a representative democracy like ours, the newspapers should be on guard against their precious forum being used for distortions and manipulations of the elections. This has become necessary to emphasize today since the print media is sought to be increasingly exploited by the interested individuals and groups to misguide and mislead the unwary voters by subtle and not so subtle propaganda on casteist, religious and ethnic basis as well as by the use of sophisticated means like the alleged pre-poll surveys. While the communal and seditious propaganda is not difficult to detect in many cases, the interested use of the pre-poll survey, sometimes deliberately planted, is not so easy to uncover. The Press Council, therefore, suggests that whenever the newspapers publish pre-poll surveys, they should take care to preface them conspicuously by indicating the institutions which have carried such surveys, the individuals and organisations which have commissioned the surveys, the size and nature of sample selected, the method of selection of the sample for the findings and the possible margin of error in the findings.

1. Further in the event of staggered poll dates, the media is seen to carry exit-poll surveys of the polls already held. This is likely to influence the voters where the polling is yet to commence. With a view to ensure that the electoral process is kept pure and the voters' minds are not influenced by any external factors, it is necessary that the media does not publish the exit-poll surveys till the last polls is held.

2. The Press Council, therefore, request the Press to abide by the following guideline in respect of the exit-polls:

Guideline:

No newspaper shall publish exit-poll surveys, however, genuine they may be, till last of the polls is over.

Press Council of India frames Guidelines for Financial Journalists.

The Press Council of India counselled reporters/financial journalists/ newspaper establishments to refrain from receiving any gift/grants/concessions/ facilities, etc., either in cash or kind which are likely to compromise free and unbiased reporting on financial matters.

1. The Council in its Report observed that the financial journalists today enjoy considerable influence over readers' minds and, therefore, they owe it to them to present a balanced and objective view of the financial

dealings, status and prospects of a company. It observed that some companies are given excessive news coverage in the newspapers/ magazines because they have issued advertisements to that print media. Sometimes, adverse reports are published of those companies which do not give advertisements to the newspapers or magazines. Again, when a media is not happy with any company/management for whatever reason, the negative aspects of the company are highlighted, while in the reverse situation, no negative aspects are brought to light. Some companies are also known to give gifts, loans, discounts, preferential shares, etc., to certain financial journalists to receive favourable and positive reports of the companies. At the same time, there is no mechanism for investors' education or for raising public opinion against such unhealthy practices.

2. The Council feeling concerned over the malpractice in the Corporate Sector and after holding detailed deliberations and discussions with the representatives financial institutions and journalists, has recommended the guidelines enumerated below for observance by the financial journalists:

   - The financial journalists should not accept gifts, loans, trips, discounts, preferential shares or other considerations which compromise or are likely to compromise his position.
   - It should be mentioned prominently in the report about any company that the report is based on information given by the company or the financial sponsors of the company.
   - When the trips are sponsored for visiting establishments of a company, the author of the report who has availed of the trip must state invariably that the visit was sponsored by the company concerned and that it had also extended the hospitality as the case may be.
   - No matter related to the company should be published without verifying the facts from the company and the source of such report should also be disclosed.
   - A reporter who exposes a scam or brings out a report forpromotion of a good project, should be encouraged and awarded.
   - A journalist who has financial interests such as share holdings, stock holdings, etc., in a company, should not report on that company.
   - The journalist should not use for his own benefit of his relations and friends, information received by him in advance for publication.
   - No newspaper owner, editor or anybody connected with a

newspaper should use his relations with the newspaper to promote his other business interests.
–   Whenever there is an indictment of a particular advertising agency or advertiser by the Advertising Council of India, the newspaper in which the advertisement was published must publish the news of indictment prominently.

Portrayal of Women in Media (1996)

The Central Government in February 1995 forwarded to the Press Council for its views, the recommendations of Maharashtra Government on the possible role of audo-visual and print media in the advancement of the cause of women. A Sub-Committee of the Council interacted with prominent film/media personalities and other eminent persons. Its report was adopted by the Council on January 8, 1996. While concurring with and endorsing the recommendations of Maharashtra Government's Policy for Women, the Council made seventeen more recommendations, prominent among them being (a) stories of atrocities on women should be published but without sensationalising them; (b) efforts of the media should be directed towards highlighting the positive achievements of women; (c) the downward slide in the moral ethos has to be checked by combating obscenity and vulgarity; (d) the Press Council of India on its part should accord priority to consideration of complaints brought before it on charges of denigrating women and build up further guidelines etc. In conclusion, it was emphasized that fructification of such a policy document will be possible only through the cohesive will of the people of all strata of society.

Problems of Small and Medium Newspapers (1996)

A sub-committee of the members of the Council had been set up to go into the problems of small and medium newspapers in the country. The sub-committee in its report to the Council, while identifying the problems faced by the small and medium newspapers, made some concrete long-term/short term recommendations in the matter: (a) a Small and Medium Newspaper Development Corporation should be set up as an autonomous body with a view to promote and ensure the development of small and medium papers or in the alternative they be encouraged to form cooperative society; (b) the government should devise a suitable advertisement policy in keeping with the guidelines framed by the Press Council of India; (c) the DAVP should display the list of those newspapers which are granted advertisements every quarter; (d) all advertisement bills of the papers should be settled by the Directorate of Audio-Visual Publicity and Directorate of Information and Public Relations within 45 days of the receipt thereof; (e) while printing paper be brought within the purview of newsprint and a specific quantity thereof be earmarked for small and medium newspapers; (f) 75 per cent advertisements like those of biogas chulha, which do not concern the urban areas, should be given to the small and medium newspapers. These recommendations which were twenty-two in all were unanimously adopted by the Press Council.

Closure of Newspapers and Problems of Urdu Newspapers

The Council had undertaken a study to gauge the reasons for increase in closure of newspapers over the past few years. The Committee of the Council had studied the situation in various regions all over the country. In the meantime the specific problems being faced by the Urdu papers were also brought to its attention.

Favour to Journalists

The public outcry in 1998 over the reported attempts to win over the media through gifts and favours had prompted the Press Council of India to undertake a comprehensive study of the issue with regard to all kinds of favours/benefits, either in cash or in kind in the form of concessions, gifts, lands, house facilities etc., extended to journalists (both editors and other than editors) news agencies, newspaper establishments and owners by various authorities during the 10 year period from 1985-95).

The Committee in its report, as adopted by the Council on 22.1.1998, listed the undue favours as apart from these facilities for journalistic work and observed that ultimately the strength of the moral fabric of the press itself shall decide whether or not to be swayed by the inducements and enticements thrown its way by those in power.

Legislations Examined

The Council considered in depth the provisions of the Press and Registration of Books (Amendments) Bill, 1988, and held that it went beyond the statement of its objects. It did not implement properly the recommendations of the Second Press Commission relating to the subject. Though some of the provisions were of a positive nature, certain others were fraught with mischief leading to consequences perilous to the freedom of the Press. The Council suggested many radical changes in the Bill. The government later withdrew the Bill.

Similarly, the Council examined suo motu the Jammu and Kashmir Special Powers (Press) Bill, 1989. It also heard the State Ministers and representatives of various organisations of the Press on September 29, 1989 on the provisions of the Bill. After that the Council held that the J & K Government already had sufficient powers in its armoury in the form of existing State and Central legislations which could be effectively used to deal with cases of gross misconduct by the Press over the entire ground for which fresh powers were sought under the Bill.

The Council said that preventive laws with wide powers of pre-censorship and forfeiture would, by muzzling the Press, give free rein to rumours and destroy the credibility of the entire print and broadcast media within J & K and in the rest of the country. The Council was of the view that pre-censorship was inherently inimical to the freedom of the press. It recommended that the Bill be withdrawn. It also recommended revival of the Press Advisory Council in the State. The Bill was later withdrawn by the J & K Government in the State Assembly.

The Council also examined the Karnataka (Freedom of the Press) Bill, 1988, and the Karnataka Legislature (Powers, Privileges and Immunities) Bill, 1988, and gave various suggestions to make them more effective in respect of the freedom of the Press.

The Council made concrete and comprehensive recommendations regarding the repeal/amendment of the Official Secrets Act, 1923. It was first done in 1982 and again in 1990. In 1990, the Council said that the existing Act should be repealed in toto. It is no use amending a bad law. The Official Secrets Act is repugnant to open government and also militates against the ethos of the Constitutional guarantee of freedom of speech and expression enshrined in Article 19 (1) (a). A new legislation should be enacted which may be called "Freedom of Information Act." In event of this not being done, the Council suggested many amendments aimed at removing the deleterious affects of the various provisions of the Act on the Press.

The Council discussed Shri V.N. Gadgil's (MP) Right to Reply in the Press Bill, 1994 and considered it in all its ramifications in response to a reference made to it by the Union Government. It communicated its view that 'the proposed legislation is vulnerable from the stand-points of its necessity, propriety, viability, workability and above all, its constitutional validity'. The bill has since been withdrawn.

In response to another reference from the Central Government on publication of newspapers in India by foreign interests, the Council communicated its opinion on June 22, 1992, "that it does not favour publication of foreign newspapers/news journals in India involving equity and management participation", adding that "the present arrangements could be reconsidered or reviewed after 3 to 5 years". After a Cabinet Sub-Committee headed by Shri N.K.P.Salve was set up to make recommendation for any modifications in the policy decisions taken by Government on the subject in 1955 - 56, the matter was again referred to the Council for its comments. The Council has reiterated its views conveyed in June 1992.

Studies

The Press Council Act, 1978, empowers the Council to undertake studies in regard to matters concerning the Press. The Council in collaboration with the Indian Law Institute has conducted various studies *viz.*, Official Secrets Act 1923, (recommendations since updated in 1990) Contempt of Courts Act, 1971, Parliamentary Privileges and Law of Defamation etc., in so far as they relate to the Press. This is a major accomplishment. These publications help the mediapersons understand the scope of their rights and the limits of their functioning.

Protection of Confidential Sources of Information

In Contempt of Court proceedings the press usually makes the plea that it should not be forced to disclose Confidential source. "Such a plea for justification has been permitted on a limited basis. The Press's right to hold on to its sources of information has been balanced against other aspects of public interest. By way of tail piece, it has also been added that the press often demands the right to break confidence more than they plead the right to hold on to their own confidential sources. It is only fair that each claim should be balanced against other claims without conceding total primacy to the press in respect of its investigative and truth verification functions".

In 1983, the Law Commission of India sent a questionnaire soliciting the views of the Press Council, inter alia, regarding disclosure of source of information by a journalist acquired by him in confidence for the purpose of his profession. In response to the Law Commission's question on the subject, the Press Council expressed as follows:

"In the opinion of the Council, the provision contained in Section 15 (2) of the Press Council Act, 1978 incorporates the latest trend and principles on the subject. Although under the above Act it is confined only to the proceedings under the Act it is strongly recommended that it should be made a part of the general law of the land." "It is equally strongly felt that if any exception is to be made, it should be done in cases of extreme nature where disclosure is altogether unavoidable in the interest of the administration of justice. But the powers to order disclosure should be conferred only on competent court and that also in confidence to the presiding officer in the first instance, who may then, if satisfied that it is germane to the decision of the case, take such steps as may be necessary to make it a part of the evidence on record".

The Law Commission of India submitted its 93rd Report to the Government of India on 10th August, 1983 recommending for insertion of Section 132A in the Indian Evidence Act, 1872, as under:

"132A - No court shall require a person to disclose the source of information contained in a publication for which he is responsibile, where such information has been obtained by him on the express agreement or implied understanding that the source will be kept confidential".

"Explanation: In this section -

(a) 'publication' means any speech, writing, broadcast or other communication in whatever form, which is addressed to the public at large or any section of the public.

(b) 'source' means the person from whom, or the means through which, the information was obtained".

It seems that the Government of India has not taken any step to get this recommendation of the Law Commission, implemented. The same can be said about the relatively moderate recommendations of the Press Commission/or of the Press Council of India, on this subject.

Lectures by the Chairman of the Council and other activities

The successive Chairman of the Council have been invited to address seminars or deliver lectures arranged by various organisations and institutions where they have stressed the need for ensuring objective and factually correct reportage by the Press, the need to safeguard and strengthen Press freedom and to help in maintaining peace and harmony between different communities.

All earlier Chairmen have also been participating in such activities and spreading awareness about the need to preserve and protect Press freedom and to observe high ethical standards of journalism as also about the role and functioning of the Press Council in this behalf.

Students of journalism from various universities which impart instructions on the subject have been visiting the office of the Press Council and the Chairman have addressed them about the objects, functioning and working of the Council and the rights and responsibilities of the Press. The Press Council of India is also a member of World Association of Press Council which seeks to promote self regulation at international level. The present Chairman of the Council Justice P.B. Sawant is the current President of the body.

Press and Registration Appellate Board

Section 27 of the Press Council Act, 1978, entrusts the Council with the functions of the Press and Registration Appellate Board, constituted under sub-section (1) of Section 8C of the Press and Registration of Books Act, 1867, to hear appeals against unlawful cancellation of declarations of newspapers or non-authentication thereof by the District Magistrate. The Board consists of the Chairman and another member to be nominated by the Press Counci of India from amongst its members. The Board has rendered a number of important judgement since it was first constituted in 1979.

INDIAN MEDIA IN THE AGE OF GLOBALISATION

The commercialisation of the electronic media was given a boost as globalisation hit India, bringing about the transformation of Indian television in the early 1990s, accelerated by the combined impact of new communication technologies and the opening up of global markets. Economic liberalisation, deregulation and privatisation contributed to the expansion of Indian media corporations, facilitated by joint ventures with international media conglomerates. Such developments revolutionised broadcasting in what used to be a heavily protected media market, certainly the most regulated among the world's democracies. Gradual deregulation and privatisation of television has transformed the media landscape, evident in the exponential growth in the number of television channels – from Doordarshan the sole state-controlled channel in 1991 to more than 70 in 2000. Out of these, 19 are in Hindi or English and therefore national in reach, while others cater to regional audiences in their own languages.

The privatisation of broadcasting made many western transnational media players enter the 'emerging market' of India – potentially one of the world's biggest English-language television markets. With a huge middle class – estimated between 200-300 million – with aspirations to a western lifestyle and a well-developed national satellite network linking the vast country, their task does not appear to be too demanding.

Sectors of the Indian economy, such as information technology, have demonstrated exceptional growth in the past decade. This has stimulated changes in the broadcasting industry, benefiting also from a fast-growing advertising sector, making the Indian television market attractive for transnational broadcasters.

The entry of global media conglomerates into India opened up a new visual world for Indian audiences, first through the live coverage of the 1990-91 Gulf crisis by the Cable News Network (CNN) and later through Hong Kong based Star (Satellite Television Asian Region) TV, part of Rupert Murdoch's News Corporation. Star's five-channel satellite service in English (Plus, Prime Sports, Channel V, the BBC World and Movie), originated in 1991, became a major hit with the English-fluent urban elite and the advertisers, who saw in these channels a way to reach India's affluent middle class.

Buoyed by advertising revenues, cable and satellite television increased substantially from 1992, when only 1.2 million homes received it. By 1999, India had 24 million cable TV homes, receiving programmes from major transnational players – notably, CNN, Disney, CNBC, MTV, Star, Sony Entertainment Television and BBC – and from scores of Indian channels. After an initial infatuation with western English-language programming, noted for its liberal attitudes to sexual subjects, hitherto a taboo on Indian airwaves, it became apparent that the Indian audience preferred television in their own languages, prompting global media companies to adapt their programming strategies to suit the local marketplace. Star started the process of hybridisation when it realised that its mainly US-originated programming was being viewed by only a very small urban elite. It therefore started adding Hindi sub-titles to Hollywood films and dubbing popular US soaps into Hindi. In 1996, Star's India specific channel, Star Plus, began telecasting locally made programmes in English and

Hindi. The sheer logic of market pressure – localising the products to reach a wider consumer base and increase advertising revenues, was at the heart of this localisation strategy.Western-owned or inspired television encouraged mixing of English and Hindi and the evolution of a hybrid media language – 'Hinglish'. The emergence of a mixed media idiom, characterised by the growth of Hinglish, has dominated cultural production in the India of the 1990s. Hinglish has been identified by the burgeoning mass media as the language of the youth of a 'liberalised' and 'modern' India. While a form of Hinglish had been in existence in urban north India for decades, it was popularised by Zee TV, India's first domestic, Hindi-language private television channel, launched in 1992.

GLOBALISATION OF INDIAN MEDIA

The emergence of networks such as Zee raises interesting questions. It is indisputable that the proliferation of satellite and cable television channels, made possible with digital technology and growing availability of communication satellites, has contributed to the increasing diversity of the global cultural landscape. The role of television in the construction of social and cultural identities is more problematic in the age of globalisation than in the era of a single national broadcaster and a shared public space, such as characterised television in most countries in the post-war years. Though national broadcasters continue to be important in most countries and still receive the highest audience shares, the availability of a multiplicity of television channels has complicated the national discourse. In the multi-channel era, a viewer can have simultaneous access to a variety of local, regional, national, and international channels, thus being able to engage in different levels of mediated discourses.

A clearer analysis of the complex process of international cultural flow reveals that the traffic is not just one way, from north to south, even though it is overly weighted in the favour of the former. Evidence shows that new transborder television networks are appearing, with some flow from the periphery to the metropolitan centres of the media and communication corporations. The extension of satellite footprints and the growth of DTH broadcasting have enabled networks such as Zee to operate in an increasingly global environment, feeding into and developing what has been called as the emergent 'diasporic public spheres'.

The deregulation of broadcasting, which has been a catalyst for the extension of private television networks, has also made it possible for private satellite broadcasters to aim beyond the borders of the country where they are based – unlike state broadcasters who have traditionally seen their role in terms of the nation state. Apart from the major powers, whose broadcasting has had an international dimension, most public broadcasters, particularly in the South, saw their audience as a domestic one. By contrast the private channels, primarily interested in markets and advertising revenues, had a more liberal media agenda. This basic difference between state-centric and market-oriented broadcasting has been a key factor in the expansion of many southern broadcasters into the lucrative northern markets, aiming to reach the diasporic communities. Being part of global conglomerates has given them the technical and managerial support to operate as a transnational channel.

Globalisation and the advent of satellite television ensured that the migrant communities of South Asians in the Middle East, Europe and North America became a new target as audiences and consumers. Zee was among the first to recognise the potential of overseas markets for its programming. In its zeal to rope in pan-Indian audiences scattered throughout the world, Zee developed a new idiom which by virtue of sheer reach of the medium contributed to making Indian television available internationally. After Star TV purchased 50 per cent of Asia Today (the Hong Kong-based broadcaster of Zee TV) in 1993, it became Zee's partner in India, facilitating Zee network's expansion both within India and beyond. Following their 1992 launch in the Middle East, Zee TV entered the lucrative British market in 1995, when it bought TV Asia, already established in the UK. By 2000, Zee was available on the Sky network and claimed to have one million subscribers in the UK and continental Europe. It became one of the first channels to go digital in the UK, offering programming in Hindi and four other South Asian languages: Bengali, Urdu, Gujarati and Punjabi. Having acquired a base in the UK, Zee expanded into mainland Europe and is also very popular in Africa, where it has a joint venture with a South Africa-based platform operator, MultiChoice.

Today, Zee claims to be 'the world's largest Asian television network,' covering Asia, Europe, US and Africa, and catering to the Indian diaspora. In Asia, where it boasts a total viewership of 180 million, the network spans more than 43 countries and offers round-the-clock programming on four channels - Zee TV, Zee Cinema, Zee TV India and Music Asia. Having reached more than 23 million homes in the Indian sub-continent and United Arab Emirates, Zee's strategy is to expand its operations in the lucrative North American market.

After Star started making programmes in Hindi, it became a direct competitor for Zee, creating business rivalry between the two operations of News Corporation in India. In September 1999, in an unprecedented action, Zee bought back Star's 50 per cent share in the company, ending years of acrimony and establishing Zee as a major media player in its own right. Taking a cue from its former business partner Murdoch, Zee has also invested heavily in making sure that the company owns communication hardware as well as programming.

With this in view, in 1999 Zee announced the construction of Agrani, the regional satellite project which, when operational in 2002, will provide direct-to-home satellite TV and long distance telephony to consumers in South Asia. This was followed by Zee acquiring a 25 per cent share in the British satellite telecommunication company ICO (International Communications Ltd) which is to have a network of satellites beaming voice and data signals around the world. Such control will make Zee a major global player. Its success is reflected in the network's financial gains – in 1999 it recorded revenues of $100 million, rising about 30 per cent annually. By 2000, Zee's media and Communication Empire included cable and satellite channels in four continents, along with interests in film production, publishing, cable distribution and satellite telephones. Other India-based channels are also increasingly looking to international markets. Star TV now supplies programming to an ethnic American pay channel, EABC, and to Channel East in Britain, while Sony Entertainment Television is available in 126 countries.

In recent years India has witnessed extraordinary growth and overseas success in computer software and cinema exports, making it a global force to be reckoned with. A recent report on the Indian entertainment business prepared for the Federation of Indian Chambers of Commerce and Industry estimates that the Indian entertainment industry, currently valued at ₹ 154 billion, will grow to nearly ₹ 600 billion by 2005. According to the report, Indian film exports, worth ₹ 4.5 billion in 1999, are estimated to rise to nearly ₹ 120 billion by 2005; the Indian music market, currently pegged at ₹ 12.5 billion, is projected to touch ₹ 22 billion, and TV software revenues are expected to soar from the present ₹ 12 billion to ₹ 90 billion in 2005.

Among the non-western film-producing countries, India is one of the few that have made their presence felt in the international market place. India's 50 billion-rupee Hindi film industry makes more films each year than Hollywood – in the decade 1989-98 India produced 787 feature films compared with 591 in the US. Hindi films are especially very popular in the Arab world, in central Asia and among many African countries. This made it imperative for producers to invest in sub-titling to widen the reach of Indian films. The changing global broadcasting environment and the availability of digital television and online delivery systems will ensure that Indian films will be available to new audiences.

Until recently, the film industry has not received official encouragement as a major foreign exchange earner. This is set to change with the Indian Government giving films the status of an 'industry'. In 1999, the Government passed a law exempting export earnings from films from tax. Plans are afoot for joint ventures between India film producers and Hollywood giants as they discover the Indian version of the tinsel world. These will receive a boost with the decision of the Government, announced in February 2000, to allow foreign companies to invest in the Indian film industry. Now major Hollywood companies such as Columbia Tristar, Paramount and Universal Pictures are flirting with co-productions in India. Already overseas rights contribute nearly 40 per cent to a film's return – given the money power of the so-called Non-Resident Indian (NRI), especially based in the two major markets (the UK and the US), the industry is likely to grow further. The unprecedented expansion of television in the 1990s has also been a boost for the movie industry, as many dedicated film-based pay-channels have emerged. In June 2000, the first international Indian film awards, billed as the 'Bollywood Oscars' ceremony from London's Millennium Dome, was broadcast to more than 122 countries reaching 600 million viewers. It brought together along with Indian film and music stars US Oscar winner Angelina Jolie, Chinese star Jackie Chan and Australian pop singer Kylie Minogue.

However, the increasingly international orientation of television seems to have excluded the majority of India's people (the poor, especially those living in the countryside) who are remarkably absent from programmes on channels such as Zee. According to a 1998 survey, less than two per cent of Zee viewers live in rural areas. (Satellite and Cable TV, 1999) A socially relevant television agenda, therefore, does not fit well with the private television networks, who appear to be interested only in the demographically desirable urban middle class or the NRIs, with the disposable income to purchase the products advertised on such channels. The 'mission statement' of Zee is unambiguous: '...to establish the company as the creator of entertainment and infotainment products and services to feast the viewers and the advertisers. Through these services, we intend to become an integral part of the global market. As a corporation, we will be profitable, productive, creative, trendsetting and financially rugged with care and concern for all stake holders'.

Given these constraints a development-oriented television remains largely under-explored, primarily because it does not interest advertisers. It is ironic that the country that pioneered the use of space technology for education, with the Satellite Instructional Television Experiment (SITE) of 1975-76, which brought TV to the poorest villages in the most inaccessible areas, and where 40 per cent of the population is still illiterate – according to the United Nations, 30 per cent of all Indian children aged six to 14 years, about 59 million children, do not attend school – has ignored the educational potential of television. (UNDP, 2000)

Though Doordarshan receives substantial support from the Government, which has extended its reach and added new channels (in 2000, it had 21 channels), it is under pressure to provide entertainment as well as education. One result of such competition is the ideological shift in television culture from public-service to profit-oriented programming. The growing commodification of information and the trend towards western-inspired entertainment can adversely affect the public-service role of television, whose egalitarian potential remains hugely under-explored in India.

As television is driven by the ratings wars and advertisers' demand for consumers, and given that visuals can be a powerful instrument for propagating dominant ideology, the electronic media can play a key role in the creation of a marketplace in which their corporate clients can consolidate and expand. Rather than toeing the Government line, as used to be the case with state broadcasters, are networks such as Zee instead promoting a corporate worldview?

Internationally, despite a counterflow of cultural products, as exemplified by networks such as Zee, US-led western media domination has not diminished. There is a temptation to valorise such a flow, suggesting it may having the potential to develop counter-hegemonic channels at a global level. Indeed, as seen in the case of Zee, the network has been modelled after transnational corporations as a market- driven organisation for whom the most important consideration is to make a profit. Therefore, it can be safely said that the emergence of regional players contributing to a 'decentred' media and cultural imperialism is not likely to have a significant impact on western hegemony within global media cultures. More than 2,000 daily newspapers are published in India. Although English-language dailies and journals remain highly influential, the role of the vernacular press is increasing steadily in absolute and relative importance. Book publishing is a thriving industry. Academic titles account for a large fraction of all works published, but there is also a considerable market for literature. On the whole, the press functions with little government censorship, and serious controls have been imposed only in matters of national security, in times of emergency, or when it is deemed necessary to avoid inflaming passions (*e.g.*, after communal riots or comparable disturbances).

Radio broadcasting began privately in 1927 but became a monopoly of the state in 1930. In 1937 it was given its current name, All India Radio, and since 1957 it has been known as Akashvani. Television was introduced experimentally by Akashvani in 1959, and regular broadcasting commenced in 1965. In 1976 it was made a separate service under the name Doordarshan, later changed to Doordarshan India ("Television India"). Despite the government's broadcasting monopoly, rules of fairness allow opposition voices to be heard, especially during election campaigns.

EMERGENCY THE BLACK ERA OF INDIAN PRESS

Emergency was imposed by late Prime Minister Indira Gandhi on June 25,1975. During this period all opposition leaders were put behind bars, press censorship was clamped and media was muzzled, judiciary was brow beaten, form of Parliamentary democracy was allowed to exist but its soul was numbed and the power of executive landed to the handful of coterie during the nineteen month of emergency. During emergency Press was totally chained and it had lost its freedom in one go. It was like a political earthquake on the fateful night. It epicentre was Bahadurshah Zafar Road and police headquarter of the capital. It was marked by two apparent executive orders. All the prominent political opponents of Indira Gandhi were arrested in various parts of the country wherever they were. The Municipal Corporation of Delhi cut the electric power of all the newspapers of Bahadur Shah Zafar Raod. It was followed by the strictest press censorship.

This was dawn of the darkest nineteen months of Indian democracy, where in the soulless democratic form existed but it was virtual dictatorship. The Constitution was there, but it was mutilated. The Parliament was there, but all the opposition leaders were in jail. Media was there, but it was totally subservient to the power that be. Its freedom was marked by its absence. It was absolutely free to write anything in praise of the emergency and Indira Gandhi. Judiciary was there, but it was browbeaten. The Govt. told the Supreme Court that there was no fundamental right of life during emergency. Even a gentlemen like S.B. Chawhan, commented" The opposition should be grateful that they are in jail. In other countries they would have been shot." One can imagine the dictatorial arrogance of rulers by the then defence minister Bansilal's utterances of breaking the legs of the journalists and reopening "Kalapani of Andaman for Sea breeze would be good for J.P.'s kidneys". Over a lakh opposition leaders and workers were arrested, under MISA and Defence of Indira rule. The number included 253 journalists also.

Treatment meted to print media is worth recalling. Indian Express was the only mass circulated anti establishment group of papers. The group was sympathetic to J.P. Movement. The Govt. chocked its resources. Not only the Govt. advertisements were stopped, but other advertisers were scared so that the owner Ram Nath Goenka, the doyen of Indian media, was forced to toe the govt. line. But Goenka was made of tough metal. He did not bend. Then the govt. nominated board was thrust on him. Even then he did not budge, At times, employees could not be paid their salaries. During that period once R.N.G. told me "don't bother, even if I have half a chapati, I would give you a piece out of it".

Another daily The Motherland was an eyesore for Indira Gandhi. It was not a big paper, but was very important, for even before formation of Janta Party, it was a political platform of all the Janta Party forces. There was an added reason for Indira Gandhi's annoyance against it. Its editor K.R.Malkani had published an astrologer Basant Kumar Pundit's prediction that Indira Gandhi would clamp an artificial emergency and would die a unnatural death. Malkani was first to be arrested. The daily could not come out after the fateful day, not even after the emergency was lifted. Malkani told me afterwards that for days he was interrogated about Pundit's prediction in jail. During emergency news of his interrogation came out and widely circulated I wanted that B.B.C. must know it and managed to contact its correspondent. I took him to Mrs. Malkani at Rajender Nagar residence. Police was quick to surround the house, knowing fully well that whiteskinned correspondent would not be touched but I would be put under MISA, I escaped after crossing there roof tops.

J.P.'s Every men edited by Ajit Bhattacharjee and Praja Neeti edited by Prabhash Joshi too were closed forever. Over a dozen weeklies of RSS orientation, including Panchjanya and Organiser were closed, but resurfaced after emergency was lifted. Periodicals which suffered demise included March of the Nation edited by late Piloo Modi, Pratipaksha edited by Gcorge Fernandes, Himmat edited by grandson of Mahatma Gandhi, Raj Mohan Gandhi, Opinion edited by late A. D. Gorwala, Mainstream edited by late Nikhil Chakravarthy and Shankar's weekly edited by Shankar Pillai stopped publishing. Many of them did not revive even after passing of dark phase. Nehru had asked Shankar Pillai not to spare him in his cartoons, but his daughter did not spare Shankar's cartoons. Rajmohan Gandhi was fined ₹.20000 for quoting Mahatma Gandhi, his grand father. Their closure marked the death of the printed dissent for all these periodicals were prominent in their respective fields.

General mood of the journalists was that of grudging surrender to the guidelines of I&B Minister V. C. Shukla. The whole National Press fallen in line with the govt. baring a few dailies with maintained dignity even while following the guideline. Among them were Punjab Kesari group, Rajasthan Patrika and half a dozen vernacular dailies of states. Prominent newspapers were enthusiastic supporter of emergency. One prominent Hindi Editor lead a delegation of top journalists in support of emergency and censorship. One top trade union organisation of Journalist passed a resolution in favour of emergency supporting censorship.

Big Newspaper proprietors played safely and sided with govt. All the four News agencies merged to form Samachar, which dutifully toed Govt. guidelines. In the process the whole press and All India Radio lost its credibility. Focus of the listeners shifted to B.B.C. Millions listened to B.B.C. regularly. " B.B.C. has given such and such news" became the words of common parlance even in villages. On the print front a powerful and credible underground publications surfaced through out India. They carried the credibility. Initially R.S.S. net work was disrupted for most of its offices were forced to be inoperative. It took two-months to make the network in order. Political leaders and cadre of various parties including Jan Sangh and Socialist were ready by then. Gradually- facts sheets of newsletter of resistance started appearing and were secretly distributed.

Title were like Janavani, Satya Samachar, Satyavani, Lokvani. Literally thousands of copies of hundreds of newsletters become the regular feature. Photocopier was not prevalent in those days. But cyclostyling machines were in abundance. I myself was given bundle of news notes. I use to prepare news out of them and handed it over to persons like Madan Lal Khurana and others. They in turn made the copies and than that use to go to underground distribution channels. In different states and cities their more copies were made. I use to feel that important news reach to masses within ten days in the whole country. Whenever the news is more important we somehow managed to make it available to B.B.C. once it came in B.B.C. we used to feel that now the whole world knews it. The resistance gradually gathered momentum. The masses were angry except that of South India, Indira Gandhi and her coterie were blissfully unaware. When the occasion arised people taught the lesson to the authoritarian ruler. Lessons of emergency must be a part of history textbooks, so that there is internal vigilance to guard the democracy.

Popular publications in urban India in 2005:
- *Aikya* (Leading Marathi daily from Satara)
- *Dainik Bhaskar* (Hindi daily) 22.5 million readers (NRS 2005)
- *Malayala Manorama* (Malayalam daily)
- *Mathrubhumi* (daily)
- *Dainik Jagran* (Hindi daily) 19.2 million readers (IRS 2005)
- *The Times of India* (English daily) 7.05 million readers (IRS 2005)
- *Amar Ujala* (Hindi daily)
- *Anandabazar patrika* (Bengali daily)
- Grihshobha (Hindi)
- India News (India Daily)
- Eenadu (Telugu daily)
- *Lokmat* (Hindi daily)
- *India Today* (weekly; Hindi edition most popular)
- *Sambhaav* (Gujarati daily)
- *Gujarat Samachar* (Gujarati daily)
- Daily Thanthi (Tamil daily with 14 editions and a circulation of 790,900)

Popular English dailies in urban India in 2003:
- The Times of India
- Hindustan Times
- The Hindu
- The Telegraph
- Deccan Chronicle
- The Asian Age
- The Economic Times
- The New Indian Express
- Mid-Day
- Deccan Herald
- Indian Express
- India today
- Outlook

NEWS AGENCIES

News agencies provide regularity and authenticity to news. K.C. Roy is credited with establishing the first Indian news agency, which became The Associated Press of India (API). However, it soon became a British-controlled agency unwilling to report about the national freedom movement. The Free Press of India News Agency came into existence under the management of S. Sadanad who had served Reuters. The United Press of India, The Orient Press, The Globe News Agency, The NAFEN News Agency, The United News of India and a number of syndicates later came to serve the news business.

The Non-aligned News Agencies Pool (NANAP), formally constituted in 1976 for the purpose of correcting imbalances in the global flow of information, is an arrangement for exchange of news and information among the national news agencies of non-aligned countries, including Asia, Africa, Europe and Latin America. Its affairs are managed by a coordinating committee elected for a term of three years. India is at present a member of the coordinating committee. The cost of running the pool is met by the participating members. The Press Trust (PTI) continued to operate the India News Pool Desk (INDP) of the NANAP on behalf of the government of India. India continued to contribute substantially to the daily news file of the Pool Network. The reception of news into the Pool Desk during the year 1998-99 has been in the range of 20,000 words per day. INDP's own contribution to the Pool partners during the year has averaged 7,000 words per day.

The organization and structure of Indian news agencies has been undergoing a controversial transformation for quite sometime. This represents a mutual mistrust between privately owned news agencies and governmental structures. Their autonomy, believed to be crucial for objectivity and fairness, is based on their role as cooperatives and non-profit groups. News agencies in general are discouraged from taking any governmental favours. There is nothing in the Indian constitution, however, that can prevent government to nationalize its news agencies. There are four dominant news agencies in India: The Press Trust of India (PTI); the United News of India (UNI); the Hindustan Samachar (HS); and Samachar Bhatia (SB).

Press Trust of India

PTI began its operations in 1949, but its origin goes back to the early years of the 20th Century when its forerunner - the Associated Press of India (API) - was launched by an enterprising Indian, Keshab Chandra Roy. The first Indian to function as a Political Correspondent at the British imperial capital, Roy was a high-school dropout who made a success of a journalistic career and rose to be a nominated member of the Central Legislative Assembly as a distinguished journalist. Working for more than one newspaper at a time, including The Tribune of Lahore, the Indian Daily Mail of Bombay and the Amrita Bazar Patrika of Calcutta, Roy found it easy to have a news pooling arrangement with European journalists to carry on with his work. It was from this experience that the idea of a news agency grew in Roy's mind. Soon he collaborated with three of his professional colleagues - Usha Nath Sen, Durga Das and A.S. Iyengar - to float and run API. According to the book 'Reuter's Century: 1851-1951' by Graham Storey, it was started in 1910. K C Roy finally gave up in 1919 his brave effort to run an Indian-owned domestic news agency and Reuters became the sole supplier of foreign and domestic news to the government and to the newspapers of India.The London-based Eastern News Agency, owned by Reuters, merely used the name Associated Press of India. API was to be registered as a private limited company, wholly owned by Reuters, much later in September 1945.

The seven men who subscribed initially to the shares of PTI were K Srinivasan, Editor, 'The Hindu', Madras, Khasa Subba Rau, Editor, 'Swatantra', Madras, S.S Vasan, Editor, 'The Anandavikatan', Madras, S. Sadanand, Managing Editor, 'Free Press Journal', Bombay, C.R. Srinivasan, Editor, 'Swadesamitran', Madras, A.A. Hayles, Editor and Director, 'The Mail', Madras and S.V. Swamy, Editor, 'Free Press', Madras. India's largest news agency, Press Trust of India is a non-profit sharing cooperative owned by the country's newspapers. PTI subscribers include 450 newspapers in India and scores abroad. All major TV/ Radio channels in india and several abroad, including BBC in London, receive the PTI Service. With a staff of over 1,300 including 400 journalists, PTI has over 80 bureaus across the country and foreign correspondents in major cities of the world including Bangkok, Beijing, Dhaka, Jerusalem, Johannesburg, Islamabad, Kathmandu, Kuala Lumpur, London, Moscow, New York, Washington and Sydney. In addition, about 400 stringers contribute to the news file at home.

It has arrangements with the Associated Press (AP) and Agencies France Presse (AFP) for distribution of their news in India, and with the the Associated Press for its Photo Service and International commercial information. PTI exchanges news with nearly 100 news agencies of the world as part of bilateral and multilateral arrangements, including Non-Aligned News Agencies Pool and the Organisation of Asia-Pacific News Agencies.

Services

English News Service

Available in two forms. The 'core' service covers major developments in diverse fields in a compact form. A more comprehensive segmented service allows papers to pick additional inputs from segments of their choice. National/ Regional, Economic/Commercial, International, and Sports. Core service puts out about 40,000 words and the full segmented service upto 100,000 words per day.

BHASHA

Bhasha is the Hindi language news service of PTI. With its own network in the Hindi-speaking states and drawing on PTI files, Bhasha puts out about 40,000 words per day.

United News of India (UNI)

Started in March, 1961, and has grown into one of the largest news agencies in Asia. During these years, UNI have acquired an enviable reputation for fast and accurate coverage of all major news events in India and abroad in all areas — politics, economics, business, sports, entertainment, stock markets and so on.

Today, UNI serve more than 1000 subscribers in more than 100 locations in India and abroad. They include newspapers, radio and television networks, web sites, government offices and private and public sector corporations.

UNI communication network stretches over 90,000 Km in India and the Gulf states.

UNI has bureau in all the major cities and towns of India, including all the state capitals. Having more than 325 staff journalists around the country and more than 250 stringers, covering news events from remote corners.

UNI has Correspondents in major world cities such as Washington, London, Dubai, Colombo, Kathmandu, Islamabad, Dhaka, Singapore, Sydney and Vancouver, bringing to our subscribers stories of interest to Indian readers..

UNI has collaboration agreements with several foreign news agencies, including Reuters and DPA, whose stories distributed by UNI to media organisations in India. It also has news exchange agreements with Xinhua of China, UNB of Bangladesh, Gulf News Agency of Bahrain, WAM of the United Arab Emirates, KUNA of Kuwait News Agency, ONA of Oman and QNA of Qatar.

UNI is currently a major modernization programme as part of which most of its major bureaus are already linked through a computerized network. UNI's wire service is available in three languages — English, Hindi and Urdu. UNI launched UNIVARTA in Hindi in 1982 and pioneered a wire service in Urdu in 1992. In 1981, UNI became the first Indian news agency to serve subscribers abroad and earn foreign exchange for the country by selling its wire service directly to newspapers in the gulf States and in Singapore through satellite channels.

UNI has always adopted an innovative approach. UNI is first news agency in the country to launch a Financial Service, a Stock Exchange service and a National Photoservice. UNI has other services like UNIDARSHAN (Television News Clips and Features), UNISCAN (News Display on Television sets for Hotels, top Government officials and corporate clients), UNI*Direct* (for top executives in the government, corporate and other sectors) and UNI GRAPHICS (Computer-designed Graphics in ready-to-use form).

CENSORSHIP AND REGULATION

Although freedom of the press in India is the legal norm—it is constitutionally guaranteed—the scope of this freedom has often been contested by the government. Press censorship was imposed during the Emergency starting in 1975 but quickly retracted in 1977. Government advertising accounts for as much as 50 per cent of all advertisements in Indian newspapers, providing a monetary incentive to limit harsh criticism of the administration.

Until 1992, when government regulation of access to newsprint was liberalized, controls on the distribution of newsprint could also be used to reward favored publications and threaten those that fell into disfavor. In 1988, at a time when the Indian press was publishing investigative reports about corruption and abuse of power in government, Parliament passed a tough defamation bill that mandated prison sentences for offending journalists. On vociferous protests from journalists and opposition party leaders, the government withdrew the bill. Since the late 1980s, the independence of India's press has been bolstered by the liberalization of government economic policy and the increase of private-sector advertising provided by the growth of India's private sector and the spread of consumerism.

Before the invention of communication satellites, communication was mainly in the form of national media, both public and private, in India and abroad. Then came 'transnational media' with the progress of communication technologies like Satellite delivery and ISDN (Integrated Services Digital Network), the outcome: local TV, global films and global information systems.

In such an era of media upsurge, it becomes an absolute necessity to impose certain legal checks and bounds on transmission and communication In the due course of this article, we would discuss the various aspects of media and the relevant legal checks and bounds governing them.

HISTORICAL PERSPECTIVE OF MASS MEDIA LAWS

Mass Media laws in India have a long history and are deeply rooted in the country's colonial experience under British rule. The earliest regulatory measures can be traced back to 1799 when Lord Wellesley promulgated the *Press Regulations*, which had the effect of imposing pre-censorship on an infant newspaper publishing industry. The onset of 1835 saw the promulgation of the *Press Act*, which undid most of, the repressive features of earlier legislations on the subject.

*Gagging Act*on 18th June 1857, the government passed the *'Gagging Act'*, which among various other things, introduced compulsory licensing for the owning or running of printing presses; empowered the government to prohibit the publication or circulation of any newspaper, book or other printed material and banned the publication or dissemination of statements or news stories which had a tendency to cause a furore against the government, thereby weakening its authority.

Then followed the *'Press and Registration of Books Act'* in 1867 and which continues to remain in force till date.

Vernacular Press Act

Vernacular Press Act, 1878 a highly controversial measure repressing the freedom of vernacular press. The regime of viceroy lord lytton is particularly noted for his most controversial press policy which led to the enactment of the Vernacular Press Act on 14 March 1878. Earlier dramatic performances act (1876) was enacted to repress the writing and staging of the allegedly seditious dramas. Vernacular Press Act (1878) was aimed at repressing seditious propaganda through vernacular newspapers. Introducing the Bill the Law Member of the Council narrated how the vernacular newspapers and periodicals were spreading seditious propaganda against the government. The viceroy Lord Lytton strongly denounced newspapers published in the vernacular languages as "mischievous scribblers preaching open sedition". He remarked that the avowed purpose of most of the vernacular newspapers was an end to the British raj.

The papers that made the government worried were Somprakash, Sulabh Samachar, Halisahar Patrika, Amrita Bazar Patrika, Bharat Mihir, Dacca Prakash, Sadharani and Bharat Sanskarak. All these papers were said to have been leading the seditious movement against the government. The Act provided for submitting to police all the proof sheets of contents of papers before publication. What was seditious news was to be determined by the police, and not by the judiciary. Under this Act many of the papers were fined, their editors jailed. Obviously this repressive measure came under severe criticism. All the native associations irrespective of religion, caste and creed denounced the measure and kept their denunciations and protestations alive. All the prominent leaders of Bengal and of India condemned the Act as unwarranted and unjustified, and demanded for its immediate withdrawal. The newspapers themselves kept on criticizing the measure without an end. The succeeding administration of Lord Ripon reviewed the developments consequent upon the Act and finally withdrew it..

However, the most significant day in the history of Media Regulations was the 26th of January 1950 – the day on which the Constitution was brought into force. The colonial experience of the Indians made them realise the crucial significance of the *'Freedom of Press'*. Such freedom was therefore incorporated in the Constitution; to empower the Press to disseminate knowledge to the masses and the Constituent Assembly thus, decided to safeguard this *'Freedom of Press'* as a fundamental right.

Although, the Indian Constitution does not expressly mention the liberty of the press, it is evident that the liberty of the press is included in the freedom of speech and expression under Article 19(1)(a). It is however pertinent to mention that, such freedom is not absolute but is qualified by certain clearly defined limitations under Article 19(2) in the interests of the public. It is necessary to mention here that, this freedom under Article 19(1)(a) is not only cribbed, cabined and confined to newspapers and periodicals but also includes pamphlets, leaflets, handbills, circulars and every sort of publication which affords a vehicle of information and opinion.

Thus, although the freedom of the press is guaranteed as a fundamental right, it is necessary for us to deal with the various laws governing the different areas of media so as to appreciate the vast expanse of media laws.

The Freedom Of Press and the Freedom Of Expression can be regarded as the very basis of a democratic form of government. Every business enterprise is involved in the laws of the nation, the state and the community in which it operates. Newspaper publishers find themselves more 'hemmed in' by legal restrictions than many other businesses do – despite the fact that the freedom of press is protected by the Indian constitution. The various Acts, which have to be taken into consideration when dealing with the regulations imposed upon the Print Media, are:

- The Press and Registration of Books Act, 1867 – This Act regulates printing presses and newspapers and makes registration with an appointed Authority compulsory for all printing presses.
- The Press (Objectionable Matters) Act, 1951 – This enactment provides against the printing and publication of incitement to crime and other objectionable matters.
- The Newspaper (Prices and Pages) Act, 1956 – This statute empowers the Central Government to regulate the price of newspapers in relation to the number of pages and size and also to regulate the allocation of space to be allowed for advertising matter.

When dealing with this statute, it will be worthwhile to mention about the case of *Sakal Papers Ltd.* v. *Union of India.* In this case, the *Daily Newspapers (Price and Control) Order, 1960*, which fixed a minimum price and number of pages, which a newspaper is entitled to publish, was challenged as unconstitutional. The State justified the law as a reasonable restriction on a business activity of a citizen. The Supreme Court struck down the Order rejecting the State's argument. The Court opined that, the right of freedom of speech and expression couldn't be taken away with the object of placing restrictions on the business activity of the citizens. Freedom of speech can be restricted only on the grounds mentioned in clause (2) of Article 19.

- Defence of India Act, 1962 – This Act came into force during the Emergency proclaimed in 1962. This Act aimed at restricting the Freedom Of The Press to a large extent keeping in mind the unrest prevailing in India in lieu of the war against China. The Act empowered the Central Government to issue rules with regard to prohibition of publication or communication prejudicial to the civil defence/military operations, prevention of prejudicial reports and prohibition of printing or publishing any matter in any newspaper.

- Delivery of Books and Newspapers (Public Libraries) Act, 1954 – According to this Act, the publishers of books and newspapers are required to deliver, free of cost, a copy of every published book to the National Library at Calcutta and one copy each to three other public libraries specified by the Central Government.
- The Working Journalists and other Newspaper Employees (Conditions of Service and Miscellaneous Provisions) Act, 1955 – It lays down the minimum standards of service conditions for newspaper employees and journalists.
- Civil Defence Act, 1968 - It allows the Government to make rules for the prohibition of printing and publication of any book, newspaper or other document prejudicial to the Civil Defence.
- Press Council Act, 1978 – Under this Act, the Press Council was reconstituted (after 1976) to maintain and improve the standards of newspaper and news agencies in India.

Although on one hand, the Constitution confers the fundamental right of freedom of the press, Article 105 (2) provides certain restrictions on the publications of the proceedings in Parliament. In the famous *Searchlight* Case[5], the Supreme Court held that, the publication by a newspaper of certain parts of the speech of members in the House, which were ordered to be expunged by the Speaker constituted a breach of privilege. Due to the restrictive scope of this Article, it is not possible for us to delve into all the other statutes; however, a few of the legislations, which are worth mentioning are the Contempt of Courts Act, 1971 and The Official Secrets Act, 1923.

Indian copyright law

The Indian copyright law is governed by the Copyright Act, 1957. The Copyright Act was based on the Copyright Act of 1911, framed by the British during the Colonial rule and also borrowed extensively from the 1956 Copyright Act of the United Kingdom.

The Act, with five amendments, in 1983, 1984, 1992, 1999 and a substantial one in 1994, adheres to the treaties of the Berne Convention, the Universal Copyright Convention, the Rome Convention and the Agreement on Trade-Related Aspects of Intellectual Property Rights (TRIPS) agreement.

Press Laws

The regulation concerning newspapers in this subcontinent was passed for the first time during the rule of the governor general Lord Wellesley in 1799. It stated that every newspaper must bear the name of the owner of the printing press, the publisher and the editor. By virtue of an ordinance of 1823 governor general Adams introduced licensing for the newspapers. This was annulled in 1835 but reintroduced in 1857. The penal code was enacted in 1860, which included the subjects of defamation and obscenity. The subjects of sedition and the act of creating class-enmity were incorporated into this law in 1870 and 1898 respectively.

The Press and Registration of Books Act of 1867 introduced the convention of registration and preservation of all newspapers and books. Vernacular Press Act of 1878 empowered the government to take action against any seditious writing. A number of provisions in the code of criminal procedure of 1898 touched the operation of newspapers. The Newspapers Incitement to Offences Act of 1908 gave a magistrate the power to seize a newspaper if it published anything malicious. The Press Act of 1910 gave government the power to ask the concerned press for a deposit if it published material instigating crimes, such as sedition and killing or homicide. The Press and Registration of Books Act, Customs Act and Post Office Act were amended in 1922 and at the same time the Acts of 1908 and 1910 were annulled. The Official Secrets Act of 1923 prohibited publication of any official secret as news.

6

Politics and Media

INTRODUCTION

The young Americans writing about television news reported a limited interest in politics to match their moderate viewing habits. Unlike their elders, they told no stories of using the news to take political actions. The young adults tended to define themselves as ineffectual and relatively powerless, seeing television news (often mentioned with the generic phrase "news media") as a potent political actor. Some essays mentioned observing cynicism in themselves · or in peers as a response to media power and their own political impotence. Although they gave a positive overall rating to the job news outlets do, they saw entertainment values corrupting the news. Somehow the media, they believed, supplanted political parties and weakened political discourse, limiting their own options. Some of the Americans saw their only option as a choice between television news and newspapers.

The essays from Spain revealed a stronger interest in politics, which also turned up in the questionnaire. The group gave itself a mean rating between "very" and "somewhat" interested in politics (1.5 on a three-point scale). Although higher than the national average, the rating reflects the group's median age (21), when Spanish youth have the highest political interest (Institute de la Juventud, 1991). The participants also linked their political interest with media use. In the questionnaire, those "very" interested in politics watched news habitually (6 days "last week"), and those "somewhat" interested said they watched slightly less (5.5 days "last week"). None reported being "not at all" interested in politics.

The Spaniards most often mentioned a type of action they call a political decision, which they usually defined as making a choice between political alternatives. Some essays also mentioned voting, and several specified other actions. "These days the news still has an impact on me," said a female regular viewer, 26, "and perhaps those are what in a given moment made me try working in a non-governmental organization or making a donation or whatever else to help out." Such levels of participation match survey results (Institute de la

Juventud, 1991), in which a majority of 18- to 29-year-olds said they voted in elections (69.2 per cent) and about half said they usually followed political stories in the media (51.9 per cent). Consonant with other statistics, only a small share of participants reported joining associations (13.8 per cent).

When they wrote about politics, the participants considered the use of power central, and they saw themselves, not television news, as capable of exercising power. The exception, a 20-year-old female, remarked, "Everyone knows perfectly well how important a politician's image is when televised. It's the only medium that they can count on to reach the entire population and share their ideas." Even this passage places the politicians, not the journalists, at centre stage and lacks the sort of cynicism found among some Americans. Instead, the Spaniards appear to play down the importance of the news media generally and television news particularly in their political world. They rated the overall job the news media do in Spain (2.4) lower as a result. An urban male, 21, said, "More than a few times the newscasts give too much importance to an exchange of insults between politicians." The Spaniards saw the shift towards spectacle in television news as confirmation of their judgement that television news can play only a partial role in their political thinking.

Such a critical stance towards television news appears to go hand in hand with their own sense of potency and independence. The Spaniards emphasized their own position as decision-makers. "I think the stories get too little coverage to be used as the only base for information," said an urban female, 21. More than a quarter of the essays described comparing the various news media (28.1 per cent). A rural female, 22, said that newscasts led her "to take a more critical view, since the different ways of presenting stories on the different television networks give you contradictory images. Only after thinking about them can you then form your own opinion."

The essays also brought newspapers into the discussion. "I always like to watch several newscasts to see the different ways journalists have of narrating the stories," said a suburban female regular viewer, 25. "I also like to contrast this with the press." The Spaniards did not treat newscasts and newspapers as competitors, between which to choose. Instead each news outlet had a use. As did their compatriots who wrote about newspapers, the television group also took a sophisticated attitude, judging television news harshly but also acknowledging its usefulness. I've always thought that assimilating information from newscasts is relatively complex.

The bombardment of information is so rapid it's difficult to absorb what they say. Now I also believe it's much more powerful seeing images on television than reading them in the paper. Television touches my emotional fibre as a spectator. a suburban female regular viewer, 25

The essays most often cited one political topic: the corruption scandals surrounding the former socialist (PSOE) government (a current issue in the news just after the 1996 election). Revelations by news outlets illustrated the importance of a free press in Spanish democracy, the essays said. More than half of the essays talked about the value of television news (56.3 per cent) since the transition to democracy. The scandal coverage, followed by a substantial young adult vote against the socialists, appeared to have especially enhanced the participants' sense of power to make political decisions, independent from the older generation that repeatedly elected socialist governments.

Instead of concluding that the media have somehow supplanted political parties and weakened political discourse, the Spaniards discounted the role of newscasts as only one source among many. They emphasized their own thinking, as well as their ongoing political discussions with family and friends.

THEORY AND METHOD

The idea of comparing nations has long been employed to build theories of politics and society. Since Durkheim and Weber, "the father of crossnational research", tried to understand modern society by holding it up against historical and primitive groups, scholars have used examples from different nations as a way to illustrate their ideas, from the social Darwinism of Spencer and the functionalism of Radcliffe-Brown, to the structuralism of Levi-Strauss. Herbert Blumer criticized these comparisons to remote societies as an exercise in nostalgia.

Comparative studies of contemporary nations, on the other hand, give observers a vantage point closer to home, reducing the danger of romanticizing a traditional or historical society. Interest in comparative research was surging, principally at the intersection between sociology and political science, when Seymour Martin Lipset wrote his classic studies. The new field, political sociology, took on several topics that cross the borders of the two fields, such as the fate of democracy, the role of the media, and the participation of individual citizens as part of different generations.

Defining and measuring "the political culture of democracy" and "the social structures and processes that sustain it" inspired the pioneer study of comparative political attitudes in the United States, United Kingdom, Germany, Italy, and Mexico. The news media clearly took part in these structures and processes. To illustrate the patterns found in survey questions about media use and political interest, the authors also conducted life history interviews.

During the early 1960s Americans facing the cold war, fearing a domino effect if small nations fell to Communism, wanted to know how to encourage the broadest democracy without causing instability. "How can the apathetic peripheral man become the aspiring participant man without a deep seachange in the psychic weather?" asked Daniel Lerner.

The answer was found in Lipset's three requirements for political democracy; a regular means to change officials, a loyal opposition, and (important for this study) a mechanism for the largest possible share of society to participate. Communication seemed to provide one of the most likely mechanisms. "In the world today - whether you like it or not, whether it is advisable or not, whether it is good policy planning or not - tremendous developments in communication," Lerner went on, "are occurring in every country".

These changes at mid-century began to shrink the global community, and several contemporary studies identify communications (including newspaper consumption) as a strong indicator of political development.

Subsequent studies have paid most attention to voting, but the news media also provide a key to citizens' involvement in democratic governments. As mass communication grows, clusters of older social, economic, and psychological commitments end, and citizens become more open to new patterns of action.

The commitment to participate in politics can clash with the roles the media play in generating economic profits, and this contradiction may limit their legitimacy and effectiveness in the political system. News media can block as well as encourage change, because "the construction of political reality is essentially a 'mediated' process". Young adulthood, when political reality takes firm shape in personal commitments, is rarely studied.

Socialization research emphasizes childhood and adolescence and pays little attention to the media, although media research shows that television often provides the earliest encounters with politics in the United States. Cross-national research on media and politics usually focuses on media content, not audiences, and mass media researchers have called for more comparative study of public communication.

This chapter on young citizens and the media has two theoretical aims. One is to describe and delineate elements in the structure of subjective experience. In his suggestions for studying the media, Blumer proposed that they do not operate within clearly demarcated and distinct outlets and forms, such as newspapers and television, but instead act within a larger zone that he called an arena. Viewed from the perspective of citizens' symbolic interactions, subjective experiences with the news arena have been little studied.

To extend understanding of the political sociology of news, this monograph employs a descriptive strategy to discover grounded theory. After identifying other groups for comparison, a principal task is to describe subjective experience in detail, thus adding to the store of empirical observations of responses to the media arena. To build theory, groups are chosen as negative cases, selected to delimit the news arena and clarify its role in young citizens' experience.

That Americans increasingly reject news invites the search for cases where a different news arena holds sway. Cross-national research looks for similarities between nations because "if the same factor produces the same effects in two very different situations, its influence tends to be confirmed". National distinctiveness makes finding the same processes less likely in more than one country, and so similarities are not only unexpected but also valuable to add to the general understanding of the media arena. Differences contribute as well, and the most important source of contrast, of course, is national history.

As they confront problems, the citizens of various countries find alternatives and reach different decisions. Their contrasting responses can be used to suggest policy options.

Another theoretical aim is to examine generational change. Generations are produced only in modern societies, where rapid changes produce longterm shifts in ideology. Events give each new group of children a different set of experiences that tie them strongly to others their age. What people know about politics is influenced by their position in a generation, and studies of generations suggest that their collective memories emerge not only from massive traumatic events such as wars and large scale demographic shifts but also from mass exposure to events shown in the media. Karl Mannheim noted that an actual generation, whose coming of age coincides with a set of common experiences, does not necessarily interpret those shared events uniformly.

The conflicting meanings they assign events divide them into what Mannheim called generational units. Maurice Halbwachs agreed that collective memories play a central role in distinguishing different social groups and classes. Mannheim further suggested that, although their life spans may overlap, different age groups experience the same moments of history differently, each generation living in its own subjective era, as he called it.

This has been borne out in subsequent research. Finally, Mannheim proposed that national differences effectively separate people of the same chronological age; citizens in Germany and China in 1800 could not form part of the same actual generation because they could share no formative experiences.

The growth of news organizations that extend beyond national borders, the consolidation of media ownership globally, and the resulting international spread of political reporting styles raise the question whether citizens of nations separated by geography and language had begun to share sufficient media experience by the end of the 20th century to form a generation in effect.

These theoretical considerations guide the study: the search for commonalities that indicate new social and political meanings for news crossing national boundaries, the observation of differences with an eye to discover alternate policies for American news organizations as they inform citizens, and the testing of boundaries of subjective experience between a political generation and its units in the United States and Spain. As a practical matter, choosing countries is the first task in any crossnational comparison. For the greatest detail and depth, a binary analysis comparing only one country to another - works best. Because it "leaves out neither the specific nor the general," binary study can contribute "to an understanding of general phenomena". The choice of countries requires a balance.

The two should share enough to make reasonable comparisons but also have enough differences to make for robust results. The United States shares with Europe many cultural, political, and economic traditions, including the modern phenomenon of youth culture. Within Europe, Spain differs from the United States perhaps more than any other nation. The United States and Spain stood as complete opposites in the early 1960s. Among developed American and European nations, Spain had the lowest newspaper circulation (70 per thousand population) and the penultimate rate for televisions (13.1 per thousand population) - only the Portuguese owned fewer sets.

During the Franco era, Spain also had no meaningful gauge of voting. By contrast, the United States had newspaper circulation in the middle of the range (326 per thousand population, compared to the United Kingdom, 506 per thousand population) and the highest number of television sets (306.4 per thousand population).

The percentage of U.S. citizens who actually voted, while not high (64.4 per cent in 1960), ranked with those nations lacking mandatory voting laws. The United States also had the highest level of college enrollment (1,983 per hundred thousand population) and Spain (258 per hundred thousand population) the lowest (Britain had 460 per hundred thousand population, but a larger share of enrollees graduated).

Perhaps because of these differences, most Americans know little of Spain beyond the tourist cliches of bullfights and flamenco, necessitating a brief overview of recent political, media, and generational history.

POLITICS

Unlike the United States, Spain experienced an extended pause from democracy during the Franco regime, which had a profound impact on the country. The "executions, the imprisonments, the torture, the lives destroyed by political exile and forced economic migration point to the exorbitant price paid by Spain for Franco's `triumphs' ". Despite these depredations, Spanish citizens remained committed to the ideal of civic culture. Under Franco, citizens in the different regions of Spain preferred democratic rule by "all of us" rather than by one caudillo, even in the most conservative strongholds. The commitment to democracy was based on the culture of Spain, rather than springing from economic factors or social structure.

In Franco's later years, Spain underwent a "Prussian-type economic development... beginning in the mid-1950s and promoted by national ruling classes". Preston characterized the 1960s as a period of robust economic growth resulting in broad social changes. Business and professional people became independent-minded in increasing numbers, and unrest from the worker movements applied growing pressure for change. The Franco regime did institute some liberalizing policies, such as the Press Law enacted in 1966. Liberalization took firm root in such places as the universities, where Marxist publications became widely available and prominent intellectuals criticized the regime, calling for reform, and where "tolerance at the ideological level was unquestionable". Spain also experienced greater contact with the outside world, through flows of migration from Europe and increases in tourism primarily from the western hemisphere.

The assassination in 1973 of Carrero Blanco, the ultraconservative head of Franco's government, "was a factor of overwhelming importance". He was replaced by Carlos Arias Navarro, who, although not progressive, did support limited reforms. In his most important act, televised on February 12, 1974, he announced that "the national consensus in support of the regime must in the future be expressed in the form of participation". Arias Navarro's speech opened the door for Francoist institutions to reflect more political pluralism, although that aim faced repeated setbacks. The regime then enacted a Statute of Associations, which allowed groups to register, although few did (and opposition political parties remained prohibited).

The hopes for reform in the early 1970s clashed with economic frustration over Franco's "paternalistic regulation of the labour market", as well as his policy of keeping Spain out of the European Economic Community.

The energy crisis put a break on increases in the standard of living for the working class, which lacked political rights and became increasingly militant. By 1975, "it had become clear that socioeconomic and institutional change as well as modifications in political beliefs at both the mass and elite level of Spanish society had eroded away the underpinnings of the authoritarian regime". Franco himself became ill, and the media kept a vigil outside the palace. The extreme measures to postpone his death, the machinations to extend the regime, and the hope of installing a new head of the Cortes (Parliament) who would resist change - these things came to light only later. At the time, Spaniards witnessed only the head of government in tears, announcing Franco's death on TVE1, the state channel.

MEDIA CRITICISM

Complaints about bias in media coverage played prominently among the Americans. Women and members of minority groups such as African Americans included examples of discrimination in their essays and vented their harsh judgements of newscasts as a result. Similar complaints of bias did not play so prominent a role among the Spanish group. Several participants from the Basque region, however, did decry the false impression television reports gave of life in their communities. A person from Jain, for example, who sees the news, must think that in the Basque country and Navarra we all go around armed and that it's almost like Bosnia. But if you live here, you realise that's not reality. - a suburban female regular viewer, 22

In general, however, the essays did not censure newscasts for discrimination. The only example parallel to the U.S. criticisms involved images of women. A suburban female regular viewer, 25, wrote: "I remember seeing a room full of men. One of them brought in a girl of seven or eight. They tied her with esparto rope... and proceeded to cut off her clitoris." The essay described this "montage of images," intended to expose discrimination, as an example of the cruelty to women "they show on television every day." Several women complained of the recent turn of television towards shocking or violent news. The essays dated the shift to the arrival of competition. They denounced the new commercial channels for trying to attract viewers without considering the repercussions:

What I like least about TV news is how very morbid they are, how, when something happens, they thoughtlessly show it all without thinking of the consequences. They only care about being as dramatic as possible, and sometimes the scenes they show... can harm the people involved. -an urban female, 19.

Although not as prominent as in the U.S. essays, such complaints mark a shift in the meaning of television news to the Spaniards. Both groups appear to share a sense that news has become degraded under commercial pressures. The transformation that the Americans noted, however, has just begun entering the situation the Spaniards describe.

The experience of television news among the Spaniards presents myriad contrasts to the U.S. group. Many of the differences result from the distinct historical contexts in the two countries.

The recent change from dictatorship helped produce a more widespread custom of news watching, which some attendant resentment hardly weakens. More of the young Spaniards became viewers without much overt parental encouragement and with little support from the schools. Instead the reinforcement of daily practice built a deep commitment.

The Spaniards, despite their constant attention to television news, tended to discount its importance. Changes in news form gave them a greater awareness of the constructedness of the newscast. The Americans, by contrast, saw their preferred content (news and weather) as information about a factual reality and responded with sadness and fear. The Spanish group reacted to news with anger, a relatively active emotion, and the women expressed less fear.

In general, the Spaniards presented themselves as more independent of television news. It influenced their actions less often, although they reported more conversations about it than the Americans did.

The most intriguing differences occurred in the political realm. The young Spaniards, at least in the particular moment after an election, took more interest in politics. They not only engaged in discussion but saw political decisions as theirs to make.

They followed politics and watched television news more than the Americans did, but at the same time they had a lower opinion of the news media. Where some in the U.S. group felt powerless, the Spaniards did not. They described themselves as free to make choices and saw an array of options for informing themselves. The Americans instead tended to see the necessity of choosing between television and newspapers, and some of them saw the media as powerful. By rejecting this view, the Spaniards avoided falling into the cynicism found among the Americans.

The U.S. television news industry cannot, of course, replicate the national historical experience of Spain, but the different experiences the Spaniards reported can recommend practices for U.S. newscasters interested in creating a high level of commitment to and critical independence from news. The Spanish example suggests a reasonable alternative to the U.S. definition of a news market, in which television must compete with newspapers in a winnertake-all contest. Such a view probably does not contribute to young adults' sense of their own options.

In Spain the media cooperate as a way of competing in the news arena. Newscasts commonly highlight newspaper stories, show images of the pages, and then go on to illustrate alternative points of view. The practice teaches viewers to read newspapers, watch the newscast, and listen to radio with the intent to learn more by comparing and drawing their own conclusions.

It is tempting to attribute the cross-fertilization among news media to the growing consolidation of media outlets in Spain. However, the television news segments highlight the main stories of all the principal newspapers. In the United States, as a result of cross-ownership such as the Chicago Tribune and the WGN super-station (Channel 9), newscasts plug only the company's own newspaper and Web version.

The case clearly differs in Spain, where anchors present news as a cooperative endeavor in which each medium has its use. Newspapers provide flexibility in time - they await the opportune moment - but their efficiency and convenience define newspapers as private reading. Television news has a programme schedule, and that inflexibility in time helps build a family ritual, although it also makes newscasts ephemeral.

By emphasizing and promoting alternative sources, the U. S. news media could provide a sense of abundance and variety similar to what the young Spaniards note. The sacrifice each medium in Spain makes in its own position as an authoritative source is small. The cooperative spirit does not dispense with competition but highlights it, producing a rising tide of news coverage that lifts all ships, for the young as well as for newspapers, electronic news, and newscasts. The young gain a sense of independence freedom to explore and make decisions. In the bargain, the news outlets get what they need most, viewers (and readers) who stay attentive and critically aware.

SIMILARITIES

The experiences of the U.S. and Spanish groups do have some important parallels. In both settings, a ritual at home supplied the most powerful and universal meanings of newscasts. Viewers acquired the practice through the rhythms of childhood experience. The temporal quality, then, came not just from the news as something new, but in the daily-ness of the process, especially in Spain. The ritual also involved the presence of parents, who shared in witnessing both the news and the family watching the news. In this sense, news watching depends on generational experience. The older generation, in Spain as in the United States, appears to have transmitted the practice through daily example more than through preachment, as predicted. Schools probably cannot reproduce the experience.

The young generation also brought its common experience to the news, and, in turn, the news of both countries contributed to the memories of the new political generation. The experience of being caught up in a national event occurred in both countries, which tends to confirm the generationbuilding effect of television news. In some cases, young adults in both countries shared the same initial news event.

The international reach of some major stories appears to tie young people in what may be an emerging trend towards actual generations, to use Mannheim's term, that cross national boundaries. That first news story does more than initiate the young generation's memory. At the same time, the common experience of the two generations, in the presence of news, ties them together in the national political identity, although as Mannheim predicted, their qualitative experiences of the event differ.

At the centre of television news stands the image. The young viewers valued the images of people and places they would not otherwise know. Such images helped them define what belongs within the nation as well as without, to the familiar us and the foreign them. The everyday procedures of news work do not often manufacture the kinds of images vital for linking young people to news. The events that tie the young generation to the old and fuse them all into national consciousness usually happen unexpectedly and overtake the newscasters at the same time. The element of surprise makes a difference. The news that marks a generation's memory transcends the daily routine of news and leaps outside the boundaries of the newscast as a temporal ritual.

One final commonality, the shift away from serious content and towards the rhythms and style of entertainment in the newscast, plagued both countries. The transformation, quite advanced in America, appears implicated in the dispirited and cynical attitudes among young citizens. The changes young adults observed in Spain presage a similar reaction among the generation to come. The stronger ritual in Spain, as well as the custom of comparing news outlets, has built sturdy links between generations, at least for the young adults studied here. However, the move towards sensational coverage and ratings competition seems most likely, in the long run, to harm Spanish broadcasters - their own reputation and position in the constellation of news options.

When developing the life history technique in the early twentieth century, Herbert Blumer attempted to create a lens for looking at the facts of his participants' childhood encounters with movies. The idea was simple: just ask them. The critique of empiricism in the intervening years suggests that life narratives, rather than simply reflecting the past, instead operate as a primary tool in the construction of identity in the present. The stories young adults wrote for this study do reveal the occasional event from history, such as the military coup in Spain, but their importance lies elsewhere. The stories give insight into subjective responses, the meanings and values young citizens assign to events in past.

Their narratives are public documents, not revelations of private goings on. The method of collecting written stories, despite the consistent offer of anonymity, generates an official version of events as the participants would like them seen. The picture they offer of themselves as audience members represents their ideal, along with a frank admission in many cases of how they fall short of that model.

In their experiences as citizens and members of media audiences, the young adults depict themselves as public persons. That image comes as close as possible to citizenship, making life histories an appropriate tool for understanding how the young adults explain their identities as citizens. In short, life narratives reveal not historical facts (although they allude to them) but symbolic interpretations, which in turn influence how the young act out their citizenship.

The success of the news industry in the United States and elsewhere depends on a range of decisions, from editorial content to corporate strategy, which rarely take into account the symbolic worth of the enterprise. As young Americans abandoned news over the past twenty years, the loss, although financial in the short run, has symbolic weight in the long run. Yet research has not usually examined that elusive quality, the subjective value of news. A cross-national comparison of how young citizens understand the news helps fill the gap.

The contrasts between subjective experiences in Spain and the United States shed light on the consequences of a news arena organized for market competition. Some things that U.S. journalists avoid most assiduously may in fact provide antidotes to the declining role of newspapers in the political life of young Americans and to their disregard for newscasts as an alternative. An explicit ideological position seems foremost among them. Reporting that consistently covers events from two opposing sides puts journalists in the role of neutral arbiter and leaves citizens out of the decision-making loop, as mere spectators. In the United States, the ideology of balance makes for powerful journalists but weakened young citizens, who respond by disengaging and in some cases turning cynical. Taking a political position and speaking consistently from it has had the opposite effect in Spain.

Another activity that U.S. journalists avoid may suggest a second remedy: a willingness to talk directly about the competition, its news decisions and ideological aims. When news organizations compete mainly in the market, mentioning the competition becomes a taboo, an unseemly intrusion of money matters into the high-minded business of public information. Fairly uniform coverage, which accompanies the silence about competitors, enhances the authority of journalists as professional news-handlers and leaves citizens with branded versions of what amounts to the same news product. In the United States, the limited choices reduce young citizens to mere consumers, who respond with boredom and indifference. Talking about the many points of view available in competing news outlets creates a vibrant news arena with the opposite effect among elite young adults in Spain.

The similarities in subjective experience between Spain and the United States suggest further remedies. In both countries the key that opens newspaper reading and news watching to more young citizens is daily ritual, observed in the example of parents and teachers. Didactic methods such as those employed in recent Newspaper Association of America campaigns seem ill-advised. The results reported here imply that the campaigns would have better success if built from in-school activities rather than homework, and in any case, getting parents to engage with news daily seems essential, and school work ancillary.

As news has become more professional in the United States, journalists have moved away from reporting the local and the particular, preferring to cover more significant and impressive events. In all the groups studied so far, however, young citizens report that local events most sparked their interest. The trends in U.S. journalism go against the subjective preference for news that stays close to young citizens' social worlds, reporting on familiar people and nearby places. Re-focusing on the local community, as the recent public journalism movement proposes, may help slow the decline in interest among young citizens.

In the context of remedies, it bears repeating that in the groups from both countries, models of entertainment and commercialism for news produce a similar negative response. The young adults' interpretations bring to mind the logic of the traffic jam. When passing an accident, drivers may prefer not to look but cannot resist. Despite their mounting frustration over so-called "gaper's delay," each car slows down at the scene of mayhem (which always reveals less than it promises).

Young adults react to shocking and entertaining news in much the same way, looking against their better will, but resenting their brief union with the crowd. For the purveyors of news, any short term gain in ratings or circulation from such coverage only feeds a longterm malady: the weakening subjective sense of the value first of news to citizens and then of citizenship itself.

All these recommendations interrelate. In the end, the U.S, news industry would be wise to target older adults primarily, organizing all efforts around building a daily habit. Whatever the cost in the near term, seriousness will build a more lasting commitment.

Techniques that draw from entertainment and advance commercialism may attract momentary attention from a young audience while doing damage to parents' willingness to incorporate news into daily living, thus sacrificing the next generation of viewers and readers. U.S. news businesses likewise would benefit by making their usually unspoken ideological stands overt, contrasting themselves clearly and openly to other news outlets. Whether motivated by politeness or professional brotherhood, journalists who fail to highlight honest disagreements about news in effect devalue not only political ideology but also the news itself. News deserves better. Variety and conflict between news organizations create, paradoxically, a cooperative news arena, increasing interest among the public rather than limiting the audience for news.

BUILDING THEORY

Besides the policy implications of the research, the Spanish case study and the comparison with the U.S. studies also contribute to theory. Three principal insights deserve elaboration, two that advance existing theories generations and political participation - and one that builds grounded concepts from subjective experience.

Similarities between the Spaniards and Americans help clarify the role of news in the formation and structure of generations. First, the young adults in each country share memories of particular moments in their national history covered in the news, especially, in the case of Spain, the events in the transition to democracy. That groups from both countries also share memories spanning national borders - such as the explosion of the space shuttle - suggests the emergence of cross-national generations, which were a conceptual impossibility at the time Mannheim wrote. Although probably not sufficient to form an actual generation, their common experience does point to an emerging global news arena and a potential internationalization of citizenship.

Second, the college students in each country might form a distinct unit within their own national generation. A next step should investigate groups of young adults from other socioeconomic levels. In the United States those who enter college form a large unit, but further study could profitably compare them with others who do not. Additional study seems especially appropriate in Spain, where fewer young citizens attend universities and read newspapers. That need does not, however, reduce the importance of an initial comparison of elites in the two countries.

The present study sheds light, for instance, on the persistent puzzle of participation in Spain. How could a citizenry deemed passive on many survey measures accomplish and sustain so successful a transition from dictatorship to democracy?

The evidence presented here contradicts the statistics for the population as a whole and expands the understanding of surveys focusing on youth (Instituto de la Juventud, 1991). Instead of the picture of a post-transition generation hopelessly disengaged from politics, the participants (unlike their U.S. counterparts) knowledgeably and willingly tackle political issues, foreign and domestic, while disparaging political parties and even their own government. Clearly the general indicators of knowledge, involvement, and efficacy fail to measure the dimensions of a subjective environment where, to paraphrase the classic statement by V S. Pritchett, nothing mediates - no association, party, medium, state, or church - between Spaniards and whatever power directs their world.

Capturing the particular moment of transition in Spanish history, contrary to expectation, does not diminish the importance of such results. Besides the obvious ways that the transition heightened citizens' sense of the importance of politics and their own decisions, the evidence suggests that the transition generation acted with circumspection, constraining their tendency to criticism when modeling media literacy. Nevertheless, further study should compare young adults in other countries where transitions have occurred, such as Brazil.

Finally, the study suggests a concept grounded in the contrast between young Spanish citizens and their counterparts in the United States. The comparison reveals a pattern in which several aspects of the participants' responses tend to cluster together in what can be termed a subjective posture.

On one hand stand many of the Americans, whom the earlier studies describe as responding with indifference to politics and activism, with resentment towards the media, and with a sense of fear and powerlessness. Another posture turns up in the essays by Spaniards, who have considerable interest in politics leading to activism, view the media with a detached but critical eye, and respond to news by comparing and making choices among political options. The two postures, or clusters of subjective responses, seem to mark endpoints on a continuum.

Certain kinds of enrichment or impoverishment define that range, which, for lack of a better term, might be called subjective affluence. The term affluence, of course, refers here to something other than material poverty. Both countries are relatively well off, and the groups studied enjoy substantial economic advantages. Their differing postures, where the observed personal responses cluster, have striking parallels, however, within the surrounding media environment.

The Americans experienced an arena for news driven by commercial competition. The news media avoid taking overt ideological stands, in favour of a uniform standard of coverage. A market mentality furthermore drives news outlets to employ the techniques of entertainment, along with an emphasis on private tragedy and public violence, to make the news more captivating (that is, to win higher ratings or circulation). The Spaniards experienced a very different news arena. The driving force of partisan ideology aims to present an politically coherent depiction of public affairs, and, moreover, holds up examples of other news media and their differing news judgements.

Of all the evidence presented, recent changes in Spain support most strongly the interpretation that these two arenas mark (in lived experienced) the endpoints on a continuum. Participants described a shift within the Spanish arena towards the U. S. version of things.

They bore witness not only to external events, as media outlets Americanize, but also to subjective events, as the young Spaniards themselves responded to that changing media environment. The subjective postures in the two countries link, not to their material prospects in this case, but with their responses to the symbolic arena. The subjective postures and the news arenas interact and together define the relative wealth of the subjective environment.

In short, subjective affluence describes a symbolic continuum independent to some degree from economic affluence. Despite material abundance, the Americans experience a symbolic poverty, brought on by trends that now have begun spreading to Spain. Further study of subjective affluence could clarify the complex relationships emerging between news and citizens, while examining the long-term consequences for trust and interest in the press and in politics.

MEDIA

In a study in the 1960s, the United States and United Kingdom plotted high and near the regression line correlating communications (an index computed from newspaper consumption, newsprint used, telephones installed, and mail volumes) and political development. Spain stood near the middle in communications development and the low-middle in political development, well below the average. This combination suggested a country poised, because of its communications development, to experience a spurt in political development - an accurate prediction, as it turned out.

Under the Franco regime, changes in the laws governing the press took a first step towards liberalization. The 1966 reform changed the process (but not the fact) of censorship, ending it before publication but imposing "post hoc suspension or closure", so that editors had to guess what might get censored.

"Franco, the Falange, the Army and the principles of the regime could not be criticized, but for all the limitations, the law constituted a real change, and the most reactionary elements in the regime were furious at the implications".

The policy change "gave rise to hopes of more substantial political change". Under the new law, periodicals such as the newspapers Informaciones, Ya, and Madrid and the magazine Diario 16 published criticism of the government and called for reform, working within the constraints of the regime. Publications also sprang up in regional languages such as Catalan.

Spanish television was founded as a state monopoly in the 1950s. "Under the Franco regime, television held the key to reading the eyes and ears of the Spanish population" because, unlike newspapers in the country, "television commands massive audiences". After Franco's death, government control continued over what were by then two state channels, TVE1 (also called La Primera) and TVE2 (La Dos). Newspapers gained much more freedom, and the transition saw several newspapers start up. The most important national paper to emerge, El Pais, established a left-leaning socialist editorial line, in contrast to the right-leaning monarchist position of the newspaper ABC. The strong political agendas of Spanish newspapers did not come as a novelty. Much earlier, for example, "Franco spoke of the monarchist daily ABC as an `enemy'".

During the period of socialist rule, two important shifts occurred in the Spanish news media, bringing them closer to their U.S. counterparts. On one hand, the government revised (by some accounts timidly) the broadcasting laws. "In the 1980s, Spanish television evolved from a public monopoly, with only two state channels, into a competitive multi-channel system".

Two new channels began free broadcasting, Antena 3 and TeleS, and a third emerged based on subscription, Canal Plus. On the other hand, Pedro J. Ramirez founded in the late 1980s a national newspaper, El Mundo. Ramirez, who worked as a young intern in the Washington Post newsroom the day Nixon resigned, introduced investigative journalism at El Mundo. The paper took a strongly anti-socialist line against Felipe Gonzalez and his government. Ramirez made himself a household name in Spain by pushing the stories of corruption in government to the forefront of the political agenda.

The national newspapers in Spain circulate throughout the country, alongside (and in competition with) the local and regional press, and both continue growing in circulation. By the 1990s, all the older Spanish newspapers had reformatted themselves as smaller tabloids. The press has adopted an aggressive pattern of redesigns and received a number of awards, particularly El Mundo for reporting and El Pais for design. U.S.-based journalism associations have named both of these among the best newspapers in the world. The changes in newspapers accompanied an erosion of press partisanship, with an increase in claims to professionalism among reporters and in market orientation among publishers.

Television news also has a history of partisanship in Spain, although less overt than the printed press. A study of the 1993 election, for example, shows that the state-controlled TVE1's favorable coverage of Gonzalez and the socialist government became especially pronounced in the pre-campaign period. In that election the private channels, Antena 3, Tele5, and Canal Plus, first covered the campaign in full. The entry of commercial broadcasters "has created a new audience map, and all the networks and stations are increasingly guided by ratings". As a result, public broadcasting, although still dominant, has seen a continual erosion of its audience and income.

Despite some growth, newspapers still do not receive wide readership in Spain, and total circulation reaches only one in ten of the population. The press has been expanding, however, with the number of newspapers published increasing since the 1980s. At the same time, the trends have been towards greater concentration of ownership, including the growth of newspaper chains and cross-ownership of television and radio stations and magazines. These trends have parallels in the United States.

Electioneering in the news media of various countries has begun to follow a pattern as elections become Americanized. That trend makes a clear picture of U.S. news essential for understanding the Spanish media. Historically, the U.S. news media have operated under market competition with only limited government regulation. Public broadcasting arrived late and has played a very small role. The press remains predominantly local, with competition at that level declining as newspapers have closed or consolidated.

Coverage of politics has changed substantially since the 1960s, when newspaper reporters and television correspondents gave a largely descriptive chronicle of the candidates' words and movements during election campaigns. Studies show that U.S. journalists have increasingly described presidential campaigns using the metaphors of conflict or the horse race, positioning themselves as political interpreters for the public. As a result, media organizations may have largely supplanted political parties as the principal power brokers in the selection of U.S. leaders.

Competition for readers and viewers has imposed entertainment values on U.S. news. Since the 1960s, television journalists have greatly shortened politicians' sound bites and increased the relative share of time and emphasis given to their own judgements about campaigns. Newscasts became dramatically more visual in the 1970s, at the time when they reached a pinnacle of audience share and advertising revenues. Seeing themselves in competition with television, newspapers followed suit, updating their designs at a rate that accelerated in the early 1980s.

Both television and newspapers began to face audience declines in the mid-1980s, as cable expanded the alternatives for news (including CNN and C-SPAN). Newspaper executives identified and attempted to slow the erosion of readership among young adults. By the early 1990s, news executives viewed computer networks as a potential competitor. Unlike the ideological competition among Spanish newspapers, the U.S. press sees itself as part of a news market, where television broadcast news competes with cable and radio and where newspapers - most of them local monopolies - compete with broadcasters. Driven by market considerations, the U.S. news media aim for the greatest visual and emotional impact within the constraints of the widest possible audience appeal.

THE INDIAN MOVEMENT AND POLITICAL DEMOCRACY

This work investigates the implications of the Ecuadorian Indian movement for democratic politics. While its empirical questions focus on Ecuador's political processes, a key purpose is to offer a Latin American perspective on the broader debate on the "civil society argument"; namely, the proposition that civil association has intrinsically positive effects on democracy.

The assumption herein is that particularization is essential for appraising this wide-ranging claim. Civil society and democracy are knotty concepts because they refer to complex realities that can be approached from different points of view. To cut through the complexity, this study follows a strategy of double specification, concentrating on social movements as a distinct type of civil association and demarcating discrete functional terrains to observe their bearing on democracy.

Applied to the case at hand, this strategy provides a basis for a contextualized assessment of the putative democratic benefits of civil association and offers insights on the conditions of political engagement that social movements share with other kinds of civil society groups.

The pivotal claim of this study is that civil society actors may or may not contribute to democracy and that, in the particular case of social movements, the underlying tension between the participatory and insti- tutional dimensions of democracy may be expressed through a mixed bag of favorable and unfavorable effects on the different components of political democracy. The analysis of the Ecuadorian Indian movement demonstrates that to understand the varying impact of civil activism on democracy, scholars must adopt a nuanced, context-specific approach that does not lose sight of the particularistic orientations of civil associations and that pays close attention to their definition of means and ends, the institutional responses evoked by their initiatives, and the unintended consequences of their actions. The relevance of the case cannot be overstated. The Ecuadorian Indian movement is often cited as the best-organized and most influential indigenous movement in Latin America. Its origins date back to the rise of local and regional organizations that, in the 1980s, came together in CONAIE, the Confederation of Indigenous Nationalities of Ecuador.

The spectacular battles of the 1990s transformed the movement into a powerful force that, in addition to pressing indigenous demands, took up a leadership role in the wider resistance to the imposition of neo-liberal reforms.

By 1997 CONAIE had launched the party Pachakutik to take part in elections, and its political clout had been boosted by its role in the developments that led to the fall of president Abdalá Bucaram and the convening of a constitutional assembly. In January 2000, amid an economic and political crisis of unprecedented proportions, CONAIE joined a group of military officers led by Colonel Lucio Gutiérrez in a non-violent coup that toppled President Jamil Mahuad but failed to hold on to power.

Three years later, the same actors made another bid for power as an electoral coalition, which succeeded in winning the presidential elections. The presence of Indian leaders in the government was a high point for the movement, but it did not last long. After six months of conflicts over President Gutierrez's neo-liberal turn, CONAIE withdrew its support and Pachakutik's ministers abandoned the cabinet.

Clearly, this is a movement that has reached well beyond the bounds of a bid for indigenous rights. Much more has been at stake, including matters of national economic and social policy and issues that are directly related to the struggle for political power and the fate of Ecuadorian democracy. In the context of contemporary Latin America, then, this case is highly relevant to the discussion of the various types of impact that social movements can have on democracy.

This chapter lays the groundwork for the analysis with a conceptual discussion elucidating the notion of civil society, the specificity of social movements as a variant of civil association, and the paradoxical relationship between social movements and democracy. The factors behind the rise of Ecuador's Indian movement, the broadening of its struggles, and the saliency of its political protagonism are then reviewed. The enquiry is framed as a scrutiny of the movement's consequences for the participatory and institutional dimensions of democracy. After exploring the bases of CONAIE's support, the study examines the movement's two main modalities of political engagement: its efforts to influence government policies and its struggles to conquer positions of power. The appraisal of the effects on the democratic regime covers four areas: interest representation, control of state power, legitimacy, and political socialization. The conclusions assess the significance of the Indian movement for democracy, briefly rejoining the debate on the "civil society argument" and commenting on the present challenges for Ecuadorian indigenous activists.

CIVIL SOCIETY, SOCIAL MOVEMENTS, AND DEMOCRACY

This work adopts a modified version of Michael Walzer's definition of civil society, taking it to refer to the ensemble of social practices that generate a space of voluntary association and the sets of relational networks, or social actors, that occupy that space. Within this scope, the cast of civil society actors includes all voluntary groups formed for the sake of the common aspirations and concerns of its members. This formula is useful because it grasps civil society on its own terms, avoiding the pitfalls of definitions that imply assumptions about its relationships with the political institutions, such as the idea that civil society is necessarily autonomous from the state, necessarily opposed to the state, or necessarily good for democracy.

A good antidote to the mystifying sway of prescriptive definitions of civil society is to keep in mind that the realm of voluntary association is thoroughly marked by pluralism, particularism, and inequality.

Civil society is pluralistic because its practices are based on multiple forms of participation, express many social identities, and pursue a wide variety of goals.

Civil society is particularistic because its groups have their own norms and because, with rare exceptions, they restrict benefits to members and pursue goals that reflect their own priorities-even when, as often is the case, they claim to represent the public interest.

Moreover, civil society is tied up with inequality not only because different groups have different levels of opportunity to associate and further their ends, but also because a great deal of what associations do has consequences in terms of widening, maintaining, or narrowing existing social gaps.

Social movements are a particular form of civil association. They can be defined as organized drives to promote or resist change through collective practices that are embedded in a structure of conflict, involve episodes of mass participation, and challenge existing institutions.

The reference to conflict implies that social movements confront opponents in struggles over values and claims to resources, status, or power, a feature that sets them apart from civil associations that are not involved in such confrontations (*e.g.*, social clubs, churches, and charitable foundations). On the other hand, the emphasis on events in which large numbers of people engage in non-institutional forms of action foregrounds popular participation and defiance of prescribed rules, two elements that are absent in the case of associations whose activities are carried out by small circles of activists or professionals who follow" the proper institutional channels" (*e.g.*, interest groups and advocacy organizations). To understand movements, one must ascertain what is at stake in the conflicts in which they are involved. In empirical studies, the stakes can be inferred from their goals, their actions, and the context of their struggles.

The conceptual distinction between civil and political engagement is a useful tool for initiating that enquiry. In civil engagement, the conflict is located in civil society itself. There are two variants of this kind of engagement:

construction of collective identity, in which movements seek to alter the self-consciousness of actual or potential followers; and cultural crusades, in which movements act on the general public to change dominant values or attitudes.

In political engagement, the conflict is played out through interactions with state actors or other agents from political society; that is, the arena of competition for control over the state apparatus and public policy. Here, the actions of movements are usually aimed at inducing policy changes. Sometimes, however, their struggles may turn into attempts to control the positions of power themselves.

Social movements are a modern form of participation that emerged with the changes related to the consolidation of capitalism, the national state, and liberal democracy. As a rule, movements have served as a medium for the participation of excluded groups and for the politicization of issues that the institutions are unwilling or unable to address.

By engaging in confrontational practices like marches, boycotts, and demonstrations, movements have shown that ordinary people can capitalize on numbers, unity, and determination to achieve goals against the will of the most adamant opponents or rulers. Movement practices, then, must be seen as practices of non-institutional power. Lacking other resources, excluded and powerless people use disruption. They generate might by withdrawing the tacit support that power holders derive from" business as usual," thus creating a political market in which they can trade the lifting of their sanctions for the changes they seek.

Some authors have argued that movements and revolutions are variants of contentious politics; namely, a particular kind of political activity in which challengers use non-institutional means in their interactions with elites and the state. By itself, though, the opposition of institutional and non-institutional means cannot capture the diversity that exists in civil society's political practices. In the view of this study, it should be combined with another distinction that, considering the actors' ends, marks the contrast between the politics of influence, which focus on swaying public policy decisions; and the politics of power, which are played as attempts to seize the positions from which the decisions are made. On the basis of the combinations of means and ends, identifies four alternative forms of civil society's political engagement.

As a static categorization, this matrix marks out the specificity of movements in regard to other forms of civil political involvement. But the framework can also serve as a dynamic referent for variants and transformations. Variants are relevant because movements often combine the use of non-institutional means with conventional modalities of action.

Transformations are also relevant because movements develop over time in a sequence of events that at some point is completed. At the peak of its cycle, a movement that initially focused on reforms may blend into a revolution, a sweeping challenge to the structure of power, which is usually violent and, if successful, involves dramatic changes in the organization and policies of the state. Far more frequent, however, is institutionalization, which takes partial forms when movements spawn lobbying agencies or political arms and final forms when they abandon the unconventional forms of action and reorganize themselves as interest groups or political parties.

What is the relationship between movements and democracy? To elucidate this, we must first dispel the myth that civil society activities are always beneficial to democracy. It is true that civil associations can assist democracy by disseminating its values, representing social interests, resisting state arbitrariness, and educating people for democratic participation. But although associations can fulfill these positive functions, they may not always do so.

Indeed, they may also harm democracy in various ways, such as upholding antidemocratic ideologies, using corruption to get privileges, and seeking co-optation as state clienteles. The key point is that civil society actors may or may not contribute to democracy; and in both cases, what they actually do may vary greatly.

The groups that are not helpful run the gamut from associations whose activities are devoid of political consequence to organizations that may be conspiring to subvert a democratic regime. When associations contribute to democracy, by contrast, they rarely do it by design, but as a byproduct or contingent result of their efforts to attain their own particularistic goals.

All the foregoing holds true for social movements, but with a special twist: their status in democratic polities is haunted by an intrinsic ambivalence.

Definitions of democracy can be broadly divided into procedural definitions, which view democracy as a regime based on electoral representation and guaranteed civil and political rights; and substantive definitions, which see it as a principle of participation that guides all political practices.

This counterpoint highlights a fundamental tension between two ingredients of democracy: the principle that" the people rule" and the institutional procedures that, at any given time, embody that principle. Generally speaking, institutions produce social order by imparting stability and meaning to behaviour.· In their domain, democratic institutions contribute to that order by protecting citizens' rights and providing means for their participation in politics. But institutions have a downside, aptly captured in Jean-Paul Sartre's assertion that they amount to" the systematic self-domestication of man by man". In dictating the acceptable ways of doing things, institutions foreclose alternatives, generating an effect of suppression that is magnified by their tendency to get entrenched in their own inertia.

The case of representative democracy is especially poignant because, for most citizens, the same institutions that enable them to choose their rulers also imply their exclusion from further participation. This tension underlies the paradox of social movements in democracies. As a form of political engagement that involves large numbers of normally excluded people, movements fulfill the principle of citizen participation. But their reliance on non-institutional means implies that they are often in breach of the rules that define how the polity works. What turns the inconsistency into a paradox is that it has not prevented the emergence of movements as a regular feature of political life. To the contrary, viewed from the side of democracy, the key element in the relationship is that political democracy is an open invitation to social movements. Democracy offers fertile ground because it guarantees the rights of expression and assembly and, perhaps more important, because its own claim to legitimacy, grounded as it is in a discourse of popular sovereignty, citizenship rights, and inclusion, lends legitimacy to the claims of those who do not feel represented and want changes in public policies, in the definition of rights, or in the democratic institutions themselves.

Viewed from the side of movements, however, the relationship cuts both ways. In positive outcomes, the paradox is resolved in the deepening of democracy; that is, in situations in which a movement helps make a polity more democratic by winning reforms that broaden citizenship rights and provide for greater citizen participation in politics. Europe and the United States offer many examples of movements that advanced democracy through struggles against slavery, for labor's freedom of association, for the enfranchisement of women and the poor, and for the civil rights of racial, ethnic, and religious minorities.

But there have been negative outcomes, too, including the Nazi and Fascist movements, which ushered in a catastrophic period when democratic institutions were wiped out, the political and civil rights of entire populations were revoked, slavery was reinstated, and genocide became state policy. Finally, there may also be cases in which a movement's impact is a mixed bag of favorable and unfavorable effects on different components of political democracy.

The paradox of social movements should give us pause. We cannot assume that movements always contribute to political democracy just because they involve popular participation. But it is also a mistake to think that movements automatically detract from democracy because they infringe on institutional rules. Mindful of the complexities, political philosophers have long been engaged in discussing the circumstances in which civil disobedience may be justified in democratic polities. For social analysts, the challenge is different. We must use the complications as pointers for trying to provide more nuanced answers to empirical questions about the origins of social movements, the sources of their power, and their consequences for democracy. These are the questions addressed in this work on the Ecuadorian Indian movement.

The Contentious Cycle of the 1990s

In 1979, Ecuador turned from military to civilian rule. By way of background, it is worth calling attention to three aspects of that transition. First, the Ecuadorian generals did not display the repressive and probusiness zeal that typified military rule elsewhere in Latin America. Instead, they pursued a nationalistic agenda focused on the development of oil exports, agrarian reform, and "inward-oriented" industrialization.

During the 1970s, the economy expanded, and there were ostensible improvements in the living standards of the popular sectors. This, and the absence of severe repression, fostered attitudes of support for the military regime. Second, the democratic transition was initiated and tightly controlled by the armed forces. The "handed down" democracy did not inspire the sense of commitment that could have existed if the political parties and civil society had played a greater role in wresting it from the military.

Because they had not been crafted through political compromises, moreover, the new institutions proved ill-suited for the resolution of conflict, which set the stage for relentless strife between the executive and congress, constitutional tampering in all branches of government, and a chronic exacerbation of party fragmentation, regionalism, and personalistic politics.

Third, the transition to democracy offered opportunities for the political involvement of the indigenous population. The 1979 Constitution eliminated the literacy requirement, which had excluded most Indians from the vote.

The process was boosted by the first civilian president, populist politician Jaime Roldós, who promoted the participation of Indian organizations in rural development and literacy programmes.

The downsizing of these initiatives under president Osvaldo Hurtado (from the centrist Christian Democratic party, 1981-84) and their elimination altogether by León Febres Cordero (from the conservative Social Christian party, 1984-88) provided an early rallying point for criticism and contentiousness among the Indian activists. These elements must be kept in mind to understand the developments of the 1990s. On the one hand, they draw a connection between the tumultuous nature of Ecuadorian politics and the reality that after a decade of civilian rule, Ecuador was still plagued by the flaws of its democratic institutions, the dubiousness of its politicians' allegiance to the rules of democracy, and the shallowness of its citizens' democratic political culture.

On the other hand they indicate that, by the late 1980s, favorable conditions for an Indian movement had appeared. The extension of political rights and the openings in government policy had stimulated indigenous organization. The subsequent withdrawal of state support, the policies of adjustment, and the downturn of the economy would provide strong motives for the Indian insurgency of the 1990s.

RISE OF THE INDIAN MOVEMENT

In the 2001 census, only 6.6 per cent of all Ecuadorians identified themselves as Indians. Including those who declared that they or their parents spoke indigenous languages, the proportion rises to 14.3 per cent, which is the best available approximation of the size of the indigenous population. The Quichuas of the Sierra account for about three-quarters of that population, with most of the rest distributed among smaller groups in the Amazon. Throughout Ecuador, the basic unit of Indian settlement is the community, which, despite variations, presents generic characteristics that will be discussed later.

The process of Indian organization was a classic example of bottomup networking based on local and regional associations of communities. In the Amazon, it came in response to the arrival of peasant colonists, oil companies, and state agencies. In the Sierra, the stimulus was the fight for the land, which peaked with the military's agrarian reform of the 1970s. With the return to democracy, the indigenous organizations continued to work for development and the defence of their culture and lands, coming together under umbrella federations in the Sierra and the Amazon and eventually under CONAIE, the Confederation of Indian Nationalities, in 1986.

Since its inception, CONAIE has combined livelihood goals and citizenship aspirations. The former have focused on economic improvements, education, health, and the protection of Indian lands; the latter on the redefinition of Ecuador as a plurinational state, the end of discrimination, territorial autonomy, representation in state institutions, control over education and development programmes, and official recognition and funding for the indigenous organizations.

CONAIE's first achievement came in 1988, when it negotiated with President Rodrigo Borja (the creation of a national programme of bilingual education, funded by the state and run by indigenous personnel connected with the Indian organizations. But the presentation of CONAIE's contentious credentials was the 1990 levantamiento (uprising), a huge mobilization that vented the frustrations of a rural population that had been severely punished by the adjustment policies and the long recession of the 1980s.

The uprising was a peaceful civic strike in which tens of thousands of highland Indians blocked highways and marched into cities to seize public offices. The protest continued for several days, until the government agreed to discuss the demands. There were measures to alleviate the situation in the rural areas and settle some pending land conflicts, but an issue that remained unsolved was the status of the ancestral lands in the lowlands. Two years later, CONAIE sponsored a large march from the Amazon. Once again, President Borja was forced to negotiate with the Indians, who stayed put in the capital until he agreed to demarcate and title their lands.

The Sierra uprising and the Amazon march revealed the depth of the Indians' discontent and opened the eyes of all Ecuadorians to their return as actors who could exert influence in national politics. The uprising, in particular, was a real shake-up. As a rural protest on a national scale, it had no precedent in the country's history. In most respects, it was a feat of collective creativity, the spontaneous invention of a new form of contention that turned into a blueprint for the string of mobilizations that would follow in the 1990s.

The Indian-Peasant Front

The 1992 election gave the presidency to Sixto Duran, a conservative independent candidate. His economic plan focused on deregulating trade and capital flows, reducing social spending, eliminating subsidies, and privatizing state enterprises and social security. But Durán lacked reliable support in the legislature, and his privatization initiative was also opposed by the military, which saw the state enterprises as an important legacy of the military regime. In addition, Durán encountered resistance in civil society. The main challenges came from the Indian movement, which, buoyed by its initial successes, was displacing the labour federations as the beacon of popular opposition.

The first confrontation took place in 1993, over the plan to cut the social security budget and liquidate the health service for rural areas. CONAIE and other peasant organizations supported the strike of the social security employees and a massive protest of the beneficiaries of the rural health service. After two days of blockades and demonstrations, Durán was compelled to restore the budget and reaffirm the continuity of the health service.

The success of this struggle proved that well-organized protests could thwart an antipopular policy. In addition, it was an important precedent of collaboration between the Indian movement, other peasant organizations, and the unions from the public sector.

Next came the battle over the government's Law of Agrarian Modernization. The bill sought to abolish the legal basis for land expropriation, concentrate state support on capitalist agriculture, eliminate communal property, and privatize irrigation water. CONAIE sponsored the formation of the Coordinadora Agraria Nacional (CAN), a coalition that included smaller Indian and peasant organizations, such as FEINE (Indigenous Evangelical Federation) and FENOCIN (Federation of Peasant and Indigenous Organizations, influenced by the Socialist Party). CAN proposed its own bill and staged public debates on the issue.

In June 1994, the Coordinadora Agraria called an uprising that, once again, paralyzed the country for several days. Eventually, President Durán was forced to negotiate the bill. In its final version, the law defined peasant agriculture as deserving full state support, reaffirmed that water was a public resource, and recognized the legality of communal and cooperative forms of ownership.

The Popular Front

By 1995, CONAIE and its allies had participated in the formation of the

Coordinadora de Movimientos Sociales, a broad coalition that included Indian and peasant organizations, unions from the public sector, and a large number of neighbourhood associations, feminist groups, and human rights activists.

Meanwhile, President Duran had called for a referendum that proposed constitutional reforms to strengthen the executive, weaken the unions, and allow the privatization of the state enterprises and social security.

While the business sector generously financed the "yes" advertising campaign, the Coordinadora de Movimientos Sociales and the labour federations mounted an intense grassroots effort to bring out the "no" vote. On the day of the referendum, the voters rejected all the reforms. The defeat closed the books on Durán's initiatives, leaving in place an empowered popular coalition.

The success of the "no" campaign reinforced the position of the activists who had been calling for electoral participation. In its December 1995 assembly, CONAIE launched a political party that was intended to be based on the Indian movement and its allies. The Pachakutik Movement of Plurinational Unity (Pachakutik means "time of resurgence" in Quichua) entered the scene in the elections of 1996, in alliance with an independent group led by television commentator Freddy Ehlers. Ehlers did not qualify for the second presidential round, but Pachakutik won 10 per cent of the congressional seats and significant representation in provincial legislatures, local councils, and mayoralties.

The victory of Abdalá Bucaram in the 1996 election opened a period of enhanced turbulence in Ecuador. This clownish politician led the Roldocista Party, a populist force with its main base of support in the suburbs of Guayaquil. As mayor of that city, Bucaram had earned a reputation for corruption, but he had also extended his clientelist networks. During the campaign he attacked "the oligarchy" and Durán's aborted reforms.

As president, however, he focused on dividing the Indian movement, creating a Ministry of Indigenous Affairs and trying to buy the support of some Indian leaders. At the same time, Bucaram stuffed the government with relatives and friends, and it soon became evident that the country was sinking to new depths of corruption. Bucaram's discourse had also changed. Now he spoke about promarket reforms, trying to ingratiate himself with the International Monetary Fund and inviting Domingo Cavallo, the architect of Argentina's neo-liberal programme, to be the consultant for his economic plan.

Bucaram announced that plan at the beginning of 1997, when the labour unions and CONAIE were preparing a rally opposing neo-liberal policies, corruption, and the Ministry of Indigenous Affairs. The measures included stiff budget cuts, higher electricity and gas rates, labour reforms, and a timetable to tie the currency to the dollar. The rally turned into a mobilization for the president's removal, and was supported by the main political parties.

As Quito swarmed with Indian demonstrators, Congress removed Bucaram on grounds of mental incompetence and named its speaker, Fabian Alarcón, as acting president. In the process, CONAIE and the other organizations extracted the promise that an assembly would be convened to reform the constitution. The 1997 elections for that assembly gave Pachakutik 10 per cent of the seats. Its delegates pushed through several reforms, including sections that defined Ecuador as a multicultural state and recognized social, cultural, and political rights for the indigenous peoples.

The next presidential election was won by Jamil Mahuad, from the Christian Democratic Party. The new president faced strong pressure from the IMF, which was vexed by the stagnation of Ecuador's reforms. At the same time, he confronted a popular coalition that rejected those reforms and had proven its oppositional power. To top it off, the economy sank into its worst recession since the 1930s.

The economic collapse of 1998-99 was triggered by the fall of oil prices and the devastation of the coast by the climatic phenomenon of El Niño. When the banana and shrimp exporters stopped repaying their loans, the banks plunged into crisis and, despite Mahuad's billion-dollar bailout programme, the financial system collapsed. A massive flight of capital ensued, the gross domestic product shrank by 7.1 per cent, and it became obvious that the country would not be able to pay its external debt.

Mahuad devalued the currency, froze bank accounts, and focused on securing the support of the Social Christian Party, traditional advocate of the coastal exporters and banks. But the IMF's conditions for a stabilization loan were tough: eliminate all subsidies, privatize public enterprises, raise taxes on income and rent, and refrain from saving the banks. Mahuad's situation became untenable. On the one hand, the popular opposition fought back against the cuts and privatization. In 1998 and 1999, Mahuad had to deal with three large mobilizations in which the popular front led by CONAIE broadened to include middle-class sectors, such as truckers, bus operators, and small and medium-sized entrepreneurs. On the other hand, the IMF's insistence on tax reform and forsaking the banks alienated the business sectors. When the Social Christian Party pulled out of the negotiations, it became clear that Mahuad's presidency would not last long.

In the last days of 1999, Mahuad announced a plan to dollarize the economy and implement the IMF measures. Assisted by soldiers, Indian crowds flocked to Quito demanding his dismissal and occupying Congress and the Supreme Court.

On January 21, 2000, indigenous activists and young military officers cheered in Congress as Colonel Lucio Gutiérrez and CONAIE's president, Antonio Vargas, proclaimed a "government of national salvation." After frantic consultations among generals, politicians, and U.S. diplomats, however, the armed forces announced that they were restoring constitutional order by installing Vice President Gustavo Noboa as the new president.

Gutiérrez and the other officers involved in the coup were arrested, and the Indian leaders were forced to order the protestors to retreat.3 In the ensuing months, the detainees were granted amnesty and discharged from the army. While dollarization was maintained, the IMF negotiations were eventually abandoned without an agreement.

Much speculation has been offered about who manipulated whom in the military-Indian coup. In some versions, the conspirators appear as victims of a plot to get rid of a weakened president and proceed with dollarization. But the truth is that the colonels had been pressing their superiors for decisive action against Mahuad and that their contacts with the Indian leaders intensified after the Parlamento Popular, an assembly in which more that three hundred delegates of CONAIE and other groups called for Mahuad's removal and the formation of a popular government.

Thus it is unquestionable that the coup's organizers were acting on their own initiative. Their inability to hold on to power, however, proved that the whole enterprise had been utterly misguided.

Disillusionment and Demobilization

In preparation for the 2002 elections, Colonel Gutiérrez founded the Patriotic Society Party, PSP, which put forward his candidacy for president. After failed attempts to forge a centre-left coalition, CONAIE and Pachakutik decided to form an alliance with the PSP. Benefiting from the Indian vote and a fragmented field of 11 candidates, Gutiérrez won the first round with 20.4 per cent of the total. In the second round he defeated banana tycoon Alvaro Noboa, an independent conservative, by 9.6 per cent. Like previous presidents, Gutiérrez lacked majority support in Congress, where the PSP-Pachakutik alliance had won only 17 of the 100 seats.

After the coup, Gutiérrez had cultivated the image of a progressive populist. As the elections approached, however, he toned down his discourse and included business leaders among his advisers. He visited Washington to meet with IMF and U.S. officials and, immediately after his election, started to talk about austerity measures. The new attitude was reflected by the make-up of his cabinet. Although Gutiérrez appointed some Pachakutik ministers, the posts responsible for economic policy were assigned to the advisers who had been functioning as links with the business sectors and the IMF.

Gutierrez's priority task was a deal with the IMF, which wanted the fiscal deficit elminated. Knowing that an agreement would open the door to loans for social investment and development, Pachakutik's cabinet ministers went along with the austerity measures, doing their best to moderate them. The result was a salary freeze in the public sector and higher prices for fuel, transportation, and electricity. Many activists saw this as a betrayal. The Indian federation of the Sierra, Ecuarunari, demanded the resignation of the responsible ministers.

CONAIE echoed Ecuarunari's reproofs, calling for a rectification of the government's economic policies.

By mid-2003, disagreements over several issues, including the government's handling of strikes by teachers and oil workers, had aggravated the tensions in the coalition. Gutierrez's intense proselytizing in rural areas irritated the indigenous activists, who decried it as a scheme to bypass CONAIE and form clientelist networks. While the cabinet was torn by mutual accusations, the "allies" maneuvered in opposite directions in Congress, where Pachakutik tried to form a centre-left block and the PSP courted the Social Christian Party. The alliance collapsed in August 2003, when Pachakutik refused to support a bill that modified labour contracts in the public sector and Gutiérrez dismissed its ministers.

With the end of the alliance, CONAIE's internal divisions rose to the surface. Amazon groups criticized the leaders for leaving the government, and radical sectors of the Sierra reproached their delay in breaking with Gutiérrez. Meanwhile, Gutiérrez went on the offensive to weaken CONAIE further, issuing a decree that allowed him unilaterally to appoint the personnel of the state agencies that dealt with indigenous issues. This ended the practice by which the officials were nominated by CONAIE and ratified by the president. The next step was the replacement of the agencies' staff with activists who had signed up with the PSP and leaders from FEINE and FENOCIN.

By the end of his first year in office, Gutiérrez was facing accusations of nepotism and corruption. He had not succeeded in winning support from the Social Christian Party (Notisur 2003d). CONAIE proposed a rally to demand his dismissal, but the Amazon groups opposed it, and the other organizations ignored the call. FEINE had chosen to back Gutiérrez in exchange for programmes for the Protestant indigenous communities, and some of CONAIE's own groups, particularly in the Amazon, were involved in similar dealings. Despite the warning signs, CONAIE staged a protest in February 2004. The Indian federation of the Amazon and the other organizations refused to participate; the grassroots response was decidedly weak; and by the end of the first day, the mobilization was called off. Four months later, CONAIE organized another protest. The outcome was the same, aggravated by the Amazon groups' public support of Gutiérrez, who had just appointed his former fellow coup leader, Antonio Vargas, minister of social welfare. Vargas, himself a Quichua from the Amazon, had left CONAIE in 2002, eventually joining FEINE and becoming a staunch supporter of Gutiérrez.

The failure of the 2004 protests exposed CONAIE's crisis. But Gutierrez's success in neutralizing the movement did not solve his problems in Congress. In November he barely survived an impeachment vote amid charges that he had bribed legislators and had secured the Roldocistas' support by promising the return of their exiled leader, Bucaram. Then Gutiérrez dismissed 27 of the

31 Supreme Court justices, installing docile judges who overturned Bucaram's corruption convictions. On April 15, 2005, after three months of constitutional upheaval, Gutiérrez declared a state of emergency and ordered the police to repress protesters in Quito. The move backfired when the radio stations opened their microphones to an outpouring of indignation against his attempts to assume dictatorial powers. Following a week of demonstrations, the military withdrew its support, Gutiérrez abandoned the presidential palace, and Congress replaced him with Vice President Alfredo Palacio.

Once again, an Ecuadorian president had been ousted on the crest of street protests. This time, however, the main protagonists had been the urban crowds of Quito. CONAIE's leaders were slow in deciding to join in the protests, and when they finally did, their calls brought few Indians to the capital. Ironically, the fall of Gutiérrez offered further evidence of the prostration of the indigenous movement.

The Indian Movement and Democracy

This section elucidates the implications of the Indian struggles from the point of view df democracy. First, it looks at participation as a source of power for the Indian movement. Next, it assesses the consequences, through separate enquiries into the politics of influence and the politics of power. The last part examines the various impacts on Ecuador's democratic institutions.

The Secret of the Indians' Power

The Indian movement became a significant force because it was able to compel governments to pay heed to its demands. It was a classicexpression of the power that grows out of the effective use of disruption. To determine the sources of that power would entail exploring many factors, including the geopolitical assets of the Indian groups (strategic location in places where they could block the main national highways), the functional capabilities of their activists and organizations, and the financial and logistical assistance of external allies, such as progressive sectors of the Catholic Church and a variety of domestic and foreign NGOs. Some of these elements were addressed in a previous study; therefore the focus here is on what can be considered the main source of the effectiveness of the mobilizations: at the grassroots level, people were willing and ready to participate in them.

Throughout Ecuador, the decisions to respond to CONAIE's mobilization calls were taken by the Indian communities. Legally recognized as rural neighbourhood associations, these communities have roots that go back to the colonial system of resguardos, or reservations. Their revitalization was boosted by the land struggles of the 1960s and 1970s, which, insofar as they involved appeals to primordial loyalties of extended kinship and reciprocity, reinforced the old community as the natural framework for these relationships. At the same time, the agrarian reforms diluted the landowners' power, creating spaces in which the communities, by taking up the representation of the Indian peasants, gained prominence as relevant actors in local and regional politics.

Today, Ecuador has about 2,100 Indian communities, functioning as self-regulated entities based on the authority of their asambleas (in which everybody participates) and cabildos (executive committees of five members). All important issues are discussed in the asambleas, where agreement is usually reached by consensus rather than by voting. The decisions are binding for all members, with formal and informal mechanisms to ensure compliance. Thus, joining in a mobilization is always the result of a decision of the community, which exerts its influence to make sure that the members join in the roadblocks and rallies.

The secret of CONAIE's power, then, lies in its ability to harness the resources for collective action that exist in the Indian communities. Pierre Bourdieu's concept of social capital helps elucidate this process. Bourdieu sees social capital as the aggregate of resources linked to the possession of a network of relationships of mutual acquaintance or recognition. Members of a group that, like the Indian community, is based on reciprocity and solidarity can claim access to the resources of their peers by virtue of belonging to the group. But the group as such can also use the resources embedded in the network. Indeed, the accumulation and use of social capital are always guided by contextual norms and institutions. This is particularly visible in communal groups, whose formal and informal rules define the available resources, the ways they can be claimed, and the sanctions that enforce delivery. The rules circumscribe and aggregate social capital, ensuring that its use is restricted to members and taking advantage of the effect of concentration to maximize benefits. In such circumstances, social capital is an asset that belongs to the group, which can institute itself as collective beneficiary in activities that benefit the group as a whole.

In practical terms, this means that a community that joins a mobilization is making a claim on its social capital, and that the members' readiness to participate is a resource that they owe to the community. As Alejandro Portes has shown, different motives may be at play when members contribute resources, including feelings of obligation (internalized norms), expectations of future repayment (norm of reciprocity), identification with the group (bounded solidarity), and fear of sanctions (enforceable trust). The same motives can explain the behaviour of each individual community within the networks of communities that make up the Indian movement. The general point is that the Ecuadorian Indian movement operates as a network of networks, whose activities can be analysed as a process of accumulation, concentration, and deployment of the social capital embedded in its grassroots community structures. By bringing that social capital to bear on the political system, CONAIE has been effecting its conversion into political capital; that is, into leverage that can be used to wrest concessions from governments or to compete for direct access to power.

The Politics of Influence

In the politics of influence, social movements seek changes in public policy decisions. We are interested, then, in these questions: On which issues did the Indian movement try to influence government policy? What was at stake in those issues? and How effective were the mobilizations in achieving their goals? Here, we should keep in mind that the issues changed with the evolution of the struggles. Initially, when the Indians were fighting alone, they focused on their own demands. Later on, CONAIE's coalition-building initiatives broadened the confrontation, incorporating issues that were relevant to the other rural groups and, eventually, to the popular sectors at large.

Through the issues we can discern the stakes. The Indians' demands focused on achieving the status of recognized ethnic groups with terri- torial rights and some degree of autonomy. This challenged the existing notions of nationhood and citizenship; the former by defying the assumption that white-mestizo identity was the foundation of Ecuadorian identity, and the latter by questioning the liberal axiom that citizen rights could only be individual, not collective rights. The Indian claims, then, sought changes in the existing conditions. By contrast, the struggles over agrarian and national economic policy matters were attempts to resist changes. The fights over the Seguro Campesino and the Agrarian Modernization Law focused on thwarting initiatives that would have worsened the situation of the rural population. Similarly, the national protests against neo-liberalism were defensive responses to attempts to unload the burdens of reform onto the shoulders of the popular sectors. The stakes, then, had to do with the distribution of the costs of adjusting the economy to the new conditions of global capitalist development.

Did the struggles achieve their goals? We may start with the opposition to the neo-liberal agenda, the results of which are trickier to appraise. Studies have shown that Ecuador ranks among the least effective reformers in Latin America. Clearly, the popular struggles played a role in this outcome, but their influence cannot be disentangled from the effects of the lack of political support and the hostility of the business sector to some reforms. Besides, we should not forget that neo-liberalism was never really defeated in Ecuador, as its setbacks were always followed by renewed attempts to enact its reforms. We can conclude, then, that in this area the struggles had limited success. Interacting with other factors, they delayed the reforms and, in some cases, mitigated their impact on the popular sectors; but they were unable decisively to vanquish the neo-liberal agenda.

On the rural-agrarian front, CONAIE and its peasant allies were much more effective. After soundly defeating the attempt to scrap the rural health service, they succeeded in influencing the new agrarian legislation to keep water in the public domain, secure the status of communal property, and restore the state's support to the peasant economy. Eventually, the 1998 constitutional reform enshrined all these attainments in the Ecuadorian charter.

Concerning Indian ethnic demands, the initial fights established CONAIE's contentious credentials and led to significant gains on the land rights front, particularly in the Amazon. Later, the confrontations over broader national policy issues became an effective means for attaining the particularistic goals of the Indian movement. In the give and take after the fall of Bucaram, for example, CONAIE won one of its most important achievements: the creation of CODENPE (Ecuadorian Council of Indian Nations and Peoples), the agency that now coordinates all support programmes for indigenous groups with participation of their own organizations. Further concessions were wrested from Mahuad in the battles of the late 1990s, including an investment fund for Indian areas, the legalization of traditional medicine, and budget increases for the state's indigenous agencies. On the whole, the movement was able to accumulate an uneven but substantial record of success in influencing government policies. One upshot was that CONAIE could reinvest political capital earned through the mobilizations in other forms o   f action and more ambitious goals. On the one hand, its lobbying drives yielded significant gains without having to resort to protests, including the creation of PRODEPINE (Development Programme for Indian and Black Populations, initiated in 1997 with World Bank funding), the establishment of a health programme for Indian communities, and the launching of CODENPE projects of infrastructural works, water and irrigation, soil improvement, rural housing, and organizational capacity building. On the other hand, the Indian movement took steps to establish itself as a contender in the struggle for political power.

The Politics of Power

In the politics of power, agents participate in contests to occupy the positions that control and direct public policymaking. The three main manifestations of the Indian movement's struggles for power were the fight for control over the state's agencies of indigenous affairs, Pachakutik' engagement in electoral politics, and CONAIE's involvement in the coup against Jamil Mahuad.

For the Indian movement, the agencies in charge of bilingual education and indigenous health; the council of indigenous peoples, CODENPE; the development programme PRODEPINE; and the indigenous investment fund constituted a first major arena of power contestation. Steered by the movement, the agencies of indigenous affairs could serve as a means to attain objectives while fulfilling the programmatic ambition of exercising autonomy. Controlled by governments, they could be turned into tools of clientelistic domination. In the heat of the struggles, CONAIE wrested from the government an informal deal whereby the officials were appointed on the basis of its nominations. Later, however, President Gutierrez's actions showed that, in a less favorable climate, CONAIE's grip could be easily broken. The situation was complicated by the rivalry among indigenous-peasant organizations. Under the initial arrangement, CONAIE monopolized the representation of the Indians; this had always been resented by smaller groups like FEINE and FENOCIN. Thus, Gutierrez's repeal of CONAIE's privileges was more than a step to exclude it from the agencies' resources. It was also a gambit aimed at luring the other organizations into a network of patronage and using their example to entice CONAIE's local and regional chapters onto the clientelistic bandwagon.

The second front in the struggle for power was electoral competition. Pachakutik was launched in 1996 as a party based on CONAIE and its closest allies. In practice, however, it has been the political arm of the Indian movement, which provides most of its candidates for office. The best indicator of Pachakutik's overall strength are the congressional elections, in which its candidates have won, on average, 7.5 per cent of the seats. While this falls short of the estimated size of the indigenous population, it can still be seen as a fair result for a new party. Moreover, the 2002 presidential election proved that Pachakutik's vote can be decisive, since Gutiérrez qualified for the second round by a margin of less than 5 per cent. But it is at local and regional levels where Pachakutik's results have been especially significant. In the 2000 elections it won 4 governorships, 17 mayorships, and substantial representation in the provincial, municipal, and parish councils of the Highlands and the Amazon. The party's performance was similar in 2004, with 3 governors and 20 majors elected. Thus, while Pachakutik has not yet fulfilled its potential, it is clear that it is serving as a vehicle for self-government in the main indigenous areas.

We do not have enough studies to draw a panoptic picture of Pachakutik's performance at the different levels of government. One area in which the outcome can be readily recognized is the country's charter. In the 1997 constitutional assembly, Pachakutik negotiated important provisions, including the definition of Ecuador as a multicultural state, the designation of the indigenous groups as peoples, and the recognition of their rights to preserve their culture and their forms of political organization and administration of justice. Together with other clauses about the creation of indigenous territorial entities, these rights offer a framework for some degree of autonomy. But implementation depends on further legislation by Congress, where Pachakutik's moves have been conditioned by its minority status and its role as an opposition party focused on undercutting initiatives coming from the executive.

In contrast to its adversarial role in Congress, Pachakutik's gains in local elections created real opportunities for exercising power. The initial research on these experiences has focused on counties with dense Indian populations or visibility as touristic or artisanal centers, including Guamote, Otavalo, Cotacachi, Saquisili, and Bolívar.

The studies cast light on innovative efforts to encourage grassroots participation, establish practices that are free of corruption and clientelism, foster fairness in the distribution of resources, and promote multiculturalism by adapting traditional indigenous institutions. But they also show that the progress has been uneven and that, in some cases, Pachakutik's local authorities have been disappointing.

The third and by far the most dramatic incursion of the Indian movement into the politics of power was the January 2000 coup against Mahuad. In that episode, CONAIE conspired with military officers to overthrow the government and assume the powers of the state.

One way of coming to terms with the outcome is to look into the reasons for the coup's failure. In retrospective accounts, the Indian leaders have mentioned the generals' betrayal, the machinations of the elites and the U.S. embassy, the hostility of the press, the lack of popular response in the cities, and their own unpreparedness to take power. From this, one can conclude that the coup failed because it was marked by improvisation and, ultimately, because it reflected a gross misreading of the political scene.

Another way of assessing the coup's significance is to consider its repercussions for the Indian movement itself. The evidence indicates that there was public support for the removal of Mahuad but not for a military-Indian takeover. In the polls taken on the day of the coup, only 6 per cent believed that Mahuad could continue, 71 per cent approved the protests, and 79 per cent thought that Mahuad had to be replaced without breaking the constitutional order.

Two days later, the polls showed that 80 per cent were pleased that democracy had been maintained, 77 per cent supported the investiture of Vice President Noboa, and only 13 per cent would have preferred to keep the military-Indian junta. The overall pattern is clear. While CONAIE fulfilled a well-regarded role in expressing public discontent, its attempt to take power by force was rejected. The payoff for the Indian movement was also ambivalent. At the time, its image as a powerful player may have been boosted and its undemocratic behaviour may have been glossed over amid the general complacency with Mahuad's removal. But in the long run, CONAIE's collusion with the colonels put it on track for further blunders whose consequences would be far more damaging.

Recapitulating, what can we make of the Indian movement's involvement in these diverse forms of the politics of power? As we saw in the conceptual section, it is not rare for a movement to launch a party and combine protest with electoral participation. The juxtaposition of CONAIE's struggles over the indigenous agencies and Pachakutik's electoral ventures, then, are an example of what a movement undergoing institutionalization typically does.

The coup, though, was a very different matter. If we were dealing with a revolutionary group, we might think about the use of force as part of the strategy of" combining all forms of struggle." But CONAIE and Pachakutik have never claimed to be revolutionary organizations.

We are left, then, with the sense that the coup was an anomalous deviation from the path that the movement had been following.

To account for it, one could make allowances for the magnitude of the crisis, the intensity of the public's outrage, and the leaders' rashness and lack of vision. What is difficult to fathom is why, to this day, the activists have not conducted a real evaluation of those events and their fallout.

In the absence of soul searching, the naive opportunism that transpired in the coup kept haunting the Indian movement. Indeed, the leaders' decision to support Gutiérrez in the 2002 elections can only be seen as an attempt to cash in on whatever political capital they believed they had gained from the January 2000 adventure. Gutiérrez won the election, but the quick unraveling of the alliance showed that the move had been another serious mistake. The Indian movement could not stop Gutiérrez's neo-liberal turn, Pachakutik was forced to leave the government, and CONAIE was weakened by divisions. But the worst damage came from the disappointment at the grassroots, where Pachakutik's presence in the government had been hailed as an opportunity to access the resources that had been always denied to the Indians. Combined with the effects of Gutierrez's clientelist strategy, the loss of trust at base level became a major factor in the failure of CONAIE's latest mobilizations.

Impact on Democracy as a Political Regime

This assessment of the Indian movement's impact on the regime is grounded on elaborations of four ways that civil associations may impinge on democratic institutions.

The first of these is interest representation. In democratic regimes, political parties are the prescribed medium for representing citizen interests. Very often, however, party systems cannot express the diversity that exists in society. Civil associations can compensate for this deficit by conveying the interests of specific sectors to the political system. The Ecuadorian Indian movement exemplifies this function.

It gave voice to excluded groups, projected their concerns into the public agenda, and opened new areas for policymaking. Furthermore, its strategy of alliances was instrumental in aggregating and expressing the demands of all the rural groups and, eventually, the popular sectors at large.

To this we can add the creation of a party that incor-porated marginalized interests into the system and spurred indigenous participation in elections.

Interest representation by civil associations can help fulfill three principles of democratic governance: responsiveness (serving all sectors), consensus orientation (mediating among different interests), and equity (treating everyone equally). Realizing this potential, however, does not depend on the civil groups alone.

It also depends on the institutional actors' willingness to consider their views and adhere to democratic principles. In Ecuador, incumbent governments had many opportunities to hear what the indigenous and popular sectors wanted and to fulfill their side of the democratic governance bargain.

But those governments chose to ignore the input that came from below. Insisting on the imposition of unpopular reforms, they wasted the opportunities for building the kind of consensus that would have strengthened democratic governance.

This calls attention to a second function of civil associations: the control of state power. Liberal formulations emphasize the notion that citizens should protect themselves from state intrusion in private affairs and from violations of civil and political rights. Broader interpretations, however, include additional issues related to transparency and accountability. Once again, we find a connection with the principles of democratic governance, since the contribution of civil associations consists in holding governments responsible for fulfilling those principles.

In Ecuador, the popular opposition to neo-liberal governments repudiated the governments' insensitivity to the concerns of the majority, unwillingness to compromise, and unilateral commitment to the priorities of the business elites and the IMF. Thus, in the process of defending the interests of the popular sectors, the Indian movement and its allies were also fulfilling the watchdog role of trying to counterbalance what was widely seen as an unfair use of authority.

The foregoing interpretation leads to a third function: legitimation. In democratic polities, governments are acutely dependent on legitimacy because it is the people's support that justifies the right to exercise authority. Citizen groups can reaffirm legitimacy in two ways: explicitly, through actions that convey support; or tacitly, by doing nothing that might be construed as opposition.

The denial of support, however, must take the form of explicit oppositional action if it is to be understood as such. It is also worth noting that, in democracies, legitimation is rarely an all-or-nothing matter. The reason is that civil associations can legitimate or delegitimate authority at different levels.

Opposition to a policy does not necessarily imply disaffection with a government, and disaffection with a government does not necessarily entail rejection of the regime. Indeed, a common result of challenges at lower levels is the reinforcement of legitimacy at higher levels, as illustrated by cases in which a negotiated solution of a policy conflict boosts the image of a government, and situations in which the constitutional replacement of an unpopular government reaffirms the credibility of a democratic regime.

The legitimacy issue is particularly sensitive in the case of social movements because their motives are oppositional and their activities assume non-institutional forms. Still, taking into account the nuances of legitimation, there is much room for their fulfillment of this function.

The Ecuadorian Indian movement was certainly shoring up the political institutions when it created a party and urged its base to go to the polls. Beyond that, the routine challenges of the movement focused on policy matters that did not question the legitimacy of the governments or the regime as such. Through a different route we return to the point that, if the Ecuadorian governments had been more open to negotiation, the results could have enhanced their standing. Instead, their inflexibility became a factor in the escalation of conflict that led to their delegitimation. It was against this background that the Indian movement played an active role in the demise of two presidents. In the fall of Bucaram, the legitimacy of the regime was not at stake. The ousting of Mahuad was different because it involved a conspiracy to usurp power, which, had it succeeded, would have implied the breakdown of democracy. But the coup failed, and as a result, its actual impact on regime legitimacy is difficult to assess.

Intuitively, one would think that, by exposing the frailty of the institutions, the affair may have eroded their credibility. This inference, though, is not supported by the evidence. Over the last decade, the Latinobarómetro polls have shown a general softening of support for democracy, but the trend has been much less pronounced in Ecuador than in the rest of the Latin America.

Comparing the periods 1996-99 and 2000-2004 (before and after Ecuador's January 2000 coup), support for democracy declined by 12 per cent in the region as a whole but only by 6 per cent in Ecuador. One can speculate that, to some extent, Ecuadorians felt reassured that their democracy had survived the crisis.

Speculations aside, the movement's attempt to subvert the regime raises questions about a fourth function attributed to civil society: political socialization. In one of the most prominent formulations of the "civil society argument," associations are presented as frameworks in which citizens acquire the values and dispositions that are needed for a workable democratic polity. This claim relies on two basic assumptions about political socialization: that it is a matter of the formation of individuals, and that its results can somehow "free-float" into the public sphere as a resource that can be readily harnessed for the benefit of democracy.

What these assumptions miss is the significance of the mediation of the group, which becomes a collective subject of its own socialization process, inculcates its particularistic norms along with the more general dispositions, and regulates the use of the resources that make up the network's social capital. In so doing, civil society groups invariably condition the impact their socialization may have on the political system.

Taking this into account, we can tackle what appears to be one of the most puzzling questions about the Ecuadorian Indian movement. This study has demonstrated that the movement's struggles have induced vast changes in the behaviour of the indigenous groups. Because those changes would not have been possible without processes of socialization, it is clear that the movement has been doing a massive job teaching people to work together, cultivating interest in policy issues, and providing knowledge and skills for participating in public activities, such as mobilizations and elections.

The seemingly puzzling question is how these contributions to political socialization, which, according to the celebrated claim, should be functional to democracy, square with the attempt to take power by force. The matter is less baffling if we keep in mind that movements do not socialize people to help the workings of democratic regimes; they do it to attain their goals. The real question, then, concerns the movement's lack of commitment to Ecuadorian democracy.

This lack of commitment can be traced to three sources. One is the conviction that Ecuador's democracy is a fraud. Time and again the Indian militants have decried what they view as a corrupt democracy, with institutions that are discriminatory and governments that benefit the elites at the expense of the common people. Another source is the disrespect of all the political players for the rules of democracy. Willy-nilly, the indigenous activists have "learned the ropes" of practical politics within a system of interactions in which the prevailing attitudes are not distinguished by reverence for constitutional conventions.

The third source is the tension between the principles that inspire the indigenous internal practices and the liberal notions of democracy. At one level, it is a matter of the contrast between direct and indirect democracy; the former embodied in the participation of all in communal decisionmaking, and the latter in the elected officials who decide for all citizens in the broader Ecuadorian polity. At another level, it is a contrast between two canons of representation.

When the communities elect representatives to the associations, and when the associations elect representatives to the next-level federations, the elected persons function as delegates, whose powers are limited to specific mandates and whose authority can be revoked at will by those who elected them. In a liberal democracy, by contrast, elected officials operate as fiduciaries who use their discretion to interpret the interests of the represented and act on their behalf.

This raises the question of what the Indian movement's democratic ideals are, and whether these ideals and the standards of Ecuador's democracy are so incompatible as to justify the repudiation of the latter by the activists. In a political declaration approved in 1993, CONAIE called for a "plurinational communitarian democracy" based on equality, liberty, fraternity, and social peace. This goal would be achieved through a political reorganization aimed at guaranteeing the full participation of the Indian peoples and the other social sectors.

The platform adopted by the first congress of Pachakutik in 1999 was more specific, proposing a "radical democracy" based on a semiparliamentary system, decentralization, civil society representation in some state agencies, and direct participation through citizen initiatives, referenda, and recall of elected officials. These proposals could be easily integrated into an agenda to "deepen" the democratic character of existing institutions. The activists' lack of commitment, then, is not rooted in an unbridgeable programmatic rift.

Rather, it seems to result from a double ideological distortion: a view of Ecuadorian democracy that chooses to dwell on its deficiencies (ignoring that the conquest of indigenous rights and the Indian movement itself would hardly have been possible without it), and an exaggerated sense of the contradiction between the indigenous principles and those of the existing institutions.

This work has investigated the consequences of the Ecuadorian Indian movement for democracy. Its enquiry was based on conceptualizations that defined the specificity of movements as a form of civil society's political engagement and offered guidelines for studying their effects on the participatory and institutional dimensions of democracy. The analysis showed that the Indian movement had roots in communal mechanisms of direct democracy, that its multilayered structure had been built through bottom-up networking based on delegative representation, and that its protagonism in the contentious cycle of the 1990s marked a historic milestone for the involvement of the indigenous groups in Ecuador's public life.

The participatory breakthrough came on two fronts. Practicing the politics of influence, the movement forced new issues onto the public agenda, wrested concessions from governments, and led alliances that repeatedly hindered the imposition of neo-liberal reforms.

Engaging in the politics of power, it contested the control of the state's indigenous agencies and spawned a party that made strides in the electoral representation of the Indian groups, the procurement of their collective rights, and their progress towards self-government. These initiatives fulfilled important functions for Ecuador's democratic institutions. In the areas of interest representation and control of state power, the demands and protests provided ideas and contributions for improving the quality of democratic governance and imposed restraints on policies that were widely rejected by civil society. The launching of a new party was also significant as a development that upheld the legitimacy of the democratic regime.

It is unquestionable, then, that the Indian movement has made remarkable contributions to Ecuadorian democracy. Yet we have also seen that the swell of activism was not an unmitigated blessing for democratic politics. The critical drawback was the January 2000 attempt to subvert the constitutional order. At that point, CONAIE transgressed the threshold beyond which, in a democracy, an opposition becomes disloyal. The analysis here showed that the coup was inconsistent with the behavioural pattern of the Indian movement and that its negative impact was mitigated by its own failure and by the special conditions under which it happened. But the extenuating circumstances cannot absolve the movement of responsibility for threatening the democratic regime. Further scrutiny emphasized the reality that political socialization within the Indian movement had not fostered a sense of commitment to Ecuadorian democracy.

This evidence of contradictory consequences is consistent with the critique that the "civil society argument" plays up beneficial effects and ignores the possible downside. It also underscores that in Latin America, the study of the impact of civil associations on democracy cannot overlook three crucial points. The first is that the realization of the democratic potential of any civil society initiative depends on how the political institutions process it. Democratic governance is enhanced when decisionmakers take the concerns of civil associations into account. Conversely, democracy suffers when governments ignore citizen feedback, treat it perfunctorily, or demonstrate biases in their reactions to the bidding of different sectors.

The second point is that when civil associations mobilize broad support, the institutional responses to their functions of interest representation and control of state power can be highly consequential for regime legitimation. The legitimacy of democratic politics is strengthened when governments take notice of popular sentiment; but democratic regimes may fall into a tailspin of delegitimation when· the inputs from below are repeatedly rebuffed.

The third point is that it is a mistake to view civil society groups as neutral purveyors of citizens trained for democracy. Like other social capital resources, the results of political socialization remain embedded in the networks of interaction that produce them. As collective structures that constitute the primordial source of social capital, regulate its uses, and mediate between individuals and society, civil associations impart their particularistic slant to socialization and influence its fallout in the political system.

For Ecuador's indigenous activists, the stark contrast between the successes of the 1990s and the more recent frustrations underscores the urgency of rethinking their bearings.

To a large extent, their present predicament is a result of their own inability to respond to the complexities of the movement's institutionalization process. Two tasks in particular were sorely neglected. One was in the area of strategic development. To maintain coherence in situations of partial institutionalization, social movements must define a roadmap for combining protest with the use of prescribed means, and they must do it in such a manner that the two forms of action reinforce rather than interfere with each other.

The other neglected task was ideological elaboration. In the politics of influence, social movements can afford to condemn unstintingly the poverty of democracy. But in a democratic system, whatever its shortcomings, a movement that acts in the name of democracy cannot make the transition to the politics of power without taking a more constructive stance towards the existing institutions.

Essentially, it is a matter of reframing the movement's ideology by shifting the emphasis from antisystem representations to imageries of democratic renovation from within. In Ecuador, the lack of strategic guidelines and the shortsighted attitude towards the democratic institutions jumbled the responsibilities of CONAIE and Pachakutik, muddled their priorities, and paved the way for the missteps that weakened the Indian movement.

It may be a commonplace to say that a crisis can be turned into an opportunity, but that is precisely the challenge that the Ecuadorian indigenous activists face today. Whether or not they succeed will depend on their willingness to recognize that the time for reckoning and self-criticism is long overdue.

IMPLICATIONS FOR MEDIA AND JOURNALISM

The Internet has grown in a way distinctly different from any medium before it. As a result, it's difficult to predict how the Net will change mainstream media and to what magnitude. To say that media will undergo a "paradigm shift" might be an understatement. Consider that today 1 billion computers are connected to the Internet, most dialing in through telephone lines. By the end of 2010, Intel predicts that more than 1.5 billion computers will be connected via high-speed broadband and another 2.5 billion phones will have more processing power than today's PCs. Yet, only one-tenth of the world's population, or 600 million people, can access the Internet today. What will happen when many of the rest join in seeking others with whom to collaborate and share information? That's a revolution already underway, but it's one that's easy to miss. It's quiet. Revolutions on the Net happen at the edges, not at the centre.

Economist J. Bradford Long explains: "As the action spreads from producers (the few) to users (the many), it becomes much, much harder to get an overview of the revolutionary things occurring. We have anecdotes of brilliant new uses and applications, but do they add up to an enduring boom or just a few isolated pops that make good copy?" And that is the problem facing media companies, the entertainment industry and even governments. How do you put together the pieces of a puzzle without knowing what the final picture looks like? First, you find the edges. While we may not be able predict how the media landscape will shift, there are places we can begin looking for change and their likely impacts.

DEMOCRATIZATION OF MEDIA

Those who believe the democratization of media will have little effect on big media often point to the "zine" business. In the late '80s and early '90s, desktop publishing allowed many small, independent publications to spring up. To some degree, the magazine business became more democratized with the addition of more viewpoints. But those publications generally expanded the reach of magazines without toppling the more established titles. In the same way, some see little evidence that micromedia will displace established media today.

An important distinction to remember is that the economics of production and distribution in the magazine business, while less costly than before, were still substantial — keeping the number of new competitors to a handful. Moreover, competing with magazines that had larger circulation usually required considerable marketing budgets and years to build a large subscriber base. On the Web, the barriers to entry are next to nothing. The costs associated with distributing content online are so low that anyone can join and experiment with the democratization of media.

And that experiment is quickly moving into the mainstream. Recently America Online announced it would get into the weblog game, putting simple and powerful publishing tools into the hands of more than 30 million members. Millions will own a press, making everyone a potential media outlet. With the ability to publish words and pictures even via their cell phone, citizens have the potential to observe and report more immediately than traditional media outlets do.

Challenges to the Media's Hegemony

A democratized media challenges the notion of the institutional press as the exclusive, privileged, trusted, informed intermediary of the news. According to a recent Sports Illustrated story, "there is little doubt that fan web sites are breaking — and making — news and dramatically reshaping the relationship between college coaches and the public. "Mainstream news media, SI included, monitor web site message boards to take the public's pulse and, in some cases, look for news tips." Are respected news operations such as SI likely to be eliminated as one of the primary intermediaries of sports news any time soon? That's unlikely, but Web communities and even search engines are becoming valued outlets of news, which guide and direct their readers to information of interest. The role these sites play — as filters, simplifiers and clarifiers of news — is adding a new intermediary layer. They might not be the ultimate authority, but the new intermediaries — forums, weblogs, search engines, hoax-debunking sites — are helping audiences sort through the abundance of information available today.

Many newspapers and TV stations have had years to establish the trust of their audiences. Yet participatory news sites, with their transparent and more intimate nature, are attracting legions of fans who contribute and collaborate with one another. In addition, recent surveys suggest people are beginning to place more trust in online sources and are seeking increasingly diverse news sources and perspectives.

Credibility becomes Redefined

What are the implications of a distributed, collective pool of knowledge on credibility? Arguably, the stakes go up. Online communities require transparency of sources and reporting methods. Experts emerge through the recognition of their online peers rather than by anointment by the mass media.

For example, Glenn Fleishman, a freelance journalist in Seattle, has become one of the world's leading experts on wireless technology. He uses his weblog to both report on the latest developments in wi-fi and to interact with readers who might point him to a new wrinkle in the fast-moving field. In a digital medium, reputations form through a synthesis of consistency, accuracy and frequent comparison by the reader.

Says author Howard Rheingold: "I think people who are dedicated to establishing a reputation for getting the story right and getting it first don't necessarily have to work for The Washington Post or The New York Times." Individuals, institutions, the government and even reporters use the Web to maintain a record of their encounters with other media. The Department of Defence routinely posts transcripts of interviews with the Secretary of Defence and other high-ranking officials.

The motivation for self-publishing interviews appear to be twofold: To ensure that their words aren't misconstrued or misreported by the news media and to publish a complete public record of what the person being interviewed is saying. Even well-intentioned journalists may misinterpret an interviewee's meaning. Annotating provides the interviewee the opportunity to give his or her comments the kind of nuance, heft, context and thoughtfulness that might be left on the cutting-room floor in a news outlet's notoriously shrunken news hole. One of the better examples of user-generated content actively challenging the media's credibility is product reviews. While mainstream readers might not actively seek news reports or political opinions from amateurs, many are willing to consult reviews contributed by strangers before they make a purchase. Commerce sites like Amazon or product review sites such as Epinions.com or Edmunds.com put a great deal of emphasis on user-generated reviews and discussions. Many manufacturing companies like Subaru have taken notice and actively monitor discussion boards to understand what online communities think about their products.

THE RISE OF NEW EXPERTS AND WATCHDOGS

News organizations have spent much time and effort trying to position their journalists as more than impartial observers. They have in many ways tried to present them as experts in a field or interpreters of events. This approach in a print or broadcast model makes perfect sense. Online, the world of opinion and expert commentary is not restricted to the privileged. But forward-looking media companies don't view that development as a threat. News organizations still have the resources to become known as the definitive authority on various subjects. They will have to make way, however, for readers who want pick up the tools of journalism to contribute to a more informed citizenry and a more robust democracy.

For example, the news media and consumer non-profits no longer have a monopoly on serving as a watchdog on government and private industry. Individuals and citizen groups are stepping in to fill the void they believe has been created by lapses in coverage by big media. One of the more ambitious attempts is the Government Information Awareness (GIA) project by the MIT Media Lab, created in response to the government's Total Information Awareness project, which aims to collect personal information on citizens and foreigners and analyse it to pre-empt terrorist activities.

In a sense, GIA hopes to be Big Brother's Big Brother: "To allow citizens to submit intelligence about government-related issues, while maintaining their anonymity. To allow members of the government a chance to participate in the process." The Centre for Responsive Politics' Opensecrets.org site tracks campaign contributions and corporate connections of government officials, from the president's administration to every member of Congress. Citizens are also taking up a media watchdog role when it comes to chronicling perceived evidence of the news media's political bias, censorship or reporting inaccuracies. Controversies surrounding the invasion of Iraq have fuelled the launch of many sites. Mainstream media has been criticized for under-reporting both coalition force and Iraqi civilian casualties. In response, two sites — Iraq Coalition Casualty Count and Iraq Body Count — have attempted to establish independent databases that tabulate deaths by reviewing military and news reports. Each provides greater detail and accuracy than currently found in mainstream news reports. The sites also provide a transparency of sources and methodology rarely found in other media.

The Memory Hole, run by Russ Kick, is an example of a watchdog site that attempts to preserve and share information that has been removed from other sites on the Web or is difficult to find. FAIR.org scrutinizes media practices that "marginalize the public interest." Established in 1986, the organization highlights neglected news stories, opposes efforts at censorship and defends First Amendment precepts.

In a similar vein, the Tyndall Report monitors the three major U.S. television networks' nightly newscasts and the time devoted to each story. In England, where the BBC is funded by public tax monies, groups like bbcwatch.com have sprung up to make sure the broadcast organization stays true to its charter, which pledges journalism that is impartial and comprehensive.

In the wake of corporate scandals and greater influence-peddling in Washington, grassroots organizations are also turning a watchful eye towards corporate responsibility. CommercialAlert.org, a 4-year-old consumer organization in Portland, Ore., tries "to keep the commercial culture within its proper sphere, and to prevent it from exploiting children and subverting the higher values of family, community, environmental integrity and democracy."

Media Organization and Culture

Three incidents in the spring of 2003 point to the disruptive effects that the Internet has begun to sow in newsrooms — a disruption that threatens the status quo of news organization culture and policy.

- In April 2003, The Hartford Courant required a travel editor and former columnist, Denis Horgan, to stop posting commentary to his weblog.
- A month earlier, CNN reporter Kevin Sites was told to discontinue posting to his blog, which featured first-hand accounts of the war in Iraq. According to a CNN spokesperson, "CNN.com prefers to take a more structured approach to presenting the news.... We do not blog."
- Similarly, Time magazine editors instructed reporter Joshua Kucera to stop posting reports from Kurdistan to his weblog.

The resistance in media organizations to these newer forms of expression is not surprising. But such incidents, which are likely to multiply, raise questions about the nature of the relationship between journalists and their employers. Is a journalist, by virtue of his or her newsroom employment and access to newsmakers, not permitted to express a personal opinion outside of the office? Do media companies own an employee's free time? Do such prohibitions apply only to working journalists or to newsroom executives as well?

A chief concern on the part of news organizations is one of liability. Allowing reporters to write when off the clock might expose a company to a lawsuit. In addition, news outlets may perceive a reporter's weblog as competition, since it potentially draws eyeballs away from a media company's advertisers. Yet, as media companies gear more of their operations to an online audience that expects a more interactive dynamic, things will have to change. The collaborative and fast-paced nature of online news will require new policies, technologies, organizational structures and workflows. The assembly-line nature of broadcast and print media is not well-suited to developing content for smaller, more targeted audiences. Content will likely be published in a more continuous manner by teams or communities acting as an extention of the enterprise. Eventually, licensing and copyright policies will need to be reexamined to come into harmony with a collaborative audience model.

Moreover, measuring and managing the success of such collaborative ventures might be a challenge and force some rethinking about how such projects are gauged within the larger organization. Some news sites are experimenting on a small scale by co-opting successful participatory media models. MSNBC.com's Weblog Central section hosts a variety of analysts and columnists such as Instapundit.com's Glenn Reynolds and Eric Alterman of The Nation. Some of the more ambitious efforts have come from the United Kingdom. Whereas many larger news sites keep links to other sites to a minimum, Britain's The Guardian maintains many weblogs that guide readers to the best of the Web, including other news sites.

The BBC has announced plans to make its entire archives available for non-commercial use. Called the BBC Creative Archive, it will offer more than 80 years of radio and broadcast programmes free to anyone. The BBC's director general, Greg Dyke, said the decision was made based on their sense of where the Internet was heading: "I believe that we are about to move into a second phase of the digital revolution, a phase which will be more about public than private value; about free, not pay services; about inclusivity, not exclusion. "In particular, it will be about how public money can be combined with new digital technologies to transform everyone's lives."

When some media outlets start making participatory media work effectively, media companies that dig in their heels and resist such changes may be seen as not only old-fashioned but out of touch.

Journalism and the Media Workforce

Assuming that issues related to newsroom culture can be overcome, there are more hurdles facing the media. Along with a rethinking of journalism's role in the online medium, new skills and attitudes will be required. Staffs will need to be motivated to collaborate with colleagues, strangers, sources and readers. After years of working their way up the professional ladder, some reporters will undoubtedly need to discover a newfound respect for their readers. Arrogance and aloofness are deadly qualities in a collaborative environment.

To be successful, reporters will need to be more than skilled writers. They will have to hone their skills in growing communities around specific topics of interest. "That's one of the great challenges to us as news gatherers and journalists," said Joan Connell, executive producer for opinion and community at MSNBC.com. "How do we discover information and share it in creative ways with people? Give them the information they need to make the choices in their lives as citizens."

MSNBC.com believes that the editing process brings a higher degree of journalistic integrity to the news equation, and that's one factor that sets news organizations apart from personal weblogs.

"One of the values that we place on our own weblogs is that we edit our webloggers. Out there in the blogosphere, often it goes from the mind of the blogger to the mind of the reader, and there's no backup....I would submit that that editing function really is the factor that makes it journalism."

Universities will also need to shape their journalism curricula to help students prepare for working in this new media ecosystem and the fast-changing tools needed. A larger unknown for investigative reporters will be the impact of the Internet on sources. Now that we live on the cusp of a world in which everyone has the potential to be a reporter and a source, will that affect the behaviour of sources when they are approached by mainstream journalists?

Advertising and Marketing

Clay Shirky believes that mass media are dead. In his essay "RIP the Consumer 1900-1999," he suggests that mass media depend on two important characteristics of the audience: size and silence. According to recent Nielsen ratings reports, the TV audience continues to become more fragmented, with new channels continuing to proliferate. (Nightly network news viewership dropped in half from 1993 to 2002.) Today, an unqualified ratings champion is a fraction of what it was several years ago. Audiences, while still fairly large, are diminishing in size.

To Shirky, silence means that the audience remains passive. The Internet has helped to fracture mass media by empowering the audience to take a more active role when interacting with media. "The Internet heralds the disappearance of the consumer altogether," Shirky writes, "because the Internet destroys the noisy advertiser/silent consumer relationship that the mass media relies upon. The rise of the Internet undermines the existence of the consumer because it undermines the role of mass media. In the age of the Internet, no one is a passive consumer anymore because everyone is a media outlet."

There are a number of challenges facing media companies in the long run, if Shirky's argument is valid.

First, traditional media may need to rethink how to measure economic success. One option is to explore avenues for targeted, personalized advertising aimed at individuals or small identifiable groups. Another is to consider the possibility of moving away from an advertising-supported business model and towards subscriptions and other pay-for-content models. Real-time data about readership and viewership might lead to new pricing rules where fixed pricing is replaced by real-time market adjustments.

In addition, media companies will likely have to devise new ways to present audiences to advertisers. Typically, standard demographics are the measure of an audience. It may be that more creative and descriptive measures of audiences, based around psychographic characteristics, will be devised. Such changes cannot happen without expecting a change in the relationship between businesses and their customers. While many news sites have experimented with personalization as a means to identify more targeted advertising opportunities, they have only fleetingly experimented with new ways to allow consumers to interact with advertisers.

Citizens as Stakeholders in the Journalistic Process

Increasingly, audiences are becoming stakeholders in the news process. Rather than passively accepting news coverage decided upon by a handful of editors, they fire off e-mails, post criticism of perceived editorial shortcomings on weblogs and in forums, and support or fund an independent editorial enterprise. In June 2000 the NOW Legal Defence and Education Fund launched Women's eNews, a news service run by a small staff of professional journalists who work with a national network of free-lance writers. Devoted to coverage of women's issues, the site became a fully independent operation in early 2002. In July 2003 it won four journalism awards from the National Federation of Press Women and continues to probe issues often overlooked by the mainstream media.

Occasionally, readers will dig into their own pockets to finance a journalism effort they find worthwhile. Freelance journalist Christopher Allbritton received $14,334 from 320 people who funded his trip to Iraq to report his first-hand observations of the war zone. He filed daily dispatches on his Web site, Back-to-Iraq.com, about the fall of Tikrit and reported on the region's ethnic tensions.

A freelance journalist from Maine, David Appel, asked readers of his weblog to pony up to let him pursue an investigative story. After receiving more than $200, Appel investigated a sugar lobbying group's attempt to get Congress to kill funding for the World Health Organization, whose policies had offended corporate sugar interests. While war reporting and investigative reporting remain the province of trained journalists, more often citizens are taking up the tools of journalism to write about favourite topics. Columnist J.D. Lasica calls these do-it-yourself entries "random acts of journalism," as when Jessica Rios, a 22-year-old woman in Los Angeles, attended a Coldplay concert and wrote a review of their performance on her weblog.

The author Howard Rheingold is representative of a new kind of reader who spends more time with favourite weblogs and collaborative media than with traditional media. "The things I'm interested in, from pop culture to wireless policy to copyright, you have to go to the fanatics," he said. And those fanatics are more easily found in niche online media.

Potential Benefits of we Media

Participatory journalism is not going to disappear any time soon. Communication, collaboration and sharing personal passions have been at the heart of the Internet since its inception more than 30 years ago. David Weinberger, author of Small Pieces Loosely Joined, says that this is because the Web is not just a giant marketplace or an information resource. Rather, "it's a social commons on which the interests of a mass of individuals are splayed in universally accessible detail and trumpeted in an effectively infinite array of personal voices." According to Scott Rosenberg, managing editor of Salon.com, what Weinberger reminds us is that "every Web site, every Internet posting matters to the person who created it — and maybe to that person's circle of site visitors, whether they number 10 million or just 10."

"Individually, these contributions may be crude, untrustworthy, unnoteworthy. Collectively, they represent the largest and most widely accessible pool of information and entertainment in human history. And it's still growing." If media companies are going to collaborate with their audiences online, they must begin to consider a news and information Web site as a platform that supports social interaction around the stories they create. These interactions are as important as the narrative, perhaps more so, because they are created and owned by the audience. In a networked world, media whose primary value lies in its ability to connect people will win.

This chapter explores the potential benefits to media companies and businesses that adopt participatory journalism in meaningful ways. Possible examples include enabling editors and reporters to publish a weblog about the subjects they cover; hosting, moderating and participating in discussion forums or groups about news; encouraging audience contribution of editorial content for distribution on a Web site or in a traditional media product; enabling your readers to purchase online advertising through affordable text ads. The possibilities are limitless, as long as it includes an effort to engage the audience in an authentic conversation and collaboration. An involved, empowered audience could well bring a number of potential benefits to media companies. From our research, we have compiled the following list of benefits:

Increased Trust in Media

According to a USA Today/CNN/Gallup Poll in June 2003, only 36 per cent of those polled believe the news media generally "get the facts straight." News media have their work cut out in restoring their reputations and their readers' sense of trust. Participatory journalism provides media companies with the potential to develop a more loyal and trustworthy relationship with their audiences.

This can happen, for example, with a reporter who writes a weblog, asking the audience to fuel her efforts by providing tips, feedback and first-hand accounts that confirm a story's premise or that take it in a different direction. We Media can also provide the audience a deeper level of understanding about the reporting process by illustrating, for example, how a reporter must balance competing interests. This communication can lead to a lasting trust.

Time magazine media critic James Poniewozik explains how this is possible, when he describes the perception gap between the audience and the media about trust. "Journalists think trust equals accuracy. But it's about much more: passion, genuineness, integrity." Honest conversation and passionate collaboration could instill respect and trust into the relationship between both parties. Involving an audience, either small or large, in the creation of content also gives them a sense of ownership — an affinity with the media brand that they believe they are not getting today — as well as a more intimate relationship with the storytellers.

Shared Responsibility in Informing Democracy

An audience that participates in the journalistic process is more demanding than passive consumers of news. But they may also feel empowered to make a difference. As a result, they feel as though they have a shared stake in the end result. According to Bill Kovach and Tom Rosenstiel, authors of the book The Elements of Journalism, citizens must take an active, collaborative role in the journalistic process if we are to realize an effective journalism that appropriately informs a democracy.

"Journalists must invite their audience into the process by which they produce the news," Kovach and Rosenstiel write in their book. "They should take pains to make themselves and their work as transparent as they insist on making the people and institutions of power they cover. This sort of approach is, in effect, the beginning of a new kind of connection between the journalist and the citizen. It is one in which individuals in the audience are given a chance to judge the principles by which the journalists do their work."

"The first step in that direction has to be developing a means of letting those who make up that market finally see how the sausage is make — how we do our work and what informs our decisions." Many journalists who are already weblogging are doing just that — exposing the raw material of their stories-in-progress, posting complete text of interviews after the story is published, and inviting comments, fact checking and feedback that contribute to follow-up stories.

7

Online Journalism and Ethics

INTRODUCTION

Online journalism is mistakenly equated with the print and broadcast variety, given the inclusion of elements from all known media on the Internet. But the nature of the beast is such that unexpected challenges have arisen in the very definition of what journalism is, who a journalist is and how one evaluates online journalism's performance and sets guidelines for good practice and behaviour in cyberspace.

The proliferation of blogs (weblogs) in the Arab world has added to the choices of news consumers by turning some into news producers. But can anyone with the technical know-how be classified a journalist? Are we so overwhelmed by gadgetry and high-speed access as to have lost sight of solid content, context, balance, fairness and ethics? The new media have spawned a new breed of citizens' media. How reliable are they? Can they, and do they, compete with traditional and well-established media? What are the ethical implications of blogging?

Haven't traditional media come under attack for publishing in print (and increasingly online) material considered objectionable by consumers? Should news consumers take matters into their own hands and turn the tables on the media by creating and producing their own content?

French author Alexis de Tocqueville wrote that if one wishes to know the real power of the press, one should pay attention, not to what it says, but to the way in which it is listened to. "It only cries so loud because the audience is becoming deaf," he argued. But today, the opposite may be the case, wrote Brad Badelt, adding that the audience has been crying loudly for some time and the mainstream media have been slow to respond. *(The Rise of the Pajama Clad Scribes; How Weblogs Are Reshaping the Not-So-Free Press, Brad Badelt, Thunderbird magazine, University of British Columbia, http://www.journalism.ubc.ca/thunderbird/archives/2005.01/blog.html).*

Although chat rooms have been a natural extension and complement to news sites, in June 2005, the portal Yahoo closed its user-created chat rooms following a TV exposé that showed an online service had attempted to exploit children for sex. Key advertisers pulled their commercials from Yahoo's site because of the TV report.

According to the press story, Yahoo's "terms of service" agreement stipulates that users must agree not to use any of the company's products or services to "harm minors in any way" or to e-mail or transmit "vulgar" or "obscene" content. It added that, that was not the first time Yahoo's image had been brought to question and that in 2001 an FBI investigation had targeted certain Yahoo users and led to the arrest of over 100 people in the U.S. who were seeking to lure children or trade pornographic material involving minors.

Jordanian general security officials organized a workshop on computer/ Internet crimes against children, the first such event in the Middle East, in a bid to help protect families, find missing children and prevent or lessen the adverse effects of cyber crime against minors.. It's a step in the right direction, but a drop in the ocean.

How does one legislate for the Internet, notably since one man's proverbial meat is another man's poison? If freedom of expression advocates in one country publicize their hardships on the Web to attract international attention to their plight, should legislators across their borders be passing laws barring the dissemination of such news if it could benefit others and bring about positive change?

News media analysts suggest that practitioners and organizations need clear ethical standards to guide behaviour. But lawyers have shied away from formal codes because they provide other lawyers representing injured parties with documents and proof that can be used against journalists if the procedures and rules are not strictly followed. Given the reach of globalization, the pervasiveness of satellite TV channels that transcend borders and the very changing nature of news as we have known it, I'd like to examine the evolving dynamics of online journalism and the concomitant challenge of trying to establish ethical standards and laws to define "do"s and "don't"s in cyberspace.

Moreover, I will examine whether new media and good governance are mutually reinforcing, and whether online news outlets have kept reporters in the office and off their beats, thereby depriving consumers from credible and ethical coverage. But first, let's examine how journalism is being defined.

CONTENT ANALYSIS OF ONLINE NEWS

The landscape of news consumption is in the midst of a dramatic transition. As online news attracts more news consumers than ever before, Yahoo!News and Google News have, for now, established a stronghold in the news aggregation market. Aggregators produce little original news content, instead providing a platform for established news producers and access for users to multiple news sources. Arguably the most popular online news portal,

Yahoo!News3 allows users to identify favourite topics-politics, business, science, entertainment-from various sources including Associated Press (AP), Agence France-Presse (AFP), Reuters, CNN, and others.

A recent Pew study determined that 23 per cent of online news consumers chose Yahoo!News, and while Yahoo!News usage has continued to increase, competitor aggregators, such as Google News, and online news providers, such as MSNBC.com and CNN.com, have lost users. In the fickle world of online credibility ratings, YahooiNews is considered by consumers to be as trustworthy as national television and newspaper producers' Web sites and more credible than the online versions of local news media. And Yahool's customers are satisfied, with satisfaction scores increasing from 2006 to 2007.

This increased reliance on online news consumption brings with it many opportunities and challenges for mass communication research. Rich sources of text and images fundamental to mass communication research have never been more accessible, and while data can be gathered relatively easily, the sheer volume of available data can be overwhelming. The choice of appropriate sampling procedures is always a critical methodological decision, but unlike traditional print and broadcast media, the question of how much is enough to adequately represent online news content is yet to be rigorously addressed.

This chapter evaluates constructed week samples in terms of efficiency for representing online news content. Five sample sizes, ranging from one week (n=7 days) to five constructed weeks (n=35 days), are compared for their ability to accurately represent six months of content. Eight different content measures are used: four different news categories, plus average length of story, average number of photos, average number of videos, and the average number of "most popular" stories. In addition, the results are compared with the results from two other sampling techniques: simple random sampling and consecutive day sampling.

In her review of nineteen studies that applied content analysis techniques to the World Wide Web, McMillan found that few provided any discussion of sampling decisions and some applied statistics that "assume a random sample to analyse data sets that were not randomly generated." She concluded that the findings and conclusions of such studies must be viewed with caution and that the requirement for rigour in drawing a sample "may be one of the most difficult aspects of content analysis on the Web."

Sample selection is a critical content analysis design decision and must assure that each unit has the same chance of being represented in the collection of sampling units.10 In the early 1990s, Riffe and Lacy began a programme of research on sampling standards in the content analysis of traditional news media coverage. The recurring question for content analysts is, they argued, "how many sampled edition dates are needed to adequately represent the population during a particular period in time?"

More than half a century of news media research, beginning with Stempel's 1952 study of sampling daily newspapers, has shown that "the cyclic nature of media content can render simple random sampling inefficient compared to other types of sampling." Stratified sampling that yields constructed weeks has been the most convincing response to the problem of systematic content variation in media content. Constructed week samples "involve identifying all Mondays, and randomly selecting one Monday, then identifying all Tuesdays, and randomly selecting one Tuesday, etc., to 'construct' a week that ensures that each source of cyclic variation-each day of the week-is represented equally."

For example, after comparing different sampling methods, one study found that one constructed week was adequate for representing a six-month "population" of editions for a daily newspaper, but that two constructed weeks were better. While stratified sampling has some efficiency compared to random sampling for weekly newspapers and magazines, the influence of cycles in weekly or monthly content is not as strong, and so the relative efficiency of stratified (constructed) sampling compared to random sampling is not as high.

When studying sampling efficiency for nightly network newscasts, researchers found the selection of two days stratified by month to be most efficient. In contrast, simple random sampling demanded selecting thirty-five days to match the efficiency of the twenty-four-day-per-year sample required using stratified sampling.

The requirement for stratification has also been explored in the context of longitudinal studies of news content. In a study of sample size for newspaper content over multiple years, researchers deemed the selection of nine constructed weeks from five years to be more efficient than selecting two constructed weeks from each year or ten weeks in total, but only when the variables being measured had small variations. An important caveat for this finding was that, when variations in the variables under consideration are large, the sample size of ten constructed weeks should be used.

A review of online news research applying the content analysis method shows limited evidence of the application of random sampling techniques that might lend efficiency and support claims of representativeness and generalizability. Most researchers opt for sampling approaches that are purposive, convenience, consecutive days, or some combination therein. Stratification of sampling in published studies of online news is rarely discussed and even more rarely applied.

Sampling stratification decisions in the content analysis of online news coverage continue to be guided by the conventions developed by Riffe, Lacy, and others for traditional print and broadcast contentnewspapers, magazines, and network newscasts.

For example, Hoffman compared the content of online and print newspapers for differences in the frequency of mobilizing information, selecting a sample of one constructed week for each version to represent a seven-week period. This sampling approach assumed no difference between print and online news, and cited guidelines for sampling for newspapers from Riffe, Lacy, and Fico. In Lim's cross-lagged analysis of agenda setting among online news media, a sample of two constructed weeks was selected to represent a twelve-month period.

Bucy content analysed the home pages of four network affiliates, sampling purposively during approximately the same time (mid-October) in two years-1998 and 2000. The reasons for choosing this sampling approach are given limited explicit attention.

To compare online news sites with their printed counterparts, Boczkowski and de Santos collected online news content from three Argentine sites on two days per week, Monday through Friday only, for ten weeks. Schwalbe recognized that generalizations beyond the days and sites studied could not be made in her content analysis of the home pages of twenty-six mainstream news sites on every Wednesday for the first four weeks of the 2003 Iraq war.

Despite extensive research into sampling issues for newspapers of various types, as well as TV news broadcasts and news magazines, little is known about sampling for studying online news content. In the few instances where researchers have attempted to randomly sample online news content, they have relied on the research from traditional news media to guide sampling decisions. Do the same guidelines apply? Is online news content affected by daily variation similar to that in daily newspapers? How much content needs to be sampled to estimate the content in a longer time period? To address these issues, this study attempts to answer two research questions:

> *RQ1:* What is the minimum number of randomly constructed weeks necessary to accurately generalize to a population of six months of online news?

> *RQ2: Is a constructed week sample more efficient than simple random or consecutive day samples of comparable size?*

METHOD

Testing sampling efficiency for generalizing to a six-month population of online news content requires knowledge of population parameters to compare with obtained sample statistics. This study used data from a content analysis of news content on the Yahoo! News portal collected daily between 11 a.m. and 2 p.m. (EST) from December 15, 2005, to June 15, 2006. Data collected included the top five stories listed for each of the three wire services (Agence France Presse-AFP; Associated Press-AP; and Reuters), two newspapers (Christian Science Monitor-CSM and USA Today) and one cable TV news channel (CNN). Also captured were users' top five most-viewed, most-recommended, and most-e-mailed stories.

After approximately twelve hours of training, five coders examined each of the 7,438 separate articles collected during the 183-day period. Coding categories included news source, article length (in paragraphs), whether the story was a news source's top story, and whether the story was one of the top five most viewed stories, most e-mailed (one of the top five stories most often e-mailed by a reader to someone else), or most recommended story (one of the top five stories based on user ratings). Also coded were whether the story had a link on the home page and whether it was accompanied by still images, video footage, or audio clips. Additionally, adapting the YahooiNews categories, coders organized the articles into one of nine topics: world, business, entertainment, sports, health, technology, U.S. government/politics, science/education, and odd news. The coders used data from days not coded in this study to pretest the coding schedule and work out coding disagreements.

Intercoder reliability was calculated with Holsti's coefficient of reliability using data from the first seven days of December and the first fourteen days of February (11.5 per cent of the data). Agreement was 100 per cent for the "Most Popular" variable and 98 per cent for "Story Length," "Photos," and "Video." For the nine news topic categories, the intercoder reliability outcomes are as follows: "World," 93 per cent; "Business," 92 per cent; "Entertainment," 97 per cent; "Sports," 100 per cent; "Health," 99 per cent; "Technology," 90 per cent; "U.S. Government/Politics," 90 per cent; "Science and Education" 99 per cent; and "Odd News," 90 per cent.

For this study, the 183 days were treated as the population, and data were used to create, for this study's purposes, eight variables describing the content for each day. The eight variables showed a degree of variation in their means and standard deviations that would provide a more conservative test than using just a single variable. The variables were:

- *News Category 1*: Percentage of "Odd News" stories each day
- *News Category 2*: Percentage of "Sports" and "Entertainment" stories each day
- *News Category 3*: Percentage of "Health," "Tech," "Science," and "Business" stories each day
- *News Category 4*: Percentage of "U.S. Government/Politics," and "World" stories each day
- *Story Length*: Average number of paragraphs in each story coded each day
- *Photos*: Percentage of stories containing photos/slides each day
- *Video*: Percentage of stories containing video each day
- *Most Popular Stories*: Percentage of stories each day that are simultaneously featured as a Top 5 story among online users (most e-mailed, most viewed, or most recommended) in addition to being a Top 5 story for at least one of the news sources.

Once population parameters were known, the first step involved drawing constructed week samples in sets of fifty. Originally, fifty samples of one constructed week (n=7) were drawn, as were fifty samples of two constructed weeks (n=14), fifty samples of three constructed weeks (n=21), and fifty samples of four constructed weeks (n=28). However, after analyzing these samples, an additional set of fifty samples of five constructed weeks (n=35) was also drawn.

The second step involved drawing comparable sets of fifty samples for comparison using both simple random sampling and consecutive day sampling. Fifty 7-day samples were randomly selected, as were fifty 14-day samples, fifty 21-day samples, fifty 28-day samples, and fifty 35-day samples.

For consecutive day samples, fifty random starting points were generated and, for each, seven consecutive days were selected to form a sample week. The same process was used, again with random starting points, to create fifty two-week (fourteen consecutive days) samples, fifty three-week (twenty-one consecutive days) samples, fifty four-week (twenty-eight consecutive days) samples, and fifty five-week (thirty-five consecutive days) samples.

The third step was to compare the efficiencies of the various sampling methods and sample sizes. These comparisons are based on the distribution of sample means predicted by the Central Limits Theorem. Because this distribution is based on a normal curve, in 68 per cent of the samples, the population mean should fall within plus or minus one standard error of the sample mean, and in 95 per cent of the samples, the population mean should fall within plus or minus two standard errors of the sample mean.

The percentage of times the population mean fell within the ranges predicted by the theorem was then computed for each sample size and sampling method.

The CV is the standard deviation divided by the mean and represents the variability of the units in the population. A higher CV indicates more variation among the cases. In this population of news stories, three variables show relative low variation: News Category 4 (CV=.11), average Story Length (CV=.10), and Photos (CV=.17). On the other hand, two variables, News Category 1 (CV=.86) and Most Popular Stories (CV=.81), have very high coefficients of variation. Past research has shown that high variability requires larger sample sizes in order to be representative of the population.

RQ1 asked: What is the minimum number of randomly constructed weeks necessary to accurately generalize to a population of six months of online news? As noted earlier, constructed week sampling assumes that there is systematic, or cyclic, variation of content by day of week. For example, Sunday has the highest average number of sports and entertainment stories (News Category 2), but the lowest average number of health, tech, science, and business stories (News Category 3) as well as the lowest average number of videos.

Data present the results for fifty samples of 7-, 14-, 21-, 28- and 35-day constructed week samples for each variable. Each underlined percentage indicates that the sampling percentage exceeded the values determined by the Central Limits Theorem (68 per cent for plus or minus one standard error; 95 per cent for plus or minus two standard errors).

Based on the decision criteria used in previous research,36 sample size was efficient if both its percentages equaled or exceeded the expected percentages, provided that the next larger sample size did not drop below either of the expected percentages.

Using these criteria, a sample of two constructed weeks (n=14) was efficient for four of the variables. These four variables, News Category 3 (CV =.31), News Category 4 (CV=.ll), Photos (CV=.17), and Video (CV=.49), had coefficients of variation that were less than.50.

The remaining four variables still did not meet the efficiency criteria when an additional week was added to form a sample of three constructed weeks (n=21). Instead, a sample of four constructed weeks (n=28) was required for two variables, News Category 2 (CV=.48) and Average Story Length (CV=.10), despite the fact that Average Story Length had the lowest CV of any variable tested.

The Most Popular Stories (CV=.81) variable did not meet the efficiency criteria until five constructed weeks (n=35) were used. None of the sample sizes tested were efficient for the variable with the highest CV, News Category 1 (CV=.86). This variable reached the expected percentages with one constructed week (n=7), but then dropped below the criteria levels for the remaining sample sizes.

RQ2 asked: Is a constructed week sample more efficient than simple random or consecutive day samples of comparable size? For simple random samples, only the 21-day sample for one variable (Video) and the 28-day sample for one variable (Most Popular Stories) meet both sets of decision criteria (equaling or exceeding the expected percentages, provided that the next larger sample size did not drop below either of the expected percentages). For the consecutive day samples, the 28day sample for one variable (News Category 3) is the only sample meeting both sets of decision criteria. Compared to constructed week samples, simple random and consecutive day samples are much less efficient.

Based on the results of this study, sampling requirements for online news content are somewhat different from those of traditional media. Constructed week sampling is still the most efficient type of sample, but sample size needs to be much larger. While previous research concluded that a single constructed week would allow reliable estimates of content in a population of six months of newspaper editions, this study shows that, at a minimum, two constructed weeks are needed. Moreover, as many as five constructed weeks may be needed for some online news content depending on the type of variables being analysed. In addition, both simple random and consecutive day samples performed particularly poorly and should probably be avoided.

As a general rule, variables with high variability need larger samples. Among the variables in this study, the one with the highest level of variability, News Category 1 ("Odd News," CV=.86), never reached the established efficiency criteria for the sample sizes tested, while the variable with the second most variability, Most Popular Stories (CV=.81), needed at least five constructed weeks to represent six months of content. On the other hand, some low variability samples such as News Category 4, Photos (CV=.17), and News Category 3 met the efficiency criteria with just two constructed weeks.

Previous research suggests using a coefficient of variation of .5 as the criterion for increasing sample size. The results of this study imply that this approach may not be sufficient. Two variables in this study, Video (CV=.49) and News Category 2 ("Sports" and "Entertainment;" CV=.48), had almost identical coefficients of variation but required very different sample sizes, two and four constructed weeks, respectively. One possible explanation is the difference in population percentages. The population mean for the Video variable (15.24) was higher than the population mean for the News Category 2 variable (9.50). A similar pattern is seen in comparing the four news category variables.

The two news category variables with highest population means (News Category 3 and News Category 4) also require the smallest sample sizes, two constructed weeks. In addition, the variable with the lowest CV (.10) and a relatively low population mean, Average Story Length, required a sample of four constructed weeks to meet the threshold while other variables with low CVs but higher population means required only two constructed weeks. Future research should investigate the relationships between population means and CVs, along with other indicators of variability, as criteria for determining sample size.

Of course, this study cannot be generalized to all online news content because only one news aggregator, YahooiNews, was examined. Additional research is needed to examine other sources and types of online news content. In addition, news content was gathered only once each day. Research is needed to determine if variation in news content throughout the day affects sampling requirements.

Like most of the previous research on sample size for content analysis of the media, the variables in question are the types that are simply counted. Future research using different types of variables common to media content analyses (tone, frames, etc.) would also be a very useful contribution to the content analysis sampling literature.

Research shows a decline in voter turnout since the 1950s, while other forms of political participation also have declined over the past four decades.

Reduced newspaper readership has been named as one precursor to this falloff in participation, with newspaper readership decreasing from 47 per cent in 2000 to 42 per cent in 2004.

Some scholars hail the Internet as a possible route for reinvigorating the democratic process and encouraging citizens to become more involved. Others have argued the Internet could negatively affect the electorate, much like other media such as the telephone and television, which at first were thought to enhance participation. However, a study by Kraut et al. suggests that such negative effects of the Internet have dissipated. "Changes in the Internet environment itself," they noted, "might be more important to understanding the observed effects than maturation or differences between samples."

Those seeking news online increased from 23 per cent in 2000 to 29 per cent in 2004. Reading political news is also popular: 40 per cent of Internet users reported this activity in 2002. This suggests that news and politics online could have substantial effects and that systematic analysis of this content could be fruitful.

Communication scholars have long advocated examination of content10 in addition to time spent with a medium. Content, more than just the diverse materials presented on various media, changes from day to day. Analysis of content is important in understanding what information people are exposed to, above and beyond measures of time spent with media.

Content analyses of the Internet, though, have generally focused on how messages are presented rather than what is communicated. Thus, in the absence of a true theoretical framework, many Internet studies fail to come to replicable conclusions.

Bucy asserted, "Web content is often measured and described in a theory-free context, adding little to our conceptual understanding of the online medium." Although effects cannot be ascertained from a content analysis, the absence of content research in the Internet-effects debate ignores the importance of studying content before effects. As Riffe, Lacy, and Fico argued, "in the long run, one cannot study mass communication without studying content." One type of content that has been studied in analyses of news and that is the focus of this study is mobilizing information (MI), defined simply as information found in news that aids people to act on attitudes they already hold.

THEORETICAL FRAMEWORK

The introduction of a new communication technology, such as the Internet, allows scholars to "rethink, rather than abandon, definitions and categories," including conceptualizations like MI. This shady seeks to answer the question: Does the presence of MI differ in online versus print newspaper contexts? Eveland suggested applying uniform analyses to media, assessing "mixed attributes" to differentiate media. This study assesses print and online content in as uniform a way as possible to evaluate whether new technology has changed the content of newspapers.

Importantly, new technology alters the sociology of news production, which suggests that content differences may be found. For instance, Pavlik predicts that new media will encourage journalists to move beyond norms of objectivity. Some cases of what Pavlik calls "contextualized journalism" have already occurred. For example, reader feedback via e-mails to journalists has changed the way future stories are written, readers can create unique content, and journalists have relinquished some control to consumers who can customise their news experience. Newspapers, in particular, are being forced to make their Web sites "commercially viable" to compete with other sources.

Boczkowski found that online newsrooms differ from print newsrooms in the amount of autonomy they have, policies, and definitions of Web site users. He suggested that online, news "moves from being mostly journalist-centered...to also being increasingly audience-centered." The Internet could also have advantages over other media because reduced material cost can provide more incentive for consumers to search for political information as well as decrease production costs for news producers.

THE INTERNET AS A PARTICIPATORY MEDIUM

Much debate surrounding the Internet as a political and participatory medium relates to its ability to create new relationships; function as a virtual forum; or enhance social networks. Findings generally show that this social aspect of the Internet is ineffective in producing social trust or engagement. Some research has found, however, that online users who search for information and exchange e-mail, rather than those who chat or play games, are more active in civic life.

Thus far, no empirical research directly links the Internet to political participation. Indirect effects have been monitored, and "political learning and motivation for participation are enhanced through various types of communication, which in turn increases the level of political participation." In this way, the information that so many users seek online could encourage participation.

MOBILIZING INFORMATION

MI can be found online via hyperlinks, contact information, and linked content on other Web sites. Although it does not inherently motivate citizens, MI enables them to act on existing motivations by providing information on how to follow through with an action. Research on MI has declined since the 1980s, yet the concept continues to be cited in the context of media's role in mobilizing political participation and civic engagement, as well as in health communication. MI is relevant to the discussion of media effects and political participation because MI has the potential for directly encouraging citizens to become involved in politics.

Lemert and his colleagues, credited with the term, acknowledged that MI originated in publications on environmental and media studies. Two articles, published mere months apart, are cited as the concept's inspiration. Murch's content analysis of newspapers revealed that local media focused more on national rather than local pollution issues, excluding information that could provide information on which to act.

Rubin and Sachs's report correlated increased public interest in environmental issues and increased media discourse on the environment during the 1970s. While "mobilizing information" was not referenced explicitly, Rubin and Sachs referred to "specific information, and the day-to-day alerting which is necessary for any citizen to participate effectively in the legislative process," which "the public at large still expects the news media to provide." They asserted that the public does not have access to such information outside the media and "one cannot become involved without at least knowing when and where hearings are being held, and who it is that should be contacted in order to voice an opinion."

THREE TYPES OF MOBILIZING INFORMATION

Locational MI provides information about the time and place of an activity; identificational MI provides names and contact information for people or groups; and tactical MI is the explicit and implicit instructions for certain behaviours, such as tactics used in a strike. Because some MI could be controversial or even harmful, Lemert argued that mainstream media are reluctant to provide coverage of such events, let alone publish information that might encourage participation. Lemert also differentiated between "political MI," (locational, identificational, and tactical) and non-political MI (such as advertisements, cooking recipes, or garden tips). He admitted, however, that MI "needs to be described in more detail" and that it is "a relatively new concept, and our thinking about it is still changing."

How does one move forward, then, in a meticulous study of MI in news content? Lemert provided calls for research, most of which centered on reasons MI is excluded from media content. He claimed, however, that there is so little MI in news that it becomes difficult to test for it. Previous work on MI has focused on environmental or specialized contexts. The present study seeks to analyse the concept in a more general news context.

Where Is Mobilizing Information? MI is essential in advertising; the advertiser wants potential customers to know where and how to purchase a product or service (*e.g.*, "in your grocer's freezer"). In news, however, MI varies depending on the type of news presented. Positive and non-controversial items are most likely to include MI because they are "harmless" or "good for the

published previously, both conceptual and operational definitions of locational, identificational, and tactical MI were constructed for this analysis. Although MI can be found within different contexts, this study examines only political news, as derived from Perloff's definition of politics: "a process whereby a group of people, whose opinions or interests are initially divergent, reach collective decisions which are generally regarded as binding on the group, and enforced as common policy."

Therefore, political MI contained only those news stories about decisions that are regarded as binding on the group and enforced as common policy. Specifically included were stories in National, International, Political, and Local/Metro sections.

Only MI that fit this definition of "politics" was coded. Operationally, this means that to be included, each instance of MI had to represent a decision to be made regarding public policy or government. Because this is still quite broad, an example may help demonstrate criteria for inclusion. An announcement for a neighbourhood social where community members are welcome to share food and play games would not be included, while an announcement for a neighbourhood meeting to discuss new regulations enforced by city council would.

The question to be answered in deciding what content should be included was, "Does this represent the fact that multiple opinions exist and a common policy should or will ultimately be enforced by political actors?"

The three types of MI are not mutually exclusive and more than one type may exist in a unit of analysis, particularly with tactical MI (*i.e.,* a unit may describe specifically how to accomplish an activity, but also provide the time and place for that activity).

Locational MI provides information about a time and place for an activity. Excluded from examples of locational MI were programme listings for television and radio, as well as obituaries. The fundamental attribute of locational MI is that it provides a time and place for a political activity or event. An example of locational MI from this study's sample provided information about a Philadelphia City Council committee: "The committee meeting will be at 3 p.m. tomorrow in Room 696 at City Hall."

Online, there are multiple opportunities for locational MI that may not exist in print. A meeting announcement might be hyperlinked from a story about a new residential development, or a hyperlink could link to details on a weekend rally. For both print and online, the question to ask when assessing locational MI was, "Does this give me enough information to attend an event in which I might be interested?"

Identificational MI provides names and contact information for a political candidate or representative, interest group, political party, corporation, or government agency. Examples include names and addresses or phone numbers;

names and positions in relatively stable, easily locatable organizations (*i.e.*, Vice President Dick Cheney); and company or group names.

Again, the emphasis is on strictly political or publicpolicy contexts and the key element is contact information. Online, a hyperlink is inherently identificational if it links to an e-mail address or a Web site of a person or organization. Reporters often provide a link to their e-mail address in their byline. Because this study examined political news, these links were included, as they allow readers to act on information they read. Not all newspapers provided this information. However, the Philadelphia Enquirer, for example, provided both a phone number and e-mail address for each article. Tactical MI makes available explicit and implicit behavioural models for action.

In this study, only explicit tactical information was coded. Explicit tactical MI tells a person exactly how to accomplish a political activity without necessarily providing a time, place, or contact information. The chief component of tactical MI is that it tells a reader how to do something, such as how to participate in a rally or how to affect the legislative process.

An example comes from the San Francisco Chronicle, which encouraged citizens to contact officials when things went wrong in their neighbourhoods. The Chronicle provided specific information on how to make a complaint to be published in the newspaper and, once complaints were published, contact information for officials in charge was given. This represents tactical MI because explicit directions are provided for how to accomplish the activity. The question asked in ascertaining tactical MI was, "Does this give me enough information to become involved in some way, based on the attitudes I may already hold?"

PROCEDURE

Print articles were collected through subscriptions to each newspaper during the sampled period. Online articles were collected using WebZIP software (version 5.0.5.896) from Spidersoft and were downloaded only at the first level-the news article page and subsequent pages for that same article. The content beyond the news article page(s) was not downloaded for analysis.

Online and print articles were selected based on whether they fit the coding criteria, then assigned numbers. Links were assessed for mobilizing information based on the information they provided on the news article page(s) (*i.e.*, if information provided on the page indicated that MI was accessible by clicking on that link). An a priori power analysis was conducted using GPOWER software (version 2.0) in order to minimize the sample size while maintaining sufficient power. The total sample before this analysis was 1,418 articles. It was concluded that 65 articles per version of each newspaper (online and print) were adequate to maintain power, and the sample was reduced to 780 articles. Because some issues did not include enough articles to reach this total, the final sample was 763.

RELIABILITY

Two coders assessed reliability after being trained with coding rules and definitions. Reliability was analysed for locational, identificational, and tactical MI. Eighty-seven articles were sampled from the same seven-week period from days on which sampling did not take place. This meets Wimmer and Dominick's recommendation of coding 10 per cent to 20 per cent of the total sample for reliability. Krippendorf's alpha was used because it takes into account chance agreement.

All reliability coeffiecients met standards set by Krippendorf and Riffe, Lacy, and Fico (above.80), except tactical MI in online text (0.76), tactical MI in print text (0.72), and locational MI in online text (0.66). Latent content is admittedly more difficult to assess; therefore, those coefficients above.65 were deemed acceptable. Disagreements were addressed by the coders until understanding was reached before actual coding began. In order to prevent biases due to coder fatigue or repetitive stress, care was taken not to code articles in any systematic order and coding was completed in one- to two-hour increments.

MI IN NEWSPAPERS BY TYPE

Of all MI found in the sampled articles, identificational was the most plentiful. Lemert's definition, which stated simply that this type of MI "usually requires" both identification (such as a name) with locational information, did not provide specific coding rules or operationalizations. Therefore, coding rules were created. This may explain the differences in MI found here when compared to Lemert's and colleagues' findings.

Hungerford and Lemert found that 20 per cent of environmental stories had some form of MI, while Lemert, et al. reported that 22.8 per cent of main news stories had some form of MI. Similar results were gleaned from Stanfield and Lemert who found that, in two mainstream dailies, between 13 per cent and 17 per cent of all stories had some form of MI. Perhaps because of a more inclusive operationalization of identificational MI, 99.5 per cent of articles in the present study contained some form of identificational MI, while 9 per cent of all articles contained locational MI, and 5.1 per cent contained tactical MI.

MI by Medium: Online versus Print. Hl predicted more MI overall in online newspapers than in print because of added space, technological advances, and relative freedom. But even with the inclusion of hyperlinks, video/audio links (of which there were zero occurrences with MI), interactive links, and online artwork, this hypothesis was not supported. There were indeed more occurrences of MI online than in print, but this relationship were not significant. When all the online-specific links were excluded, and only MI in text was included (*i.e.*, the body of the story without any links), print newspapers had slightly more MI in text than online newspapers. Again, results were below the standards for marginal significance.

RQ1 asked whether one type of MI was more prevalent in print and online newspapers. There was significantly more identificational MI than locational MI online. Identificational MI also occurred more frequently in print than locational. Online, identificational MI had significantly more occurrences than tactical MI. In print, identificational MI occurred significantly more frequently than tactical MI.

The comparison between locational and tactical MI yields the only non-significant difference, and this is specific to print. There were no more occurrences of locational MI than tactical MI in print. The difference online, however, was significant, with more locational than tactical. Thus, identificational MI occurred with more frequency in both print and online contexts than either locational or tactical MI, and locational MI occurred more frequently online than in print. However, this last difference is most likely due to the enormity of the San Francisco Chronicle's archival links in its "ChronicleWatch."

Online newspapers do not differ significantly from print newspapers in terms of presence of mobilizing information, and look much like the "shovelware" versions Singer suggested.

The relative similarity between print and online versions of the newspaper-even accounting for value-added items such as links to archived content, audio/video links, and discussion boards-is startling.

This was not a print-to-print or text-only comparison; on the contrary, this analysis took into account those elements that make online newspapers different from print newspapers. This would suggest that the same fears Lemert cited as reasons journalists exclude MI in print newspapers might also apply to those publishing online.

That said, however, online newspapers are certainly not the only political and news content available online. There are countless government and interest-group Web sites, discussion boards, and "blogs," as well as non-traditional news sources unavailable in other media formats.

Moreover, non-newspaper sites may create "run-off" to newspaper sites. Therefore, although this study was limited to print and online newspapers, it provides a first step in examining MI online.

In addition to journalistic fears of endorsement, partisanship, or libel, there might be other factors acting to keep online newspapers similar to print versions. It has been argued that powerful media corporations establish norms and routines that keep journalists deferential to the media structure and that normalize content. Journalists who adhere to these routines are considered professional and rewarded, while those who oppose them might be reprimanded.

The most widely discussed of these norms is objectivity or neutrality-the desire to be fair and present "both sides" of an issue-a norm particularly widespread in American journalism.83 The adherence to norms could deter journalists from publishing MI online that threatens the status quo. However, online newspapers might simply be seeking consistency with their print counterparts in order to maintain a common voice. Interviews with online journalists could provide useful insights into these dynamics.

This study operationally distinguished among the three types of MI-locational, identificational, and tactical. Past research has focused on the reasons MI is excluded from news, and recent work on political participation that alludes to, or sometimes assumes, the presence of MI in news often fails to differentiate among the three types.

The near exclusion of tactical and locational MI in this study indicates that explicit MI is rare in both print and online newspapers. This raises questions about the validity of differentiating among these types that occur so infrequently. However, the volume of identificational MI begs important new questions: Is identification of a political individual enough to mobilize action on the part of the reader? Moreover, in this era-when to find more information, all a person has to do is "Google" someone-are mobilizing possibilities greater than they were before these technologies were available? Surveys and experiments with online users could provide us with answers.

Future studies could expand on this analysis by conducting similar research in health, environmental, and other contexts. Health communication researchers have already adopted the MI concept, although the conceptual and operational definitions used here have diverged substantially from those in the political and environmental contexts. A useful study would apply the same operationalizations to each context. Additionally, Lemert and Ashman, as well as Dunwoody and Griffin, examined mobilizing content in controversial or negative contexts, suggesting that tone also influences inclusion of MI.

A second, and laudable, addition to this content analysis would be an expanded examination of all content in online newspapers, including that found on discussion boards, chat rooms, hyperlinked sites, and audio/video clips. This information is inherently different from what is in print newspapers.

An expanded sample of newspapers including more regional variation might also find more differences. Examining news content on blogs, portal sites, and search engines could also yield new and interesting findings. Additionally, as Tremayne found, Web sites affiliated with broadcast networks are more "linked" than those affiliated with newspapers. An interesting direction for research would be to compare these two in terms of their mobilizing information.

Beyond examining MI in content, researchers could assess the cognitive processes involved in reading and understanding MI. Eveland and Scheufele argued that those in a community with higher SES are more likely to see MI and, perhaps more important, "they possess the information processing strategies and cognitive skills necessary to identify mobilizing information, even if it is less prominently placed or mentioned only implicitly." Individual and socioeconomic differences could play a key role in the usefulness of MI. Finally, a reliability assessment for inclusion of political news in the sample would make the interpretation of these results more powerful. Print newspaper readership has consistently been correlated with higher rates of political participation, voter turnout, and civic engagement. If Internet news use is on the rise while print news use declines, what does this mean for the link between political participation and media use?

This study suggests that online newspapers provide content that simply reinforces print content. But even if mobilizing information in print and online newspapers is not significantly different, the effects may differ across readers. Because this study examines only content, effects cannot be ascertained, but this is clearly an area for further research. Indeed, the Internet could draw new readers who would not have otherwise been exposed to mobilizing content. In this case, more people may be exposed to more mobilizing information, despite declines in print newspaper readership.

Some researchers have noted that higher levels of Internet use are associated with higher levels of political participation. Johnson and Kaye asserted that Internet users represent "model citizens" and are more likely to be politically interested, efficacious, and seek information from the media. Moreover, evidence suggests that both gender and race gaps in Internet use are closing or closed, and children increasingly use the Internet at school and home. Improved understanding of how individuals use the Internet, as well as what content they view, will clearly add meaning to the present study's findings. The changing nature of the Internet environment demands that researchers take into account how both its audience and its content must continually be monitored.

PRINCIPLES OF GLOBAL JOURNALISM ETHICS

Journalism, at its best, is one of the arts of democracy. Journalists provide the news and analysis by which a society communicates with itself, allowing some measure of self-government. The public absorbs a daily barrage of news images that, over time, help to define one's sense of place in society and within a global community. News stories parade our injustices, vanities, power struggles, disasters, accomplishments and peculiar interests. Citizens, following the major issues in the press, become aware of their shared and competing values. Through journalism, a society debates how to reform its institutions and face the future. Vigorous journalism is the lifeblood of a deliberative democracy.

Journalism, at its worst, is an art of the demagogue and the despot. It is the propaganda tool of powerful interests who subvert popular self-governance by manipulating the channels of information. Journalism is debased if it falls into the hands of unethical media owners and journalists, or when editorial resources are squandered on entertaining stories. Journalism falters when it fails to question the powers that be, and when budget cuts strangle investigative journalism. Journalism degenerates when the business of journalism overwhelms its democratic functions, seeking profit through every cheap trick in the history of popular printing – jingoism, sensationalism and fear mongering. Journalism is an anti-democratic art when news organizations wield power without responsibility and journalists forsake their public responsibilities for fame and money.

Five centuries after the first periodic papers were introduced, journalism still struggles to avoid debasement, let alone to live up to its democratic duty. In today's climate of fear, terrorism and regional conflict, the democratic function of journalism is sorely needed. The news media bear a substantial responsibility in helping citizens control their armed forces and shape security policy. In theory, the media should contribute to democratic oversight through revealing information, sharp analysis, thoughtful commentary and in-depth investigation. In reality, the news media provide adequate oversight only if many conditions are satisfied. A self-governing society requires an aggressive press led by major news organizations willing to spend time and resources on testing official positions and offering alternative views. Journalists Stephen J. Ward Draft – Please do not quote February 8, 2003 2 must have sufficient education and skill to pursue the issues and make them intelligible to others.

Reporters and editors must be able to act independently of commercial and ideological pressures inside and outside the newsroom. Self-governance needs a supportive legal and political climate. There must be mechanisms that guarantee access to government records and mechanisms that force bureaucracies to be open and accountable. In addition, the general public must support a critical and watchdog press, not only in times of peace but also in times of uncertainty. A sufficient cross-section of the population must not be alienated from public life, but willing to play a part in policy deliberation and political action.

Often, these conditions are not satisfied. In Canada, we have witnessed a worrisome pattern over the past year and a half. The ability of government to monitor the daily behaviour of its citizens has increased while the ability of citizens to oversee its government has decreased. Under the banner of "anti-terrorism," the Canadian government has introduced laws that allow officials to compile dossiers on every citizen, and to monitor e-mail and other communications.

More laws may follow. These initiatives buttress an already entrenched attitude of secrecy in government. The freedom-of-information commissioner of Canada has called this attitude a "culture of secrecy" while the privacy commissioner of Canada has accused the government's new security initiatives as risking a "permanent loss" of basic civil rights and freedoms.

The privacy commissioner's warning caused only a ripple of interest in Parliament and in the news media. The federal bureaucracy is so protective of its public records that the Canadian Association of Journalists hands out an annual "Code of Silence" award to the most secretive government department in Canada. Last year, the 'award' went to the federal Department of Justice for giving itself the power, under new anti-terrorism legislation, to override the Access to Information Act and withhold information relating to international affairs, national security and defence that it deems sensitive. Two year's ago, the winner was the Ontario Ministry of the Environment for withholding information about the Walkerton water tragedy, in which a town's contaminated water supply claimed seven lives and sickened hundreds more.

The Canadian legal environment works against a vigorous investigative journalism. Canadian reporters do not have American-styled "shield laws" that protect them from being forced to hand over video, audio tapes, pictures and notebooks to state prosecutors. Canadian reporters do not work under a First Amendment. Reference to a free press in the Canadian Constitution is briefly mentioned in Section 2(b) of the document. It is preceded by Section 1, which notes that such 1 George Radwanski, Privacy Commissioner of Canada, interview on "The House," CBC Radio One, Feb. 1, 2003. Stephen J. Ward draft – please do not quote February 8, 2003 fundamental freedoms can be abridged under certain broad conditions. Canada does not have "whistleblower" legislation that protects officials who make important information public. Canadian libel laws are much tougher on journalists than in the United States.

Moreover, the public has reason to be skeptical about whether today's news media can play a serious role in democratic self-governance. Skeptics can point to the prevalence of soft, superficial or sensational news. For at least a decade, intense commercial and technological pressures have prompted editors to ignore or "dumb down" complex issues, or to treat issues as a conflict between hostile camps. The process of public policy is portrayed as a cynical power game, of interest only to insiders and elites. As a result, the public credibility of the news media spirals downward, making it more difficult for journalists to claim that the news media are a legitimate watchdog. A depressing number of citizens fail to see a clear distinction between a journalist and a media personality, or between journalism and 'media' in general. After years of cost-cutting, staff reductions and closing down of foreign bureaus, how many newsrooms have the knowledge, the sources and the resources to cover complex international stories?

Nevertheless, the terrorist attacks of September 11th rudely awakened journalism from its superficial slumbers. The serious, unavoidable, implications of living in a connected world stared us in the face. Both citizens and journalists have been put in a difficult position, torn between the need for security and the need for liberty. Recent polls indicate that Canadians share this ambiguity about their world. Polls show that Canadians feel that the world is a more dangerous place, and therefore there is a need for increased security. Yet the polls also indicate that some Canadians fear limitations on free speech. They fear that police and security personnel will abuse the increased powers. Equally interesting is polling that shows that Canadians believe that understanding the world beyond their borders is a necessary condition for coping with this new environment. The hypothesis of this chapter is that journalists and news organizations, to carry out their democratic role, need to adopt a different ethic to guide their practice.

Radical changes in news media and in society call for a radical reformulation of journalism ethics, its standards and goals. I argue that journalists, media scholars and others should work towards what I call *global journalism ethics* for a global media environment. Journalism should transcend its centuries-old parochialism and seek a more cosmopolitan attitude. Once we start to adopt the perspective of global journalism ethics, however, common principles of journalism ethics, such as objectivity and serving the public, become unclear. I suspect that nothing short of a wholesale conceptual Stephen J. Ward draft – please do not quote February 8, 2003 revolution will do. By itself, the adoption of a new ethic won't create a better news media; but it is a step in that direction.

By global journalism ethics, I mean an approach that defines the primary responsibilities of the news media from a global perspective. The essential features of this approach are as follows: Acting as global agents: Journalists should see themselves as agents of a global public sphere, with new and increased responsibilities. The goal of their collective actions is a well-informed, diverse and tolerant global 'infosphere' that provokes citizens to become engaged in issues and provides a counter-balance to the lies of tyrants and the manipulation of information by special interests.

Serving citizens of the world: The journalist's primary loyalty is to citizens of the world. Journalists should not define themselves as attached primarily to factions, specific causes, or even to the public of their countries. Serving the public means more than serving one's local readership or paying audience. Journalists are answerable, ethically, to the information needs of world citizens. Non-parochial understanding: The journalistic duty to inform takes on the demanding task of framing issues broadly, using a diversity of sources and providing multiple, critical perspectives. The aim is help citizens gain a nuanced, in-depth understanding of issues.

This form of journalism opposes all attempts to define issues according to narrow ethnocentrism or patriotism. Global Journalism helps to reduce the power of slanted information and simplistic claims to spread xenophobic ideas and spark conflict. New international initiatives: Journalists should promote a global ethic by developing new international organizations, by initiating 'media training' programmes and by taking advantage of new interactive forms of communication to strengthen the media system and encourage rational deliberation in the global public sphere.

Why should journalists contemplate an ambitious and still vaguely defined, global ethic? Because journalists work increasingly in a global news environment. Their reports, via satellite or the Internet, reach people around the world and influence the actions of governments, militaries, humanitarian agencies and warring ethnic groups. Their reports help to shape the way that See polling on Canadian attitudes towards military and security matters by Ipsos-Reid Corp. from September 2001 to Stephen J. Ward draft – please do not quote February 8, 2003 citizens see the world and their place in it. Journalists now report for a large virtual community spread around the globe. The impact of writing or broadcasting or posting a story transcends borders. From an ethical point of view, the distinction between local and non-local stories begins to crumble when news Web sites are accessible from anywhere and everywhere in the world.

With this increase in reach and impact come new and more onerous responsibilities. Journalism ethics changes and expands. Journalists now must consider the potential impact of their work on an electronic diaspora of readers and Internet users. If quality global media can inform the global community, irresponsible and parochial journalism can help to wreak havoc. Unless reported accurately and with diversity, North American readers may fail to understand the causes of violence in Middle East, or a drought in Africa. Jingoistic reports can portray the denizens of other regions of the world as possible combatants, bloodthirsty lunatics or part of a shadowy, undefined threat. In times of insecurity, the news media can amplify the views of fear-mongering officials who want to stampede populations into joining a call to arms, or to supporting the swift removal of the civil rights for minorities. Not all newsrooms will bear the same responsibility for widening the journalistic ethical viewpoint.

A small newspaper in rural British Columbia will bear less responsibility than major news organizations such as CNN, the BBC, the Canadian Broadcasting Corporation, the major news agencies, leading newspapers and widely accessed Web sites. Moreover, no one can expect realistically that news organizations will completely transcend the perspectives of the country in which the majority of their journalists live. There are strong economic, psychological and cultural forces that keep new organizations focused on specific demographical and geographical audiences. Nevertheless, journalists cannot evade the potential or actual global influence of their work. They should not ignore their contribution to a less tolerant and less enlightened global public sphere. Global journalism ethics requires that such organizations do everything possible to enlarge the perspectives of their newsrooms, their stories and their audiences. In journalism, the term "globalization" does not refer only to the development of global communications and global corporations. The term has an ethical sense, referring to the professional standards that should guide this expanding news media. January 2003.

IMPLICATIONS OF GLOBAL JOURNALISM ETHICS

What global journalism ethics entails for journalism and democratic oversight is yet to be determined. However, we gain some insight by examining three topics: new forms of communication, pluralism and patriotism.

NEW FORMS OF PUBLIC COMMUNICATION

The future of oversight of the security sector must take into account two large-scale changes in the media environment. One change is that journalists now report upon pluralistic societies in a pluralistic world. Another is the evolution of new forms of communication and public dialogue through what is called the "new media" – the Internet and other communication technologies. Initiatives to support democratic oversight that ignore these new forms of communication will miss important opportunities for deliberation, monitoring and self-governance. A significant portion of the mainstream news media and media-savvy elites tends to think of oversight according to a traditional model of journalistic communication. According to this model, oversight happens as a result of the public receiving information, analysis and argumentation contained in major newspapers and television broadcasts. Armed with the facts, members of the public form their own judgements on the issues before them and judge the performance of their politicians, institutions and government agencies. Oversight is the product of the formation of rational public opinion that, at least in democracies, restrains governments and militaries.

This model is a modern formulation of the 19th century liberal theory of the press, which preceded the 20th century notion of public self-governance through objective reporting. On the liberal view, the journalist acts like a tutor of the public, creating and shaping public views through weighty opinion pieces and strong political coverage.

The journalist acts as a watchdog of government abuse of its powers on behalf of the public. With the rise of the doctrine of objectivity in the early 1900s, an additional idea was added to the doctrine of self-governance. The objective journalist laid the facts before the public in an impartial manner. Citizens made their own judgements, based on the facts. The objective journalist attempted to be an independent voice amid the cacophony of partisan voices in the public sphere.

This model of oversight continues to operate as a background assumption in many articles on the news media, despite the fact that the liberal theory of the press has been subjected to withering criticism. Much of the criticism is based on Stephen J. Ward draft – please do not quote February 8, 2003 the belief that the free marketplace of ideas and the formation of public opinion are neither rational, nor open, nor fair. The development of global technologies signals the arrival of new forms of public communication and new means of oversight. Citizens with common interests have new ways to seek out information for themselves and to debate issues. Citizens consult weblogs, interactive Web sites, Web forums, and alternative on-line journalism for diverse perspectives. They use the Internet to "drill down" into the deep background and history of a topic, or use hyperlinks to access the original documents that prompted yesterday's news reports. Citizens can see for themselves much of the material that reporters used, making perspicuous any "spin" in the news article.

Moreover, the informal nature and inter activity of on-line communication is creating a web of participants who expect to have an opportunity to engage in 'real-time' debate among their list serve colleagues and experts from around the world. All of this means a decreasing role for the old forms of mediation practiced by the journalistic gatekeeper in mainstream newsrooms. New forms of public discourse are emerging and with them, new habits and expectations among information-hungry audiences. On-line public discourse displays a distinctive and far-reaching feature: it addresses people as participants in an interactive process. It is not content with the old Transmission Model of journalism, where the journalist is active and the audience is relatively passive. In the old model, the journalist is one who writes with 'authority.' The journalist, not the audience, gathers the sources, does the research, and verifies the facts. Journalism is not a dialogue. It is, rather, the transmission of results structured according to the various genres of journalism.

The emphasis is on the final product, not the process. Communication in the Transmission Model is one-to-many and non-interactive. In new on-line communication, the journalist is more an initiator of conversation than a transmitter of pre-digested facts or settled opinion. On-line communication is multi-media and non-linear. Stories on the Internet combine text, audio and video, supplemented by hyperlinks and chat forums, to put forward certain perspectives and debate public issues. The audiences expect to be given the opportunity to engage in debate, to pursue their own research on the Net, and to respond immediately by e-mail to what the journalist writes. This new environment changes how journalists see themselves and how they regard public deliberation. Instead of claiming to write the last word, many on-line journalists acknowledge that their articles are perspectives on complex topics. A commentary is a fallible stab at a defensible point of view.

Readers are expected to use a plurality of perspectives to come closer to the truth. John Pavlik, a new-media expert at Columbia University, thinks that the Internet's ability to Stephen J. Ward draft – please do not quote February 8, 2003 provide layers of information should result in a more "contextualized" journalism for a pluralistic public sphere. Jon Katz, the American columnist, has described how writing commentary on-line contrasts with writing editorials for a newspaper. Within minutes of posting his articles on the Internet, a host of experts from around the world use e-mail to provide Katz with counter-evidence, counter-argument, original documents, graphics and new studies. Katz often finds himself writing not one article on a topic, but a series of articles with updated facts and alternate perspectives. Katz says inter activity can be a humbling experience: "The only thing I can compare it to is being tied to the back of a car and dragged through the street." These evolving modes of communication have implications for ethics and democratic oversight.

The first implication is that if NGOs, international organizations and other groups wish to strengthen public discourse and oversight in the years ahead, they should consider how public deliberation could be fostered through new media. On-line communication could be used to help members of the public inform each other on security issues. In mainstream news media, the transmission of facts, expert analysis and the results of investigations will carry on. The mainstream news media will continue to be important to oversight, given their central role in the media system. But a good deal of the conversation in the future will occur outside traditional forms of journalism. To participate in and facilitate this conversation, journalists need to design coverage of issues in ways that encourage active engagement by citizens, both in their newspapers and on their Web sites. The nature of media oversight is changing.

It is no longer the specialty of the "beat" or investigative journalist, who digs up information, checks sources, places facts in context and sends it off to readers. Democratic oversight is becoming a multi-media dialogue among journalists, experts, freelancers, Web site providers, video journalists, human rights groups and ordinary citizens. Journalists will have to act more like Sherpas, leading people to other sites and perspectives. One benefit of the new media may be the swift distribution of information that governments and militaries would rather keep hidden from view. In an age of portable cameras, powerful communications satellites and the ability to send video over the Internet, more people will be able to participate in the exchange of information on the activities of para militaries, armies and security forces on the ground in previously remote areas of the world. The new media also present problems for oversight and accurate information exchange.

With all new forms of communications come new ways to spread rumour, lies, hatred and manipulated images. The challenge of media oversight in the future will go beyond finding ways to access and distribute information globally; it will include finding ways to confirm information as reliable.

Another challenge will be to make sure that the interaction of participants does not fragment into a plethora of parochial discussions. Effective oversight will require that there are forms of media and communication used by a substantial cross-section of citizens from around the world. Deliberation on politics or social issues will lack impact if the global public sphere becomes a universe of many small 'publics' engaging in arcane discussions that are intelligible only to relatively small groups of enthusiasts or experts. Another challenge will be to use the global public sphere to enlarge perspectives through provocative and critical exchanges of informed views. The new media will not foster public understanding and oversight if on-line communication is dominated by Web sites that only reinforce existing beliefs and prejudices.

Nor will democratic oversight improve if on-line communication is used to rant, rather than rationally exchange views and information. At least some portion of the new public sphere will have to embody a culture of critical, but tolerant, communication where journalists and non-journalists subject their claims global public scrutiny. Achieving this goal in a time of acute cultural tensions will not be easy.

Writing for a Pluralistic World

A primary rationale for global journalism ethics is political and cultural pluralism. Pluralism represents one of the greatest challenges of our age. The world is not a cozy McLuhan village where the media act as electronic extensions of humankind's nervous system, bringing us all closer together in a benign manner. Our world *is* connected electronically like never before, but this grid of connections co-exists with a collision of cultures, values, customs, religions, social structures and philosophies. The assertion of universal rights and the transmission of a global commercial culture co-exist with a resurgence of particular traditions, religions, languages and ethnic politics. Cosmopolitan attitudes run up against communal perspectives. To compound matters, this pluralism is refracted through the prism of a news media of striking images of angry, conflicting voices and of powerful, manipulative agents. It remains to be seen whether we, as a species, have the ability to evolve mentally and ethically to live in this pluralistic world.

Will we blow ourselves off the planet, degrade the environment and continue to live in a world of grave inequities and the threat of terrorism? Will humankind's penchant to divide people into "us" and "them" remain dominant?

One of the important roles for Global Journalism in the future will be assisting groups who have radically different ideas of what is 'good' in life to negotiate a way to live together.

A pluralistic society cannot hope to achieve consensus on what the 'goods' of life are among religious, ethnic and other groups. But it can hope to achieve an "overlapping" consensus among groups on fair procedures for resolving disputes. In one sense, global journalism ethics is an extrapolation of this viewpoint to journalism, and to the international scene. The global journalist belongs to one of the institutions that can help groups negotiate and agree on ways to live together and resolve disputes, short of war or terrorism. To act as an international "go-between," the journalist must become a sort of anthropologist, sensitive to nuances in cultural differences, knowledgeable in the history and ideas behind movements, and able to convey the meaning of puzzling behaviour to people outside that culture. Journalists must be careful about how they "frame" stories. Special efforts need to be made to find viewpoints and experts from all countries involved in internationals issue, rather than relying heavily on local officials.

The model of "public journalism" developed in the United States in the 1990s offers some ideas for how to approach Global Journalism, if we think of public journalism on the international stage. Public journalism has its critics, but what is of value is the idea of journalists as active and inventive facilitators of public discussion. Public journalism seeks to overcome the alienation of citizens from the political process by using all forms of media to invite citizens to participate in the solution of community problems. Public journalists seek out different voices in their communities, hold town hall meetings and avoid the 'conflict' model of reporting that portrays each issue as an uncompromising struggle between two camps for power. Public journalists reject the image of the journalist as a disengaged, cynical observer looking down on society as it screws up. Instead, the journalist is a fair, well-researched catalyst of public deliberation. I suggest that this image of the journalist is part of the identity of the global journalist.

Writing for a pluralistic world has implications for journalism education. The issues that face journalism education in the West are not primarily issues of technological training but issues of liberal education. We need journalists with critical thinking skills, cultural awareness, expertise in crucial topics, and knowledge – about science and technology, and national and international institutions. Journalism education should shift from industrial training, linked to an apprenticeship model, to the education of journalists as critically aware world citizens. In the long run, better skills and education will have an impact on journalism and, eventually, media oversight.

They will perpetuate the prejudices of their times and their local environments. One of the greatest obstacles to Global Journalism is narrow patriotism and excessive parochialism. In every crisis, in every war, journalists come under pressure to be patriotic. Journalism history is redolent with examples of how journalists discarded any pretense to objectivity for jingoism, ethnocentrism and even xenophobia, especially when their country was in trouble, or their leaders sounded a call to arms. Patriotism, in this context, is not just a love of one's country; it is an extreme, emotion-driven patriotism that demands that all citizens "get on side" and support uncritically the government's actions.

The social pressure that such patriotism can exert on both the public and the news media has never been clearer than since September 11th. Patriotism puts pressure on journalists to suspend or water down the standards of journalism: to root for the home team, to minimize dissent, to censor the "enemy" and to maintain morale. Supporting the home effort becomes a primary aim, overriding other journalistic functions such as acting as a watchdog and providing a forum for diverse views. Journalists, caught up in such mass emotions, ignore or forgot that government will use fear and uncertainty to push for major restrictions on civil liberties, including press freedom, and that a nervous public will be less inclined to object voraciously.

The idea that special times call for special measures is fraught with danger. The primary ethical duty of journalism, even in times of crisis, is *not* a patriotism of blind allegiance, or even a journalism of muted, careful criticism. The primary duty of journalists is *not* to the state, but to the public. That public duty calls for hard-edged news, investigations, analysis and multiple perspectives on the most important issues. We need a journalism that, more than ever, assumes some responsibility to "prepare" the public for difficult decisions ahead. Journalists serve the citizens of their country and the world by being critical, independent journalists.

Canadian journalists, for example, need to ask whether their government will follow the lead of the United States in its War on Terrorism, and where that path leads. Journalists need to help citizens to unearth the historical roots of their troubles and deepen their understanding of other religions, other cultures. News organizations need to help the public debate the difficult decisions ahead. Journalists should maintain skepticism towards all sources, test facts, detect hoaxes, reject rumors, and report controversial opinions. They must protect their independence in dealings with governments and military leaders.

All avenues of influence, all forms of inducement will be used to shape the war coverage. Most of all, journalists must avoid the temptation to write stories that portray the military and defence options as reducible to a Stephen J. Ward draft – please do not quote February 8, 2003 medieval engagement of the forces of light against the forces of "pure evil." Journalists must deal with the stubborn complexity of the world, not shrink it down to digestible sound bites. Journalists are not indifferent to acts of terrorism or to the fate of their country. But, knowing that they, like all people, have such feelings is all the more reason to be vigilant that no one manipulates these honest emotions. In the fog of war, truth is the first casualty. Appeals to patriotism, if not challenged, only thicken the fog.

Concrete Steps

Journalists, media scholars, foundations and other groups can foster a fledgling Global Journalism by taking a number of concrete steps. They should consider forming new international alliances and organizations to promote journalism from a global perspective. Some international groups exist, such as Reporters Without Frontiers and the International Communications Forum. Often, these groups are focused on only one issue, such as reporters killed or thrown in jail. Other groups lack strong links to major journalism organizations. We need alliances between scholars, institutes, journalism organizations and unions, schools of journalism that take a broad interest in professional standards from a global perspective. These coalitions could provide resources and educational programmes for journalists writing on specific issues. They could sponsor international journalism fellowships, journalism sabbaticals and study opportunities abroad.

They could monitor the news media for good and bad coverage, speak out against clamp downs on the press and expose attempts to manipulate the facts. International alliances could publish an annual report on the state of Global Journalism and the free press. Global Journalism organizations could provide moral, financial and legal assistance to journalists and news organizations struggling to be an independent voice in certain countries. Such organizations could liaise between journalists and the growing list of international agencies whose activities may impinge on the work of journalists, such as International Criminal Tribunal for the former Yugoslavia in The Hague. More news organizations, NGOs, and other agencies could support attempts to develop a free and responsible news media in developing and war-torn societies. 9 Ethically, journalists and other media professionals could begin to draw up statements of journalism principles that begin to articulate the common values that news media around the world should be embracing – or at least discussing and debating.

We need a debate on the 9 A Global Journalism perspective will be crucial to the development of such programmes. Western journalism programmes should be sensitive to cultural differences. Journalism development should not be an unreflective exporting of Western media values to a foreign country, or a "top-down" process where elite journalists 'talk down' to local Stephen J. Ward Draft – Please do not Quote February 8, 2003 principles of global journalism ethics. An example of an international statement of principles is The Sarajevo Commitment adopted in September 2000 by participants to a World Media Assembly in Sarajevo. The commitment commits the participants to independent, fair and factual informing and to opposing "hypocrisy, oppression, exploitation." The commitment states: "We shall not cease to strive until every gun is silent, every injustice righted and every human being enabled to live a life of satisfaction and purpose." The commitment is idealistic, to be sure. But it points towards an increased ethical commitment of the media towards a safer and more humane world. Declarations could be bolstered by UN conferences on media and information rights, and the protection of journalists. Scholars should also show leadership. Interdisciplinary studies and journals by ethicists, communication scholars and experts on international affairs could explore the economic, political and ethical implications of a global media. Ethicists can contribute by showing how the concepts of current codes of ethics are too parochial and need to be changed to reflect the global media environment.

Perhaps the best place to start is to hold workshops, round tables and conferences where participants develop ideas for ethical handbooks and manuals. The process will involve a fundamental re-thinking of our basic journalism concepts. We will have to face tough questions such as how journalists can be independent and objective yet also act as global agents. A media that has taken on global proportions is still constructing stories according to the standards and practices of a pre-global media of the 20th century. Most discussions of ethics refer to the duties of the individual journalist, an individual news organization or the ethics of a country's media system. Many ethical codes are the codes of specific organizations or a particular medium like photography. The codes speak of impartiality but in times of conflict, the patriotic impulse soon reveals that the journalist's impartiality exists within a larger zone of partiality.

There is a need for more international journalism forums on the Web that stimulate multi perspective discussions. My editorship of *Global Journalism Ethics,* an interactive forum on the Web site of the World Press Institute in St. Paul's, Minn., is a small step in that direction. Ethical analyses of media issues are posted on the site, and journalists and ethicists from around the world respond with comments and criticisms. I can foresee the day when there will be many more forums like this, linking major journalism organizations on every continent. journalists. Development programmes should be flexible enough to allow local journalists to interpret and apply the principles of journalism in ways that speak to their situation and cultural values.

In the West, the 18th century saw journalists of the daily press begin to address citizens in the new public sphere. Nineteenth century journalists became standard-bearers for an ascendant liberalism – as partisan essayists, as news-writers, as reformers, and as revolutionaries. The 20th century journalist became an employee of the business of news, an informer and entertainer for a mass society of consumers.

As the 20th century progressed, chains of newspapers developed into multi-media, global media empires. With each revolution in journalism, the ethics of the press evolved to articulate the new relationship between journalist and reader. The ethic of a fourth estate arose by the late 1700s, liberalism gave birth to the idea of a maximally free press that directed public opinion. A mass commercial press encouraged the doctrine of news objectivity. Given the new media environment at the start of the 21st century, I expect another evolution in journalism ethics. This evolution must walk between the extremes of native idealism and despondent cynicism. Native idealism underestimates the economic and political forces that would debase journalism. Cynicism despairs at those forces. In the aftermath of the First World War, Walter Lippmann, the influential American columnist, began to doubt the liberal theory of the press. He questioned whether public opinion was formed in a rational manner in the public sphere. He pointed to the unreliable practices of the press and their lack of professionalism. He noted with alarm the growing legion of press agents manipulating public consent. Lippmann called public opinion a "phantom" and doubted the ordinary person's ability to understand complex policy options.

Lippmann was, in effect, questioning two major assumptions of the liberal theory of the press:

(a) A press freed from government control would be a serious informer of citizens and advocateb of progressive causes, not a superficial provider of 'content' for consumers.

(b) The public sphere was a democratic sphere, an open marketplace of ideas.

He warned that if liberty depended on factual news from the media and a truly informed citizen, then liberty and democracy were truly in trouble. Today, Lippmann's warnings are still worth pondering. But we should not despair and we should not lose faith in ordinary citizens. Instead, we should take up the challenge to create a more reliable, truly informative news media. As citizens of the world, must do what we can to construct communication systems that provide some degree of genuine oversight over governments. As scholars, we need to study the nature of new forms of communication and articulate the values that should guide such powerful Stephen J. Ward draft – please do not quote February 8, 2003 technology.

As journalists, we should strive to act as engaged, public informers and intellectuals, not aim to be media stars or 'personalities.' Only if these new values and ideals are embraced will globalization in journalism mean something more than the development of satellites, broadband connections, smarter computers, converging media and global media companies.

Only if journalists re-examine their ethical role amid these changes, will they survive as critical informers and not become mere "content providers." Journalism must strive to be one of the arts of democracy in a global context, a force for humanity, for toleration, for peace and for cross-cultural understanding.

Established in 2000 on the initiative of the Swiss government, the Geneva Centre for the Democratic Control of Armed Forces (DCAF), encourages and supports States and non- State governed institutions in their efforts to strengthen democratic and civilian control of armed and security forces, and promotes international cooperation within this field, initially targeting the Euro-Atlantic regions. The Centre collects information, undertakes research and engages in networking activities in order to identify problems, to establish lessons learned and to propose the best practices in the field of democratic control of armed forces and civil-military relations.

JOURNALISM ETHICS AND STANDARDS

Journalism ethics and standards comprise principles of ethics and of good practice as applicable to the specific challenges faced by professional journalists. Historically and currently, this subset of media ethics is widely known to journalists as their professional "code of ethics" or the "canons of journalism". The basic codes and canons commonly appear in statements drafted by both professional journalism associations and individual print, broadcast, and online news organizations. While various existing codes have some differences, most share common elements including the principles of — truthfulness, accuracy, objectivity, impartiality, fairness and public accountability — as these apply to the acquisition of newsworthy information and its subsequent dissemination to the public.

Like many broader ethical systems, journalism ethics include the principle of "limitation of harm." This often involves the withholding of certain details from reports such as the names of minor children, crime victims' names or information not materially related to particular news reports release of which might, for example, harm someone's reputation.

Some journalistic Codes of Ethics, notably the European ones, also include a concern with discriminatory references in news based on race, religion, sexual orientation, and physical or mental disabilities. The European Council approved in 1993 Resolution 1003 on the Ethics of Journalism which recommends journalists to respect yet the presumption of innocence, in particular in cases that are still *sub judice*.

EVOLUTION AND PURPOSE OF CODES OF JOURNALISM

The principles of Journalistic codes of ethics are designed as guides through numerous difficulties, such as conflicts of interest, to assist journalists in dealing with ethical dilemmas. The codes and canons provide journalists a framework for self-monitoring and self-correction as

CODES OF PRACTICE

While journalists in the United States and European countries have led in formulation and adoption of these standards, such codes can be found in news reporting organizations in most countries with freedom of the press.

The written codes and practical standards vary somewhat from country to country and organization to organization, but there is a substantial overlap among mainstream publications and societies. The International Federation of Journalists launched a global Ethical Journalism Inititiative in 2008 aimed at strengthening awareness of these issues within professional bodies.

One of the leading voices in the U.S. on the subject of Journalistic Standards and Ethics is the Society of Professional Journalists. The Preamble to its Code of Ethics states:

...public enlightenment is the forerunner of justice and the foundation of democracy. The duty of the journalist is to further those ends by seeking truth and providing a fair and comprehensive account of events and issues. Conscientious journalists from all media and specialties strive to serve the public with thoroughness and honesty. Professional integrity is the cornerstone of a journalist's credibility. The Radio-Television News Directors Association, an organization exclusively centred on electronic journalism, maintains a code of ethics centring on—public trust, truthfulness, fairness, integrity, independence and accountability. RTDNA publishes a pocket guide to these standards.

COMMON ELEMENTS

The primary themes common to most codes of journalistic standards and ethics are the following.

Accuracy and Standards for Factual Reporting

- Reporters are expected to be as accurate as possible given the time allotted to story preparation and the space available, and to seek reliable sources.
- Events with a single eyewitness are reported with attribution. Events with two or more independent eyewitnesses may be reported as fact. Controversial facts are reported with bnfkof the publisher is desirable
- Corrections are published when errors are discovered
- Defendants at trial are treated only as having "allegedly" committed crimes, until conviction, when their crimes are generally reported as fact (unless, that is, there is serious controversy about wrongful conviction).
- Opinion surveys and statistical information deserve special treatment to communicate in precise terms any conclusions, to contextualize the results, and to specify accuracy, including estimated error and methodological criticism or flaws.

Slander and Libel Considerations

- Reporting the truth is never libel, which makes accuracy very important.
- Private persons have privacy rights that must be balanced against the public interest in reporting information about them. In Canada, there is no such immunity; reports on public figures must be backed by facts.
- Publishers vigorously defend libel lawsuits filed against their reporters, usually covered by libel insurance.

Harm Limitation Principle

During the normal course of an assignment a reporter might go about—gathering facts and details, conducting interviews, doing research, background checks, taking photos, video taping, recording sound — harm limitation deals with the questions of whether everything learned should be reported and, if so, how. This principle of limitation means that some weight needs to be given to the negative consequences of full disclosure, creating a practical and ethical dilemma. The Society of Professional Journalists' code of ethics offers the following advice, which is representative of the practical ideals of most professional journalists. Quoting directly:

- *Show compassion for those who may be affected adversely by news coverage. Use special sensitivity when dealing with children and inexperienced sources or subjects.*
- *Be sensitive when seeking or using interviews or photographs of those affected by tragedy or grief.*
- *Recognize that gathering and reporting information may cause harm or discomfort. Pursuit of the news is not a license for arrogance.*
- *Recognize that private people have a greater right to control information about themselves than do public officials and others who seek power, influence or attention. Only an overriding public need can justify intrusion into anyone's privacy.*
- *Show good taste. Avoid pandering to lurid curiosity.*
- *Be cautious about identifying juvenile suspects or victims of sex crimes.*
- *Be judicious about naming criminal suspects before the formal filing of charges.*
- *Balance a criminal suspect's fair trial rights with the public's right to be informed.*

PRESENTATION

News Writing

Journalism: Ethical standards should not be confused with common standards of quality of presentation, including:

- Correctly spoken or written language (often in a widely spoken and formal dialect, such as Standard English)
- Clarity
- Brevity (or depth, depending on the niche of the publisher).

SELF-REGULATION

In addition to codes of ethics, many news organizations maintain an in-house Ombudsman whose role is, in part, to keep news organizations honest and accountable to the public. The ombudsman is intended to mediate in conflicts stemming from internal and or external pressures, to maintain accountability to the public for news reported, and to foster self-criticism and to encourage adherence to both codified and uncodified ethics and standards. This position may be the same or similar to the public editor, though public editors also act as a liaison with readers and do not generally become members of the Organisation of News Ombudsmen.

An alternative is a news council, an industry-wide self-regulation body, such as the Press Complaints Commission, set up by UK newspapers and magazines. Such a body is capable perhaps of applying fairly consistent standards, and of dealing with a higher volume of complaints, but may not escape criticisms of being toothless.

ETHICS AND STANDARDS IN PRACTICE

Journalism Scandals

Journalism scandals are high-profile incidents or acts, whether intentional or accidental, that run contrary to the generally accepted ethics and standards of journalism, or otherwise violate the 'ideal' mission of journalism: to report news events and issues accurately and fairly.

JOURNALISTIC SCANDAL

As the investigative and reporting face of the media, journalists are usually required to follow various journalistic standards. These may be written and codified, or customary expectations. Typical standards include references to honesty, avoiding journalistic bias, demonstrating responsibility, striking an appropriate balance between privacy and public interest, shunning financial conflict of interest, and choosing ethical means to obtain information.

Journalistic scandals are public scandals arising from incidents where in the eyes of some party, these standards were significantly breached. In most journalistic scandals, deliberate or accidental acts take place that run contrary to the generally accepted ethics and standards of journalism, or otherwise violate the 'ideal' mission of journalism: to report news events and issues accurately and fairly.

Common Characteristics

Journalistic scandals include: plagiarism, fabrication, and omission of information; activities that violate the law, or violate ethical rules; the altering or staging of an event being documented; or making substantial reporting or researching errors with the results leading to libelous or defamatory statements. All journalistic scandals have the common factor that they call into question the integrity and truthfulness of journalism. These scandals shift public focus and scrutiny onto the media itself. Because credibility is journalism's main currency, many news agencies and mass media outlets have strict codes of conduct and enforce them, and use several layers of editorial oversight to catch problems before stories are distributed.

However, in many of the cases listed below, investigations later found that long-established journalistic checks and balances in the newsrooms failed. In some cases, senior editors fail to catch bias, libel, or fabrication inserted into a story by a reporter. In other cases, the checks and balances were omitted in the rush to get an important, 'breaking' news story to press (or on air). Furthermore, in many libel and defamation cases, the publication would have had full support of editorial oversight in case of yellow journalism.

FREEDOM AND GOVERNANCE IN ONLINE JOURNALISM

We're toying with the Arabization of URLs and Arabic domain names, in a move endorsed by the League of Arab States. It's part of an overall plan to produce Arabic domain names across the region and aided by the Saudi Centre for Web Information at the King Abdel Aziz City for Science and Technology. Egypt, Palestine, Syria, Tunisia and several Gulf countries are enrolled in the scheme that was expected to be launched on an experimental basis in November 2005.

In 2004, the Arab League organized a conference in Egypt aimed at promoting Arabic-language search engines. According to a survey conducted by Spot On, a public relations firm based in Dubai, Internet use in the Arab world hasn't been fully realized through cell phones (SMS) because users were still unaware of the potential this vehicle provides them for obtaining online news and information. The shortfall was also attributed to poor marketing of available services, despite the immense potential for revenue generation and competitiveness vis-à-vis other information carriers in the region.

Activists are urging press freedom advocates to resort to the Net, particularly blogs, to get their message out, saying it's a substitute for missing democracy. But analysts concede that language may still be an obstacle in trying to bridge the cultural divide between the Arab world and the West – read America – since few Americans know Arabic and Arabs are not always well versed in the nuances of American parlance.

Moreover, many U.S. media have for years been accused of stereotyping and denigrating Arabs and Muslims, a tendency that has been exacerbated by the events of September 11, 2001 and the resultant hostility and mis-communication between the two sides.

But Arab media representatives in the U.S. have also been remiss in arguing their case vis-à-vis the West, lamented longtime Arab-American activist Jean Abinader. Their lack of relative freedom to openly explore many issues makes them resort to their own stereotypes, he said. He urged Arab media to do more to develop ties with American media.

"There is a need for more Arab media in the U.S. to have a dual role– to report the news and to build networks of relationships with U.S. media that will lead to greater awareness of Arab sensibilities, concerns and perspectives on the part of reporters and editors," he said. "This may also in time lead to greater access beyond news features for Arab media in the U.S., for example, stories in English on Arab society, reform, cultural issues and similar topics that could be featured on American media outlets."

He complained, as do many of us, that Arab media and Arab journalists quite often lack the basic language skills to communicate with "the other," although they often lambaste "the other" for failing to understand them. "If reaching American audiences is a priority, then Arab media will have to develop a competency in English reporting that will allow them to be fed directly into the American media," he added. *(Ibid)*.

It should also be a priority to evolve into knowledge societies in the Arab world through the development of adequate and equitable information and communication technologies (ICTs).

UNESCO has been campaigning for such a goal and has given much thought to restrictions on information flows.

A UNESCO-organized conference on Freedom of Expression in Cyberspace held in Paris in February 2005 stressed that the free flow of information was a fundamental premise of democratic societies, where individual freedom was respected and honored.

It premised one of the sessions on the belief that everyone had the right to freedom of opinion and expression, which includes the right to seek and receive information. It also discussed the sensitive issue of the choice between security and openness and where limits should be placed to the free flow of data, as well as the need for free media. But participants were faced with the challenge of determining whether creativity should be hampered by codes and restrictions.

Censorship, the great Arab bugaboo, is a matter of interpretation, depending on the country one is dealing with. In Myanmar (Burma), it may mean one thing, while in Egypt quite another. "Egyptian law censors content to defend 'public morals,' regulating faulty or ill-motivated rumours or agitating news if the objective thereof is to disturb public order, induce fear in people or cause harm to public interest.

The Egyptian laws have been invoked frequently." So is there room for Internet governance given the Arab world's media landscape? Not only do developing countries need to get a grip on production of good and professional content, they also need to be well versed in, and capable of handling the technical administration of the Net, or at least their part of it. Unfortunately, many countries are not even up to par on that front and have different standards of operation.

"To date, the involvement and participation of developing countries on most ICT and Internet governance issues and mechanisms has been scant and certainly not consistent over time," reads a task force report on the subject issued last year. That's because developing countries often confuse government with governance and end up having government officials representing them to decide on matters perhaps better left to private or quasi-governmental organizations. A "Report of the Working Group on Internet Governance" (WGIG) meeting at Chateau de Bossey in June 2005 recognized that one of its overarching priorities "was to contribute to ensuring the effective and meaningful participation of all stakeholders from developing countries in Internet governance arrangements."

It further recognized that any organizational form for the governance function/oversight function should adhere to: no single government having a pre-eminent role in relation to international Internet governance; a multilateral, transparent and democratic form of governance by governments; full involvement of governments, the private sector, civil society and international organizations in the process; and, involvement of all stakeholders. Which brings us to the question: Who rules the Internet? And should they? The Internet Corporation of Assigned Names and Numbers (ICANN) is the U.S.-based organization established in 1998 to oversee the system of Web addresses. Perhaps the prickliest issue is who runs ICANN and whether its hegemony on the Internet should remain undisputed, since it is not accountable to governments but, critics claim, is under the control of the U.S. government since most Internet regional registries are located in America.

The World Summit on the Information Society (WSIS), begun in Geneva in 2003, and followed up in Tunis in November 2005, has had to grapple with the issue of governance. "Some groups fear that the Internet is controlled by commercial interests instead of being a global resource that is equally available to all; on the other hand, others fear that calls for reform of Internet governance mask a desire on the part of some governments to control content and limit freedom of expression on the Internet," according to the Panos Media Toolkit on ICTs.

According to the document, the Internet does not have a system of governance and is a humongous, and sometimes unruly body of information. Opinions differ on whether the Internet's governance system should address the question of controlling undesirable content – pornography, hate-content, crime, etc. – or whether this is covered adequately by existing legislation in each country, the toolkit said. In the post-9/11 climate of fear and everything being laced with terrorism, the International Federation of Journalists has expressed concern that media freedoms may have been curtailed on both sides of the divide for misguided reasons. It prefaced its "Journalism, Civil Liberties and the War on Terrorism" report by quoting Ben Franklin, who said: "Those who sacrifice liberty for security deserve neither liberty nor security." In its Middle East and North Africa segment, the report said that the media in most Arab states "continue to exist in a twilight world of harsh regulation and governmental influence, despite the excitement and undoubted progress that has accompanied the growth of independent satellite television (and web sites) in the region."

Equally frustrating to the IFJ is that following 9/11, the United States and Canada introduced anti-terrorism laws "which were supposedly implemented to protect citizens against terrorist threats. However, the impact of national security measures and restrictions on basic rights and freedoms appear to be both disproportionate and repressive."

The IFJ's secretary general, Aidan White, told a UNESCO conference marking World Press Freedom Day in Dakar, Senegal, in May 2005 that governance was about rights, the rule of law and the manner in which they were administered. Not only were good administrators required, he said, but there's also a need for "journalism practiced in an atmosphere of access to reliable information, where reporters can use a variety of sources and where they have the freedom to work safely."

He added that it was difficult to speak of good governance when journalism was under such pressure. "Governments appear oblivious to the fact that the mechanisms they choose to fight terrorism – military action, increased power for police, risk profiling, immigration controls, propaganda and manipulation of media — also nurture anxiety and more fearfulness within society," he explained.

Touching on calls for responsible journalism by government officials, a euphemism for "don't rock the boat," Larry Kilman, communications director at the World Association of Newspapers, told the same conference that what media contribute to good governance was exactly what some government officials find revolting: "freedom to be annoying, to make trouble, to embarrass, and, yes, to be obnoxious and insulting." He said the free press' role is not to cooperate with government but to question and be skeptical, to dig beneath the surface, and to take nothing at face value.

But to thrive in a free environment requires a certain amount of government cooperation – an increasingly rare commodity in our day and age. A year after 9/11, Reporters Without Borders issued a report entitled "The Internet on Probation," in which it said that cyberspace can be added to the list of "collateral damage" caused by security measures.

"As a result, basic cyber-freedoms have been cut back." Add to that copyright matters and the environment could be stifling. A paper prepared by the U.S. Congressional Budget Office in August 2004 on "Copyright Issues in Digital Media" saw obstacles to copyright enforcement such as infringement by individuals and on the international level. "The ease of replication and

redistribution of creative works in digital form facilitates the instantaneous, global availability of copyright-infringing works. Consequently, the effectiveness of any nation's efforts to protect the rights of its copyright owners depends increasingly on international coordination of enforcement efforts and the harmonization of copyright law across countries," it said. But developing countries already pinched by their inability to attain governance of the Internet may be reluctant to go along with such a high-minded request.

Bibliography

A.S. Shukla: *Journalism Today : Concepts and Practices*, Rajat Publications, Delhi, 2010.

Ajay Das: *Mass Media And Journalism*, Omega Publications, Delhi, 2010.

C.S. Shrivastava and R.K. Parekh: *Media Journalism*, Crescent Publishing Corporation, Delhi, 2012.

Dhawal Paramjeet Singh: *Medical Journalism*, Anmol Publication, Delhi, 2011.

Diwakar Sharma: *Modern Journalism Reporting and Writing*, Deep and Deep Publication, Delhi, 2005.

Gurdarshan Singh: *Major Trends In Commercial Journalism In The World*, Arise Publication, Delhi, 2006.

J K Singh: *Media and Journalism*, APH Publication, Delhi, 2007.

Jagadish Chakravarthy: *Journalism: Changing Society, Emerging Trends*, Authors Press, Delhi, 2003.

Jitendra Kumar Singh: *Modern Journalism : Issues and Trends*, APH Publication, Delhi, 2009.

Krishna Menon: *Media Communication and Photo Journalism*, Manglam Publication, Delhi, 2008.

M H Syed: *Journalism Writing Techniques*, Anmol Publication, Delhi, 2006.

M H Syed: *Mass Media and Journalism*, Anmol Publication, Delhi, 2006.

M H Syed: *Modern Journalism*, Anmol Publication, Delhi, 2006.

M.S. Bisht: *Journalism, Advertisement and Public Relations*, Cyber Tech Publications, Delhi, 2011.

Manoj Dixit: *Modern Journalism and Public Relations*, Enkay Publishing House, Delhi, 2013.

Manoj Kumar Singh: *Mass Communication And Journalism : In New Millennium*, Saad Publications, Delhi, 2009.

N.C. Pant: *Modern Journalism : Principles and Practice*, Kanishka Publication, Delhi, 2002.

Narendra Arya: *Media and Journalism Laws*, Anmol Publcation, Delhi, 2011.

Neelam Dubey: *Media, Journalism and Prostitution*, Surendra Publications, Delhi, 2010.

Pramod Pandey: *Modern Journalism : At a Glance*, Sublime Publication, Delhi, 2010.

S P Phadke: *Media and Journalism Ethics*, ABD Publication, Delhi, 2008.

S P Phadke: *Modern Journalism : Tools and Techniques*, ABD Publication, Delhi, 2008.

S.C. Sharma and Sweta Bakshi: *Modern Journalism and Mass Communication*, A.K. Publication, Delhi, 2009.

S.N. Dixit: *Journalism: A Guide to the Reference Literature*, Pearl Books, Delhi, 2008.

S.N. Dixit: *Journalism: Reporting, Writing and Editing*, Pearl Books, Delhi, 2008.

S.N. Dixit: *Management in Journalism*, Pearl Books, Delhi, 2011.

Shailendra Sengar: *Journalism, Advertisement and Public Relations*, Anmol Publication, Delhi, 2008.

Suraj Singh: *Liberalization and Journalism*, Centrum Press, Delhi, 2010.

T Rajsekhar: *Media and Sports Journalism*, Sonali Publication, Delhi, 2007.

T Rajsekhar: *Modern Media and Television Journalism*, Sonali Publications, Delhi, 2007.

T.J.S. George: *Lessons in Journalism: The Story of Pothan Joseph*, Viva Books, Delhi, 2007.

Veena Sharma: *Journalism with New Challenge*, ALP Books, Delhi, 2012.

Index